CONSTITUTIONAL OPTIONS
FOR A
DEMOCRATIC SOUTH AFRICA

CONSTITUTIONAL OPTIONS

FOR A

DEMOCRATIC SOUTH AFRICA

A Comparative Perspective

Ziyad Motala

HOWARD UNIVERSITY PRESS

WASHINGTON, D.C.

Howard University Press, Washington, D.C. 20017

Manufactured in the United States of America

This book is printed on acid-free paper.

10 9 8 7 6 5 4 3 2 1

Library of Congress Cataloging-in-Publication Data

Motala, Ziyad, 1962-
    Constitutional options for a democratic South Africa : a
comparative perspective / by Ziyad Motala.
        p.   cm.
    Includes bibliographical references and index.
    ISBN 0-88258-187-2 (alk. paper) : $39.95.—ISBN 0-88258-180-5
(alk. paper) : $19.95
        1. Africa—Politics and government—1960-   2. Comparative
government.   3. South Africa—Constitutional law.   4. Federal
government—South Africa.   5. Democratic centralism—South Africa.
I. Title.
JQ1872.M69   1994
342.68—dc20
[346.802]   94-6680
                                                          CIP

Contents

■ ■ ■

CONTENTS

Acknowledgments

■ ■ ■

In writing this book, I owe a debt to many people who deserve special gratitude. First, I want to acknowledge the immense contribution of all those people in South Africa who inspired me throughout my life, particularly relatives such as my uncle Abdul Samed Motala, my grandparents, and my parents. I acknowledge the many people who in many ways touched my life and inspired me in different ways as I watched them struggle for a just and better order in South Africa.

I owe an immense debt of gratitude to professors Victor G. Rosenblum and Leonard S. Rubinowitz, both of Northwestern University School of Law, who were tremendous sources of inspiration and encouragement. I wish especially to thank Professor Rubinowitz for the many hours he spent reading the project and for his helpful and detailed critical comments.

This book would not have been what it is without the assistance of the library staff at many institutions, particularly the staff at Northwestern University library. I owe a debt to my research assistant Mr. David Ritchie for his help in so many areas, particularly for the copious checking and correction of references. I would also like to thank the staff of Howard University Press and Ms. Ruby M. Essien in particular for their support in the publication of this book.

I would like to thank three very important people in my life: my wife Farhana, and my children Irshad and Tasnim for their patience and love.

I finally thank God for his infinite support.

CONSTITUTIONAL OPTIONS
FOR A
DEMOCRATIC SOUTH AFRICA

Introduction

■   ■   ■

T HIS STUDY EVALUATES constitutional options for a post-apartheid, antiracial, and democratic South Africa. We do not seek to devise a constitutional blueprint but instead to outline the broad parameters of constitutional choice and the direction in which "constitutional engineers" should be thinking.

The premise of the study is that any constitutional order must meet certain interrelated requirements if it is to achieve legitimacy and stability. First, it must provide a certain standard of democracy that encompasses widespread participation (beyond elite decision making) in the decisions that affect people's lives. Second, it must have the capacity to effect a socioeconomic transformation that will bring the majority, who have suffered centuries of oppression and discrimination, out of the squalor, poverty, and ignorance of apartheid. Third, the new order must integrate the various divisions the apartheid order has created over the last few decades into a unitary South Africa.

We do not suggest that a constitution is a panacea for all social and economic problems, nor do we suggest that a constitution is an instrument for pursuing happiness. The resolution of societal problems depends on a myriad of social, political, and economic forces whose analysis is beyond the scope of this study. All countries, however, find it necessary to describe the major institutions and parameters within which government can operate. A constitution serves as a framework for pursuing the goals of society, though it can also serve to retard the achievement of those goals. Our focus is to map out the broad parameters of constitutional choice in terms of whether any of the various models will serve as a viable framework for achieving the major goals defined in this study.

The mode of enquiry we have adopted is the comparative approach, looking at constitutions in different societies—particularly those of independent African countries, which share common social and political features. We evaluate constitutional models in terms of their potential for success in achieving the goals of democracy, socioeconomic transformation, and national unity, and we search for general laws based on an area study of constitutional experimentation in African countries.[1] Many of the popular constitutional models establish terms of order that are inappropriate to the society in which the model is established. It is conceivable that the reproduction in South Africa of many of the constitutional models that were introduced and failed in independent African countries could produce similar results in South Africa.

Two important and interrelated components to our enquiry are the jurisprudential/philosophical and the actual selection of a constitution and institutions. Because of the interrelationship of the two, this study combines comparative constitutional law with political philosophy. The philosophical aspect is dealt with in terms of two components, namely, the "pure" jurisprudential/philosophical aspect and the political economy component. The jurisprudential question relates to the actual philosophical basis on which state law is going to operate. The three broad schools of thought competing for the hearts and souls of Africans are liberalism, scientific socialism, and African socialism. Each of these schools has a separate conception of democracy and different assumptions about the way society should be organized. Each will be investigated in terms of its influence in African countries and on political movements and leaders in South Africa. Each will be further investigated in terms of the way its constitutional theory outlines how public authority should define and exercise power. Finally, the core institutions associated with the different schools of thought will be evaluated in terms of their capacity to meet the concerns of South African society. The way we look at law and the place we give it in society affect the nation in terms of its social aspirations.[2] Constitutions and the institutions they promote enhance the values and goals people hold important. The institutional structures in turn shape public policy, the priority that issues are accorded, and the actual outcome of policy.[3]

The political economy component explains the basis of South African society and the way it has come to be structured the way it is. In the current constitutional debate, this enquiry is extremely crucial, given the many constitutional options for a post-apartheid South Africa that presuppose South Africa to be a strife-torn "plural" society.[4] A fundamental tenet of this study (which departs from almost all popular liberal assumptions) is that the notion of pluralism is an inappropriate way to describe and understand South African society, not least because it is ahistorical and fails to explain the apartheid basis of the divisions in South African society. The constitutional prescriptions of the plural constitutional theorists contain core features that will cloud priorities of South African society such as socioeconomic change and promotion of national unity.[5]

Many problems have to be met in a new South Africa. Considering different constitutions in different environments seems to us the best mechanism for making generalizations about their effectiveness.[6] In South Africa the constitutional debate is often waged in terms of the British unitary constitution and the United States federal system. The comparative approach allows us to go beyond the popular assumptions of "negative" government and to investigate how different societies deal with problems of national unity, democracy, and socioeconomic disparity. For example, the social welfare constitutions contain provisions that impose constitutional duties on the state to provide certain social and economic rights to all citizens. Our approach also allows an evaluation of alternate strategies (more suited to realities) to meet the problems of South African society.[7]

The study concerns itself with the values that should underlie the constitution as well as the institutions needed to direct the new order toward the goals of a new South Africa.[8] In devising institutions and structures, constitution makers should be mindful of the culture and the context in which institutions are introduced.[9] We pay attention to the problems and difficulties of introducing institutions that are not accessible to the majority of the population, or whose intricacies may not be understood.[10] The study involves an investigation of the legal institutions and rules as well as the appropriateness of both to the South African social context.

The institutions of Western liberal systems[11] and Communist systems[12] are investigated in terms of their capacity to cope with the problems of national unity, socioeconomic transformation, and democracy, and of how the institutions from these different systems have fared when they were replicated in independent African countries. We will look at how the institutions in the different orders work to promote national unity and democracy, and how the system deals with the distributive function in society.

This study operates on the assumption that a constitution does not and cannot provide a neutral political framework and that it is irrational to separate law and politics.[13] Legal institutions are designed to carry out political purposes. The priorities and needs of South African society must be identified in the process of constitution making. The constitution should determine the parameters within which the government can and should act in terms of social, political, and economic goals.

REFERENCES

1. For the merit of conducting contextually limited generalizations based on area studies, see Fred Eidlin, "Area Studies and/or Social Science: Contextually Limited Generalizations Versus General Laws," in Fred H. Eidlin and Henry W. Ehrmann, eds., *Constitutional Democracy: Essays in Comparative Politics—A Festschrift in Honor of Henry W. Ehrmann* (Boulder, Colo.: Westview Press, 1983), 199–202.

2. For an exposition of this view, see Ian Harden and Norman Lewis, *The Noble Lie: The British Constitution and the Rule of Law* (London: Hutchinson, 1986), 16. The relationship between legal theory and social policy will be further developed in chapters 2 and 3.

3. W. C. Mitchell, "The Shape of Political Theory to Come," in Seymour M. Lipset, ed., *Politics and the Social Sciences* (New York: Oxford University Press, 1969), 124.

4. South Africa is described as a country made up of a number of groups in conflict with each other. The popular argument that a federal constitution is most appropriate to a plural society is discussed in chapter 4. The entire notion of the plural society is discussed in chapter 7.

5. See chapter 7.

6. This is the problem-oriented approach. See Roy C. Macridis, *The Study of Comparative Government* (Garden City, N.Y.: Doubleday, 1955), 71.

7. Chapter 11 deals with a judicial structure based on the Continental model.

8. In the words of Ogwurike, we need to ascertain the province of jurisprudence for a post-apartheid South Africa. Chijioke Ogwurike, *Concept of Law in English-Speaking Africa* (New York: NOK Publishers International, 1979), 6.

9. In this regard the institutions and structures must be accessible to the population, which is largely illiterate.

10. Chijioke Ogwurike, *Concept of Law in English-Speaking Africa* (New York: NOK Publishers International, 1979), 7.

11. Chapters 4 and 5.

12. Chapter 8.

13. In subsequent chapters the evolution and development of the South African legal and constitutional systems will be evaluated in order to understand the historical relations between law and politics in the South African order.

CHAPTER TWO

Philosophical Origins of Liberal Constitutions

■ ■ ■

A LMOST ALL COUNTRIES deem it necessary to draw up a constitution,[1] to describe the major institutions of government and lay down the way power is to be exercised. To many states the constitution is a symbol of nationhood.[2] In newly emergent nations (particularly those finding themselves free from colonial rule), the constitution is used to articulate a newly emergent order.[3] The origin of modern constitutions is thus attributed to a desire by the people to make a fresh start. This requires an outline of the new form of government.[4] A constitution is especially important to a nation-state in its infant stages. In this context, constitutions provide the rational, legal basis for the present order, though the functions constitutions serve differ across different orders. This chapter examines the philosophical notions of a constitution from the perspective of the Western liberal tradition.[5]

There is a dichotomy in thinking as to whether a constitution is associated with a normative system or whether it is purely a set of rules regulating government functions and agencies. This dichotomy reflects the difference between the views of a constitution as simply a set of legal rules that define and regulate the agencies of government and the principles of constitutionalism whereby limits are imposed on the power of states to encroach on certain liberties.

The Constitution and Legitimacy

To some extent the drawing up of constitutions provides a moral and legal basis for the way power is to be exercised; that is, it provides a basis for legitimacy.[6] Legitimacy involves the extent to which the system can engender and maintain the belief that the existing political institutions are the most appropriate for the society.[7] Some view constitution making as a science: if the correct structural principles are employed, freedom and justice will materialize.[8] But invariably, all constitutions ultimately claim their power from the people.[9] The question of legitimacy (whether the people believe the existing arrangements are appropriate) goes to the heart of any debate on constitutions and the exercise of power.[10] Many political systems experience crisis because of the failure to resolve the legitimacy question. The basis of this legitimacy varies between the principles of natural law or what is considered "the natural order of things" under Western systems, and the "rights of the working class" in Communist systems.

Constitutional Law and Constitutionalism in a Liberal Political System

CONSTITUTION VERSUS CONSTITUTIONALISM

Today, some Western constitutional lawyers make a distinction between constitutions and constitutionalism. The term *constitution* is used in the sense of describing the codes and rules that allocate and regulate the functions, duties, and powers of the various government agencies, the officers of the government, and the relationship between all of these and the public,[11] and is not used in an overtly prescriptive sense.[12]

The term *constitutionalism*, on the other hand, is a reference to a constitutional system associated with a highly normative system, particular institutional frameworks, and the protection of individual and property rights.[13] However, the distinction between constitutions and constitutionalism can become blurred. The Western constitutional lawyer's evaluation of a constitution is invariably weighed against the principles of constitutionalism, and when he or she refers to a constitution he in fact really means constitutionalism. In the words of one author, the constitution is both the symbol and instrument of constitutionalism.[14]

THE CORE PRINCIPLES OF CONSTITUTIONALISM

Constitutionalism is clearly linked to a set of political ideals. Some commentators have equated the difference between constitutions that conform to the principles of constitutionalism and those that do not as the heart of the cold war.[15] The core principles of constitutionalism are the limitation of government power and the guaranteeing of individual and civil liberties enforceable by the courts.[16] In essence, constitutional government is limited government. The limits imposed on the government are of two kinds. First, the scope of government powers is restricted. Second, the procedure the government is to follow in exercising its powers is spelled out.[17] The control or limitation of government is effected in terms of two major doctrines, the separation of powers and the rule of law. Both of these doctrines are related to natural law theory.

Constitutionalism and the Separation of Powers. Constitutionalism seeks to introduce certain institutional arrangements to restrict the scope of government power. Constitutionalism operates on the premise that there are certain demonstrable relationships between institutional forms and the attainment of certain values.[18] The issue is presented as an ongoing contradiction between government and the people. Power is in the hands of the government and has to be brought under control. One way of achieving this control is to fragment and distribute the power of government among different government agencies. The judiciary is the main agency for exercising this control.[19] An independent judiciary constitutes the pivotal point in the institutional arrangements under constitutionalism.

Consequently, the first important aspect of constitutionalism in respect to the institutional arrangements is the doctrine of separation of powers. This doctrine can be traced back to the writings of Montesquieu, who argued that the way to control power is to fragment it. Montesquieu advocated the classification and division of government power into legislative, executive, and judicial branches.[20] Some writers link the doctrine to the notion of checks and balances, while others view it as an institutional arrangement for limiting government.[21] The notion of checks and balances seeks to make the separation of power effective by balancing the power of one agency against that of the other. The strict notion of separation of powers stands for the complete separation of the agencies of government, at the institutional level and in the composition of personnel.[22] Despite different interpretations of the theory, the one thread common to all interpretations is the belief in the separation and independence of the judiciary from the executive and legislative branches of government.[23] The judiciary is seen as the bulwark that protects the fundamental values of liberal society. The separation of powers is seen as necessary to achieve liberty. The notion of liberty in this instance is perceived in negative terms in that it essentially seeks to weaken government.[24]

At a second level, constitutionalism amounts to accountable government, holding of free elections, the existence of pluralism in political organizations (multiparty political system), and legal guarantees for civil liberties.[25]

Constitutionalism and Political Ideology. Constitutionalism today is the philosophical and legal shell under which liberal democracy exists. The origins of modern constitutionalism can be traced to liberalism and capitalism.[26] Its main focus is on the individual and individual rights, which are the libertarian aspects of the doctrine. Today many of these individual rights are classified as "natural" rights.[27] Under ancient law, the constitution was seen to be the mere enactment of the prince or emperor. In the modern setting, with the influence of natural law,[28] the constitution is seen to derive its validity from some higher law beyond the prince and the constitution. This higher law could be fundamental law, the law of reason, or the law of God or nature.[29] This higher law is today referred to as natural law, and provides a barrier beyond which government should not venture. Natural law is posited as preexisting positive law, and state law is derived from the former. State violation of this natural law is illegitimate and therefore void.[30]

What did natural law thinkers understand the law of nature to be? Although opinions differ about the proper philosophical basis of the doctrine, they all share some guiding threads. The first is a focus on individualism and the protection of individual rights.[31] The second (no less important) is the belief in and concern for the protection of private property.[32]

The priority of the individual was seen to be derived from a previous state of nature in which no prior group had existed.[33] Similarly, private property was seen to exist in the presocial state and was therefore also seen as a natural law not subject to modification.[34] Today, the expression of these individual rights is termed *fundamental human rights*, essentially what we know as civil liberties[35] and economic freedom. A major component of both individual rights and economic freedom is the right to individual property.[36] The protection of property and individual rights is proclaimed to be beyond the encroachment of any government, and any such encroachment would be a violation of the law of nature. The protection of these rights has become part of the normative structure of Western societies.[37]

In a state of nature man's natural rights are subject to constant flux and invasion by others. So man enters into a society and forms the state to guarantee and protect these natural rights.[38] Rousseau argues that the human race would perish in the state of nature.[39] Entering into a society constitutes a social contract,[40] an effort to protect natural rights that requires the partial surrender of political power to the state,[41] specifically, the power to prevent violent conflicts and the power to protect natural rights.

Since a social contract is formed to protect the individual's natural rights, it is necessary to limit the powers of government to prevent it from transgressing the boundaries of natural law. It is unthinkable that on entering into a social contract people would wish to relinquish such rights as liberty and property.[42] The control of government is thus to be effected by the other crucial doctrine in constitutionalism, the rule of law.

Constitutionalism and the Rule of Law. The rule of law is an important doctrine in Western constitutional systems and is used as a yardstick to judge whether a political system is "just" and "free."[43] In the Western systems it is "the symbol of the legitimating force of the whole notion of constitutionality."[44]

The main tenet of the rule of law is limited government in terms of clear, preannounced rules of law.[45] A second tenet is the actual limiting of government power to do certain things.[46] In the first instance, whether an action is lawful depends on whether it conforms to preexisting rules; that is, there should not be any punishment for an action that was not a crime when the act was committed.[47] According to Locke, in a state of nature power is not arbitrary. Once part of that power has been relinquished to a legislature, it must not be exercised in an arbitrary manner.[48] Moreover, man enters into the social contract to prevent fluxes and uncertainties. Hence, the law should be open and clear so that people may structure their actions accordingly.[49]

THE SOCIOECONOMIC SYSTEM
AND LAW IN THE LIBERAL ORDER

The theory of law in liberal systems is an outgrowth of classical economic theory,[50] which is not practiced in its pure form despite its growing appeal.[51] The form of law is, however, very much related to the broad economic philosophies of liberal societies. In its pure form, classical liberal economic theory is best represented by the writings of Adam Smith,[52] and its modern variant by Milton Friedman.[53] The writings of Adam Smith and the works of modern laissez-faire theorists are based on natural law and what they consider to be the natural order of things. Economic freedom is seen as a prerequisite for political freedom, and the two can only exist under conditions of free competition.[54] Individuals should be permitted to conduct their affairs in an atmosphere free of restraint, which will benefit all members of society. Individuals must be free to engage in whatever economic activity they choose, and consumers must be free to purchase what they please. Any interference will result in a state of disequilibrium that will affect the prosperity of the entire economy. The cardinal emphasis is again on individual rights and individual property, the guaranteeing of which should be the main purpose of government. Since the function of government is to act as an umpire to guarantee the requisite rights of individuals, government must be given sufficient power to fulfill this purpose and no more. In this sense, the government is seen more as a necessary evil.[55] There is an ongoing conflict between private and public existence, and the role of the state must be confined to those areas identified as part of the public domain.[56] Among the important government powers are those of defense, that is, the protection of society from invasion by others, the administration of justice, and the erection of certain public works to facilitate commerce in the society.[57] The dispersion of government power manifested, among other things, in the separation of powers is designed to constrain it to its "necessary" purposes.

The libertarian influence commits constitutionalism to the preservation of political liberty in terms of a particular conception that favors liberty over equality.[58] In the first instance, the government is prohibited from doing certain things[59] that constitute the libertarian aspects of the theory. A vital aspect of liberty is the protection of the institution of private property, which is tied to the notion of individual rights. As part of the notion of individual rights, various important freedoms such as the freedom of speech and assembly are championed. Moreover, the institutional arrangements linked to constitutionalism are viewed as auxiliary means of protecting liberal interests.[60] The overall institutional arrangements and the notion of liberty are essentially geared to weakening government and to promoting a negative conception of political liberty as imposing restraints on government. Positive government directed toward economic and social change is viewed as acting against the principles of constitutionalism.[61]

The point has repeatedly been made about the supposed autonomy of the law and the neutrality of institutions of the state.[62] Today, liberal theorists increasingly reject the notion of the neutrality of state institutions. When norms are established and institutions designed to weaken and limit the competencies of government, the procedures used to achieve these ends are clearly value charged.[63] Once introduced, the institutions of the state may operate in a neutral manner, but they are merely a means of achieving the values deemed essential.[64]

The South African Constitution in Historical Focus

South African authorities have been particularly fond of associating their system with Western democracy and claim to be part of the Western legal system.[65] Historically, the South African constitution has been an outgrowth of the British Westminster system of government. Such features as weak separation of powers, a parliamentary government, and an independent judiciary, however restricted in terms of pronouncing on substantive aspects of legislation, have been inherited from the British tradition.

Great emphasis was placed on the rule of law as an absolute requirement.[66] But at the level of practice, there were fundamental points of difference. In the British tradition, the common law has acted as a powerful break on legislative powers. In the South African tradition the rule of law has lacked normative content and never limited the principle of parliamentary supremacy.[67] The popular definition of the rule of law in South Africa (particularly from the perspective of the ruling group) was to see its observance in the government acting in terms of clear, pronounced rules. This is the narrow definition of the rule of law in terms of the legality principle; that is, an action is valid provided it is taken in terms of some valid law.[68] In terms of this definition, no judgment was made on the content of the law regardless of how harsh its effects on society. For example, no judgment was made on the power of the government to detain persons indefinitely or to banish them to certain areas or to treat citizens differently. It suffices that actions were taken in terms of some prescribed law.[69]

Clearly, here the rule of law does not entail "good" law or democracy in the liberal sense. It does not say anything about how the government is formed, that is, whether it is a dictatorship or based on the consent of all the people. In South Africa the black majority have historically been excluded from the central political process. Successive governments have been formed exclusively at the whim of the minority white electorate.[70] The legality doctrine does not address itself to notions of fundamental liberty such as freedom of speech, property, or movement, tenets that are today considered essential in liberal society.

The element of natural rights—particularly the right of all persons without regard to color to enjoy the same rights and privileges—so crucial to liberal societies was lacking in South African society. The Group Areas Law restricted freedom of movement, residence, and ownership of property.[71] The act confined the designated groups to reside and own property only in specifically demarcated areas. Freedom of movement was also restricted by virtue of the power given to the executive to ban certain individuals or restrict their movement. For example, the minister of law and order could restrict the movement of persons he had reason to suspect were a danger to the security of the state.[72] The minister could confine such persons to a particular area or house for a specified period of time and prevent them from meeting others. A further encroachment on individual freedom and freedom of movement was the power conferred on the minister as well as police officers to detain persons they considered dangerous to the security of the state for prolonged periods and without explanation.[73] The executive had widespread discretionary powers to curtail the freedom of organizations to meet publicly.[74] The act allowed the executive on petitioning a magistrate to ban a public meeting.[75] Moreover, freedom of organization could be severely restricted by banning an entire organization, thus making its activities illegal.[76] Freedom of opinion and belief was also severely restricted. Widespread discretion is still given to the executive to ban any literature or film considered undesirable.[77] The powers conferred in terms of the act have been used repeatedly, particularly against publications critical of the government and which the government sees as promoting Communism.[78]

However, the notion of the rule of law here departs fundamentally from the legality notion of the rule of law that Western theorists like von Hayek claim to be its proper definition. For von Hayek, the legality notion of the rule of law calls for a government bound by fixed rules announced beforehand so that the individual will know in advance how to conduct him or herself.[79] Such a rule allows extensive poverty, denial of human rights, racial inequality, and persecution so long as the certainty of the law is fulfilled.[80] Even in terms of the narrower meaning of the rule of law as government according to law and certainty in the law, the rule of law was lacking in the apartheid South African legal system. This can be seen from the wide array of discretionary powers which were available to the executive in the system.[81] In exercising these powers, the agents responsible neither answered nor were subject to the control of any body, and in many instances did not need to provide details of their actions. Many of the sections of the Internal Security Act were so ambiguously phrased it was impossible to know whether a person had fallen afoul of its provisions. For example, the detention provisions of the act did not make clear when an individual's activities were considered to endanger the interests of the state.[82] In terms of von Hayek and Rawls's criteria, no fixed rules are known beforehand on which an individual can structure his or her behavior. Similarly, it is not always clear when a publication is obscene or dangerous to state interests.[83]

Today, with the rise of the welfare state, a great deal of discretionary power is given to administrative bodies. The tendency has been for the courts to require that these bodies provide reasons for their actions in terms of precise rules. However, in South Africa, statutory provision allows for arbitrary action.[84] The most serious instance of arbitrary power given to the executive is the emergency powers provided under the Public Safety Act.[85]

Most countries allow the exercise of emergency powers in situations of war.[86] However, the statutory state of emergency in South Africa confers on the executive widespread discretionary powers in nonwar situations. Under the Public Safety Act, the state president can proclaim a state of emergency if he believes that events in the country pose a threat to the public safety. To date the statutory state of emergency has been declared three times since 1960, most recently in June 1986.[87]

The proclamation confers widespread powers on the security forces. The police have the power to search and seize materials from anyplace or premises without a warrant. They can impose curfews in any area as well as remove persons from particular places. Freedom of the press is severely restricted, limited to reporting only such activities of the security forces and matters relating to the unrest as are approved by the government. Civil disobedience and boycott activities are prohibited. Any person who contravenes the state of emergency faces a prison sentence of up to ten years and or a fine of up to twenty thousand rand.

Thousands of people, including many children, were detained in the past. There have been numerous complaints of police brutality and torture of detainees. But no civil or criminal proceedings could be brought against the state president, police, or other government official acting under the state of emergency even if it leads to injury or death.

The South African Constitutional Order in Theoretical Context

The reality of the legal order in South Africa demonstrates that law does not operate in a neutral fashion. The law, particularly the constitutional system for the main part, is used to maintain order and implement the policies of the ruling group.[88] In this sense, the South African legal system conforms to the orthodox Marxist criticism of being part of the repressive machinery of the state.[89] Moreover, the legal system institutionalizes the privileged position of a sector (white) of the population and legitimates the inequalities in the system.[90]

The South African Constitution and Western Liberal and Soviet Socialist State Theory

The South African economic order is essentially capitalistic. However, it is a capitalistic system of a particular nature where race has assumed an important dimension in the determination of the class composition of the society. Unlike other capitalist countries that over a period of time have accepted freedom of association and a single legal system for the entire population, the South African system has failed to incorporate the majority of the working-class black population into its social and political institutions.[91]

Many of the discretionary measures available to the executive resembled the flexibility in the law characteristic of the legal system in the former Soviet Union. Similarly, the level of state involvement in the South

African economy was also uncharacteristic of most liberal systems. However, despite the controls and state involvement in the economy, there is no central planning of the economy. Moreover, the ideological orientation of the apartheid system was the antithesis of Communism.

The myriad of repressive laws and discretionary powers have mostly been employed against the black majority population in the interests of the white sector. In a practical sense, the South African constitutional system under apartheid can be characterized as liberal democratic in regard to the white population, who largely enjoyed the liberal democratic rights so common to Western society. This has led some commentators to characterize the South African order as displaying a dual legal system. Particularly in the area of private law, the white population suffered little political intrusion, and laws were administered by an "impartial" judicial system.[92] Here, the state assumed the passive role of arbiter of disputes characteristic of other liberal states.[93]

REFERENCES

1. Herbert J. Spiro, *Government by Constitution: The Political Systems of Democracy* (New York: Random House, 1959), 11–12.

2. Carl J. Friedrich, *Constitutional Government and Democracy,* 4th ed. (Waltham, Mass.: Blaisdell Publishing, 1968), 584.

3. See K. Lowenstein, "Reflections on the Value of Constitutions in Our Revolutionary Age," in Harry Eckstein and David E. Apter, eds., *Comparative Politics: A Reader* (New York: Free Press of Glencoe, 1963), 149.

4. See Kenneth C. Wheare, *Modern Constitutions,* 2d ed. (London: Oxford University Press, 1966), 6. Wheare refers to the U.S. Constitution of 1787, the Soviet constitution of 1917, and the French constitution of 1946; Istuan Kovacs, *New Elements in the Evolution of Socialist Constitution* (Budapest: Akademiai Kiado, 1968), 12.

5. This tradition is a reference to those societies committed to the free enterprise system and the upholding of individual rights and property. For a discussion of the concept of the Western liberal tradition, see Mary Ann Glendon, Michael Wallace Gordon, and Christopher Osakwe, *Comparative Legal Traditions: Text, Materials and Cases on the Civil Law, Common Law and Socialist Law Traditions, with Special Reference to French, West German, English and Soviet Law* (St. Paul, Minn: West, 1985), 14–38.

6. Gaetano Mosca, *The Ruling Class,* trans. Hannah Kahn (New York: McGraw-Hill, 1939), 70. Mosca argues that the ruling class does not justify its exercise of power by mere possession of it, but tries to formulate a moral and legal basis for it.

7. Seymour M. Lipset, "Social Conflict, Legitimacy, and Democracy," in William Connolly, ed., *Legitimacy and the State* (New York: New York University Press, 1984), 88.

8. Fred I. Greenstein and Nelson W. Polsby, eds., *Handbook of Political Science, vol. 5, Governmental Institutions and Processes* (Reading, Mass.: Addison-Wesley, 1975), 1.

9. A reading of virtually all constitutions begins with a phrase or statement claiming power from the people.

10. For a detailed discussion on the concept of legitimacy, see the articles in Connolly, *Legitimacy and the State.*

11. Samuel E. Finer, ed., *Five Constitutions* (Brighton: Harvester Press, 1979), 15.

12. Wheare, *Modern Constitutions,* 1.

13. Giovanni Sartori, "Constitutionalism: A Preliminary Discussion," *American Political Science Review* 56 (1962): 853–59.

14. Benjamin O. Nwabueze, *Constitutionalism in the Emergent States* (London: C. Hurst, 1973), 23.

15. Carl J. Friedrich, *Limited Government: A Comparison* (Englewood Cliffs, N.J.: Prentice Hall, 1974), 37.

16. Nwabueze, *Constitutionalism*, 1, 10; Wheare, *Modern Constitutions*, 137; Denis V. Cowen, *The Foundations of Freedom, With Special Reference to Southern Africa* (Cape Town: Oxford University Press, 1961), 197.

17. William G. Andrews, *Constitutions and Constitutionalism*, 3d ed. (Princeton, N.J.: Van Nostrand, 1968), 13.

18. Maurice J. C. Vile, *Constitutionalism and the Separation of Powers* (Oxford: Clarendon Press, 1967), 8.

19. Greenstein and Polesby, *Handbook of Political Science*, 36.

20. Carol Harlow, "Power from the People? Representation and Constitutional Theory," in Patrick McAuslan and John F. McEldowney, eds., *Law, Legitimacy, and the Constitution: Essays Marking the Centenary of Dicey's Law of the Constitution* (London: Sweet and Maxwell, 1985), 67.

21. For a discussion on the theory of separation of powers, see William B. Gwyn, *The Meaning of the Separation of Powers: An Analysis of the Doctrine From its Origin to the Adoption of the United States Constitution* (New Orleans: Tulane University, 1965), especially chapter 1.

22. To some extent, the arguments over the different meanings of the doctrine of separation of powers revolve around the debate over preference for the U.S. presidential system as opposed to the British parliamentary—or Westminster—system of government. See Geoffrey Marshall, *Constitutional Theory* (Oxford: Clarendon Press, 1971), 97–100.

23. Ibid., 103.

24. At times the weakening of government inhibits it from fulfilling many of its social and economic functions. See, for example, Vile, *Constitutionalism,*, 14.

25. S. A. de Smith, *The New Commonwealth and Its Constitutions* (London: Stevens, 1964), 106.

26. Friedrich, *Constitutional Government and Democracy,* 6.

27. This focus on individuality has been attributed to, among other things, Christianity, which eventually gave rise to the notion of natural rights. P. Sigmund, "Carl Friedrich's Contribution to the Theory of Constitutionalism—Comparative Government," in J. Roland Pennock and John W. Chapman, eds., *Constitutionalism* (New York: New York University Press, 1979), 37.

28. Andrews, *Constitutions and Constitutionalism*, 15.

29. Greenstein and Polsby, *Handbook of Political Science*, 28.

30. Brendon F. Brown, *The Natural Law Reader* (New York: Oceana Publications, 1960), 2.

31. See generally John Locke, *Two Treatises on Government*, ed. Peter Laslett (London: Cambridge University Press, 1960); Otto Friedrich von Gierke and Ernst Troeltsch, *Natural Law and the Theory of Society 1500–1800* (Boston: Beacon Press, 1957), 96–98.

32. Franz Neumann, *The Rule of Law: Political Theory and the Legal System in Modern Society* (Dover, N.H.: Berg, 1986), 119.

33. Gierke and Troeltsch, *Natural Law*, 96.

34. Huntington Cairns, *Legal Philosophy from Plato to Hegel* (Baltimore: Johns Hopkins University Press, 1949), 359ff.

35. The main civil liberties are freedom of speech, assembly, movement (interstate migration), press, religion, and political freedom.

36. Neumann, *Rule of Law*, 37.

37. In the United States the protection of these rights is secured by the first ten amendments to the Constitution, collectively known as the Bill of Rights.

38. John Locke, "An Essay Concerning the True Original Extent and End of Civil Government," in Ernest Barker, trans., *Social Contract: Essays by Locke, Hume and Rousseau* (London: Oxford University Press, 1952), 73.

39. Jean Jacques Rousseau, "The Social Contract," in Barker, *Social Contract*, 179.

40. Ibid., 180.

41. Gierke and Troeltsch, *Natural Law*, 44–45.

42. Locke, "An Essay Concerning the True Original Extent," 75, 82; Rousseau, "The Social Contract," 197–98, in Barker, *Social Contract*.

43. Albert V. Dicey, *Introduction to the Study of the Law of the Constitution*, 10th ed. (New York: St. Martin's Press, 1959), cvii.

44. Ian Harden and Norman Lewis, *The Noble Lie: The British Constitution and the Rule of Law* (London: Hutchinson, 1986), 32.

45. Friedrich A. von Hayek, *The Road to Serfdom* (Chicago: University of Chicago Press, 1980), 54. There are different interpretations to the rule of law. Some favor the view that the rule of law is simply government according to law. Others advance the view that the rule of law means both procedural and substantive justice. See, for example, Anthony S. Mathews, *Law, Order and Liberty in South Africa* (Berkeley: University of California Press, 1972), 1–20, for the different notions of the rule of law. Mathews attempts to separate the notion of the rule of law from that of natural law, arguing that to link the rule of law with natural rights is to prefer a political ideology. His argument and presentation of the Diceyian theory of the rule of law as a value-free theory is untenable. The Diceyian theory of the rule of law is value laden as it is also premised on individual rights and the institution of private property, which for Dicey were elements that allow the rule of law to flourish.

46. There is a debate in Western liberal thinking whether the rule of law means only the first aspect, that is, government according to law, or whether it means government according to "good" law. See discussion in E. C. S. Wade and G. Godfrey Phillips, *Constitutional and Administrative Law* (London: Longman, 1977), 92. In a sense, linking the rule of law to limitation of government powers subsumes the doctrine into constitutionalism. There are theorists who reject the association of the rule of law with "good" law or substantive justice. See Robert L. Cunningham, ed., *Liberty and the Rule of Law* (College Station, Tex.: Texas A & M University Press, 1979), 3–4. To theorists like Cunningham, the rule of law is limited to only the first definition. See also views of Mathews, *Law, Order, and Liberty*, who argues that to expand the concept to associate it with civil rights would be to associate the concept with liberal democracy. However, under liberal systems it is generally appreciated that the two are mutually interdependent. Wade & Phillips, *Constitutional and Administrative Law*, 90. See also J. Raz, The "Politics of the Rule of Law," *Ratio Juris* 3 (1990): 3. Raz argues that the rule of law can only flourish when civil rights are respected. In this study, the rule of law will be used in terms of legality and both substantive justice, which are accepted tenets of constitutionalism.

47. Friedrich August von Hayek, *The Political Ideal of the Rule of Law* (Cairo, 1955), 12.

48. Locke, "An Essay Concerning the True Original Extent," in Barker, *Social Contract*, 79.

49. Ibid., 80.

50. Neumann, *Rule of Law*, 189.

51. Both the United States under Ronald Reagan and Britain under Margaret Thatcher were more committed to implementing the principles of classical economics in their respective countries. The fervor with which they went about pursuing these programs has not been equaled in any other country since World War II.

52. See Adam Smith's classic, *An Inquiry Into the Nature and Causes of the Wealth of Nations*, ed. Edwin Cannan (New York: The Modern Library, 1937).

53. See, Milton Friedman, *Free to Choose: A Personal Statement* (New York: Harcourt Brace Jovanovich, 1980).

54. Ibid., 3.

55. G. J. Schochet, "Constitutionalism, Liberalism and the Study of Politics," in Pennock and Chapman, *Constitutionalism*. 37.

56. Ibid.

57. Smith, *Wealth of Nations*, book 5, chap. 1.

58. Wheare, *Modern Constitutions*, 137.

59. See the first ten amendments to the U.S. Constitution.

60. Greenstein and Polsby, *Handbook of Political Science*, 35–36.

61. See Sartori, *Constitutionalism*, 862. The author considers economic policies in the constitution as frivolous, and a move away from constitutional telos. See also Greenstein and Polsby, *Handbook of Political Science*, 3, for the view that positive government after the Great Depression was incompatible with the principles of constitutionalism.

62. For a discussion of law being autonomous from political processes see Talcot Parsons, "Evolutionary Universals in Society," *American Sociological Review* 29 (1965): 353.

63. G. Kateb, "Remarks on the Procedures of Constitutional Democracy," in Pennock and Chapman, *Constitutionalism*, 217. Institutions are clearly important for achieving goals and objectives. This aspect is explored in chapter 7.

64. Ibid.

65. Cowen, *Foundations of Freedom*, 49–50.

66. *Krohn v. Minister of Defence*, 1915 A.D. 191.

67. Laurence J. Boulle, *Constitutional Reform and the Apartheid State: Legitimacy, Constitutionalism, and Control in South Africa* (New York: St. Martin's Press, 1984), 95.

68. Peter Randall, ed., *South Africa's Political Alternatives* (Johannesburg: SPRO-CAS, 1973).

69. Wade and Phillips, *Constitutional and Administrative Law.*

70. Notwithstanding the partial reforms that brought "coloreds" and "Indians" into the central government in the new tricameral Parliament introduced in 1984.

71. Group Areas Act 36 of 1966.

72. Internal Security Act, sec. 19.

73. Internal Security Act, sec. 28 and 29.

74. Internal Security Act 8232 of 1982, chap. 5, sec. 46.

75. Ibid.

76. Internal Security Act, sec. 4.

77. Publications Act 42 of 1974.

78. J. C. W. Van Rooyen, *Censorship in South Africa: Being a Commentary of the Application of the Publications Act* (Cape Town: Juta, 1987), 110–11.

79. von Hayek, *The Road to Serfdom*, 54.

80. J. Raz, "Liberty and the Rule of Law," in Cunningham, *Liberty and the Rule of Law*, 4.

81. There is an ongoing tension between the rule of law and discretionary powers. Today flexibility in administrative decisions is recognized by most theorists as important for the efficiency of the modern state. However, officials must give public reasons for their decisions and the administrative machinery must follow certain procedures. See J. Raz, "The Politics of the Rule of Law," 332. The administrative discretions that officers of the state enjoy in South Africa depart from basic administrative rules found in most Western systems.

82. Internal Security Act, sec. 28 and 29.

83. Publications Act, sec. 47(2); Internal Security Act, sec. 5.

84. H. R. Hahlo and Ellison Kahn, *The Union of South Africa: The Development of Its Laws and Constitution* (London: Stevens, 1960), 134.

85. Act 3 of 1953.

86. For example, in England the government has at its disposal the prerogative powers of the Crown. This is found in most constitutional systems. See S. Finer, "The Governments of Europe," in Finer, *Five Constitutions*, 58–59.

87. Proc. 108 of 1986 in Government Gazette 10279 of 12 June 1986 (hereinafter referred to as the 1986 proclamation). The restrictions in terms of the state of emergency have from time to time been amended and tightened.

88. R. S. Suttner, "Law, Justice, and The Nature of Man," in Ferenc Madl, ed., *Acta Juridica* (Budapest: Akademiai Kiado, 1963), 180.

89. For comments on the Marxist state, see chapter 8.

90. For the view that South Africa conforms to the repressive model of law, see John Hund and Henrik W. Van der Merwe, *Legal Ideology and Politics in South Africa: A Social Science Approach* (Lanham, Md.: University Press of America, 1986), 11.

91. Trapido, "South Africa in a Comparative Study of Industrialization," *Journal of Development Studies* 7 (1971): 313.

92. Hund and Van der Merwe, *Legal Ideology,* 28.

93. Ibid.

CHAPTER THREE

Democracy: Meaning and Interpretation

■ ■ ■

F EW WORDS EVOKE so much controversy as the word *democracy.* At the outset let us emphasize the distinction between democracy as a social idea and democracy as a system of government.[1] Many commentators allude to the immense difficulty in defining democracy.[2] The word *democratic* has become a catchword for all kinds of political systems and governments, each claiming authority for its beliefs.[3] According to Robert Dahl, there is no democratic theory but only democratic theories, each with its own ideological underpinnings.[4]

In this chapter we trace the origins and development of democratic theories from various perspectives. We consider present conceptions of democracy in Western liberal and Communist systems, as well as conceptions of democracy in traditional African societies. This enquiry is crucial to understanding the link between theory and the different constitutional models that are considered afterwards.

The examination shows that much of the current debate tends to ignore democracy as a social idea, and just assumes that those countries called democracies are democratic. In this approach, "application determines meaning" as opposed to "meaning determining application."[5] The chapter concludes with a more viable democratic theory for a future South Africa.[6] We explore the elite nature of present notions of democratic theory, which subsequently will be shown to be inappropriate for African countries.[7]

Evolution of Democracy in Liberal Thought

To the ancient Greeks, democracy denoted rule by the citizen body (the common people), as opposed to rule by the rich.[8] In this sense it was very

19

much a class affair,[9] calling for the full participation of all citizens in the political and legal matters of the community.[10] Decisions were made in full meetings of all citizens who voted.[11] It follows from its early setting that democracy meant rule by the people, and the participation of the people in the decision-making processes of the community.[12] The type of society that Athenian democracy applied to was essentially a nonclass or one-class society. As a rule, the citizen population was not dependent on others for employment and everyone owned their own property.[13]

In liberal thought today, a crucial debate is waged concerning the purpose and nature of participation in society.[14] The models reveal different assumptions about the way society should be structured and the nature of people in a political system.[15] The arguments have been formulated in terms of a debate between traditional, classical or orthodox thinkers, and modern or revisionist thinkers.

TRADITIONAL TENETS

Traditional thinking on democracy argues for the greatest participation of the individual in the political affairs of the community. Its single most influential proponent was the French philosopher Jean Jacques Rousseau, as revealed in his *Social Contract*.[16] For Rousseau, man is born free, and the only way of ensuring this freedom is to vest sovereign power in the hands of the people.[17] Democracy and participation are not merely institutional arrangements: participation has certain essential psychological and educational effects on the members of society. The latter aspect is central to Rousseau's thinking. It is through participation that a private citizen learns to become responsible in political action, linking his or her individual interests with the public interest.[18] The system once created becomes self-sustaining, as participants develop the qualities necessary to maintain it.[19]

For Rousseau, the system of representative democracy was untenable: "Sovereignty, being no more than the exercise of the general will, can never be alienated."[20] The general will would be arrived at if the people were adequately informed, and if they could communicate their thoughts to one another. This general will tends to the good of society.[21]

Private property is an essential right in Rousseau's model, though he imposes conditions on this right. People must only occupy as much land as is necessary for their subsistence. And they must take possession of the land with the intention of working it.[22]

Extreme inequality in wealth is inimical to liberty. Nature has provided amenities for the common use of mankind, and one part of society cannot deprive others of these amenities by excessive appropriation. Rousseau envisaged a system where no person would be dependent on another for well-being or employment.[23] Differences in the amount of property result in a division into different classes with divergent interests. In such circumstances, it is impossible to arrive at the general will because each of the contending groups has a separate interest to protect and champion. Arriving at the general will requires economic "homogeneity" in the form of a one-class society.[24] Rousseau's call for a homogenous economic order is what distinguishes his thought from present-day liberal democratic models.[25]

REVISIONIST/MODERN THINKING

The core concern of modern (revisionist) thinkers is a rejection of direct democracy. They argue that the mass of the people cannot decide complex political matters and that this necessitates representation.[26] They see the formation of oligarchical and bureaucratic party organizations as inevitable.[27] Moreover, direct democracy as an ideal or theoretical system is beyond the limit of human possibilities.[28]

Since direct democracy is impossible, it is time for a revision in the thinking on democracy.[29] The modern age is an age of realism and this realism is irrevocable.[30] According to G. Sartori, there is an unbridgeable gap between traditional theory and reality;[31] the modern theorists set out to provide a theory of democracy more fitting to reality.[32]

Modern theorists question and criticize the basic postulates on which traditional thinkers on democracy based their arguments. First, they assert it is impossible to talk about arriving at a common will. If one is going to argue about a common will, then one must firstly demonstrate the rationality of each voter, with respect to the voter's powers of observation and interpretation, and ability to make decisions.[33] On the basis of several studies and investigations, the revisionists claim that voters do not display the level of interest in politics traditional theory credits them with.[34] The general picture is of a citizenry uninterested in politics and civic affairs.[35]

Even when citizens do display interest, they are ignorant of issues and policies, and consequently their voting behavior is irrational.[36] The idea of a rational citizen is a legal fiction.[37] With this reduced sense of reality, political groups are able to manipulate the irrational or illogical voter in a manner similar to commercial advertising.[38]

Apart from portraying voters as generally uninterested in political affairs, the revisionists make the additional claim that such apathy is good for the system overall because the mass of the people are not in a position to decide complex political questions. An increase in participation by the citizens is seen as dangerous to the stability of the system.[39] Even if all voters showed rationality, interest, and knowledge, the result would be detrimental to democracy.[40] For the system to hold together, the type of population required is a heterogeneous and pluralistic social organization.[41] Some members of society must be well informed and others less informed, some conservative and others liberal, and some interested and others uninterested.[42]

Modern theorists reject the traditional notions with their heavy emphasis on norms and values. They assert that since the present era is an age of realism,[43] modern theory should be empirical and grounded in the facts of life.[44] Democracy should not have any idealistic orientations. Taking this "reality" into account, democracy for Joseph Schumpeter "is that institutional arrangement for arriving at political decisions in which individuals acquire the power to decide by means of a competitive struggle for the people's vote."[45] Since traditional thinking rested on false premises, namely, the supposed rationality and participation of the people, the revised definition attempts to cure this defect. According to the revisionists, political decisions are taken by an elite leadership, and the democratic process is the competition between contending elites for the support of the people. In this context, democracy does not mean the people contribute or initiate decisions. It only means that the people have the choice of electing rulers from among candidates.[46] It is the leaders who decide the issues. This Dahl characterizes as rule by minorities.[47] According to the revisionists, it is political institutions that permit the election and alternation of elites that distinguishes a democratic system from a nondemocratic system.

The actual institutional arrangements are described by Dahl and can be summarized as the right of all adults to elect government officials entrusted with decision-making powers.[48] There should be equality in that all adults should have the right to run for political office, and freedom of speech (including the right to criticize the government) should be guaranteed. There should be freedom to form political associations to achieve these rights.[49] These, together "with frequent alternations in office from one party to the other," are the defining characteristic of democracy.[50]

Modern thinkers' notion of equality means the abolition of socioeconomic distinctions and not the abolition of the class system. In its application, it means an equality of opportunity to select leaders and not an equality of power. Modern thinkers recognize that the majority are denied access to power because of their socioeconomic status and lack of resources.[51] However, this lack of access to power is not seen as contradictory to democracy, because in the choice between equality and liberty, the latter is considered more important. According to Milton Friedman, if equality means material equality (as opposed to equality of opportunity and treatment under the law), then equality is contrary to liberty.[52] The preference for liberty is consistent with the liberal view of placing the core emphasis on individual rights.

An important question that theorists raise is what the precise relationship between representatives and the people should be. Should representatives be bound by the instructions of their constituents, or should they be in a position to judge on their own what is good for the people? According to the modern liberal view, elected representatives have the greater knowledge in political affairs and are in a better position to make choices,[53] that is, the electoral mass is incapable of action, so leaders must perform the initiating.[54] In the institutional arrangement, representatives enjoy considerable autonomy in making choices on policies and programs. The public view is not directly taken into consideration.

This view conceives the public as passive and does not invite initiative. Direct control by citizens over their representatives is viewed as undemocratic.[55] According to Sartori, the people must react to the initiatives of the leaders as opposed to taking initiatives on their own. To do otherwise would lead to totalitarianism.[56] Despite the absence of traditional requirements, the revisionists claim their system of democracy still continues to work and flourish.[57]

The modern liberal theory of democracy primarily concerns itself with providing a description of prevailing systems as they exist and providing rationales for why a system should continue the way it is. In terms of the latter function, the theory is more concerned with legitimating the existing order and destroying expectations that endanger it. The selection of leaders is "an intermediate goal which leads to the final goal of system stability."[58] Stability is provided in several ways. First, only informed and interested persons will be elected to leadership positions. These persons are most likely to share values that are consistent with the continuation of the system.[59] Second, the election of leaders in a competitive system contributes to the legitimacy of the system.[60]

The people's participation does not in any way constitute a meaningful contribution in the framing of issues or the outcome of decisions. All that the people do is vote for representatives, which may provide individual satisfaction and a feeling of participation by "stirring people up and giving them a sense of their own potential significance, and attaching their sentiments to symbols which comprehend the entire nation."[61] In this context, elections are more allegiance maintaining and fulfill a more ritual function.[62] Overall, the system enjoys legitimacy, and "the belief and ritual aspects of political participation are more important than its substantive policy results."[63]

Criticism of modern democratic theory takes aim at its descriptive nature. It describes the system in terms of what it is instead of what it ought to be. Its assumption of political equality in the absence of legal bars is erroneous. In theory, all sectors of the population have the same power to influence the political process. In practice, those sectors of society with greater material resources are more influential politically.[64] Political equality cannot be claimed in the absence of economic equality. Despite equal access to the vote, those citizens with significant financial resources control politics as well.[65] The wealthy can get their own candidates elected and ultimately their views accepted.[66] Nowhere is this reality more stark then in the U.S. political system. Arthur Miller asserts that those sectors with greater financial resources have the ability to manipulate the political process.[67] Modern elections require vast amounts of money for advertising and getting a candidate's message across to the public. Not surprisingly, more often than not the candidate with financial resources or backing is more likely to succeed in an election against a candidate with less resources at his or her disposal, a situation Arthur Miller characterizes as an illusion of equality.[68] It is a situation that also leads to a perception that the government is representative of special interests.[69]

Several liberal writers following along the lines of traditional thinking have called for greater citizen participation in political affairs. The question is whether greater participation is possible under a liberal system of government, and if not what the limitations are. The type of society that Rousseau posited for participatory democracy to function was essentially one with no gross inequality. Stratification of class engenders class conflict. In a society with class antagonisms, mutual agreement (Rousseau's general will) would not be possible because of contradictory interests. Modern liberal democratic theory departs fundamentally from this ideal in its acceptance of the market forces that lead to class divisions in society.[70] The requirements for participatory democracy as outlined by Rousseau are incompatible with unfettered free enterprise.[71]

Democracy and Socialism

Marxist theory is like participation theory in its emphasis on change as opposed to merely providing a description. However, states claiming to represent the tenets of Marx have been oppressive and authoritarian. Consequently, there is a dichotomy between Marxian theory and regimes that espouse Marxism that has to be explored when considering the notion of democracy under Marxism.

KARL MARX AND DEMOCRACY

Karl Marx saw Communism as democracy in its best form and as the only system of true government of the people. For Marx, governments under a capitalist system perpetuate alienation and exploitation in that the ordinary person is separated in one form or another from the process of governing. The root of this alienation is the institution of private property, which is the cause of political and social divisions.[72]

Marx's theory of democracy is highly moralistic. Capitalist society is associated with class rule, where one class by force maintains control over

24

the others. The resolution of class exploitation requires overthrowing the capitalist system and replacing it with a socialist order in which all class distinctions are abolished;[73] only then can human beings achieve their humanity.[74] Capitalist systems offer various civil liberties that Marx welcomed as a step in the right direction. He was as much concerned with the positive aspects of liberal democracy as with its limitations. However, for him the struggle for democracy must be linked to the struggle for socialism.[75] Civil rights were not in themselves sufficient. Marx linked the achievement of these civil rights to a state of political emancipation, which he asserted could only be achieved by a transformation of the economic and social order.[76]

Democracy for Marx was very much a class state where the legal basis of capitalism was abolished. The means of production should be placed in the hands of the lower classes and workers and utilized for their benefit.[77] The goal for Marx was "to raise the proletariat to the position of a ruling class, to win the battle of democracy."[78] In this sense Marx's notion of democracy is consistent with the agelong interpretation of democracy as meaning the ascendancy of the lower classes.[79] Some writers go so far as to say that Rousseau provided the inspiration for Marx's political theory,[80] but there are fundamental points of departure between the two thinkers. Marx's conception of history is materialist and he views events in a historical and material context,[81] what he calls concrete reality. Marx's version of democracy also goes beyond Rousseau and the ancient notions by conceptualizing how the liberation of a class will result in the liberation of humanity.[82] In terms of their conception of democracy with respect to their demand for maximum participation, however, Rousseau and Marx share a number of ideas.

Marx placed the masses at the forefront of society in terms of economic and political decisions—raising workers to what he called the "dictatorship of the proletariat." The meaning that Marx and Engels gave to the phrase is crucial to understanding their conception of democracy. Both Engels and Marx refer to the Commune of Paris of 1871, which existed for a brief period following the reign of Louis Napoleon in France, as providing the best expression of democracy.[83] For Marx, the Paris Commune overcame the distinction between members of civil society and members of political society in that state power and society were not separated.[84] The Commune was made up of paid officials who were elected by universal suffrage, ordinary working people who were subject to recall at any time. In this sense the Commune was a working body and not a body of representatives. The officials were simply public employees who received wages.[85] The working body combined executive and legislative functions, was at all times accountable to the electorate, and in all instances had to act on instructions. The franchise was not simply an act of choosing who was to represent the people: the people at all times exercised control over the officials.[86]

The power of the working body was the antithesis of elite rule. Marx's notion of representation was severely critical of representatives or delegates who turned out to be masters over the people. The lack of accountability of delegates to the people creates a situation where the delegates become accountable to parliament, instead of being deputies of the society, "linked to their electors by an instruction, commission or mandate."[87] Moreover, with lack of control over the deputies, the latter become an organ that decides what is in the best interests of the people. The masses then have to assume a position of trust in instead of control over the deputies.[88]

The aspect of control by the people is the cornerstone of Marx's theory of democracy. For Marx this control must be exercised by the lower classes at all stages in their struggle. Moreover, the struggle must be conducted according to the wishes of the lower classes as opposed to those of the leadership. The point of control by the lower classes is incessantly impressed. It has to be borne in mind, because present practices by governments that claim the Marxist tag reveal fundamental points of departure from the tenets of democracy as emphasized by Marx and Engels. Some of the differences in practice and the rationale underlying it have affinities with the revisionist liberal democratic theory.

The Paris Commune was for Marx the model of democracy primarily for two reasons. First, it did away with the capitalist system of production.[89] Second, it gave people a system of self-government, a model Marx urged should be replicated at every level of society.[90] A number of villages or towns in a region should select their deputies for a district assembly, and the latter in turn should select deputies to serve at a national assembly. However, delegates should act in terms of the mandate given to them, which could be revoked at any time.[91] Marx's scenario envisaged the "amputation" of authority that existed above society, which was what he considered the system of selecting delegates once in three or any number of years.[92]

Before considering the practices of former Communist countries, as exemplified in the former Soviet Union, it is worth mentioning other common features between Rousseau and Marx with regard to their position on democracy. Orthodox Marxism also does not assume that people are irrational, but emphasizes that human behavior depends on the immediate situation. Moreover, rational people are not a prerequisite for democratic institutions. Instead, political institutions must be developed in a way that makes maximum participation possible.[93] It is through participation that the citizen develops the capacity to make rational judgments.[94]

LENINISM AND THE DRIFT TOWARD ELITE RULE

According to Marx and Engels, the organized proletariat would be the agent for effecting the transformation to democracy. The form of democracy that existed in the former Soviet Union and the former East European countries based on elite rule is a far cry from that advocated by Karl Marx. The trend toward elite rule can be traced to the writings of Lenin and the founding of the Bolshevik state in the Soviet Union. In the beginning, elite decision making was an essential component of Lenin's theory, apparently based on the conditions prevailing in Soviet society prior to the Bolshevik revolution. Elite rule became the enduring feature of former Communist countries, with its most extreme manifestations seen in the reign of Stalin.

Marx had prophesied that the proletariat would come to acquire revolutionary consciousness and would eventually adopt the revolutionary option. Lenin was faced with this expectation at the turn of the century, but to his disappointment, it was not realized in Russia. It was in this context that Lenin revised essential aspects of Marx's doctrines and replaced them with the notion of a vanguard movement.[95]

For Lenin, the workers do not possess the necessary consciousness to transform the system—a consciousness has to be brought to them from outside. Left to themselves, workers do not aspire beyond trade-union consciousness.[96] The masses have tremendous energy, but conducting the overall struggle requires a brand of professional people who must make the struggle their full-time occupation. The core of professional people must be small and it must conduct its activities in secret.[97] Lenin envisaged setting up committees and organizations operating at various community and workplace levels. However, he saw the function of these bodies more as agents to carry out the decisions of the core group. In addition he called for specialization of activities and, more importantly, centralization of decision making.[98] In Lenin's words, the "strictest centralization and discipline are required within the political party . . ., in order that the organizing role of the proletariat . . . may be exercised correctly, successfully, victoriously."[99] This control has to be maintained by the iron hold of the party.[100]

Marx's state organization did not allow for a separation of the executive and legislative functions, as this was not compatible with the mandate system, though it did not preclude an executive organ. The essential point was that the executive should not enjoy special privileges but should only work for a salary. These aspects of Marx's ideas were criticized by constitutional theorists in Communist countries as unrealistic. A distinction was made between preconstitutional models outlined by Marx and Engels and actual constitutional models in socialist countries. The early models were criticized as being unsound because they were formulated on the basis of insufficient data.[101] Only after the effects had been felt could a correct model be put forward, as was done in the former Soviet Union. In a sense, it was empirical in merely assuming that the organizational form under their system was democratic while actually debasing democracy of its essential participatory qualities.

Lenin's revised notion of democracy shares similarities with the revisionist liberal school and departs fundamentally from both Marx and Rousseau's notions. For Marx, the proletariat is the agent for change and the struggle can only be waged on its terms. For Lenin, it is impossible to wait for majority support. Like the revisionists, Lenin refers to the people as irrational and unable to make proper decisions. Therefore, choices have to be made on their behalf. He also conceives the masses as passive. It is unclear whether Lenin considered this elitist element to be an everlasting feature or something only in the buildup to the overthrow of the old order. For example, in his later writings Lenin also speaks about drawing all members of society into the practical work of administration.[102] However, the elitist element of rule began with Lenin and proved to be an enduring feature of Communist countries many years after the "revolution." The idea of vanguardism is not democratic and like revisionism required from the majority of the people deference on political matters. Communist countries were run strictly from top to bottom and permitted only a minority to decide on matters.[103] The Soviet view was that important matters could not be left to the masses to decide, but had to be referred to the central committee of the party. Under the former Soviet system what one saw was a narrowing down of decisions from the entire population, the party, the central committee to just a few people, and under Stalin, to just one person.[104]

Democracy and the Exercise of Power in Traditional African Systems

African leaders often protest against the tendency of Western scholars to study African problems in terms of theories and concepts "established on the basis of western experiences."[105] Much is made of traditional African institutions and notions of democracy, which are advocated as better-suited to the African condition. Democracy in the traditional setting will be examined. At the outset, we emphasize that Africa, being a vast continent, was not a homogeneous entity. The kinds of political systems that existed varied from highly centralized to decentralized forms of rule. However, there were common practices across many parts of Africa, which permit broad generalizations of traditional practices.

TRADITIONAL EXERCISE OF POWER AND LEGITIMACY

Under Western political systems control of government power is seen in terms of a highly normative system of constitutional checks and balances, and separation of powers. In traditional societies the law existed outside the framework of the nation-state as it is known in the present setting. Obedience to law—and social control—was maintained through custom and religion,[106] which also played a crucial part in legitimating the rule of the leader.[107] Like present systems of government, the traditional ruler's power claimed to derive from an authority—for instance, the myth of the founding father or other ancestor, similar to the "mysterious" God of Western natural law theory.[108]

DEMOCRACY AND THE EXERCISE
OF POWER IN TRADITIONAL SYSTEMS

The most influential personality in traditional African systems was the chief or king. The chief enjoyed "mystical" qualities and in most instances was a charismatic personality. Although the chief had considerable power, he did not rule on his own but was subject to a host of controls. The most important of these controls was the elders[109] of the community. In most instances, the chief did not arrive at a decision on his own but "sounded out the elders" and solicited their opinion.[110] The elders constituted an effective check on the chief, and in some societies the chief was obliged in all instances to act on the advice and concurrence of the council or risk being deposed.[111] When the chief gave his verdict, he was not giving his personal opinion but was providing the consensus among the elders.[112] The chief and the elders were responsible for the administration of the region, and together they were the government.[113] They met on a regular basis to decide matters of concern, and the elders would communicate the decisions to their respective lineages.[114]

Hence, the king did not rule on his own but was subject to pressures from diverse interests represented by the elders, who in a sense represented the political elite.[115] The elders could represent other lineages, regions, or the military. The various interest groups competed to influence policy decisions.[116] In effect, the exercise of political power was circumscribed or restrained by social institutions—the customs and traditions of the society.[117]

In traditional systems decisions were arrived at after a prolonged process of consultation and discussion.[118] This aspect of talking things over has often been characterized as a unique feature of African societies. Opposition was articulated, but the final decision summed up by the chief reflected the general opinion of the group.[119] In the process, all parties were allowed to voice their opinions without threats or abuse. Kofi Busia makes the point that even the young and ordinary people participated in decisions either directly or through their chosen representatives.[120] In this sense there was a high premium on freedom of opinion.[121] Studies in southern Africa have shown similar evidence of assemblies of people where issues of concern to the community were discussed by all in an atmosphere of free speech.[122]

In most traditional African systems chiefs were chosen by a system of election. However, the choice was limited to elderly males from the right lineage.[123] In the end the acceptance of a particular chief was dependent on the approval of the elders.[124] The elders were the representatives of the people, and in most instances were men of knowledge and integrity.[125] The elders were elected by the senior people in the respective lineages.[126]

CONSEQUENCES OF ABUSE OF POWER

The general description of the way power was exercised and controlled in traditional societies does not mean there were no abuses on the part of leadership. Africa prior to the advent of colonialism had a number of despots as well. In the context of southern Africa the most controversial has been King Shaka, who has been called southern Africa's Napoleon.[127] The reign of Shaka was an exceptional period in which many atrocities were committed against the people of southern Africa. This is something that traditional leaders have recognized,[128] though authoritarian patterns of behavior were a departure from the norm,[129] and were exercised at the peril of the despot.

While the customs served to control society, they also regulated the conduct of the leader. In those instances where a leader departed from the norm, numerous sanctions were available, the most severe being the removal of the chief from the leadership position. Subjects could also withdraw economic services to the chief or withhold the payment of taxes.[130] Busia identifies instances in which a leader was removed from office for drunkenness, greed, abusive behavior, or being physically or mentally unfit for carrying out the duties of office.[131] In this sense the king was generally restricted in terms of his scope of action. The customs of the society were an extremely powerful instrument in obtaining conformity to general practices. The conformity to these norms can be said to be built into the political institutions. In particular, the requirement that a chief consult his council was a very strong practice.[132] In turn, members of the council had to act on the advice of their lineages or face the prospect of being penalized by the members of the community.

SOCIOECONOMIC ARRANGEMENTS
IN THE TRADITIONAL SETTING

Widespread participation in an essentially egalitarian order was a prevalent feature of traditional systems. The socioeconomic system was communal.[133] The traditional society was a mutual society whose priority was to see to the welfare of all its members. The economic benefits were shared by all, and all property was held for the mutual benefit of the society. The individual had the right to use the land to produce food for himself and his family but that right did not extend to individual ownership. The institution of private property seems to have been a nonexistent feature in all African societies. The society generally provided security for all its members.[134] In this sense the conception of equality extended beyond individualism.

REFERENCES

1. J. Dewey, "Search for the Great Community," in L. Earl Shaw, ed., *Modern Competing Ideologies* (Lexington, Mass.: Heath, 1973), 297.

2. William N. Nelson, *On Justifying Democracy* (London: Routledge and Kegan Paul, 1980); Crawford B. MacPherson, *The Life and Times of Liberal Democracy* (Oxford: Oxford University Press, 1977); Keith Graham, *The Battle of Democracy: Conflict, Consensus, and the Individual* (Brighton: Wheatsheaf Books, 1986), 1.

3. MacPherson, *Liberal Democracy,* 3. MacPherson asserts that democratic theory should not simply be equated with Western liberal systems, as other systems also claim the title of democracy.

4. Robert A. Dahl, *A Preface to Democratic Theory* (Chicago: University of Chicago Press, 1956), 1.

5. Barry Holden, *The Nature of Democracy* (New York: Barnes and Noble Books, 1974), 7.

6. The failure of constitutional models that provide for "democracy" based on elite rule will be considered in chapters 5, 7, and 8.

7. Ibid.

8. Moses I. Finley, *Democracy Ancient and Modern* (London: Chatto and Windus, 1973), 12–13.

9. MacPherson, *Liberal Democracy,* 5.

10. Howard P. Kainz, *Democracy, East and West: A Philosophical Overview* (New York: St. Martin's Press, 1984), 15.

11. Ibid.

12. However, in the Greek setting all the people were not included, as women and slaves were still excluded. See Graham, *Battle of Democracy,* 12.

13. MacPherson, *Life and Times,* 11–12.

14. Lee Ann Osbun, *The Problem of Participation: A Radical Critique of Contemporary Democratic Theory* (Lanham, Md.: University Press of America, 1985), v.

15. MacPherson, *Liberal Democracy,* 5.

16. See J. Rousseau, "The Social Contract," in Ernst Barker, trans., *Social Contract: Essays by Locke, Hume, and Rousseau* (London: Oxford University Press, 1952).

17. Charles F. Strong, *Modern Political Constitutions: An Introduction to the Comparative Study of Their History and Existing Form,* 6th rev. ed. (London: Sidgwick & Jackson, 1963), 35; Rousseau, "The Social Contract," Book 2.

18. Carole Pateman, *Participation and Democratic Theory* (Cambridge: Cambridge University Press, 1970), 25.

19. Ibid.

20. Rousseau, "The Social Contract," 190.

21. Ibid., 194.

22. Ibid., 187.

23. Ibid., 217.

24. MacPherson, *Liberal Democracy,* 17.

25. This theme is developed in the ensuing section.

26. Holden, *Nature of Democracy,* 29.

27. Robert Michels, *Political Parties: A Sociological Study of the Oligarchical Tendencies of Modern Democracy* trans. Eden and Cedar Paul (New York: Collier Books, 1962), 65, 72.

28. Robert A. Dahl, *Dilemmas of Pluralist Democracy: Autonomy vs. Control* (New Haven: Yale University Press, 1982), 6.

29. See generally Joseph A. Schumpeter, *Capitalism, Socialism, and Democracy,* 2d ed. (New York: Harper & Brothers, 1947). Schumpeter is widely perceived to have laid the framework for the revisionist theory of democracy.

30. See L. Hartz, "Democracy: Image and Reality," in William N. Chambers and Robert H. Salisbury, eds., *Democracy in the Mid-Twentieth Century: Problems and Prospects* (Freeport, N.Y.: Books for Libraries Press, 1971).

31. Giovanni Sartori, *Democratic Theory* (Westport, Conn.: Greenwood Press, 1973).

32. There is no specific school of modern or revisionist theory of democracy, but there are several writers who share similar perspectives on the proper role and definition of democracy in modern society. For the merits of this approach see Osbun, *Problem of Participation,* 1. Also see Holden, *Nature of Democracy,* especially chapters 3 and 6. Holden also adopts the dichotomy of traditional democratic theory and modern democratic theory.

33. Schumpeter, *Capitalism,* 256.

34. Mark A. Abrams and Richard Rose, *Must Labour Lose?* (Harmondsworth: Penguin Books, 1960), 73.

35. Abrams and Rose, ibid.; Bernard Berelson, Paul F. Lazarsfeld, and William N. McPhee, *Voting: A Study of Opinion Formation in a Presidential Campaign* (Chicago: University of Chicago Press, 1954), 310; Graham, *Battle of Democracy,* 131; L. Hartz, "Democracy: Image and Reality" in Chambers and Salisbury, *Democracy in the Mid-Twentieth Century,* 13–29.

36. Holden, *Nature of Democracy,* 143.

37. Ibid.; Berelson, Lazarsfeld, and McPhee, *Voting,* 310.

38. Schumpeter, *Capitalism,* 263.

39. Pateman, *Participation,* 10.

40. Berelson, Lazarsfeld, and McPhee, *Voting,* 313.

41. The argument goes that it is better to have multiple centers of power in society to ensure a modicum of liberty and social harmony. See Shaw, *Modern Competing Ideologies,* 281.

42. Berelson, Lazarsfeld, and McPhee, *Voting,* 314.

43. See Chambers and Salisbury, *Democracy in the Mid-Twentieth Century,* 15–17.

44. Pateman, *Participation,* 3.

45. Schumpeter, *Capitalism,* 269.

46. Dahl, *Preface to Democratic Theory,* 84.

47. Ibid., 132.

48. Dahl, *Dilemmas of Pluralist Democracy,* 10–11.

49. Ibid.

50. Robert A. Dahl, *Who Governs? Democracy and Power in an American City* (New Haven: Yale University Press, 1961), 311.

51. Pateman, *Participation,* 9.

52. Milton Friedman, *Capitalism and Freedom* (Chicago: University of Chicago Press, 1962), 195.

53. See John Stuart Mill, *On Liberty and Considerations on Representative Government* (Oxford: Blackwell, 1946), 233; Benjamin O. Nwabueze, *Constitutionalism in the Emergent States* (London: C. Hurst, 1973), 11.

54. Schumpeter, *Capitalism*, 270.

55. Pateman, *Participation*, 5.

56. Sartori, *Democratic Theory*, 77.

57. The success of the system is measured by the lack of widespread revolt to overhaul the existing system. Lester W. Milbrath, *Political Participation: How and Why Do People Get Involved in Politics?* (Chicago: Rand McNally Press, 1965), 143.

58. Osbun, *Problem of Participation*, 12.

59. Ibid., 13.

60. Ibid.

61. Edward A. Shils, *Political Development in the New States* (Gravenhage: Mouton, 1962), 38.

62. R. Rose and H. Mossawir, "Voting and Elections: A Functional Analysis," in *Political Studies* 85 (June 1967): 177. See also, Murray J. Edelman, *The Symbolic Uses of Politics* (Urbana, Ill.: University of Illinois Press, 1985), 2–3.

63. Osbun, *Problem of Participation*, 15.

64. See the dissent of Justice White in *Buckley v Valeo* 424 U.S. 1 (1976). Justice White in his dissent recognized that money talks in politics. Ibid., 262.

65. Jack Lively, *Democracy* (Oxford: Blackwell, 1986), 28–29.

66. See the dissent of Justice White in *First National Bank of Boston v Bellotti* 435 U.S. 765 (1978). Justice White pointed to the dangers of corporations using their wealth to gain an unfair advantage in the political process. Ibid., 809.

67. Arthur Miller, "On Politics, Democracy, and the First Amendment: A Commentary on *First National Bank v Bellotti,*" *Washington and Lee Law Review* 38 (1981): 23.

68. Ibid., 25.

69. See Leventhal, "Courts and Political Thickets," *Columbia Law Review* 77 (1977): 362. Leventhal refers to political polls conducted over the years pertaining to the people's perceptions with regard to their confidence in the government. In 1974, 70 percent of the people polled felt the government was controlled by a few big corporations looking out for their own interests.

70. MacPherson, *Liberal Democracy*, 20.

71. See Leventhal, "Courts," 370. Leventhal says that the perception that politicians represent special interests is not a new phenomenon. He refers to senators of the nineteenth century who represented various special interests such as insurance, lumber, railroads, banking, and manufacturing.

72. Karl Marx, Friedrich Engels, and Vladimir Lenin, *On the Dictatorship of the Proletariat: A Collection* (Moscow: Progress Publishers, 1984), 5.

73. Karl Marx, *The Class Struggles in France, 1848–1850* (New York: New York Labor News, 1924).

74. Karl Marx and Friedrich Engels, *The Communist Manifesto*, trans. Samuel Moore, II (New York: New York Labor News, 1948); MacPherson, *Real World of Democracy*, 14.

75. John Hoffman, *Marxism, Revolution, and Democracy* (Amsterdam: B. R. Gruner Publishers, 1983), 93.

76. Ralph Miliband, *Marxism and Politics* (Oxford: Oxford University Press, 1977), 8.

77. Marx, *Dictatorship of the Proletariat*, 7.

78. Marx, quoted in Graham, *Battle of Democracy*, 180.

79. Lively, *Democracy*, 33.

80. Lucio Colletti, *From Rousseau to Lenin: Studies in Ideology and Society*, trans. John Merrington and Judith White (London: NLB, 1972), 185.

81. Karl Marx, *A Contribution to the Critique of Political Economy*, trans. S. W. Ryazanskaya (London: Lawrence and Wishart, 1971), 20.

82. MacPherson, *Real World of Democracy*, 15.

83. For a full view of Marx's thoughts on the Paris Commune, see Karl Marx, *Der Bürgerkrieg im Frankreich* [The Civil War in France] (New York: International Publishers, 1933).

84. Karl Marx, *Political Writings, vol. 3, The First International and After,* ed. David Fernbach (Harmondsworth: Penguin Books, 1973).

85. Marx, *Civil War in France,* 42.

86. Ibid.

87. Marx's critique of Hegel's theory of representation quoted in Fine, *Democracy and the Rule of Law,* 76.

88. Ibid.

89. Marx, *Civil War in France,* 44.

90. Ibid., 41.

91. Ibid.

92. Ibid., 42.

93. This comes out clearly in Marx's comments on the Paris Commune. See Marx, *Political Writings, vol. 3,* 36.

94. Ibid., 37.

95. Guenter Lewy, *False Consciousness: An Essay on Mystification* (New Brunswick, N.J.: Transaction Books, 1982), 6. The relative merits or weaknesses of this approach in the objective conditions of European society in the nineteenth century will not be considered, only its implications for democracy.

96. Vladimir I. Lenin, *What is to Be Done?* trans. Joe Fineburg and George Hanna (London: Penguin Books, 1988), 31.

97. Ibid., 107–9.

98. V. I. Lenin, *Detskaia bolezn' "levizny" v kommunizme* ["Left-Wing" Communism, An Infantile Disorder], 5th ed. (Moscow: Progress Press, 1968), 53; *What is to Be Done?* 123, 127.

99. Lenin, quoted in Marx, *Political Writings, vol. 3,* 15.

100. Ibid.

101. Bihari, *Constitutional Models,* 24.

102. Lenin, quoted in Marx, *Political Writings, vol. 3,* 32.

103. The way the state institutions operate will be considered in chapter 8.

104. Graham, *Battle of Democracy,* 210.

105. P. F. Gonidec, *African Politics* (Boston: M. Nijhoff, 1981), 1.

106. Osita C. Eze, *Human Rights in Africa: Some Selected Problems* (Lagos: MacMillan Nigeria, 1984).

107. Christian P. Potholm, *The Theory and Practice of African Politics* (Englewood Cliffs, N.J.: Prentice Hall, 1979), 25.

108. F. Olisa Awogu, *Political Institutions and Thought in Africa: An Introduction* (New York: Vantage Press, 1975), 47. Awogu further describes this exercise of power by the ruler as being similar to the notion of a social contract.

109. The term *elders* is a reference to the older members of society.

110. Jaramogi Oginga Odinga, *Not Yet Uhuru: The Autobiography of Oginga Odinga* (London: Heinemann, 1967), 12.

111. Kofi A. Busia, *Africa in Search of Democracy* (New York: Praeger, 1967), 23.

112. Odinga, *Not Yet Uhuru,* 12.

113. Kofi A. Busia, *The Position of the Chief in the Modern Political System of Ashanti: A Study of the Influence of Contemporary Social Changes on Ashanti Political Institutions* (London: Cass, 1968), 14.

114. Ibid., 16–17.

115. P. C. Lloyd, "The Political Structure of African Kingdoms," in Michael Banton, ed., *Political Systems and the Distribution of Power* (London: Association of Social Anthropologists, 1968), 73.

116. J. Maquet, *Power and Society in Africa*, trans. J. Kupfermann (London: World University Library, 1971), 92–93.

117. Potholm, *African Politics*, 25. See also A. Jinadu, *Structure and Choice in African Politics* (n.p., 1979), 43.

118. Unfortunately, like Athenian society, the consultations were limited to the male members of the society only.

119. Lloyd, *African Kingdoms*, 80.

120. Busia does not indicate how the representatives were chosen. Busia, *The Position of the Chief*, 9–10.

121. Busia, *Africa in Search of Democracy*, 29.

122. See Edwin W. Smith, *The Golden Stool: Some Aspects of the Conflict of Cultures in Africa* (London: Holborn Publishers, 1927), 164. The author describes the Basutho Pitso (national assembly).

123. J. Fletcher-Cooke, "Parliament, The Executive, and the Civil Service," in Alan C. Burns, *Parliament as an Export* (London: Allen & Unwin, 1966), 161.

124. See Busia, *The Position of the Chief*, 19–20. The author describes at length how the chief is elected among the Ashanti.

125. Odinga, *Not Yet Uhuru*, 12.

126. Busia, *The Position of the Chief*, 7.

127. Motsoko Pheko, *Apartheid, The Story of a Dispossessed People* (London: Marram Books, 1984), 39.

128.. Edgar H. Brookes and J. B. Macaulay, *Civil Liberty in South Africa* (Westport, Conn.: Greenwood Press, 1973), 8.

129. J. Maquet, *Power and Society*, 101.

130. See J. Beattie, "Checks on the Abuse of Political Power in Some African States: A Preliminary Framework for Analysis," in Ronald Cohen and John Middleton, eds., *Comparative Political Systems: Studies in the Politics of Pre-Industrial Societies* (Garden City, N.Y.: Natural History Press, 1967), 361–73. Beattie selects four traditional African societies in different parts of the continent and refers to the established norm of a leader first acting on the advice of his council.

131. Ibid.

132. Busia, *The Position of the Chief*, 21–22.

133. Awogu, *Political Institutions*, 83.

134. Z. Motala, "Human Rights in Africa: A Cultural, Ideological and Legal Examination," *Hastings International and Comparative Law Review* 12 (1989): 382.

CHAPTER FOUR

State Organization and Federalism in Africa

■ ■ ■

A DISTINCTION IS OFTEN made between forms of state and forms of government.[1] *Form of state* refers to how public authority is organized in the state; that is, whether power is centrally located or dispersed. *Form of government* involves a description of those persons entrusted with determining public policy, the relationship between them and the citizens, the actual outline of the organs of government, and the way these organs function.[2] The latter term deals with the relationship between the constitutional organs exercising public power.[3] The distinction between form of state and form of government is not absolute, as one can have similar forms of government in different forms of state and vice versa. The distinction is, however, essential, as there are attributes unique to each of the two primary forms of state that affect the way power is exercised.

The ensuing discussion highlights the primary differences between the unitary and federal forms of state and shows the main attributes of federal states as adopted in Africa. Finally, we evaluate the rationale for the adoption of one or the other form of state with particular emphasis on the federal/consociational form of state.

The Federal-Unitary Dichotomy

The two primary forms of state organizations are unitary and federal. Broadly speaking, the unitary form of state is associated with a strong central government with few territorial divisions. The federal arrangement is associated with a delegation of authority and territorial divisions.

Under a unitary arrangement greater emphasis is placed on unity and central control of activities. The system aims at achieving greater homogeneity in the country, be it in the realm of economic or legal affairs. However, the system does not preclude delegation of power. Regardless of the nature of decisions (or the way they are reached), almost all states find it necessary to delegate power in the interest of efficiency.[4] An important distinction has to be drawn between local government under a unitary arrangement and the powers of the units in a federal arrangement. In the former instance, the powers of central government are not fettered by local governments, who essentially owe their existence to the central government: no smaller part of the state can impose any restriction on the central government.[5] While there may be delegation of power to lower levels (such as the different territories), this is not performed because of any ideal but more to achieve efficiency.[6] Overall, under a unitary system, for political and legal purposes of decision making the country is regarded as a single unit.

Under a federal constitution, the various local units exercise authority in certain affairs that cannot be infringed on by the central government. Despite the variety of federal systems, federal systems do have a logic of their own that distinguishes them from unitary arrangements.[7] A federal system is essentially a constitutional arrangement that allows territorial diversity in the organizational structure of the state. A national government and a territorial government both rule over the same domain, with the latter government having a prerogative over some defined interest.[8] The constitutional demarcation between the power of the central government and that of the territories is the cornerstone of Western federalism. In the words of K. C. Wheare, "[T]he general and regional governments are each, within a sphere, co-ordinate and independent."[9]

Institutions and forms of government vary across different federal systems. The diversities that may lead to federalism can be many, but the more important are religion, language, regional peculiarities, nationality, and race. A particular society or group in the society may wish to protect specific aspects or diversities, and accordingly will adopt the appropriate form of government.[10] Hence, no single form of government within a federal system is axiomatic. In the next chapter we will consider some different forms of government in terms of various federal constitutions. But the institutional characteristics of a federal system linked to constitutionalism and the scope of action of the various organs in the system depart radically from a federal arrangement not linked to constitutionalism.[11] The hallmark of Western federal models is a set of institutional arrangements designed to achieve a greater level of decentralization, such as different government agencies with separate powers[12] and the clear demarcation of authority between the center and the units. With respect to economic affairs, the doctrine of the liberal state essentially argues for free competition, with the state as the impartial guarantor. The doctrine of the socialist state argues for public ownership of the means of production, and calls for a distribution of income among the citizens. In the former Soviet socialist model, the authority and powers of the units were much more restricted and confined more to linguistic and cultural affairs.[13]

Before leaving the federal-unitary dichotomy, it is important to note a variation of the federal form of state called the consociational form of state. Some theorists prefer to treat consociationalism as a distinct arrangement. The consociational arrangement embodies many of the characteristics of a federal state and in a sense can be subsumed under the rubric of federalism. Indeed, there is considerable overlap between the two, and we treat them as variations on a similar theme. In many instances the regions in a federal arrangement coincide with differences in the population, and the federal arrangement (based on territory) grants by default a high degree of autonomy to these different groups. However, in some instances there are differences in the population with respect to language, culture, race, and religion that are not territorially distinct.[14] In such an instance dividing the country into different segments is seen as inappropriate by theorists who seek to protect the interests of the diverse groups regardless of where they reside.[15] The consociational arrangement is meant to cure this problem.

Consociational democracy is defined in terms of four characteristics. The first is a grand coalition of leaders from the different segments.[16] The second is segmental autonomy, which means all the units must enjoy maximum autonomy in matters pertaining to their personal interests.[17] The third characteristic is the need for a mutual veto. This means no important decision can be taken without the consent of each of the segments.[18] The final requirement calls for proportional representation of all groups in the major institutions of government.[19] There can be an overlap between the two; for example, Switzerland is both a federal and a consociational model.[20]

While federalism and consociationalism need not be the same in all respects, the theory and rationale underlying the two systems are invariably the same: "The federal solution shades in some circles into and encapsulates Consociationalism."[21] Federalism attempting to provide decentralized government to protect the interests of the groups is a consociational device, and consociationalism attempting to provide the protection of the interests of different groups (albeit not necessarily in a distinct territory) is a federal device.[22] Federalism, consociationalism, and variations of the two have become the dominant constitutional models among liberal academics, politicians, and constitutional theorists in South Africa.[23]

Reasons for Selecting a Form of State

Some theorists assert there are objective or rational reasons for adopting a unitary or federal constitution.[24] A unitary form of state is more conducive to central planning and better suited to a society faced with major dislocation, famine, economic crisis, and a need for welfare and social services.[25] A unitary state is less expensive than a federal state because there is no duplication of government at different levels.[26] And because there is no duplication, a unitary system is more likely to be administratively and economically efficient.[27]

The advantages or objective reasons put forward for a federal state are more contentious. First, in terms of Western liberal political theory it is associated with freedom,[28] and is seen as a framework (for new nations) that allows individual freedom to flourish.[29] While it may be inefficient, the trade-off is the greater freedom it allows.[30] A second virtue that liberal theorists see in federalism is the restriction it places on the central government by virtue of the dispersal of power territorially. The United States is the best example of a territorial division of power that clearly acts as a fetter on the central government. Third, and arguably most controversial, is the notion that a federal form of state is most appropriate for a plural or heterogeneous society characterized by cultural, linguistic, national, ethnic, or religious diversities.[31] A federal arrangement is seen as a mechanism that allows each of the diverse elements in the population a measure of autonomy with respect to matters of local concern.

However, the United States, which is the oldest surviving federal state, is a symmetrical federal state in that no social, economic, national, ethnic or cultural peculiarities are given territorial protection.[32] Although the society is heterogeneous and comprises many immigrant nationalities, these differences are not geographically defined. In this sense, the United States (like Australia) is "relatively homogeneous."[33]

Several federal states in the world today are made up of different cultural, ethnic, linguistic, and religious groups. In this sense, they are asymmetrical federal systems composed of political units that correspond to the differences of interest and makeup that prevail within the society.[34] The federal form of state is meant to allow the people of each of the units to express their peculiarities within their territory.

South Africa and Pluralism

Historically, the form of state organization and constitutional arrangement in South Africa took its inspiration from the British Westminster example.

Ever since the Union of South Africa, the form of state in South Africa has been unitary. Today, the federal form of state organization (either territorially or non-territorially defined, that is, consociational) is particularly popular among many liberal[35] political theorists in South Africa as a viable constitutional option. The attractiveness of the federal model flows from their classification of South Africa as a plural society.

Pluralism has been applied extensively by social scientists and academics to describe South African society.[36] Initially, it was used by the government as an argument for its separate development policy. Today the notion figures prominently in National Party descriptions and liberal (opposed to apartheid) characterizations of South African society and constitutional programs for South Africa.[37]

In politics the term *pluralism* has a wider meaning and is used to denote the dispersal of power among various agencies in society. For example, in the United States power is divided between the center (which is represented by the federal government) and the states. At the central level it is divided among the various agencies of government. Moreover, the membership of the various branches of the government can belong to different political parties. A plural society in a sociological sense is a heterogeneous society marked by significant cultural, religious, linguistic, or ethnic differences. It is the latter interpretation that sociologists and political commentators apply to the South African context.[38]

The notion of a plural society is not without its conceptual difficulties in that almost all societies can be characterized as being composed of diverse nationalities and groups. The United States is perhaps the most diverse country, consisting of immigrant populations from almost all parts of the world. Even a unitary state such as Britain is composed of Scottish, Welsh, Irish, Asians, Africans, and Caribbeans. There has been no attempt to stratify these societies along racial, cultural, and ethnic lines to prevent possible conflict. Proponents of the plural notion in South Africa distinguish South African society from the previous examples by differentiating between mutually reinforcing and crosscutting or overlapping cleavages.[39] The first example posited is a nonantagonistic form of pluralism:[40] multiple and overlapping membership of groups allows common loyalties to form and a state of equilibrium to be achieved, which reduces conflict.[41]

In contradistinction, the second model of a plural society considered is a conflict model. This model is derived from the writings of the sociologist John Furnivall, who described the workings of colonial societies characterized by sharp cleavages.[42] Furnivall observed that these societies have a mix of people living side by side who do not mix with each other except for their interaction in the marketplace.[43] Beyond this each group maintains its own identity, language, culture, and religion.[44] Smith extends the analysis further and asserts that in a colonial context such societies are characterized by domination by one unit that is a cultural minority.[45]

South Africa is characterized as falling into the category of a plural model of the conflict variety.[46] It is described as "a house divided among itself."[47] Its history is one of strife among various groups with conflict between various "tribes" and between blacks and whites.[48] It is a society that has a multitude of different groups, with the extreme cultural influences of three continents.[49] Moreover, there is little or no social interaction between the groups. Each has its own lifestyle, language, and identity, which coincide with political divisions and create a situation of conflict. Boulle maintains that not only is South Africa a highly plural society, but it also shares the domination by one unit, whites, over coloreds, Indians, and Africans.[50] The only mixing between the groups occurs in the economic sphere.[51]

These factors have determined identity patterns that act as important determinants of political alignments and conflicts.[52] According to the plural theorists, it is not possible to blend these disparate elements into a single coherent nation because fear and prejudice are so deeply rooted.[53] The conflict between the groups in South Africa is described as particularly severe[54] and any attempt to interfere with it will not only fail but will reinforce the divisions.[55] Similarly, modernization will not in any way reduce these conflicts but will exacerbate them.[56] Race and separateness are seen as rooted in the South African situation, and subnational solidarity is an everlasting factor in determining politics.

But despite the differences in the population, proponents of the plural view assert that pursuing a completely separate course is not possible because the groups in South Africa are highly dependent on each other economically.[57] The only constitutional alternative is to keep South Africa as a single geographical entity but to provide a form of state that allows maximum autonomy to each of the different groups with respect to matters that affect its interests.[58] Thus the federal model, particularly in the consociational form, is posited as ideally suited to a plural society such as South Africa's.[59]

Pluralism and the Federal State in Africa

Pluralism has also been applied by social theorists extensively to describe other African societies. Before Nigeria became independent, various conferences were held in London to investigate the proper form of constitution for the country.[60] All the major Nigerian leaders were of the opinion that a federal arrangement was the most viable form of state and that a unitary constitution would not work in the Nigerian context.[61] Some Nigerian leaders argued that in a society where there is diversity of language, religion, and nationality a unitary constitution would be a source of bitterness and conflict.[62] Any attempt to integrate the communities into one community would be a disaster.[63] A federal state would allow each of the national and linguistic groups regional autonomy.[64]

Similarly, in the Congo (now Zaire) prior to independence, several of the leaders called for a federal constitution because of the "tribal" composition of Congo society.[65] Those in favor of the federal arrangement wanted considerable local autonomy.[66] Federalism was seen as the only realistic model to protect the interests of the minority groups.[67] Although the independence constitution did not explicitly characterize the Congo as a federal state,[68] the country was divided into twenty-one units with the units having considerable budgetary and fiscal control.[69]

In Kenya, Uganda, and Ghana a federal form of state was adopted at independence as a concession to "minority tribes." The leadership of the minority groups felt they would be overwhelmed by a strong central government.[70] Again, the rationale was that given the ethnic and plural character of these societies, the best form of arrangement was one that permitted autonomy to the various groups.[71] In Uganda, the region of Buganda was most concerned about exercising the greatest measure of autonomy granted to it in the independence constitution.[72] In Kenya, the minority Kenya African Democratic Union Party (KADU) wanted a federal arrangement, arguing that a unitary form of state results in a form of government that concentrates power in the hands of a single person or group.[73] The alternative was to spread power among the regions, which was the option adopted in all of the above three instances.[74] Consequently, power was divided between the center and the regions.[75]

The adoption of a federal form of state was made a sine qua non (by the British) for independence, and in almost all instances the federal formula was opposed by the majority of the population or by the majority party.[76] It was invariably accepted as a compromise measure to speed up the process of independence. All the federal forms of states adopted in Africa fit into the category of symmetrical federations in that the units coincided with ethnic or religious differences. The overall arguments for federalism encompass all the popular ideological grounds; namely, it acts to ensure checks and balances, it is a means of local government, and it is a system that allows diversity in the population and promotes maximum freedom.[77]

REFERENCES

1. M. Hough, "Forms of State, Government and Authority," *South African Journal of African Affairs* 9 (3/4) (1979): 160.

2. Alessandro Pizzorusso, et al., eds., *Law in the Making: A Comparative Study* (Berlin: Springer-Verlag, 1988), 63.

3. Ibid.

4. Ivo D. Duchacek, *Power Maps: Comparative Politics of Constitutions* (Santa Barbara, Calif.: ABC-CLIO, 1973), 93.

5. Charles F. Strong, *Modern Political Constitutions: An Introduction to the Comparative Study of Their History and Existing Form*, 6th rev. ed. (London: Sidgwick & Jackson, 1963), 64.

6. Ivo D. Duchacek, *Comparative Federalism: The Territorial Dimension of Politics* (New York: Holt, Rinehart and Winston, 1970), 3.

7. Preston T. King, *Federalism and Federation* (London: Croom Helm, 1982), 71.

8. This definition is consistent with that given by W. H. Riker. See W. H. Riker, "Federalism" in Greenstein and Polsby, *Handbook of Political Science*, 101.

9. Kenneth C. Wheare, *Federal Government*, 4th ed. (New York: Oxford University Press, 1964), 10.

10. W. S. Livingston, "A Note on the Nature of Federalism," *Political Science Quarterly* 67 (1952): 91.

11. We will consider federalism in terms of the Soviet constitution in chapter 8.

12. This applies more specifically to the U.S. system, as some federal systems—such as the Canadian and German systems—have a weak separation of powers.

13. Pizzorusso, *Law in the Making*, 69.

14. S. Venter, "Some of South Africa's Political Alternatives in Consociational Perspective," *South African International* (1981): 131.

15. Laurence J. Boulle, *Constitutional Reform and the Apartheid State: Legitimacy, Constitutionalism, and Control in South Africa* (New York: Basic Books, 1986), 53.

16. Ibid., 47.

17. Ibid., 51.

18. A. Lijphart, "Federal, Confederal, and Consociational Options for the South African Plural Society," in Robert I. Rotberg and John Barratt, eds., *Conflict and Compromise in South Africa* (Lexington, Mass.: Lexington Books, 1980).

19. See D. Geldenhuys, "South Africa's Constitutional Alternatives," *South African International* (1981): 213.

20. Ibid. The model of Switzerland being an example of both a federal and constitutional state will be examined in chapter 5.

21. Rotberg and Barratt, *Conflict and Compromise*, 8.

22. N. J. Rhoodie, "Value Consensus as a Prerequisite for Consociationalism in Southern Africa," in D. J. Van Vuuren and D. J. Kriek, eds., *Political Alternatives for Southern Africa* (Durban: Butterworth's, 1983), 486.

23. See Geldenhuys, *Constitutional Alternatives*, 205 and 219–24. Geldenhuys summarizes the political programs of the major white political parties, namely, the National Party, the former Republican and former Progressive Federal parties, which mostly encapsulate the principles of consociationalism and federalism. The reasons why the federal and constitutional models are most attractive to liberal theorists in South Africa will be examined in chapters 6 and 7.

24. M. Bothe, Final Report in F. Gerster, *Federalism and Decentralization: Constitutional Problems of Territorial Decentralization in Federal and Centralized States* (n.p., 1987), 412.

25. Kenneth C. Wheare, *Modern Constitutions*, 2d ed. (London: Oxford University Press, 1966), 11.

26. D. Rothchild, "Majimbo Schemes in Kenya and Uganda," in Jeffrey Butler and A. A. Castagno, eds., *Boston University Papers on Africa: Transition in African Politics* (New York: Praeger, 1967), 298–99.

27. Carl J. Friedrich, *Constitutional Government and Politics*, 4th ed. (Waltham, Mass.: Blaisdell Publishing, 1968), 227.

28. Nelson A. Rockefeller, *The Future of Freedom: A Bicentennial Series of Speeches* (Washington: U.S. GPO, 1976), 4.

29. Ibid., 68–69.

30. Friedrich, *Constitutional Government*, 227. See last part of chapter 5, where it is argued that the federal state offers a better opportunity for protection of individual rights and the protection of values of liberal society.

31. The merit of this view is challenged and rejected in chapter 7.

32. Tarlton, "Symmetry and Asymmetry as Elements of Federalism: A Theoretical Speculation," *Journal of Politics* 27 (1965): 861.

33. Mayer, "Federalism and Party Behavior in Australia and Canada," *Western Political Quarterly* 23 (1970): 795.

34. William H. Stewart, *Concepts of Federalism* (Lanham, Md.: University Press of America, 1984).

35. The term *liberal* is used to describe a political tendency in South Africa that is opposed to apartheid and that subscribes to the idea that apartheid has historically been inimical to the process of capital accumulation. The views of the liberal school of thought will be dealt with in chapters 5 and 7.

36. Theodor Hanf, et al., South Africa, *The Prospects for Peaceful Change: An Empirical Enquiry into the Possibility of Democratic Conflict Regulation*, trans. John Richardson (London: R. Collings, 1981), 3; J. Rex, "The Plural Society: The South African Case," *Race* 40 (1971).

37. For example, see the former white liberal opposition party's, the Progressive Federal Party (PFP), approach to South Africa as reflected in their constitutional proposals, *Report of the Constitutional Committee of the Progressive Federal Party and Policy Decisions Made by the Federal Congress of the P.F.P. at Its Federal Congress Held in Durban on 17th and 18th November 1978* [The Van Zyl Slabbert Report] (Cape Town: P.F.P., 1979). The new white liberal opposition party—the Democratic Party (DP)—maintains an identical constitutional vision. See The Democratic Party, *The Democratic Party: A Government in the Making* (n.p., 1989).

38. See Pierre L. Van den Berghe, *South Africa, A Study in Conflict* (Middletown, Conn.: Wesleyan University Press, 1965).

39. Peter Randall, ed., *South Africa's Political Alternatives* (Johannesburg: SPRO-CAS, 1973).

40. Leo Kuper, "Plural Societies: Perspectives and Problems" in Leo Kuper and M. G. Smith, eds., *Pluralism in Africa* (Berkeley: University of California Press, 1969), 7.

41. Randall, *Political Alternatives*, 82.

42. John S. Furnivall, *Colonial Policy and Practice* (Cambridge: Cambridge University Press, 1948).

43. Ibid., 304.

44. Ibid.

45. Kuper and Smith, *Pluralism in Africa*, 12.

46. W. B. Vosloo, "Consociational Democracy as a Means to Accomplish Peaceful Change in South Africa," *Politikon* 6 (1) (1979): 14.

47. Leopold Marquard, *The Peoples and Policies of South Africa*, 4th ed. (London: Oxford University Press, 1969), 28.

48. Ibid.

49. Van den Berghe, *Study in Conflict*, 38.

50. Laurence J. Boulle, *Constitutional Reform and the Apartheid State: Legitimacy, Constitutionalism, and Control in South Africa* (New York: St. Martin's Press, 1984), 36.

51. Marquard, *Peoples and Policies*, 28.

52. The term *plural society* has come to be applied to societies perceived to be characterized by divisions and fragmentations. However, the basis of these divisions may differ, and where factors such as language, religion, and culture operate the term *cultural pluralism* has been employed. See Crawford Young, *The Politics of Cultural Pluralism* (Madison, Wis.: University of Wisconsin Press, 1976), 12.

53. Hanf, *Prospects for Peaceful Change*, 9.

54. Arend Lijphart, *Democracy in Plural Societies: A Comparative Exploration* (New Haven: Yale University Press, 1977), 3.

55. Hanf, *Prospects for Peaceful Change*, 9.

56. Schlemmer, "Theories of the Plural Society and Change in South Africa," *Social Dynamics* 3(1) (1977): 4.

57. W. B. Vosloo, "The Executive" in John Benyon, ed., *Constitutional Change in South Africa: Proceedings of a Conference on Constitutional Models and Constitutional Change in South Africa* (Pietermaritzburg: University of Natal Press, 1978), 168.

58. Lijphart, "Federal, Confederal, and Consociational Options," 238.

59. Rotberg and Barratt, *Conflict and Compromise*, 8.

60. Kofi A. Busia, *Africa in Search of Democracy* (New York: Praeger, 1967), 113.

61. Obafemi Awolowo, *Thoughts on the Nigerian Constitution* (London: Oxford University Press, 1966), 29.

62. Ibid., 48.

63. R. B. Neuberger, *Concepts of Nationhood in the Thought of Selected African Leaders* (n.p., 1975), 204.

64. Nnamdi Azikiwe, *Zik: A Selection From the Speeches of Nnamdi Azikiwe* (Cambridge: University Press, 1961), 48; Arnold Rivkin, *Nation-building in Africa: Problems and Prospects*, ed. John H. Morrow (New Brunswick, N.J.: Rutgers University Press, 1969), 100; Benjamin O. Nwabueze, *A Constitutional History of Nigeria* (Essex: Longman, 1982), 147; T. O. Elias, *Nigeria: The Development of Its Laws and Constitution* (London: Stevens, 1967), 121.

65. R. C. Good, *Congo Crisis, The Role of the New States* (n.p., n.d.), 5.

66. Kwame Nkrumah, *Challenge of the Congo* (London: Nelson, 1967), 67.

67. Crawford Young, *The Rise and Decline of the Zairian State* (Madison, Wis.: University of Wisconsin Press, 1985), 41.

68. Ibid.

69. Ibid.

70. D. Rotchild, "Majimbo Schemes in Kenya and Uganda," 293; Benjamin O. Nwabueze, *Presidentialism in Commonwealth Africa* (New York: St. Martin's Press, 1974), 139.

71. Nwabueze, *Presidentialism*.

72. S. A. de Smith, *The New Commonwealth and its Constitutions* (London: Stevens, 1964), 263.

73. Butler and Castagno, *BU Papers on Africa*, 294.

74. Ibid.

75. For a discussion of the actual division and nature of power exercised by the regions and center in each of the above three countries, see Nwabueze, *Presidentialism*, 140–50.

76. Ibid., 140. In chapters 6 and 7 the argument will be made that the federal form of state was the best model for both neocolonial interests and the interests of the indigenous elite who stepped into the shoes of the departing colonial powers.

77. Neuberger, *Concepts of Nationhood*, 303.

CHAPTER FIVE

Western Constitutional Models and Government in Africa

■ ■ ■

U NDERSTANDING THE WAY constitutions work is critical to analysis of a model meeting the problems of a particular society. An analysis of institutions is also important because the choice of institutions has social, political, and economic consequences.[1] Institutional structures shape public policy, the priority issues are accorded, and the outcome of policy.[2] Accordingly, when a particular constitutional model is presented as a framework for South Africa, its merits and demerits have to be considered in terms of whose interests are being enhanced.

Here we consider the different liberal constitutions and forms of government that exist in various parts of the world. One factor in choosing the models cited is the broad influence they have exerted in various parts of the world, particularly in Africa. For example, Britain and France were prone to introducing elements of their respective constitutional models into the independence constitutions of their former colonies. And historically, the South African constitution contained the major trappings of the British Westminster model. Today the great debate in constitution making in the West and in South Africa centers on the unitary and parliamentary system of government as it exists in Britain, and the federal presidential model of the United States. In white South African liberal circles the choice is greatly influenced by the extent to which a model offers the best framework for protecting the values and financial interests of the dominant white sector of the population. A second factor for discussing the model is the prominence a model (or the main features of a model) enjoys in South Africa as a viable option for the country. The federal/consociational model figures most prominently in that debate.

The final factor in selecting models is post-World War II development in some liberal constitutions away from "pure" liberalism in the direction of a constitutional welfare state, aimed at achieving a minimum standard of living for all citizens. Discussion of the social welfare constitution is intended to enlarge the debate by including models that have all but been ignored in the context of South Africa. The social welfare constitution provides a different conception of government in liberal society and additional insights into how some liberal societies have dealt with the distributive function that will be crucial in an antiracial and democratic South Africa.

A Unitary System:
British and French Constitutional Models

Most countries in the world have adopted a unitary form of government. The basic principle of unitary states is that they all display "one supreme, ultimate and unified center of authority."[3] Establishing a unitary form of government does not tell us about the relationship between the electorate and the government or the way the government is composed. Indeed, there are a great variety of institutional structures a unitary form of government can adopt. The two models that have historically been most popular in Africa are the British Westminster model and the French presidential model.

THE BRITISH WESTMINSTER MODEL

The Westminster model is a system of government that incorporates all the main features of the British constitutional arrangement.[4] In the first instance, this is a paradox because Britain does not have a written constitution as such. The main constitutional practices in Britain evolved over centuries to their present form and presently exist more as conventions than written rules. However, many of the institutions and constitutional practices in Britain have been copied in various parts of the world as part of the written constitutions of many independent nations.

The main features of the British model are first, the aspect of sovereignty or supremacy of Parliament, that is, no person or body has the authority to override or set aside an act of the legislature.[5] It means further that there are no legal fetters imposed on Parliament with regard to its legislative competence. In a positive sense this means Parliament can pass any law it wishes.[6] The principles of morality in no way impose limitations on the authority and supremacy of the legislature. The courts are duty bound to uphold an act of Parliament and cannot set aside an act of that body.[7] The corollary of legislative supremacy is a flexible constitution in that legislation can be changed very easily. No law is regarded as inviolable or sacred.

Second, the Westminster system represents a model where the head of state is not the main organ of political power. In Britain all power is exercised in the name of the head of state, the queen. In fact, little power is exercised by the head of state but instead by the government, represented by the prime minister and the cabinet in the name of the head of state.[8] In practice the effective head of government is the prime minister, who is also the leader of the majority party in the lower house.

Third, the legislature is bicameral, consisting of a lower house that is popularly elected and an upper house in which members are nominated or inherit their positions. The lower house, called the House of Commons, is the dominant chamber in which legislation is initiated. The upper chamber, the House of Lords, is more of a review chamber that scrutinizes bills and provides comments on impending legislation.

Fourth, the form of government is parliamentary in that all ministers including the prime minister have to come from one of the two chambers of the legislature. In this sense the British system has a weak separation of powers, as the members of the executive are drawn from the legislature and continue to maintain their membership of the legislature. The term *parliamentary government* is often used to describe the British system. This characterization is erroneous because in no real sense does Parliament govern.[9] The legislature oversees the activities of the executive, whose major seat of authority is the cabinet. The doctrine of collective responsibility is used to describe the relationship between the members of the cabinet. This means that the cabinet is collectively responsible for all decisions taken by the executive. The government and all members of the cabinet will defend an individual cabinet minister subjected to criticism in the legislature. All members of the cabinet are bound to secrecy with regard to executive discussions.[10]

The last major trapping of the Westminster model is an independent judiciary. The function of the judiciary is to pronounce on legal disputes and to interpret the law as laid down by the legislature. In fulfilling this function there is no interference from the legislative or executive branches of government. Members of the judiciary enjoy security of tenure and cannot be removed for unpopular decisions. It is, however, an established custom for the judiciary not to pronounce on the validity of legislative actions that would infringe on the principle of legislative supremacy.[11]

THE FRENCH PRESIDENTIAL MODEL

Under the constitution of the French Fifth Republic, the key personality and organ of power is the president.[12] The French president is popularly elected for a period of seven years.[13] The constitution confers on him a host of powers that he exercises at his discretion. The constitution further casts him in the role of mediator, a role that allows him a veto on almost every aspect of policy, be it in the realm of internal affairs, foreign affairs, or the functioning of the institutions of government.[14] The president is responsible for the selection of the prime minister.

The legislature of the French republic is bicameral, consisting of a popularly elected lower house, the National Assembly, and an indirectly elected upper house, the Senate.[15] The upper chamber is designed to fulfill the classic functions attributed to upper chambers, namely the reviewing of actions of the lower house. Unlike the British legislature, all legislation in the French system has to be passed by both houses, with the exception of the budget. Moreover, the purview of the legislature is restricted.[16]

The French cabinet is only responsible to the National Assembly. An important point of departure from the British model is that here cabinet membership is incompatible with parliamentary membership.[17] Cabinet members are allowed to participate in the parliamentary debates but are not allowed to vote. Very often members of the cabinet are drawn from the legislature, in which event they have to resign their positions in the legislature. The National Assembly can bring down a government by passing a vote of no confidence in the government. A government will also resign if the National Assembly rejects its program.[18] Hence, despite the fact that a prime minister is put into office by the president, the cabinet in France is to an extent accountable to the legislature albeit only in an indirect fashion.

The preeminent and most powerful figure in the French political system is the president. The extent of the president's power is much greater than that of the British prime minister. The French constitutional and institutional setup is suited to a unitary system with maximum central control. All major decisions of internal affairs, education, medical benefits, taxes, police, and so forth are made at the center by the president and cabinet. The decisions are in turn implemented by a chain of local function-aries with strict supervision from the center. This is done with a combina-tion of locally elected officials and officials called prefects appointed by the central government through the Ministry of Interior. The Ministry of the Interior is the primary department responsible for implementing the decisions of the central government throughout the country. The prefect is "the local agent of the central government,"[19] responsible to the minister of the interior in Paris and in most instances more powerful than the elected heads in the area. He or she supervises the activities of locally elected officials such as the mayor, and appoints many prominent officials in the civil service, such as tax collectors, teachers, and clerks.[20]

In a unitary system political uniformity is of key importance. The French institutional arrangement denies a distinction between local and countrywide concerns, resulting in an integration of local and central politics in a hierarchical chain of command emanating from Paris.[21] The consequence is a tremendous bureaucracy, and it is often remarked that France is ruled by civil servants who constitute a permanent body of administrators. The top civil servants have ready access to government ministries and the policy-making organs.[22]

The principal of judicial review is historically absent in France owing to a strict conception of separation of powers.[23] In terms of its vision, the judiciary should not be able to question an act of Parliament. It does, however, have a constitutional council called the Conseil Constitutionnel, which previews the constitutionality of an act before it is promulgated.[24] The Conseil verifies whether the act passed is consistent with the powers conferred on the legislature.[25] But the Conseil may only review legislation in the period between its enactment and promulgation.[26] Once an act has been promulgated, the Conseil cannot pronounce on its validity. We will consider the composition and method of election of members to the Council in chapter 11.

The Federal System

Today most countries of the world operate under federal constitutions. The most important influence on Western federal systems has been the U.S. Constitution,[27] which is the longest-surviving written constitution and federal system in the world. Western federal constitutions come in a great variety of forms. The major points of institutional difference between the United States and other Western federal systems will be explained, especially in relation to the consociational model.

THE U.S. CONSTITUTION

In the United States, as in most federal systems, the Constitution is supreme and cannot be easily amended. In this sense, the Constitution is definitely a superior law in relation to other statutes unlike in the unitary British system. In contrast to most unitary constitutions, the U.S. Constitution implicitly aims to limit government, which seems almost its main purpose. But the Constitution goes beyond this to spell out the primary way power is to be exercised in the U.S. system.[28]

The Constitution allocates power in two primary ways: it allocates power between the central government and the states, and it distributes power within the various organs of the federal government. The first is what distinguishes federal systems from unitary systems, that is, the aspect of two levels of government, each with its own sphere of authority.

The second element, the separation of powers, constitutes an important, though variable, aspect of Western constitutionalism.

The U.S. Constitution expressly spells out the power of the federal government and specifies that any powers not granted to the federal government "are reserved to the states respectively."[29] The federal government is therefore a government of enumerated powers, restricted to those conferred expressly in the Constitution, while the various states retain all powers not conferred on the federal government.[30] Among the powers conferred on the central government the more important are those relating to taxes, coinage, naturalization, commerce, defense, and war.[31] The first, like others, is a joint power in that the states can also impose taxes. In the event of a conflict between the actions of the states and the federal government over areas of joint power, the courts have from very early on ruled that an act of the central government has the greater effect.[32] Both the federal government and the governments of the states act directly on the subjects within their respective jurisdictions. Both have their own government apparatus—legislative, executive, and judicial.[33] Thus is government machinery duplicated at the level of the central government and across the fifty states. Each of the states has its own law enforcement, and performs many important functions in such areas as education, public health, police protection, parks, and sanitation.

The second division of power is within the various organs of the federal government, in keeping with the principle of separation of powers. The first section of Article I of the Constitution specifies that all legislative power shall be vested in the Congress. The federal legislature is composed of two houses, the Senate and the House of Representatives.[34] Members of the House of Representatives are elected from the population from roughly equally populated districts for a period of two years. The Senate in contrast consists of two members from each state elected by the adult population regardless of the size of the state.[35] At the formation of the Union, the role of the Senate was perceived to represent the interests of the states.[36] Today many federal systems have a bicameral legislature, with one chamber consisting of equal representatives from the various states regardless of the size of the states, to represent the interests of the various territories. In the United States the powers of both houses are equal with respect to the passing of all statutes.

Executive power is vested in the president. The powers given to the president are broadly framed, and he is ultimately responsible for seeing that the laws of the country are executed. The president does not owe his existence to the legislature, as he is popularly, but not directly, elected for a period of four years. Consequently, the president is not responsible or limited by the legislature with regard to his executive duties. The president selects the members of his cabinet, who again cannot belong to the legislature while they are part of the cabinet. This notion of a strict separation of personnel is an absolute feature of the U.S. federal and presidential model, in contrast to the British parliamentary system where the executive is drawn from the legislature.

The third agency in the division of power in the U.S. federal arrangement is the judiciary. Since there is a division of power both territorially and within the branches of the central government, in the United States a judiciary adjudicates over disputes concerning the authority of the units or the different branches of the government. An independent judiciary has the power to determine whether an action of the central government or states is consistent with the powers conferred on them in the Constitution. Moreover, the judiciary determines whether the actions of the legislature or executive branch of the government are in accordance with the provisions of the Constitution. In the United States the highest judicial body is the Supreme Court,[37] which has the final pronouncement on constitutional disputes.

The separation of powers in the United States is qualified by the principle of checks and balances, which allows each of the three agencies limited interference in the activities of the other. For example, while the president cannot participate in the passing of legislation, he can use his executive power to veto an act of Congress.[38] This allows the president to participate in legislative activities in an indirect way. The presidential veto can, however, be overridden by a two-thirds vote of Congress. Similarly, Congress has a check on the activities of the president in that all presidential appointments of executive officers, judges, and ambassadors require the approval of the Senate.[39]

The United States has a rigid constitution. Constitutional amendments can only be made if a two-thirds vote of both houses of Congress, and three-fourths of the states, approve the amendment, or if a special constitutional convention is held. This contrasts with the British constitution, to which changes can be made relatively easily by a simple majority in the central legislature. Western standards view a rigid constitution as an important yardstick in determining whether a system is federal or not.[40]

An additional feature of the U.S. Constitution is a Bill of Rights, which are considered fundamental and inviolable. The Bill of Rights was passed in 1789 and today consists of twenty-seven separate amendments. In terms of the First Amendment, laws cannot be passed that abridge the freedoms of speech, press, or religion. Accused persons are accorded due process protections under Amendments 5 to 8. The provisions call for, among other things, a speedy trial and the right to confront one's accusers. The Fifth Amendment also includes the provision forbidding the taking of property without just compensation. The Bill of Rights is a very important aspect of the U.S Constitution, and has served as an inspiration to other countries. Any party who feels that his or her constitutional rights have been violated can seek relief from the courts. Moreover, any statute that conflicts with the provisions of the Bill of Rights (as with the other provisions of the Constitution) can be invalidated by the courts.

Variations in Western Federal Systems

BRITISH PARLIAMENTARY
FEDERAL GOVERNMENT SYSTEMS

The United States no doubt has been the most important influence in the formation of federal systems and the distribution of power between the levels of central government and the states and territories. However, the forms of government found in other Western federal systems show considerable creativity. Even the British parliamentary system designed for a unitary state has been modified and adopted in a federal context in countries such as India and Canada. The German system as well is a federal system where the executive is drawn from the legislature.

The German, Australian, Indian, and Canadian constitutions combine elements of federalism with responsible government.[41] Under the last three systems, a parliamentary form of government exists along the lines of the British model. At the time the constitutions of the former British colonies were drawn up, the express intention was to capture the spirit of the British constitution,[42] whose most important principle is the notion of parliamentary supremacy. Consequently, a major difference between the U.S. federal system and those influenced by the British parliamentary form is the absence of a bill of rights in the latter instances.[43]

Under the parliamentary federal system, the government is drawn from the legislature and is dependent on the support of the legislature. In those countries influenced by the British model, the head of state is not the true head of government, but has to act subject to the control of the legislature.[44] In Canada, India, and Australia, there is cabinet government with the government coming from the majority party in the lower house of parliament. The prime minister in almost all instances comes from the majority party in the lower house, and his (or her) position is the most important in the government. Unlike the U.S. system, there is no strict separation of powers; the cabinet operates on the principle of collective responsibility. The doctrine of parliamentary sovereignty applies with respect to acts of parliament with one critical difference from the British example, namely, that Parliament has to act within the sphere of competence allocated to it. As a federal system attempts to distribute power between the central government and the regions, its legislature cannot act in matters the constitution reserves for the units. However, in those areas where the central government has been given competence, there are no fetters on its ability to act. Following the notion of parliamentary supremacy, the central legislature in, for example, India could pass any legislation even if it was repugnant to individual rights, unlike the United States where Congress is constrained by the Bill of Rights.[45]

An independent judiciary is an important feature of liberal constitutional systems and an important aspect of constitutionalism. In federal systems with a parliamentary form of government, an independent judiciary is also pivotal to the functioning of the system; but in these systems the judicial role operates in a different fashion.[46] All that the judiciary can enquire into is whether the central government or the units have the required competence to act in the dispute in question, as opposed to the United States where the judiciary can invalidate an act against the Bill of Rights.

Bicameralism is a prominent feature under many constitutional systems. In the unitary forms of government, the second chamber or upper house acts more as a review chamber.[47] Under federal systems a second chamber is often perceived as representing the interests of the units. The U.S. model gives equal representation to states of unequal size, with the representatives elected directly by their constituents. Other systems, like the Indian and German models, apportion the representatives from the territories based on the population in the respective units. Moreover, the representatives are not elected directly by the population but by the governments of the local legislatures.

The federal government in the United States and Australia is one of enumerated powers in that those powers not expressly given to the center remain with the units. In federal systems like Canada and India, powers not expressly given to the states remain with the central government.[48]

GERMAN FEDERAL SYSTEM
AND THE SOCIAL WELFARE STATE

The German constitutional system differs from the constitutional models considered hitherto both in terms of the way its institutions operate as well as the philosophical basis of the constitution. In the ensuing section we will evaluate both the constitution and institutions of the German state as well as the philosophical departure from laissez-faire liberalism toward what is today termed the welfare state. The development and institutionalizing of the welfare state into the constitutions of many European states since World War II is a major departure from classical liberalism and its underpinnings of limited government.

Institutions of the German State. The German federal state is a third form of federal government. It is a system that combines a parliamentary form of government with a rigid constitution protecting basic rights,[49] neither of which can be altered easily. To effect an amendment to the constitution (basic law) a two-thirds vote of the parliament is needed.[50] The structure of the German legislature is of a novel character. The legislature is a bicameral body. The members of the upper house (Bundesrat) are elected by the Lander (or state) governments. With respect to the second house, half the members of the lower house (Bundestag) are elected in single-member constituencies by majority vote. The other half of the members of the Bundestag come from a list of party candidates in each of the Lander on the basis of proportional representation. Each voter has to cast two votes in the elections to the lower house. The lower house amounts to a "personalized proportional law" with half the members elected by plurality vote in single member constituencies, and the other half by proportional representation from the state party lists.[51] Both houses are responsible for passing legislation.

The most important personality in the German system is the chancellor who is elected by the legislature. The chancellor appoints the cabinet and determines the guidelines of public policy.[52] Hence, unlike the Westminster tradition, there is no collective responsibility because executive authority is linked to the chancellor.[53] As in other parliamentary systems, the president fulfills primarily a ceremonial function.

Germany as an Example of the Welfare State. Since World War II many European countries have moved away from "pure" liberalism, with its underpinnings of completely autonomous individuals and an essentially passive state, in the direction of a welfare state. The move away from pure liberalism in large measure has been because of a perception that unrestricted private property and unrestricted individual freedom results in large concentrations of wealth and power in the hands of a few, while a large majority of the population continues to reside in poverty despite legal equality.[54] In order to prevent these disparities, the state is now called on to enter into the economy and regulate the activities of citizens as well as provide services for the population.

The German constitution defines the country as a social federal state.[55] In German terminology the concept of the social state is the equivalent of the welfare state,[56] though it is difficult to define a welfare state precisely. Most political scientists agree that a welfare state actively intervenes to provide a basic standard of living for all as opposed to leaving this function to be fulfilled in the marketplace.[57] The benefits the state typically provides include minimum education, nutrition, healthcare, unemployment insurance, pensions, and in some instances housing allowances and employment. These have to be contrasted with the welfare benefits provided in the British system or for that matter those provided by the federal and some local governments in the United States,[58] where social provisions have increased since the Roosevelt New Deal era when the government intervened following the Depression to provide relief to the worst off sectors of society.[59] In the latter instance the welfare functions are pursued more as a political response. In Germany, on the other hand, the constitution makes it compulsory for the state to make certain provisions for welfare and to construct a just social order.[60] For example, the constitution specifies that the entire education system shall be under the control of the state,[61] that the community has the duty to provide for the protection and maintenance of every mother,[62] and that equality should not be viewed only in legal terms but also in terms of the actual (social) position of the parties.[63] Moreover, it calls upon the states to adopt provisions that conform to the principles of a democratic and social state.[64]

Similar provisions are found in other European countries such as Sweden, Denmark, Norway, Italy, and France.[65] For example, the constitution of Sweden states that "the personal economic, and cultural welfare of the individual shall be fundamental aims of the activities of the community."[66] The constitution goes on to specify that every individual has the right to housing, education, social care and security, and a favorable living environment.[67] Some countries such as Norway and Sweden include in the constitution the right to work.[68]

The traditional Diceyian notion of the rule of law encompasses the concept of government operating by law in an order that guarantees important individual rights. At a conference in New Delhi in 1959 the International Commission of Jurists supported a declaration stating that the rule of law is a dynamic concept for the achievement not only of civil and political rights, but also social, economic, educational, and cultural rights.[69] It is arguable whether the German constitution with its dictates directing the state to fulfill welfare needs operates in terms of the expansive concept of the rule of law. However, the evolution toward the constitutional recognition of socioeconomic rights is consistent with developments in the human rights field, most notably the formulation by the United Nations of the Covenant of Social, Economic, and Cultural Rights.[70] In terms of this new conception of the constitutional welfare state, the classical notion of the passive state is no longer tenable. Indeed, the German Constitutional Court plays an active role in reminding the government of its social obligations toward the establishment of a just social order.[71] For example in Germany the Constitutional Court has ruled that the function of the state is not only to protect individual rights but also to be active in promoting the social and educational advancement of the community.[72]

The constitutional demand on government to intervene in social and economic affairs is a major departure from the classical liberal theory of an essentially passive government. The inclusion in the constitution of economic and social rights of the population is also a departure from a former emphasis on only civil and political rights. These departures have led some to categorize the welfare state as an entirely new legal system, both in terms of application and origin.[73] Ewald argues this is so because in the classical liberal state the social contract is conceived as a relationship between the state and autonomous individuals where the power of the former is restricted. In the welfare state the actions of individuals are measured by the state against the interests of the society at large.[74]

Legal taxonomists may continue to argue the point, but we maintain that present welfare states despite their demand for positive government fall within the broad ambit of liberalism. Existing welfare states protect the positive aspects of liberal society such as freedom of person, speech, assembly, political association, and conscience. And, despite the attempt to balance the interests of individual rights and social obligations, private property is still a decisive factor in the organization of society.

Federalism and Consociationalism

INSTITUTIONAL FEATURES
OF THE CONSOCIATIONAL MODEL

The description of federal models thus far have concerned the institutions relating to the division of authority between various territories. The consociational model contains the main principles of the federal model except that it does not necessarily have to apply to territory.[75] Historical examples of the consociational system can be found in Cyprus, the Netherlands, Lebanon, Austria, and Malaysia.[76] At the practical level there are no consociational states in existence today, the closest approximation being the Swiss federal system. The consociational model continues to enjoy great popularity among political parties and academics in South Africa.[77] It is therefore worthwhile discussing both the theoretical aspects of the model as well as its closest surviving approximation.

MAIN FEATURES
OF THE CONSOCIATIONAL MODEL

The main exponent of the consociational model is the Dutch political scientist Arend Lijphart.[78] He defines consociational democracy in terms of four elements: grand coalition of leaders, segmental autonomy, mutual veto, and proportionality.[79]

The first requirement of elite accommodation is the main element in the system. Consociational democracy is based on the principle of a grand coalition of the leaders of the various segments. The grand coalition of "a cartel of pragmatic elites" must be able to act on behalf of their segments without any mandate from their constituency.[80] There must be no danger of the elite leadership being repudiated or replaced by more extreme leadership. So the segments must to a large extent be deferential to their leadership.[81] The latter must be able to compromise and regulate political conflict in the interest of all,[82] according to Lijphart, to "recogni[ze] . . . the gravity of the problems confronting the system and the constant peril of disintegrative tendencies."[83] The consociational arrangement is viewed by theorists like Lijphart as the best framework for joint government in a grand coalition. The grand coalition can be in the form of a cabinet encompassing members of all the segments,[84] and acting together on matters of common concern.[85]

The second element in consociational theory is the notion of segmental autonomy in matters such as education, health, language, religion, and community and health services.[86] This autonomy serves two purposes: first, it permits each of the groups latitude in regard to "personal" matters,[87] and second, it fits with the principles of constitutionalism in that it serves the object of spreading power among the various segments.[88]

The third element is the mutual veto. No important decision can be taken without the consent of all the segments,[89] which thus will have a substantial influence in the decision-making process.

The last element is the principle of proportionality, which translates as proportional representation in terms of numerical strength of all segments in the major institutions of government and state including the civil service, military, executive, and legislature.[90]

THE SWISS CONSTITUTION
IN CONSOCIATIONAL PERSPECTIVE

The Swiss model is both federal and consociational in that it protects segmental autonomy in defined territories. Switzerland consists of twenty-two cantons or units,[91] sovereign in all matters not entrusted to the federal government.[92] The equality of languages is a very important aspect of the Swiss constitution: it gives recognition to four national languages and three official languages.[93] It is a recognized principle that not only should the units have their linguistic rights protected but that the linguistic boundaries should not be altered.[94]

The composition of the Swiss legislature is consistent with most federal systems, with the lower house representing the population at large from equally populated districts,[95] and the upper house representing the segments.[96] The most important principle of grand coalition is seen in the composition of the Swiss executive, termed the Federal Council. The federal executive consists of seven members elected by the members of the legislature. However, there cannot be more than one member from each canton.[97] It has also become an established and rigid convention that members of the Federal Council shall consist of members of the different regional, linguistic, religious, and political groups.[98] If a councillor representing a prominent political party or group dies, his replacement will invariably come from the same political party or group.[99] The collegial aspect is reinforced in the constitution, which provides for the election of a rotating president who holds office for only one year.[100] The president serves as a chairperson and spokesperson for the collegial executive. Thus the presidency is shared by members of the federal executive.

The apportionment of members of the federal executive on the basis of party, linguistic, and religious strength is consistent with the principle of proportionality, which extends to other areas of the state agencies. The constitution specifies that the Federal Tribunal (Supreme Court) must consist of members of all national groups.[101] A concerted effort is made to provide proportional linguistic representation in the civil service and army.[102]

The one principle missing in the Swiss model is the veto. The units or segments cannot veto a decision taken by the central government with which they disagree. Even constitutional amendments can be effected if the majority of cantons approve the changes.[103]

Federal vs. Unitary States

A federal constitution provides greater limitation on government power because a federal constitution restricts the exercise of power both spatially and functionally. By giving the local units power, a federal constitution allows the units to act as a brake on the ability of the central government to act in certain matters.[104] In most instances a federal constitution operates according to anti-majoritarian principles in that it calls for bargains and compromises in government and state problems either between the various units and the central government, and in the presidential model between the executive and legislative organs of government. In this sense federalism can rightly be associated with a weaker form of government.

The federal-unitary dichotomy in terms of the British and U.S. model has very important consequences for a "new" nation particularly when the values of liberalism are not shared by all members of the community. The unitary state in England does not endanger the principles of liberalism, because liberal values have been internalized by the majority. Even though there is no bill of rights or constitutional protection of individual rights in the British system, individual rights and liberal values are respected in the British tradition as part of the common law. In those societies where there is no consensus or majority acceptance of liberal values there is a greater likelihood of strong currents advocating a federal solution. The institutions associated with the federal system disperse power across society thus providing for a weaker form of government and offering greater protection for liberal values once they are entrenched in the constitution. Moreover, where the particular values of Western constitutionalism are not part of the traditions of the society, there is a strong argument by those parties seeking to institutionalize liberal values to promote the adoption of the U.S. model and introduce a rigid constitution and bill of rights so as to entrench these values in the system. It follows, while the U.S. and British system work to promote broadly similar values in the two societies, under given circumstances it is more likely that the U.S. model would be preferred as a better guarantee for the maintenance of liberalism and constitutionalism in areas where liberal values are not firmly embedded.

Western Forms of Government in Africa at Independence

The forms of government introduced in most of Africa at independence invariably were modeled along lines familiar to the departing colonial power. In countries subject to British rule, for example, such as Kenya, Botswana, Uganda, Nigeria, Ghana, and South Africa, the form of government was essentially of the Westminster variety. However, the form of state in many instances was federal, consistent with a desire to entrench liberal values through the mechanism of a (relatively) weak government and strong constitution.

The main features of the Westminster model such as plurality of parties, bicameral legislature, responsible and parliamentary government, and joint ministerial responsibility were characteristic features of the independence constitutions of Tanzania, Kenya, Nigeria, Ghana, and Botswana.[105] In all these countries the legislature was considered as the supreme law-making organ, subject however to the regions and bill of rights. Other features from the British model were a nominal head of state and cabinet government headed by a prime minister.[106]

In countries subject to French rule, the independence constitutions introduced were mostly of the presidential variety modeled on the French Fifth Republic. For example, in Côte d'Ivoire, Niger, and the Cameroons a centralized form of government was instituted with a popular president elected for a fixed period.[107] The legislative institutions were also identical to those of France. The president enjoyed the same powers as the French president—such as the ability to dissolve the National Assembly, to call a referendum, and to exercise emergency powers.[108] Similarly, in the Congo (now Zaire) the Belgians introduced a form of government similar to what existed in Belgium.[109]

Despite major similarities (with the mother country) in the forms of government introduced, the fact that they were introduced in a federal form of state in many instances was a major departure from the British constitutional tradition.[110] In countries such as Nigeria, Uganda, Ghana, and to a lesser extent Kenya, the Westminster system was introduced in a federal state. The federal arrangements in the former British colonies in many instances resembled the parliamentary federal arrangement in Australia with a parliamentary executive, unlike the United States' independent executive. As is characteristic of most federal states, one chamber of the legislature was designed to protect the interests of the regions. Like all liberal federal models power was distributed between the regions and the central government. In the case of Nigeria residual powers remained with the regions[111] as is the case in the United States and Australian models. Functions such as coinage, currency, customs, foreign borrowing, exchange control, and international trade were matters exclusive to the central government.[112] In Uganda the region of Buganda was given exclusive powers with regard to local government, land tenure, public service, public debt in the area, and customary matters.[113] In Ghana and Kenya as well regional units were created with powers separate from the central government.[114] In Uganda the central government was responsible for all residual matters such as currency, defense, foreign trade, and finance but shared this power with Buganda.[115] So not only was the authority over certain matters given exclusively to the regions, but the region of Buganda had the right to participate in all the decisions of the central government as well. The Uganda constitution, by giving the region of Buganda a right of veto over the decisions taken at the center, had consociational features.[116]

The second major departure from the original British model was the introduction of a bill of rights into the independent constitutions of many African states (unitary and federal), such as Nigeria, Uganda, Sierra Leone, and Kenya. The British view historically has been that a legal document should not contain political manifestos,[117] since the respect for liberal values such as individual freedom and property have become embedded in the common law. However, the British sought to institutionalize these values in the independence constitutions of African states in the form of a bill of rights to protect individual rights and property.[118]

The third major feature in many of the African independence constitutions was the rigid nature of the constitution. Under the British system the constitution is not entrenched, and Parliament can make or unmake any law it wishes. In African states the notion of parliamentary supremacy was qualified by the bill of rights and the rigid nature of the constitutions.[119]

Liberal Approaches to
Constitutional Change in South Africa

In the historical context of South Africa's unitary Westminster constitution, the "pure" liberal call would be a demand for the participation of all members of society in the institutions of state. D. V. Cowen argued in 1960 for universal franchise in a unitary state.[120] Cowen found racial federations unacceptable, as they perpetuated racial thinking in politics.[121] However, he was prepared to accept a federal system based on existing provinces where the units are not defined in terms of race.[122] Regardless of the nature of the state, he advocated a bill of rights to protect individual rights.[123] This last option was never popular among liberal circles throughout the apartheid era. Translated into reality, if applied across the whole of South Africa, it would mean a black majority government whose political and ideological persuasion was uncertain.

The more popular liberal approach was the restricted franchise. This was the approach of the old Cape liberals at the time of Union who insisted on the retention of the franchise for Africans in the Cape Province. A more recent advocate of this approach was Professor Robert Molteno whose recommendation was adopted by the former Progressive Party.[124] This option would restrict the franchise to those who had achieved a certain standard of "civilization": those "that have attained an economic level or a degree of sophistication to enable them to feel sufficient identification with society as a whole—to possess sufficient 'stake in the country'—not to fall prey to totalitarian illusions."[125] The Molteno Report equates black nationalism and the demand for equal rights and unqualified franchise with totalitarianism.[126] The report does not spell out how it arrived at this conclusion. It does reveal a perception that a black majority government could pose a threat to white and liberal interests, and advocates a bill of rights to safeguard these interests.[127] However, despite describing South Africa as a plural society, there is no reference to the units being defined in terms of racial composition.

Despite the proposal of a federal system with a restricted franchise, the previous two approaches still promote a single society with a common government representative of all the people. In this context the assumptions and principles underlying the proposals are close to the United States federal system. The process incorporates all the people into an existing political constitutional system historically reserved for whites.[128] Leo Marquard was one of the foremost liberal exponents of this view.[129] He advocated a bicameral legislature with the lower house representing the interests of the people at large and the upper house representing the regions much like the United States.[130] A wide degree of autonomy much like the United States constitution should devolve on the regions.[131] There

62

should be an independent judiciary to adjudicate over disputes and prevent violation of the bill of rights.[132] Racial equality, a common franchise, and a single legislature were the assumptions underlying this liberal view,[133] which differed from the U.S. view only in the cautious approach of some theorists to the franchise, where additional guarantees were sought to prevent the vote being exercised by those not sharing the fundamental assumptions of the system. However, the recent tendency of liberal approaches has been marked by a swing away from the promotion of a "common society."[134]

Today liberal constitutional thought has gone beyond proposing a bill of rights and federal system to protect liberal interests to a more sophisticated constitutional program advocating the protection of group rights. Consistent with the liberal conclusion that a unitary state is less conducive to protecting liberal values and the interests of the property class in an order where the values of liberalism are not rooted in the culture, and given the South African reality that the dominant class (the white minority) is not geographically limited to a few areas, the consociational model offers the best framework to protect the interests of the minority.[135]

Hence, today's liberals claim to be committed to the ideals of equality and individual rights, but they question the efficacy of the traditional liberal constitutions to resolve social and political conflict in a culturally heterogeneous society.[136] Hitherto liberal theories promoted a common society, but the underlying values were not sufficiently entrenched in their constitutional models. For example, the bill of rights in Marquard's model in itself could not prevent a black majority government under the guidance of a unified party. Even in a federal state with a rigid constitution the units could still conceivably be under the control of a single party, thus enabling uniform policies to be effected across the country. Under the Westminster parliamentary form of government this scenario is more likely to occur. Moreover, the liberals fear there is no guarantee that the ruling party and government would have the same commitment to the protection of the interests of the status quo. Underlying the new liberal approach is the recognition that "traditional" Western state models can only operate to protect liberal values if there is majority agreement on the fundamentals of liberalism.[137] The emphasis has now changed from the "simple" federal system of the U.S. model to the more complex model advocating the protection of group identity and group rights.[138] Federalism is now advocated to protect the "integrity" of community interests and promote community autonomy as opposed to simple regional autonomy.[139] The units should encompass linguistic, ethnic, and religious diversities in the population.[140]

Variations on the models are proposed by different theorists. Some liberal theorists advocate the creation of new homogeneous units while others argue that the groups need not be geographically defined. The former model is closer to consociationalism and the Swiss model of federalism. The first advocate of the Swiss model of federalism was the former South African cabinet minister Piet Koornhof.[141] More recently Frances Kendall and Leon Louw[142] advocated the creation of various cantons wherein the different groups can reside. The cantons must have considerable local autonomy to determine their own economic, labor, transport, educational, welfare, and race policies.[143] The central government must be prevented from imposing standards on the entire country, because imposed uniformity "in a heterogeneous society leads to inappropriate policies for many groups."[144] The rights of the cantons must be embodied in a rigid constitution that cannot be amended without the consent of all cantons.[145]

Both models are variations of consociationalism and aim at providing autonomy for the various ethnic and linguistic groupings in South African society as opposed to creating a common society. They seek to introduce a system where one "group" cannot interfere in the personal affairs of another. Moreover, they envisage the creation of a veto power whereby a single group can veto the decisions of the central government if the proposed decision threatens the interests of that group. These models are inappropriate for achieving the important goals and objectives of a future South African society, namely, restructuring economics and implementing democracy, because they favor the interests of the status quo—the privileged white sector of the population. Not surprisingly, the consociational model is the most popular constitutional option among liberal white South Africans, including white liberal political parties.

REFERENCES

1. See F. W. Riggs, "The Comparison of Whole Political Systems," in Robert T. Holt and John E. Turner, eds., *The Methodology of Comparative Research* (New York: Free Press, 1970), 77.

2. W. C. Mitchell, "The Shape of Political Theory to Come," in Seymour M. Lipset, ed., *Politics and the Social Sciences* (New York: Oxford University Press, 1969), 124.

3. Preston T. King, *Federalism and Federation* (London: Croom Helm, 1982), 133.

4. Benjamin O. Nwabueze, *Constitutionalism in the Emergent States* (London: C. Hurst, 1973), 77.

5. See E. C. S. Wade's introduction in Albert V. Dicey, *Introduction to the Study of the Law of the Constitution*, 10th ed. (London: Macmillan, 1959), xxxv.

6. Owen Hood Phillips and Paul Jackson, *Constitutional and Administrative Law*, 6th ed. (London: Sweet & Maxwell, 1978), 27.

7. E. C. S. Wade and G. Godfrey Phillips, *Constitutional and Administrative Law*, 9th ed. (London: Longman, 1977), 59.

8. Trevor C. Hartley and J. A. G. Griffith, *Government and Law: An Introduction to the Working of the Constitution in Britain* (London: Weidenfeld and Nicholson, 1975), 52.

9. Phillips and Jackson, *Constitutional and Administrative Law*, 27.

10. Wade and Phillips, *Constitutional and Administrative Law,* 100.

11. The ability of the judiciary to question an act of the legislature would contradict the predominant constitutional grundnorm of legislative supremacy. See Phillips and Jackson, *Constitutional and Administrative Law,* 27.

12. See Article 5 of the Constitution of France (hereinafter referred to as French Constitution). The constitution specifies that it is the President who is responsible for seeing that the constitution is respected and it is his duty to arbitrate and ensure the smooth functioning of the government and its agencies.

13. French Constitution, art. 6.

14. Roy C. Macridis, *The Study of Comparative Government* (Garden City, N.Y.: Doubleday, 1955), 106.

15. French Constitution, art. 24.

16. The French Constitution, Article 34, spells out the areas of legislative competence. Among important powers conferred on the legislature are those pertaining to civil rights, criminal law, defense, education, labor law, economic and social planning, and property law.

17. French Constitution, art. 23.

18. Macridis, *Modern Political Systems,* 110.

19. Ivo D. Duchacek, *Comparative Federalism: The Territorial Dimension of Politics* (New York: Holt, Rinehart and Winston, 1970), 116.

20. Ibid., 116.

21. Jack Hayward, *The One and Indivisible French Republic* (London: Weidenfeld & Nicholson), 1973, 19.

22. Macridis, *Modern Political Systems,* 114.

23. See Mary A. Glendon, Michael Wallace Gordon, and Christopher Osakwe, eds., *Comparative Legal Traditions: Text, Materials and Cases on the Civil Law, Common Law, and Socialist Law Traditions, with Special Reference to French, West German, English and Soviet Law* (St. Paul, Minn.: West, 1985), 64–65.

24. Bharat B. Gupta, *Comparative Study of Six Living Constitutions* (New Delhi: Sterling Publishers, 1974), 366.

25. Historically, the power of the Constitutional Council was primarily to ensure that the legislature acted only in terms of the power conferred on it and did not encroach upon the "terrain" of the executive.

26. Recently, there has been a change in the way the Conseil constitutionnel has performed its role. In 1971, when called upon to rule on a particular statute pertaining to the freedom of association, the Conseil ruled the preamble of the constitution (which reaffirmed the fundamental principles of the French revolution) was part of the constitution. This interpretation introduced a notion of there being a bill of rights in the French constitution. See Mauro Capeletti and William Cohen, *Comparative Constitutional Law: Cases and Materials* (Indianapolis, Ind.: Bobbs-Merrill, 1979), 50–51.

27. Carl J. Friedrich, *The Impact of American Constitutionalism Abroad* (Boston: Boston University Press, 1967).

28. Bernard Schwartz, *Constitutional Law: A Textbook,* 2d ed. (New York: Macmillan, 1979), 1.

29. U.S. Constitution, amend. 10.

30. David P. Currie, *The Constitution of the United States: A Primer for the People* (Chicago: University of Chicago Press, 1988), 4.

31. U.S. Constitution, art. 1, sec. 8. Over the years the domain of the federal government has been considerably extended by the last part of section 8, which allows Congress to make all laws necessary and proper for executing its powers.

32. See the decision of Chief Justice Marshall in *Gibbons v Ogden,* 22 U.S. (9 Wheat.). The Supreme Court held that New York's attempt to grant someone a monopoly to operate

a steamboat was inconsistent with the power that the federal government had in terms of the Constitution, and therefore ruled the New York action invalid.

33. Michael Conant, *The Constitution and Capitalism* (St. Paul: West, 1974), 4.

34. U.S. Constitution, art. 1, sec. 1.

35. U.S. Constitution, art. 1, sec. 3.

36. See generally Charles A. Beard, *An Economic Interpretation of the Constitution of the United States* (New York: Free Press, 1986).

37. U.S. Constitution, art. 3, sec. 1.

38. U.S. Constitution, art. 1, sec. 7.

39. U.S. Constitution, art. 2, sec. 2.

40. Duchacek, *Comparative Federalism*, 230. Clearly, if the powers of the units can be altered by the central government with relative ease, this would defeat the purpose of the federal arrangement, which is to provide autonomy to the units.

41. Responsible government means that the executive is responsible to the legislature.

42. M. Jean Holmes and Campbell Sharman, *The Australian Federal System* (Sydney: G. Allen & Unwin, 1977), 21; Seerp B. Ybema, *Constitutionalism and Civil Liberties,* (Leiden: Leiden University Press, 1973), 16; M. V. Pylee, *India's Constitution* (Bombay: Asia, 1962), 167.

43. Canada only adopted a bill of rights in 1982, which changed the constitutional powers of the courts and the country in significant ways. The discussion here will show the position of Canada prior to the adoption of the bill of rights to show the principle of federalism operating under a parliamentary form of government.

44. Pylee, *India's Constitution*, 166.

45. Ybema, *Civil Liberties*, 112, 165.

46. More specifically modeled along the Westminster model.

47. In this regard the House of Lords in England can only delay the passage of legislation but cannot prevent a bill from being enacted.

48. Charles F. Strong, *Modern Political Constitutions: An Introduction to the Comparative Study of their History and Existing Form*, 6th. rev. ed. (London: Sidgwick & Jackson, 1963), 123.

49. As laid out in its Basic Law, more particularly Article 1.

50. Basic Law of the Federal Republic of Germany, art. 19.

51. David P. Conradt, *The German Polity* (New York: Longman, 1986), 120.

52. Macridis, *Modern Political Systems*, 212.

53. Lewis J. Edinger, *Politics in West Germany*, 2d ed. (Boston: Little, Brown, 1977), 20.

54. Jorgen Dalberg-Larsen, *The Welfare State and Its Law* (Berlin: Tesdorpf, 1987), 50.

55. Ibid., art. 20.

56. K. W. Deutch and D. Brent Smith, in Macridis, *Modern Political Systems*, 203.

57. David C. Marsh, *The Welfare State* (London: Longman, 1970), 1.

58. For example the Women, Infants, and Children (WIC) program providing food stamps to lower-income households.

59. The program in the U.S. provided work, shelter, food, and medical care to those who could not afford them. See William R. Brock, *Welfare, Democracy, and the New Deal* (Cambridge: Cambridge University Press, 1988), 171–89.

60. Donald P. Kommers, *The Constitutional Jurisprudence of the Federal Republic of Germany* (Durham, N.C.: Duke University Press, 1989), 247–48.

61. The Basic Law of the Federal Republic of Germany, art. 7(1) (promulgated on 23 May 1949). For a copy see A. P. Blaustein and G. H. Flanz, eds., *Constitutions of the Countries of the World*, vol. 5 (Dobbs Ferry, N.Y.: Oceana Publications); BVerfG E 33 303 330 ff (Federal Constitutional Court Decision 33 page 303 at 33ff) [trans. by Philip Von Randow].

62. Ibid., art. 6(5).

63. BVerfGE 45 376ff (Federal Constitutional Court Decision Number 45 at 376ff) [trans. by Philip Von Randow].

64. FRG Basic Law, art. 28(1).

65. Dalberg-Larsen, *Welfare State*, 14–15.

66. Constitution of Sweden, chap. 1, art. 2, in Blaustein and Franz, *Constitutions of the Countries of the World*, vol. 15.

67. Ibid.

68. Ibid. See also Constitution of Norway, of 17 May 1814, art. 110 in Blaustein and Flanz, *Constitutions of the Countries of the World*, vol. 12.

69. International Commission of Jurists, "Declaration of Delhi," in International Commission of Jurists, *African Conference on the Rule of Law, 1st Lagos, 1961* (Geneva: ICJ, 1961), 12.

70. International Covenant on Economic, Social, and Cultural Rights, 16 December 1966, 993 U.N.T.S., 3.

71. Kommers, *Constitutional Jurisprudence*, 248.

72. BVerfG E 33 303 330 ff (Federal Constitutional Court Decision 33 page 303 at 33ff) [trans. by Philip Von Randow].

73. F. Ewald, "A Concept of Social Law," in Gunther Teubner, ed., *Dilemmas of Law in the Welfare State* (Berlin: Walter de Gruyter, 1986), 40.

74. Ibid., 41.

75. For a fuller description of the theory underlying the consociational model, see discussion in chapter 4.

76. For an account of some of these experiences see Lijphart, in Rotberg and Barratt, *Conflict and Compromise*, 62–3; F. van Zyl Slabbert and David J. Welsh, *South Africa's Options: Strategies for Sharing Power* (New York: St. Martin's Press, 1979), 66–72.

77. The political program of the government, the Democratic Party, and the former Progressive Federal Party and New Republic Party all contain elements of consociationalism. Their respective constitutional proposals will be discussed in chapter 10.

78. Lijphart in Rotberg and Barratt, *Conflict and Compromise*.

79. Ibid., 25.

80. Boulle, *Constitutional Reform*, 47.

81. Slabbert and Welsh, *South Africa's Options*, 62.

82. Lijphart, "Consociational Democracy," *World Politics* 21 (1969): 216.

83. Lijphart quoted in Rotberg and Barratt, *Conflict and Compromise, 57.*

84. Ibid., 61.

85. The term "matters of common concern" refers to core powers conferred on the central government under a federal arrangement such as—among other things—defense, coinage, and foreign affairs.

86. S. Venter, "Some of South Africa's Political Alternatives in Consociational Perspective," *South Africa International* 11:3 (1981): 130.

87. Boulle, *Conflict and Compromise*, 51.

88. Theodor Hanf, et al., *South Africa, the Prospects for Peaceful Change: An Empirical Enquiry into the Possibility of Democratic Regulation*, trans., John Richardson (London: R. Collins, 1981), 386.

89. Lijphart, in Rotberg and Barratt, *Conflict and Compromise*, 61.

90. Slabbert and Welsh, *South Africa's Options*, 45; Geldenhuys, "South Africa's Constitutional Alternatives," 213. Hanf et al., *Prospects for Peaceful Change*, 384.

91. Swiss Constitution, art. 1. For a copy of the text of the constitution see Blaustein and Flanz, *Constitutions of the Countries of the World*.

92. Ibid., art. 3.

93. Ibid., art. 116.

94. Kenneth D. McRae, *Conflict and Compromise in Multilingual Societies: Switzerland* (Waterloo, Ont.: Wilfrid Laurier University Press, 1983), 122.

95. Swiss Constitution, art. 73.

96. Ibid., art. 80.

97. Ibid., art. 96.

98. George A. Codding, *The Federal Government of Switzerland* (Boston: Houghton Mifflin, 1961), 88; Christopher J. Hughes, *The Parliament of Switzerland* (London: Cassell, 1962), 69–83.

99. Hughes, *Parliament of Switzerland*, 108.

100. Swiss Constitution, art. 98.

101. Swiss Constitution, art. 107.

102. McRae, *Conflict and Compromise*, chap. 4, especially 132–47.

103. Swiss Constitution, art. 123.

104. Carl J. Friedrich, *Constitutional Government and Politics*, 4th ed. (Waltham, Mass.: Blaisdell Pub. Co., 1968), 226–27.

105. Pius Msekwa, *Towards Party Supremacy* (Kampala: East African Literature Bureau, 1977), 1–8; J. J. Okumu, "Party and Party-State Relations" in Joel D. Barkan and John J. Okumu, *Politics and Public Policy in Kenya and Tanzania* (New York: Praeger, 1979), 44–45.

106. Okumu, "Party and Party-State Relations," 46.

107. Christian P. Potholm, *The Theory and Practice of African Politics* (Englewood Cliffs, N.J.: Prentice Hall, 1979), 140.

108. Le Vine, "Parliaments in Francophone Africa" in Joel Smith and Lloyd D. Musolf, eds., *Legislatures in Development: Dynamics of Change in New and Old States* (Durham, N.C.: Duke University Press), 143.

109. Thomas R. Kanza, *Conflict in the Congo: The Rise and Fall of Lumumba* (Harmondsworth: Penguin Books, 1972), 88; Kwame Nkrumah, *Challenge of the Congo* (London: Nelson, 1967), 18.

110. See chapter 4. In Britain, local government cannot impose any limitations on the central government in respect to the central government's scope of power.

111. Frederick August Otto Schwarz, *Nigeria: The Tribes, The Nation, or The Race: The Politics of Independence* (Cambridge, Mass.: MIT Press, 1965), 196.

112. Benjamin O. Nwabueze, *Constitutionalism in the Emergent States* (London: C. Hurst, 1973), 122.

113. Benjamin O. Nwabueze, *Presidentialism in Commonwealth Africa* (New York: St. Martin's Press, 1974), 148.

114. Henri Grimal, *Decolonization: The British, French, Dutch, and Belgian Empires, 1919–1963*, trans. Steven De Vos (Boulder, Colo.: Westview Press, 1978), 300, 313.

115. Ibid.

116. See previous discussion of consociationalism in terms of which a veto power is accorded to one or more groups over the decisions of the central government.

117. de Smith, *The New Commonwealth*, 160.

118. Ibid., 195. Southern Rhodesia, the Zimbabwe Constitution Order, 1979. Even as late as 1979 when negotiating Zimbabwe's independence from Britain, the British government insisted on voting and property safeguards that were for the protection of the minority white population. Twenty parliamentary seats (disproportionate to their number) were reserved for the white population. Ibid., sec. 38(1)(a).

119. T. O. Elias, *Nigeria: The Development of Its Laws and Constitution* (London: Stevens, 1967), 135.

120. Denis V. Cowen, *Constitution-Making for a Democracy* (Johannesburg: Anglo American Corp. of South Africa, 1960), 39.

121. Ibid.

122. D. V. Cowen, *The Foundations of Freedom*, 159–60.

123. Ibid., 175.

124. Molteno Report, vol. 1, *Franchise Proposals and Constitutional Safeguards* (n.p. 1960).

125. Ibid., 10.

126. Ibid., 13.

127. Ibid., 51.

128. W. H. Thomas, "South Africa Between Partition and Integration," *Aussen Politiek* (1979): 313.

129. Leopold Marquard, *A Federation of Southern Africa* (London: Oxford University Press, 1971), 66.

130. Ibid., 75.

131. Ibid., 76–77.

132. Ibid., 79, 97.

133. Ibid.

134. Wolfgang H. Thomas, *Plural Democracy: Political Change and Strategies for Evolution in South Africa* (Johannesburg: South African Institute of Race Relations, 1977), 16.

135. This theme is fully explored and developed in chapter 7.

136. Peter Randall, ed., *South Africa's Political Alternatives* (Johannesburg: SPRO-CAS, 1973), 129.

137. Ibid., 130.

138. The various "concrete" frameworks and proposals will be examined in chapter 10.

139. N. Holliday, *Federate or Fail: Key to a Peaceful, Politically Scientific Change for South Africa* (Alice, Ciskei: Lovedale Press, 1985), 7.

140. Ibid.

141. Quoted by Lijphart in Rotberg & Barratt, eds., *Conflict and Compromise*, 70.

142. Leon Louw and Frances Kendall, *After Apartheid: The Solution for South Africa* (San Francisco: ICS Press, 1987), 115.

143. Ibid., 126.

144. Ibid., 138.

145. Ibid., 145.

CHAPTER SIX

South African Constitutions and Government

■ ■ ■

T HE FIRST SOUTH African constitution was introduced at the formation of the Union in 1909 and took its inspiration from the British model. It was the framework of government for almost three-quarters of the century.[1] A Republic was proclaimed in 1961 but did not result in a change in the overall form of government.[2]

The Westminster model has never been introduced in identical or original form in all of Africa. The most salient departure from the "original" model is in South Africa where the Westminster model applied to the white population only. Apart from racial exclusion, most of the main features of government in South Africa have historically resembled those of Britain.

The head of state was only a nominal chief. Prior to the formation of the republic in 1961, the head of state was constituted in the governor-general, who was referred to as Her Majesty's Representative.[3] After the proclamation of the republic, the state president became the nominal head of state. He was elected by an electoral college of the two houses of Parliament at a joint sitting.[4] The form of government was "responsible government," requiring support of Parliament.[5] Similarly, all members of the executive had to be members of the legislature. The leader of the majority party in Parliament became the prime minister.

Parliament was modeled along British lines with a bicameral chamber. The members of the lower chamber, the House of Assembly, were popularly elected in single-member constituencies. The upper chamber, the Senate, was more of a review body. The members of the Senate were in part elected by the provinces and in part nominated by the state president. In 1980 following the report of the government-appointed Schlebush Commission, the Senate was abolished and replaced by a consultative body called the President's Council (PC),[6] comprising sixty members all appointed by the executive from the white, colored, and Indian communities. The exclusion of the African majority reflected the prevailing government doctrine that Africans should exercise political rights only in the homelands. The function of the President's Council was to furnish advice to the state president at his request or voluntarily if the PC felt a matter was of public interest.[7] Despite its lack of political power the PC was seen by government circles as a first step toward accommodating other groups in the central constitutional process. The abolition of the Senate marked the first step toward the move away from the main features of the Westminster system of government.

Since the formation of the Union, sovereignty of Parliament has been a major principle in the model.[8] Therefore, like Britain, South Africa had an independent judiciary that did not, however, have the power to decide on the substance of legislation. At the formation of the Union the predominant view among the delegates was that to allow the courts a testing right over legislation would amount to defeating the will of the people.[9] Supremacy of the legislature assumed the status of a predominant *grundnorm* [ground rule] in South African law.[10]

The South Africa Constitution Act of 1909 introduced a variation on the British unitary form of state by providing for the continuation of four separate provinces (Cape, Natal, Orange Free State, and Transvaal). The provinces were able to elect members of the Senate. Moreover, they were given certain powers over taxation, education, health care, and various local works.[11] Though to some it smacked of federalism,[12] the constitution did not confer on the provinces any separate powers not amenable to central control.[13] The Westminster form of government was introduced in South Africa at the time of Union in 1910 and was abolished in 1984 with the introduction of the tricameral Parliament.

FORMS OF PARTICIPATION FOR BLACKS

At the formation of the Union in 1909, Africans and coloreds were placed on a common voters roll with whites. Moreover, they were given the franchise in two provinces, Cape Province and Natal.[14] But only whites were permitted to serve as members of the legislature.[15] The reality is that very few blacks (inclusive of Africans, Indians, and coloreds, but especially Africans) exercised voting rights because of the property qualifications of the franchise.[16] Black voting strength was further eroded by the removal of income and property qualifications for whites while requirements for blacks were maintained.[17]

In 1936 Africans were removed from the common voters roll, thus precluding them from exercising franchise rights in selecting delegates to the national legislature.[18] In 1956 coloreds were removed from the roll as well.[19]

The de facto situation since the formation of the Union has been the separation of people on the basis of color.[20] With the advent of National Party control in 1948 the dominant focus of the government became the institutionalization of separate development. In 1950 the Population Registration Act[21] was passed and required every citizen of the country to register as one of the defined population groups, either white, colored, or African. Moreover, the African group was further subdivided into eight tribal units.

The removal of coloreds from the common voters roll was a further step toward the de jure separation of people, the policy of apartheid. For a short period Africans and coloreds were allowed to elect three and four white delegates respectively to represent them in the lower house of Parliament. A similar provision was made for Indians to elect three white members to the lower house to represent their interests but was never effected because the Indians boycotted it.[22] For Africans the practice of indirect representation continued until 1959; for coloreds it lasted until 1968. What followed thereafter was the creation of separate institutions for the various groups.[23] The Prohibition of Political Interference Act (1968) was passed outlawing mixed political parties.[24] The act precluded political organization across color lines in line with the National Party's program of separate development.

Coloreds and Indians. The Colored Persons Representative Council (CPRC)[25] and the South African Indian Council (SAIC)[26] were formed in 1968 as forums for their respective designated groups. These two bodies consisted partly of elected representatives and partly of members nominated by the state president. The CPRC was given authority to legislate on certain matters pertaining to colored interests, which included finance, education, local government, and social welfare subject to the approval of the state president.[27] The lawmaking power of the CPRC was never absolute. All acts of the CPRC were conditional on the approval of the central government which retained a veto over all acts. The CPRC also made recommendations and advised the government on matters pertaining to coloreds.[28] Advising and making recommendations to the government on matters affecting Indians[29] was the main purpose of the SAIC, which did not enjoy the limited legislative functions of the CPRC. The dominant Labor Party in the CPRC used the forum to voice colored grievances and the body was continually wrecked by boycotts.[30] Both the CPRC and the SAIC failed to achieve any legitimacy because of their lack of real power and their subordinate position in the government.[31]

Africans and the Homelands System. After the removal of Africans from the common voters roll, provision was made for three whites to represent them in the central lower house.[32] Simultaneously, provisions were made for the creation of a Native Representative Council (NRC) to advise the government on matters affecting Africans.[33] It had no legislative powers. The NRC consisted of some nonwhite officials appointed by the government, (both white and African) and some elected by defined black authorities.[34] As with other bodies of this nature, the council was perceived as inadequate and ineffectual and never achieved legitimacy. The NRC was abolished in 1951 by the National Party.[35]

In 1948, the exclusion of blacks from the central decision-making process took a new and somewhat sophisticated turn. The National Party's political platform was the complete separation of the races in every sphere of life. In the past Africans had been treated as a single unit; the NRC did not distinguish Africans on the basis of supposed ethnic or tribal affiliations. The National Party divided Africans into eight units with each unit having a defined territory based on ethnicity.[36] The National Party's idea was that South Africa consisted of various nations that could be geographically defined and developed to independence. The historical origins of the notion of territorial separation can be traced to the Land Act of 1913.[37] This act set aside certain defined territory for African ownership. The land area consisted of about 10 percent of South Africa and in 1936 was increased to just over 13 percent.[38] Africans were precluded from owning land outside the demarcated areas.

In the context of the policy of separate development, each African would be identified as one of the defined ethnic groups. The approach of the National government was to discourage ideas of liberal democracy among the African people and to push them in the direction of some form of "self-rule" according to traditional patterns.[39] Africans would exercise political rights as ethnic groups in the designated areas of the specific group. A corollary was that Africans would no longer exercise political rights outside the specified areas. The Bantu Homeland Citizenship Act in 1970[40] specified that every black person in South Africa was a citizen of one or another homeland irrespective of where the person was born or resided throughout his or her life. Moreover, once a territory obtained "independence," all persons identified with that homeland would be stripped of their South African citizenship.[41] To date millions of black South Africans have been stripped of their citizenship through what has been referred to as an exercise of denationalization.[42] Subsequently, the presence and movement of Africans into "white" South Africa were regulated as is done in the case of any alien by means of the Pass Law system, which demanded that every African carry an identity document outside the homelands indicating she or he was either employed in the area or had permission to be in the area in question. Africans found in an area for which their identity documents were not authorized were subject to criminal punishment.

Legal machinery was created for each of the ten territories to receive the power of self-government. Basically two stages would lead to the process of "independence." The first was a period of self-government during which a wide array of powers devolved to the homeland government.[43] A legislative and executive framework was introduced and the territory could legislate on a list of scheduled matters, though the white parliament could still exercise a veto over acts.[44] The second stage was that of "complete independence" in which all powers pertaining to the homeland devolved on the territory. The central (white) parliament divested all legislative competence over the territory, which could then legislate on any matter. The territory had the power to draw up its own constitution. To date four territories have become "independent," namely, Transkei, Bophuthatswana, Ciskei, and Venda.

Africans Outside the Homelands. The homeland governments were seen as the primary forum for African political participation. However, not all of the areas where Africans resided were incorporated into one or the other of the homelands. This was partly due to historical developments leading to the creation of major dormitory-like townships to house workers at the periphery of the major "white" cities. For the architects of apartheid it was not possible to link townships such as Soweto (outside Johannesburg) to a homeland. The reality of the situation is that almost 40 percent of the African population in South Africa lives outside the designated homelands.[45] To accommodate the "aspirations" of these urban Africans, the government had, over the years, created various bodies designed to give expression to their views.

In the 1960s the government created black councils in the urban areas.[46] These councils consisted both of elected members and members nominated by the local government. In its initial stages, the function of these bodies was primarily advisory with no decision-making powers. Over the years provisions were made for the creation of new local bodies in the urban areas with increased powers called community councils.[47] The local councils increased from being merely advisory to being bodies of local authority. Black local authorities were given power to regulate over matters pertaining to road traffic, trade, ambulance, and fire-fighting services, and licensing and control of motor vehicles.[48] The government enactment (1986) merely accorded the same powers to the black councils as to the white councils. This was the extent of participation that Africans had in the apartheid South African constitutional setup. The African majority had no say in the central decision-making process of government policy. Powers were delegated to the local authorities at the discretion of the white administration. The black councils were also dependent on the white authorities for revenue.[49]

The Last Apartheid Constitution[50]

Since the formation of Union, the tendency in South Africa had been to progressively erode the participation of blacks in the central political process. In 1983 a new constitution was passed,[51] which radically altered the Westminster tradition[52] and also pointed toward the apparent inclusion of segments of the black population, namely, the colored and Indian groups, into the central political process. The 1983 constitution extended to every white, colored, and Indian person the right to vote for the selected houses of the legislature.[53] The African majority were completely excluded from participating in the machinery created in the new constitution. The constitution operated on the premise that there are distinct "population groups" in South Africa that should enjoy separate representation as distinct entities in the central legislature. The constitution created three separate houses in the legislature.[54]

THE LEGISLATURE

The constitution proclaimed that legislative power shall be vested in the Parliament and in the state president of the republic.[55] The legislature consisted of three houses: a House of Assembly represented whites, a House of Representatives represented coloreds and a House of Delegates represented Indians. If for any reason there were no members in any house or if members failed to take their seats in a house, Parliament would continue with the house or houses that were able to take their places.[56] The number of members in each house appeared in the ratio of 4:2:1, white, colored, and Indian members respectively.[57] Most of the members were elected in single-member constituencies by members of the respective groups. In addition, members were appointed to the legislature by the state president and by the members of the respective houses.[58]

THE EXECUTIVE AUTHORITY

The head of the country was the state president[59] elected by an electoral college made up of members of the three houses in the ratio of 4:2:1.[60] Theoretically, any party with a majority in each of the houses selected the members of the electoral college. The reality was that the majority party in the white assembly selected the state president, as the ratio was stacked conclusively in its favor. Once elected into office the State President was no longer dependent on the support of the legislature for his survival.[61] The term of office of the state president was five years, which was the same as that of the legislature except that he continued to hold office after a general election until a successor was elected.[62]

The executive authority resided in the person of the state president acting in consultation with the Ministers' Council[63] or the ministers depending on whether the matter in question related to own affairs or general affairs.[64] The constitution made a distinction between matters deemed to be "own affairs" and matters deemed to be "general affairs."

Own Affairs. "Own affairs" were matters that affect a group "in relation to the maintenance of its identity and the upholding and furtherance of its way of life, culture, traditions and customs."[65] What constituted own affairs was further elaborated in schedule 1 of the 1983 constitution.[66] These included matters pertaining to social welfare; education including the syllabus and payment of salaries to teachers; health and hospital services; housing; local administration; agriculture; water supply; and the appointment of the civil service to administer matters pertaining to the affairs of the group.[67] Matters that were not own affairs were "general affairs."[68] The determination as to whether a matter fell within the ambit of own affairs or general affairs was made by the state president, who issued a certificate which denoted a particular matter or piece of initiated legislation pertained to own affairs.[69] No court of law could pronounce on the validity of the state president's announcement that a matter related to own affairs or general affairs.[70]

Once a matter was designated as own affairs by the state president, the relevant house was competent to deal with and legislate on it. However, the state president could still intervene and pronounce again by way of a certificate that a particular amendment initiated by a house extended beyond own affairs. The legislative process was halted if the amendment was not abandoned. Once legislation was successfully passed by a house, it required the signature of the state president to be effected.[71]

The constitution specified that the executive authority in own affairs was exercised by the state president acting on advice of the Ministers' Council. The Ministers' Council consisted of ministers appointed by the state president to oversee the various departments pertaining to own affairs.[72] Ministers appointed to a particular house were required to belong to the appropriate population group. The state president designated as chairman of the council a minister whom he felt enjoyed the support of the majority in the house.[73] The provision that the state president had to act on the advice of the Ministers' Council did not fetter the state president's power, as he was merely consulting with his own appointees. Moreover, no limitation was imposed on him with respect to changing the members of the Ministers' Council at his discretion.

General Affairs. General affairs essentially related to matters the state president considered beyond the interest of a single population group. The president appointed a cabinet to administer departments of state pertaining to general affairs. All members of the cabinet had to be members of the legislature.[74] The executive authority pertaining to general affairs resided in the person of the state president acting in consultation with the cabinet.[75] Again, the provision did not impose severe limitations on the president. It merely required him to consult with his own appointees, whom he could remove at his leisure.

Since general affairs related to matters that affected more than a single group, the constitution created a separate mechanism for legislation dealing with general affairs. The legislation was initiated by the cabinet and introduced to the three houses sitting separately. The three houses discussed and voted on the legislation separately; if passed by a majority in all three houses, it was presented to the state president for his signature.[76] Moreover, the constitution made provision for a permanent standing committee consisting of members of all three houses to achieve consensus on general affairs.[77]

In the event of a dispute over the passing of a bill among the various houses, the state president had the discretion to refer the matter to the President's Council.[78] The president could either refer the original bill to the PC or he could refer different versions of a bill to the PC for its recommendation. The recommendation of the PC if assented to by the president was deemed to have been passed by Parliament.[79] In this sense the legislative procedure in the new constitution was flexible and allowed for bypassing the legislature.[80]

The President's Council. The President's Council was actually an advisory body to the state president. It consisted of members appointed by all three houses of the legislature in the proportion 4:2:1. The House of Assembly selected twenty members, the House of Representatives selected ten, and the House of Delegates selected five.[81] The opposition parties in each of the houses had the right to select six, three, and one member respectively to the PC. In addition to these thirty-five members, the president had the power to appoint a further twenty-five members to the PC.

The constitution specified that the function of the PC was to advise the president on his request on any matter (excluding draft legislation) that was of public interest.[82] The President's Council assumed particular importance in the event of disagreement among the houses with respect to draft legislation. In this case the president had the power to bypass the legislature and refer the bill or bills to the PC for its advice. The PC in turn could select which bill if any was to be presented to the president for his assent.[83] Once the state president assented to the bill presented to him by the PC it became law.

OVERVIEW OF THE 1983 CONSTITUTION

The 1983 Constitution was conspicuous in its nonaccommodation of the African[84] majority in the constitutional machinery. All power pertaining to the control and administration of African people was vested in the state president.[85] He continued to exercise all power in respect to land set aside for the occupation of Africans.

More importantly, the inclusion of Indians and coloreds in the constitutional process did not really alter the status quo of white power, particularly National Party dominance of South African politics,[86] nor did it confer on the two groups significant decision-making powers. All it did was make them junior partners in the implementation of apartheid legislation to which they were also subjected. The entire constitutional machinery was designed in such a way that major decision-making power still resided in the hands of the white minority. The electoral college consisted of eighty-eight members, of which fifty came from the white House of Assembly. The 4:2:1 ratio always ensured that the choice of state president would be that of the dominant party in the white Assembly.[87]

The tremendous powers the state president had, particularly in the designation of own and general affairs, allowed him to control the legislative agenda. No court of law could pronounce on the validity of such decisions.[88] Moreover, all executive appointments relating to the cabinet and the three houses vested in the president. The President's Council was a veritable extension of the president[89] and the ruling party in the white Assembly,[90] which enabled the National Party to ensure their agenda, was in no way hampered. From a political point of view the acceptance of the idea of own and general affairs conformed completely to apartheid ideology. The constitutional demarcation of separate chambers for different groups further entrenched the belief that South Africa consisted of different groups of people who were in need of separate facilities.

TYPECASTING THE 1983
SOUTH AFRICAN CONSTITUTION

The 1983 South African constitution had features of a presidential model as well as a parliamentary system. It is therefore impossible to classify it in terms of any single model. The state president was the preeminent personality in the entire system. He was responsible for the selection of the cabinet. However, unlike most presidential models, he was not popularly elected but was instead elected by the legislature. Once elected he was not strictly dependent on the support of the legislature for his survival. In this sense he shared the independence of the French and United States presidents from the legislature. His term of office, however, was linked to that of the legislature, similar to the term of a prime minister in the parliamentary model. The requirement that all members of the cabinet be members of the legislature was again a feature of the Westminster model. However, the state president was not a member of the legislature.

The state president exerted a greater influence on the legislature than does the U.S. president on account of the strict party system in South Africa. In this sense he shared similarities with the French president in that as in France the president is responsible for determining policies of the government.[91] The South African system under the 1983 constitution has been characterized as a semipresidential system.[92]

The 1983 constitution was consistent with the Westminster tradition of excluding the power of the courts to adjudicate on the substance of legislation.[93] All apartheid and other unjust legislation thus remained intact and the majority party in the white legislature could continue legislating in a discriminatory manner without intervention by the courts. It has always been a tradition of South African constitutional law to pronounce on the procedural aspects of constitutional practice,[94] and this practice was recognized in the new constitution.[95] Moreover, so long as the constitutional procedure set out was followed, no court of law could pronounce on the validity of the state president's decisions with respect to his designation of own and general affairs.

The 1983 constitution preserved the unitary nature of the South African state. However, it was premised on the principle of group rights and group autonomy for the different "population groups," and could be construed as consociational.[96] The idea of a consociational state is one of power sharing and consensus between different groups. However, under the 1983 constitution, the autonomy and power of the designated groups were not absolute. It was always the state president who decided what affairs related to a particular group, and the separate legislatures always operated in tandem with the president. Moreover, there was no requirement for compulsory consensus between the groups, as the president could always bypass the legislature and have legislation introduced through the President's Council, nor was there any requirement that the government or executive had to comprise members of all groups. It was inevitable that the president would emerge from the majority party in the white House of Assembly. Lastly, the majority African population was excluded from the machinery. This taken together with the dominant position of the white Assembly in relation to the other houses preserved the unitary nature of the South African state.

Basson describes the 1983 constitution like its predecessor as a "race bound aristocracy."[97] It was a system that purported to introduce power sharing but in reality continued white domination. The constitution was introduced without the consent or consultation of any of the black communities. However, prior to its introduction a referendum was held among the white community to test support for the government's dispensation. In this sense it was imposed on the colored and Indian populations. The result was the boycott of the 1984 elections by almost 80 percent of eligible colored and Indian voters. Those who offered themselves as candidates for the legislature were rejected by their communities.[98] The 1983 constitution was consistent with the apartheid tradition of being an initiative imposed from the top by the white establishment. It suffered the same lack of legitimacy that all previous apartheid initiatives had experienced.[99]

REFERENCES

1. South Africa Act of 1909.

2. The proclamation of the republic merely entailed the severing of all links with the British Crown, from the perspective of the white government, therefore, it did not need any changes in the form of government.

3. South Africa Act of 1909, art. 8.

4. Republic of South Africa Constitution Act of 1961, art. 8.

5. H. R. Hahlo, et al., *The Union of South Africa: The Development of Its Laws and Constitution* (London: Stevens, 1960), 130.

6. Fifth Amendment Act 101 of 1980. The PC was the first move by the government to co-opt "Indians" and "coloreds" at some level into the constitutional process.

7. Boulle, *Constitutional Reform*, 164.

8. South Africa Act of 1909, art. 59.

9. Denis V. Cowen, *Foundations of Freedom with Special Reference to Southern Africa* (Cape Town: Oxford University Press, 1961), 139.

10. S. Venter, "South African Constitutional Law in Flux," in D. J. Van Vuuren, et al., eds., *Change in South Africa* (Durban: Butterworth's, 1983), 3.

11. South Africa Act of 1909, art. 85.

12. Henry J. May, *The South African Constitution*, 3d ed. (Westport, Conn.: Greenwood Press, 1970), 191.

13. The essential nature of a federal state is the units enjoy exclusive powers in respect to certain matters that cannot be eroded by the central government. For a discussion of the difference between the provincial system and federalism see Gail M. Cockram, *Constitutional Law in the Republic of South Africa* (Cape Town: Juta, 1975), 61.

14. Section 35 of the Union Constitution entrenched these rights.

15. Articles 44(a) and 22(a) of the South Africa Act of 1909.

16. In terms of the 1913 Land Act, Africans were precluded from owning land outside designated areas set aside for them, which in effect meant outside what was considered South Africa.

17. Boulle, *Constitutional Reform*, 80.

18. Representation of Blacks Act 12 of 1936.

19. Separate Representation of Voters Act 46 of 1956.

20. Since blacks were precluded from owning land outside prescribed areas this meant that whites and blacks lived in separate areas.

21. Act 30 of 1950.

22. Boulle, *Constitutional Reform*, 82.

23. By virtue primarily of the Promotion of Bantu Self-Government Act 46 of 1959, and the Separate Representation of Voters Amendment Act 50 of 1968. Each of the various institutions is discussed in this chapter.

24. Act of 1968.

25. Act 52 of 1968.

26. South African Indian Council Act (SAIC) 31 of 1968.

27. W. B. Vosloo, "Constitutional Democracy as a Means to Accomplish Peaceful Change in South Africa: An Evolution of the Constitutional Change Proposed by the National Party in 1977," *Politikon* 6:1 (June, 1979), 19.

28. Section 20 of CPRC Act.

29. Sections 7 and 10 of the (SAIC) Act 31 of 1968.

30. A. E. Moseneke, "An Overview of Some Aspects of Constitutional and Legal Struc-tures in South Africa," paper delivered at a Seminar on the Legal Aspects of Apartheid by the Lawyers Committee for Civil Rights Under Law, July 6–7 1985.

31. Boulle, *Constitutional Reform*, 84, 86. Both bodies were abolished with the introduction of the new constitution setting up the tricameral parliament in 1984.

32. Representation of Natives Act 12 of 1936.

33. Ibid.

34. Ibid., sec. 27.

35. By this time the National Party program for Africans was to set up "independent" homelands for the African population, and the institutions they envisaged developed in this direction.

36. Promotion of Black Self-Government Act 46 of 1959.

37. Act 27 of 1913.

38. Bernard Magubane, *The Political Economy of Race and Class in South Africa* (New York: Monthly Review Press, 1979), 85.

39. Dion A. Basson and Henning P. Viljoen, *South African Constitutional Law* (Cape Town: Juta, 1988), 309.

40. Act 26 of 1970.

41. National States Citizenship Act 26 of 1970, sec. 3.

42. J. Budlender, "A Common Citizenship," *South African Journal of Human Rights* (1985): 210.

43. The Bantu Homelands Constitution Act 21 of 1971.

44. Ibid., sec. 31.

45. J. Blenck, "Republic of South Africa: Partition a Solution?" *Aussenpolitik* 27 (1976): 29.

46. Urban Black Councils Act 79 of 1961.

47. Black Affairs Administration Act 45 of 1971; Community Councils Act 125 of 1977; Black Local Authorities Act 102 of 1982. The last act attempts to place black local government on a similar footing to that of the white local government. See Boulle, *Constitutional Reform*, 88.

48. Basson and Viljoen, *South African Constitutional Law*, 320.

49. They have no independent taxing power.

50. Republic of South Africa Constitution Act No. 110 of 1983 (hereinafter referred to as South African Constitution).

51. Ibid.

52. For example in respect to the selection of the head of state, the powers of the head of state, the composition and powers of the legislature. All these aspects are discussed below.

53. South African Constitution, art. 52.

54. Ibid.

55. Art. 30.

56. Ibid., art. 37.

57. Ibid., art. 41, 42, 43.

58. Ibid.

59. Ibid., art. 6(1).

60. Ibid., art. 7(1)(b).

61. Although he could be removed for misconduct or inability to perform his duties. Ibid., art. 9.

62. Ibid., art. 7(1).

63. Each of the three legislatures had a Minister's Council to act as a "mini-executive" with respect to matters considered "own affairs." See discussion of own affairs below.

64. Ibid., art. 19.

65. Ibid., art. 14(1).

66. Ibid., schedule 1.

67. Ibid.

68. Ibid., art. 15.
69. Ibid., art. 31(1).
70. Ibid., art. 18(2).
71. If the state president did not give his assent to the bill, the bill did not have any effect.
72. Ibid., art. 21(a).
73. Ibid., art. 21(2).
74. Ibid., art. 24(3).
75. Ibid., art. 19(1)(b).
76. Ibid., art. 33.
77. Ibid., art. 64.
78. Ibid., art. 32.
79. Ibid., art. 32(4) and 34(1).
80. In terms of Article 70(1), once the state president accepted the recommendation of the PC he could merely assent to the bill without referring the bill to the legislature for approval. The other "groups" could not challenge the power of the white executive head since the constitutional mechanisms were conclusively stacked in the white head of state's favor; the white head of state could always ensure that the white agenda was not in any way compromised. See discussion below.
81. Ibid., art. 70(1).
82. Ibid., art. 78(1).
83. Ibid., art. 78.
84. The constitution referred to them as "Blacks."
85. Ibid., art. 93.
86. The exclusive power that the state president had in designating own and general affairs allowed the dominant white group, constituted in the National Party, to control the legislative agenda. See below.
87. The members of the electoral college were chosen by the majority parties in each of the three houses of the legislature. The white legislature's share of members in the electoral college was greater then that of the other two houses combined.
88. Ibid., art. 18(2).
89. He appointed twenty-five of the sixty members to the PC.
90. They appointed fourteen members to the PC.
91. Basson and Viljoen, *South African Constitutional Law*, 48.
92. Ibid.
93. Ibid., art. 34(2).
94. That is, the courts could ensure that the legislators complied with the procedure that they themselves had set up. See *Harris v. Minister of Interior* 1952 (2) SA 428 (AD).
95. South African Constitution, sec. 34(2)(a).
96. W. B. Vosloo, "Constitutional Democracy," 23.
97. Basson and Viljoen, South African Constitutional Law, 213.
98. Following the tricameral elections the country was engulfed in a wave of violence. Ever since the elections participants in the government-created structures have come under verbal and physical attack. See *Mission to South Africa: The Commonwealth Report, The Findings of the Commonwealth Eminent Persons Group of Southern Africa* (1986).
99. In a sense, the 1983 Constitution sharpened the legitimacy problem of the South African state. The month elections were held for the Indian and Colored chambers marked the beginning of unprecedented uprisings on a national scale resulting in socioeconomic chaos and the subsequent imposition of a national state of emergency in South Africa.

CHAPTER SEVEN

Federalism and Liberal Constitutions in African States

■ ■ ■

T HIS CHAPTER FOCUSES on the constitutional experiences of independent African countries, which share a colonial history with South
Africa, and examines the success and failure of their adopted models under the complex conditions that obtain in African societies. Two
related issues are the problems associated with different forms of state
(particularly the federal model) as well as the wider problems associated
with liberal constitutions as they were introduced in African countries.

The appropriateness of a federal model for a "plural" society (which
is so often used to characterize African society) will be investigated in
light of the record of federal constitutions in many parts of Africa because,
in the words of Ivor Jennings, "constitutions are heirs of the past as well
as the testators of the future."[1] The examination will be limited to an
analysis of federal states that contain the essential elements of liberal
constitutionalism. Many of the arguments presented for a federal arrangement in other parts of Africa are today presented as arguments for the
same arrangement in South Africa. If a federal constitution (and its consociational variant) is potentially capable of producing the same results in
South Africa as in Nigeria and other African states owing to shared
"contexts of action,"[2] then what is the lesson for South Africa?

We will also investigate the notion of pluralism as a description of South
African society. Arguably the plural paradigm poses serious conceptual
problems. Demystifying pluralism is essential because of the strong prescriptive overtones it brings to the constitutional debate in calling for
federal and consociational constitutional models.

Finally, we will consider the wider problems associated with Western
constitutions (unitary or federal). There is a shortsighted tendency to look

at the success of constitutions and the particular institutions associated with them in a particular part of the world as a rationale for exporting them to a different part of the globe. The record of constitutional transfer from the colonial powers to independent African states has been a failure, because the framework exported has proved inappropriate in dealing with such issues as national unity and socioeconomic change.

The Federal Model:
Western and African Experiences

While it is true that most African states at independence consisted of various linguistic, cultural, or religious groups, the issue is whether the federal model offered a viable framework to deal with subnationalism and other centrifugal tendencies. This relates to the very important aspect of nation building in a new state. The point is repeatedly made that the borders of most African countries were artificially drawn up by the colonial powers.[3] Heterogeneous groups usually coexist without a common sense of national identity. Which form of state organization should be adopted, one that gives recognition and institutional expression to heterogeneity, or one that attempts to overcome differences in favor of a single identity? Liberal theorists prefer the federal model for a heterogenous society and argue that federalism leads to greater freedom.

However, the lessons of history have demonstrated that in many situations a federal constitution does not operate in a neutral fashion. Indeed, Western critics of the federal model also allude to its bias in favor of certain societal interests.[4] The federal model often fosters conflict between elements representing the status quo and opposed to change and elements wanting to change the system,[5] begging the question whose freedom a federal arrangement promotes. By dividing authority between various units and entrenching the rights of the units, a minority can frustrate the will of the majority. Federalism here operates to retard the freedom of the majority. William Riker asserts that the federal model in the United States historically has benefitted the privileged South.[6] The plea for states' rights has worked to guarantee the control of the minority[7] in the South over African Americans first as slaves and later as an underprivileged sector of the population over the wishes of the majority.[8] Federalism and freedom do not necessarily equate, since a majority at the national level can have their wishes blocked by a minority at the regional level.[9] Despite these criticisms the federal system in the United States has survived for over two hundred years.

There are, however, differences in the conditions under which the federal system was introduced in the United States and the conditions under which it was introduced in African countries. In looking at a federal system for a future South Africa, two interrelated matters have to be addressed: first, the overall desirability of a federal system in light of social and political circumstances, and second, the requirements for success of a federal system.[10]

The notion that a federal model is suited to societies that are culturally and linguistically diverse is questionable.[11] Although the United States is one of the most diverse countries in the world, made up of myriad ethnic and national groups, the federal units do not in any way coincide with cleavages in the population. The federal model in the United States was not designed to protect the integrity of an ethnic, linguistic, or religious group. Charles Tarlton asserts that a federal system will only work well in a symmetrical society where "each particular section, state, or region partakes of a character general and common to the whole."[12] In most societies that comprise diverse cultural or linguistic groups, the federal model has the opposite effect of stirring the groups toward greater friction.[13] It follows that there is no simple relationship between federalism and pluralism,[14] that the model is not a panacea for diversity. It is important to have "a clear understanding of the strengths and weaknesses, the benefits and liabilities, the predictability and the surprises of federalism."[15] The African independence constitutions, including the federal model, did not result in freedom and compromise, but in crisis and repression.[16]

The effect of the introduction of the federal model in Africa in most instances was to mobilize ethnic politics. The notion that minority communities should have special representation has resulted in divided loyalties and has worked against the development of national consciousness.[17] Before the Civil War in Nigeria, the federal system gave institutional expression to ethnocentric politics and tended toward crystallizing the political structure as it was when the colonial power departed.[18] The regions created (in terms of the federal plan) were all identified with major ethnic communities.[19] Each region saw itself as a distinct political entity. Not surprisingly, the parties that arose were all identified with particular regions and ethnic groups, and each party sought its support from its own base,[20] putting a great strain on the federal system.[21] The regional parties were less interested in the welfare of Nigeria than of their own region. Federal institutions failed to build national consciousness.

In Uganda the federal system was again identified with ethnic politics. The region of Buganda was given a privileged position in terms of the constitution with respect to a host of matters.[22] The leader of Buganda was identified with the traditional kingdom and claimed the loyalty of the Buganda people over that of the Ugandan state.[23] The federal arrangement created a state with divided loyalties. It gave institutional expression to a competition for loyalty between the region and the center, which threatened to destroy the Ugandan state.[24] The government of Milton

85

Obote saw the abolition of the federal state as necessary if Uganda was to remain a single country.[25] Similarly, the First Republic in Zaire was almost fragmented by provincial autonomy. The period after independence was characterized by violent ethnic riots flowing from widespread communal insecurities created by ethnic mobilization.[26]

The national question, namely the need to achieve a sense of national identity, has been a serious problem resulting in the collapse and subsequent discarding of many constitutions in Africa. Ethnicity as a basis for political organization[27] was prominent in many independent African countries. African governments adopted forms of state and constitutions that attempted to divide power between the regions, which essentially were based on "tribal" or ethnic interests, and the center. Communal representation in a federal framework has a poor track record in Africa. It has the tendency of exacerbating communal differences in that communities are stirred on to greater parochial self-consciousness, and electoral campaigns are marked by communal prejudice and strife as opposed to concern over national social and economic issues.[28] The result has been political upheavals as experienced in the Congo [Zaire], Uganda, and Nigeria.[29]

It is important to pay attention to these failures and to identify the salient factors that could provide instructive lessons for a future South Africa. The federal arrangement provided for a weak central government. Competition between the center and a region for the loyalty of the people was evident in Nigeria during the Biafran crisis when the Eastern Region attempted to secede from the federal government. A similar phenomenon was at work in Zaire with the attempted secession of Katanga. In Uganda as well, Buganda was given a special status under the federal constitution. The central government in all three instances could not effect national policies without infringing on the interests of the regions. Opposition groups thus formed around parochial loyalties, which affected both national unity and the ability of the government to act. Federalism in the postcolonial stage resulted in the entrenchment of ethnic politics. The constitutional structure under the asymmetric federal arrangement made for a weak government that endangered national unity and resources.[30]

The federal model is expensive to maintain, something which a poor and fragile state can ill afford. The dual system of local and central government consumes a great deal of resources. For example, in Nigeria, economic and social planning was quadrupled with the central and regional governments carrying out their programs in parallel, and the National Economic Council trying to coordinate the various projects.[31] Similarly, in Uganda and Kenya the duplication of legislatures and civil services imposed high administrative costs on the country.[32]

Unlike the United States, African federations came into existence at a time when attitudes toward the proper role of government had changed.[33]

A twentieth-century government is expected to play a more active role in economic and social activity,[34] and independent African countries needed urgently to deal with many problems, particularly economic development, the building of infrastructure, and equitable distribution at a central level.[35] Permitting widespread autonomy to the regions resulted in uneven economic development and progress. So whom *did* the federal model benefit in Africa, and who stands to benefit from the introduction of such a model in South Africa?

Various parties stood to benefit from a federal arrangement. Behind the drive for the adoption of the federal model were traditional leaders who feared a diminution of their authority after independence. In both Kenya and Uganda, traditional leaders sought to entrench their interests in the new constitution by adopting a federal arrangement,[36] which allowed local elites to exercise control over their affairs.[37] In Ghana local chiefs were in favor of a constitution that promoted decentralization.[38] Similarly, in Nigeria the leaders in the regions used ethnic differences to keep out rival parties and preserve their own political base.[39]

There were also crucial economic reasons for the propagation of a federal system. The parties who stood to benefit from a weak and divided state structure included local interests as well as colonial interests. For example, it is widely claimed King Baudouin of Belgium wanted a federal arrangement so that Belgium would continue to have the leverage to safeguard its financial interests in Zaire.[40] Belgium was particularly concerned about the region of Katanga, which is richly endowed in mineral resources,[41] and therefore abetted separatist tendencies there. Not wishing to share the wealth of Katanga with the rest of the country,[42] the Katanga leadership sought a more profitable alliance with Belgian interests. The regional party in Katanga was strongly supported materially, financially, and militarily by the Belgians and expatriate European population.[43]

Similar motives were at play in the Biafran conflict and the attempt of the Eastern Region, well endowed with oil deposits, to secede from Nigeria. The Igbo leadership in the Eastern Region did not wish to share the wealth of the region with the rest of the country and wanted maximum independence and control over their resources.[44] Similarly, de Smith attributes the desire to introduce a bill of rights in Kenya as an attempt to protect the properties of the European and Asian populations.[45]

In the light of this experience, who would benefit from a federal or consociational constitutional arrangement in South Africa? Unlike other African countries South Africa has long been independent. However, the socioeconomic problems of the majority in South Africa are similar to those of other African peoples in the aftermath of the colonial experience.[46] The institutions associated with Western federal and consociational arrangements would inevitably tie the hands of the central government. Since a great deal of power would reside in the regions or segments, the central government would be hard pressed to effect a socioeconomic transformation of the society. Theorists favoring the consociational option see it as imperative to devolve the maximum amount of autonomy to the segments be it in the realm of education, culture, or business.[47] But such thinking clearly favors the status quo, particularly the white population.

Moreover, there is no limitation on how the segments or units may define themselves. For example, in his federal model for South Africa Leopold Marquard states, "There is no reason why racial composition of regions should not be a factor."[48] Whites or a segment of the white population in South African society can choose to define themselves as a separate segment whose interests merit special protection.

The institutions associated with the federal and consociational arrangement have certain features that can immobilize the central government, again favoring the status quo. For example, an essential requirement of the consociational model is the principle of mutual veto, whereby one segment can veto a decision of the central government with which it disagrees.[49] No important decision can be made without the consent of all groups. Clearly, the survival of the system depends on consensus. However, it would be difficult to achieve consensus given the extreme socioeconomic disparities in South Africa, particularly between blacks and whites, with most of the wealth concentrated in the hands of the white minority. Maximum segmental autonomy, mutual veto, and a bill of rights with its protection of existing property relationships would favor the privileged white group more than any other sector. It would allow their continued economic dominance of South African society under an essentially weak black government. The central government would most likely be restricted in remedying the effects of the historical exploitative acts by the white sector by virtue of the entrenched group autonomy and veto power accorded to the minority segment. Moreover, the government would be limited in effecting any socioeconomic transformation.[50]

The model also stands to benefit an elite black group. To achieve consensus the consociational model requires elite cooperation, a feature considered to be the most important requirement of the model.[51] Elite leaders must be able to act on behalf of their constituency without any direct mandate from their group.[52] This requires a relatively passive and apolitical citizenry. So long as the leadership are able to achieve consensus, the model will survive. A disorganized political entity results, characterized by No Sizwe as "held together by a maximum unity of purpose among the elites of the 'ethnic group' on the basis of a mutually profitable collaboration".[53]

Post-independence African political experience bears testimony to the role of elite leadership under a federal constitution. The perpetuation of ethnic politics is largely a consequence of an interplay of a constitution and leader that appeals to ethnic sentiments to carve out a constituency for themselves. Despite attacks on ethnic politics made by most African leaders, many leaders manipulate ethnic values, symbols, and customs to win votes from their group and set themselves up as spokespersons for a particular group. The voter is thus called on to vote or make decisions not on the basis of policies but on the basis of the ethnic origin of the candidate.[54] Such leadership indulges in a process of retribalization,[55] exploiting the situation to keep out rival parties. This prevents politics from being conducted in terms of national issues. Once elites are in a position of influence, they are able to dispense favors and jobs, thus entering into a patron-client relationship with voters. The regionalization of politics serves the political purposes of the elite by providing them a base from which to operate.[56] Hence many of the demands for regional solutions to constitutional problems are supported by parochial elite leadership in collaboration with foreign interests.[57]

In South Africa elite rule by ethnic leaders was instituted by the government on a scale greater than anywhere else on the continent. The tricameral parliament made provision for separate representation for whites, coloreds, and Indians. The delegates appointed to the various chambers had to belong to the specific group in question. The homelands system further provided for the maximum fragmentation of the African population with each group identified with a particular area. The nine homelands had at their heads elite "leaders" who at various times professed, and some like Mangosuthu Buthelezi, still profess, to represent the interests of their ethnic constituency. Considerable power and resources were concentrated in the hands of the homeland leaders, who were able to dispense favors and patronage.[58] Not surprisingly, from within the ranks of the African community the strongest supporters for regional constitutions come from the former separate development leaders who clearly have a vested interest in promoting such constitutions.[59]

In looking at postcolonial African history it can be said that federal constitutions have thus far proved to be an inappropriate form of state.[60] The lesson to be learned from the failures of regional solutions is that no effort should be spared to unite the future South African nation in the quest to meet its urgent concerns. The notion of regional and central affairs (or for that matter own and general affairs) is problematic, because matters such as agriculture, land tenure, property, and local government converge with national interests, as does the provision of social services.[61] The duplication of government functions and agencies is costly for a developing nation, and arguments for centralizing the focal aspects of the economy and important social services are compelling. The wisdom of institutions that promote ethnic and regional politics has to be seriously questioned.[62]

The record of the failure of federal states in Africa should be a source of enlightenment for constitution-makers for a post-apartheid South

Africa.[63] De Smith asserts that federalism should be resisted and summarizes its effects most cogently by stating it "leads to fragmentation of an already weak state, tends to let in neo-colonialism by the back door, clogs up the machinery of government and makes it more expensive to run, obstructs central economic planning and introduces legal technicalities into the political process."[64] The introduction of a constitutional framework that cannot be easily removed and imposes restraints that hamper crucial government policies will result in the framework being destroyed.[65]

Theoretical Framework of the Plural Model

Considerable attention has been given to the notion that South Africa is a plural society and that the only appropriate constitution and state institutions are those that allow the diverse elements expression of their separate identity.[66] Pluralism is a central idea in all constitutional debates in South Africa. The role one accords it will greatly influence the political landscape with profound consequences for the national question, which is the Achilles' heel of so many African countries. It is important to demystify the notion of pluralism and the idea that South Africa (like the rest of Africa) consists of various antagonistic groups with few common allegiances. The plural model sees society as consisting of distinct groups, each vying for power. South African society, like many African countries, is posited as being composed of many ethnic groups with distinct language, values, and culture. For example, Pierre van den Berghe observes that South Africa is a complex and highly pluralistic society "wherein coexist several political systems, economies, and linguistic, religious, and 'racial' groups which overlap only partly with one another."[67] In the political realm each group is posited as having the protection of its own interest as its primary concern, which leads to conflict.[68] Conflict is seen as the most crucial feature of South African society.[69]

SOCIAL CLEAVAGES

It is one thing to describe South Africa as a divided society, but the more crucial question, since it affects the way we deal with it, is how to explain the divisions. The answer escapes most theorists operating within the plural paradigm. The tendency of the few who do attempt to explain it is to assume these divisions exist in a primordial way. Van den Berghe assumes there is a genetic explanation for the existence of racism and ethnocentrism.[70] He argues all organisms behave in a way that favors not only their own survival but also organisms that are genetically related to them.[71] A community can be defined in a number of ways; race or skin pigmentation is one badge for group membership.[72] Race is not only a biologically meaningful distinction but also the one most fraught with conflict. Moreover, he asserts that in instances of communal conflict violence continues unabated in an irrational way, which points to a biological basis for it.[73]

Similarly, Slabbert and Welsh maintain that ethnic conflict is more difficult to contain than class conflict because ethnicity is more deeply embedded in the human psyche.[74] Race is a factor independent of all other relations. Once ethnic hostilities are aroused, race assumes a life of its own.[75] Where ethnic and class conflict compete, ethnicity will always win and can never be transformed into a class solidarity.[76]

The major criticism of these explanations is their assumption that human beings are inherently prone to conflict on account of perceived biological or cultural differences. Human beings are assumed to have an innate disposition of hostility toward groups perceived as different from themselves. It is further assumed that these animosities are permanent features not amenable to change. Clearly, South Africa is a divided society, but these divisions have to be explained beyond mere racial prejudice against "out groups." Under what circumstances do racial or ethnic differences assume a salience and lead to situations of conflict? Apart from the few writers who assume biological reasons to be the cause of the hostility, the majority of those who subscribe to the plural paradigm fail to elaborate on their premises. They describe divisions in society without explaining how these divisions originated and how they are maintained. Understanding the nature of the political order from a historical perspective helps to unravel how the different groups have come to occupy their positions as opposed to just spelling out the different groups that are themselves the subject matter of investigation.[77]

MARXIST EXPLANATIONS FOR RACIAL DIVISIONS

The notion of conflict is also at the core of Marxist politics, but its explanation differs radically from any other theory. According to the Marxist perspective, conflict in society is a product of the class system[78] and is not inherent in human nature. It is therefore not possible to ameliorate the conflict without altering the system.[79]

The appearance of different groups each with a defined status arises as a result of a historical struggle within a power structure. The first step toward this historical evaluation is to characterize the mode of production, which requires an explanation of the economic relationships in a society.[80] Orthodox Marxism claims all social institutions "arise from and adapt themselves to the nature of the relations of production," also known as the material base.[81] All ideas, values, ideologies, and beliefs referred to as the superstructural are influenced by the relations of production; all social relations owe their origins to the economic base. Moreover, ideologies, values, and beliefs are superstructural in that they are determined by the economic base of the society in order to reinforce the existing relations of production. Yolamu Barongo asserts that "values, beliefs and ideas have their basis and reflect very fundamentally on the nature of the economic base . . . and the relations it creates among the people as well as in the historical experiences of the society."[82] Ethnocentrism and racism are posited as concern with the superstructure rather than with the social class system.[83] In terms of this crude instrumentalist approach, the appearance of different groups in South Africa with different ideological orientations owes its origins to the specific economic base. Marxists criticize pluralists for their explanation of conflict in terms of subjective feeling, such as ethnicity, which Marxists say is used to avoid a class analysis.[84]

This explanation is inadequate in that it relegates everything to the economic base without explaining the influence of social structures and institutions[85] on the consciousness and behavior of people. Harold Wolpe correctly asserts that what is needed is an analysis that investigates the legal, social, and political content of the class relationships that give the latter their specific historical character.[86] This is not to discount class theory at all. The object of class theory is to pinpoint the main line of social cleavage within a particular system,[87] that is, the structural fault to which most of the serious political conflicts can be traced. However, relationships in society are not just economic but a combination of different structures and practices, political, ideological, and theoretical.[88] Wolpe applies this to the South African situation and asserts the abstract class relationship in South Africa is capitalist whereas the specific form of the relationship is determined by apartheid.[89] So while we can use the historical materialist approach to explain social development, our examination must encompass the interconnection between the economic structure and the ideological and political elements that codetermine the particular form the social structure takes in South Africa.[90]

The Liberal-Radical Debate:
Capital Accumulation in South Africa

The liberal school of thought posits two separate and distinct elements in the investigation of South African society. The first is constituted in the economy, the second in the polity.[91] In the South African experience, the liberal school asserts the two forces have acted in opposite ways. The economy works toward the liberation of people from inferior status while the polity obstructs the progress of nonwhites.[92]

According to this view, the free market works to break down the color restrictions that exist in society. Mechanisms of control, be they state intervention in the market or color restrictions, distort market tendencies toward social and economic harmony. The presence of free competition ensures maximum efficiency in the market and dissolves prejudice, enabling underprivileged sectors of the population to share in the fruits of the economy.[93]

Apartheid policies and racial prejudice are posited as having a dysfunctional effect on the economy. For example, the system of job reservation for the whites and exclusion of Africans is wasteful and leads to industrial and administrative inefficiency.[94] Over the years (the liberal school argues) there has been a shortage of skilled labor that cannot be filled by Africans because of the job reservations.[95] Moreover, cheap labor leads to a lack of incentive to mechanize and results in a labor force that is undernourished and debilitated.[96] A mobile labor force is an essential prerequisite for capitalist development; liberals argue that South Africa's migrant labor system was counterproductive.[97]

For liberal theorists the solution to the South African problem lies in the philosophy of free enterprise.[98] The South African economy has been undermined by the stubborn pursuit of apartheid and Afrikanerdom.[99] The policies of apartheid were seen as irrational and external to the economy, pursued for political and not economic reasons.[100] For example, the control of African labor reflected sectional (white) political objectives and not economics.[101] Similarly the definition of people and their differential treatment was attributed to prejudice. This prejudice, although external to the economy, has the effect of influencing it.

Theorists operating within the radical paradigm take serious issue with the liberal notion of a separation between the economy and the polity. For example, Wolpe asserts, "Far from economic discrimination being 'foreign' to the economy, it has its origins in economic activity and is maintained both by the economic structure and . . . by the political structure."[102] Frederick Johnstone notes a marked absence of conflict between the process of capital accumulation and apartheid; in fact, apartheid and the economic system worked hand in hand.[103]

The radicals pose the question, "If apartheid is inimical to the process of capital accumulation, why is South Africa today Africa's only modern industrial giant?" In the 1960s the South African economy grew at a rate second only to Japan's. The radical view credits the laws and institutions of apartheid with this pattern of economic growth.

The radical view argues that the migrant labor system historically has not been at cross-purposes with the economy. Impediments to African progress were not due merely to racial prejudice—a view that ignores the historical role capital has played in the impoverishment of the African people in South Africa. From the very early years white farmers and mining bosses were extremely reliant on African labor to work their farms and mines.[104] But African workers were reluctant to enter into employment for the mining companies and were in a position to resist, as they were able to produce their own food and subsist on what land they had. Consequently various measures were adopted to force Africans to enter into white employment. First, a poll tax (taxing each African regardless of earning or occupation) was introduced, though it was not completely successful in reorienting large pools of African workers. A process of land alienation followed that transformed self-supporting Africans into squatters and tenants. In 1913 the Natives Land Act was passed, which set aside and restricted African ownership to about 10 percent of the total land of South Africa. This process of land alienation and the changing of the status of Africans on the land forced them into the employment of the mines.[105] Moreover, the land set aside for them was not agriculturally fertile. Other laws followed that made it impossible for Africans to reside in areas other than those designated for them. In addition to these "legal" measures, property owners—the mine owners—employed a myriad of extralegal measures to make Africans dependent on whites.[106] Not only were Africans to be conquered and decimated but they were to be made dependent on their conquerors.[107] The homelands set aside for Africans would become "concentrated areas of poverty, disease and ignorance."[108]

White property owners, particularly the mine owners, greatly benefited from this process of land alienation. Historians point to the specific nature of the gold mines in the nineteenth and early twentieth centuries, which required a large and ultraexploitable reservoir of labor to maintain profitability.[109] By pushing the African majority off the land and concentrating the wealth in their own hands, white mine owners had a massive pool of labor at their disposal. The native reserves or homelands became the reservoir of this cheap labor, first for the mines and later for the industrial sector. An agency recruited workers for all the mines, eliminating competition and keeping costs down.[110] The homelands system later served as a dumping ground for surplus labor. Employers did not have to provide social and welfare benefits to the old and sick, who were shipped back to the homelands to be replaced by a fresh supply.

Johnstone argues that it was not the richness of the gold mines that made them attractive but the fact that they could be worked efficiently by cheap labor.[111] Contrary to liberal theorists, he asserts that the mines would not have been profitable had the cost of labor been high and mobile, hence measures to ensure that the cost of labor always remained depressed.[112] All the repressive legislation that constituted the worst of the South African experience, particularly the pass and the compound systems, served the purposes of white property owners.

The pass laws made it possible for the mine owners and later the industrial sector to control and channel the movement of workers in both the desired direction and in terms of numbers. Moreover, the hated pass system served to reinforce the control of the employers to check on breaches of contract. Similarly, the compound system, which housed African workers in large prisonlike conditions, enabled the mine owners to prevent desertion by the workers and maintain discipline.[113] It is therefore not axiomatic that the best labor policy for economic growth is one that allows a free and mobile labor force to operate. Capital accumulation is compatible with a variety of forms of labor, as the South African experience has demonstrated.[114] Contrary to the liberal school of thought, the only modern industrial giant in Africa has been built with apartheid legislation.

The state also profited from discrimination against and oppression of African labor. Mining companies reaped profits that returned vast revenues to the state in the form of taxes. These taxes enabled the state to establish the infrastructure of the manufacturing industry.[115] The repressive legislation that until the 1980s prevented the operation of trade unions was greatly beneficial to the capital sector, making it possible for white employers to maintain their huge profitability while paying black employees low wages.

Liberal theorists repeatedly refer to the shortage of skilled labor and the dysfunctional effect apartheid job reservation has had on the economy, but apartheid policies historically have not been an all-or-nothing proposition. The twin goals of apartheid being prosperity and white supremacy,[116] blacks were permitted to perform jobs over the years normally restricted to whites through a process of job dilution or job redefinition[117]—and at considerably lower pay.[118] Thus white supremacy is maintained by relaxing laws that are not in the interest of the twin goals. Though white industrial owners and white workers may at times conflict in the effort to maximize their own interests, their common overarching goal of white economic prosperity forced them to compromise.[119]

Contrary to liberal thinking, there is no simple correlation between industrialization and the erosion of racial attitudes. Most liberal societies over the years have incorporated most of their population into their social and political institutions. This had not happened in South Africa where race is a dominant feature in the social structure. The cause cannot be attributed to prejudice or attitudes of the actors but to the specific nature of the South African process of capital accumulation. Contrary to what is asserted by liberal theorists, apartheid and economic development in South Africa from a historical perspective have gone hand in hand.[120] Racial discrimination and the differential treatment of black people served an important role in the overall process of capital development in South Africa.

Institutions, Laws, and Social Formation

It is crucial to understand that black South Africans did not decide the laws that sought to label them into different categories or that effectively confined them to the position of hewers of wood and drawers of water. All apartheid legislation was imposed on them. In 1950 the Population Registration Act[121] was promulgated to classify the South African population into four primary racial groups; Africans were further subdivided into eight subcategories. The "plural" structure of South African society was imposed ascriptively by the dominant white group.[122]

Similarly, blacks did not themselves choose to live in specific areas on the basis of racial or tribal identity. Legislation such as the Natives Land Act[123] and the Group Areas Act[124] (imposed in terms of the classifications created by the Population Registration Act) was passed, confining people to distinct residential areas. The Natives Land Act made provision for separate territory for each of the eight subgroups of the African population. Any attempt to reside in an area not set aside for the racial group for which a person was categorized could result in criminal penalties being imposed against them. Similarly, the schools one attended would be racially or ethnically compartmentalized. Differences of color, language, history, and culture were incessantly impressed upon the people in the schools and government-controlled media.

It is inevitable that under these conditions people would begin to behave and believe that there are fundamental and unbridgeable differences among them. Ideology and attitudes are not primordial or neutral but are shaped by experience. Any alteration of those beliefs is dependent on a change in the material conditions and political orientation of the entire population.

Failure of Western Constitutional Models in Africa

The record of institutional transfer from European countries to independent African countries has been a very dismal one with most African countries abandoning the models they inherited from the colonial countries. We examine the various reasons advanced for these collapses and highlight the important lessons to be drawn when considering a constitution for a future South Africa. The factors considered were not all present in every case of constitutional failure in Africa. However, a combination of one or more of many of these factors contributed to the instability of many independence constitutions in Africa. While there were many problems associated with the constitutions introduced, some of the reasons advanced for abolishing Western institutions were not strictly legitimate and were used by the elite as a pretext to fortify their own positions.

CROSSCULTURAL INCOMPATIBILITIES

A popular argument goes that constitutions were not suited to the societies in which they were introduced primarily owing to a mismatch between the values of the people and the new system.[125] The ideas contained in the African independence constitutions embodied ideas from Roman and Greek philosophy that over a period of time came to be the common heritage of Europe and the Western world,[126] among them ideas of individuality and property rights. But because colonial rule had not permitted Western ideas and values to be assimilated into the African political culture,[127] the values these institutions were meant to protect were not common to the society.

A further argument goes that the institutions left by the colonial powers were designed to maintain a socioeconomic system at variance with the traditional culture of the population. The most notable aspect here was in regard to property, which in the traditional setting was a communal possession as opposed to an individual right as it is under Western systems.[128] In traditional African society the group element predominates, while in the liberal constitutions the rights of the individual are the central focus. In addition, the institutions left by the colonial powers were invariably of an adversary nature requiring a government and organized opposition. Traditional African society conducts its affairs in a consensual manner through a process of mutual consultation and agreement as opposed to competition and conflict.[129]

At the forefront of most nationalist struggles in Africa was a party with an elite leadership who were the dominant actors in the shaping of the constitution.[130] In many instances the political leaders were primarily concerned with their own political aims,[131] and the constitutions and forms of state adopted reflected the aspirations of these leaders.[132] It follows that if there was a legitimacy problem, it arose because the constitutions failed to command the moral authority of the population who not only were not participants in drawing them up but also could not understand them.[133]

SOCIOECONOMIC REALITIES

The institutions suddenly introduced into African societies with the departure of the colonial power ignored both the problem of illiteracy in Africa, and the wider lack of education in Western ways.[134] The people neither had the attitudes nor knew the laws and doctrines necessary for the survival of these institutions.[135]

Every political system must be associated with the environment in which it operates.[136] The path of constitutional development in Western societies shows certain patterns in that these countries were first liberal and later democratic.[137] Industrial development took place before the franchise was extended to the population.[138] In this sense, socioeconomic values first achieved legitimacy, in most instances concurrently with the quest for a sense of national identity.[139]

The institutions born of these Western societies were dependent on a consensus of socioeconomic values, and some homogeneity of nationality and language.[140] It was only later, when the industrial property class emerged victorious in having their system and laissez-faire values firmly embedded, and a sense of national identity took root, that the issues of political participation and distribution were confronted.[141] Social welfare programs were only embarked on when there were greater resources available.[142] This pattern of development did not occur in African countries, which had to deal with all these problems at once. They had to establish a sense of national identity, work with Western forms of government and state, and provide for distribution and social welfare without the industrial base of Western societies.[143]

THE WIDER LEGITIMACY CRISIS

The failure of the overall political system to fit in with the values of the population, as well as the failure of the system to engender a belief that the institutions adopted were the most appropriate for solving their problems, can be termed the wider legitimacy crisis.[144] In the words of Karl Loewenstein, What does the constitution mean to the little man? Is it an instrument for pursuing happiness?[145] A constitution will never achieve legitimacy if it is indifferent to the realities of the lives of the people, incapable of achieving social justice, and incapable of bridging the gap between poverty and wealth.[146]

In South Africa there are many facets to economic problems to be overcome. First, distribution of resources is very unequal, which translates into an unequal distribution of income. It is estimated that the top 20 percent earns more then 56 percent of all income, while the bottom 40 percent of the population earns less then 10 percent of all income.[147] The disparities in income correspond with color, with the white population generally enjoying higher levels of income and blacks lower levels.[148] There are corresponding disparities in allocation of resources to housing, health care, education, and social welfare facilities.[149] Just as important, land and the type of land are allocated differently to blacks and whites.[150] Economic power is concentrated, with a few corporations controlling many sectors of the market and able to influence production, distribution, and exchange.[151] It is estimated that more then 80 percent of the shares in the Johannesburg Stock Exchange are controlled by four industrial "groups."[152] The crisis in South Africa can only be resolved by major economic and political transformation.[153]

ELITE RULE:

NATIONAL UNITY AND SOCIOECONOMIC CHANGE

The national question and the resolution of socioeconomic crises are not necessarily exclusive, but in Africa as in South Africa the two are inextricably linked.[154] Many conflicts in Africa characterized by "ethnic" strife originate in widespread economic disparities.[155] The failure to effect redistribution leads to a situation of strife often expressed in ethnic terms.[156] Tribalism and regionalism are a series of defensive reactions that dissipate when fears of inequality disappear.[157]

The constitution has to be an instrument and framework for resolving both the national problem and the socioeconomic crisis. It should not create a framework that allows ethnic mobilization. It should create institutions that go beyond elite decision making. Many a constitution in Africa has failed for ignoring the relationship and importance of both these factors. For example, following the coup and collapse of the federal constitution in Nigeria in 1966, the leadership in 1979 introduced a new constitution that sought to overcome parochial and ethnic tendencies. Several features distinguish this constitution from the previous one. First, it was "homegrown" in that it was drafted by Nigerian academics, politicians, and businesspeople.[158] The public was invited to submit memorandums. Second, the drafters of the new Nigerian constitution recognized the problems of the independence constitution and attempted to overcome them by making it mandatory that all political parties be representative of all the states in the country. Moreover, cabinet ministers and officeholders had to come from the different states. Most importantly, the presidential candidate had to receive support from all the states in order to be elected.[159]

The developments in Nigeria marked a move away from competing elites representing different ethnic constituencies toward the creation of a single or distinct elite separate from its institutional base.[160] The constitution provided for an American-type presidential government together with checks and balances.[161] Despite these constitutional reforms, the system collapsed, primarily because of corruption and a failure to overcome socioeconomic problems.[162] The "new" constitution and its institutions still relied on elite rule of a sort, which was not up to the job. There should be measures beyond the periodic ritual of voting for elites that link the population to their representatives and that control the representatives to prevent them from acting in terms of their own personal interests while in office. So while the new Nigerian constitution attempted to provide a constitutional order that cut across ethnic lines, it still failed because it merely replaced ethnic elites with a national elite who did not work to resolve pressing socioeconomic problems.

Constitutions and Social Transformation

Institutional transfer, which entails taking the constitution of one country and applying it in another, has been a disaster.[163] Leonard Markowitz argues that it is important to distinguish between the theoretical, or what some may consider the moral desirability of any particular form of government, and the political, cultural, and economic foundations required to make that framework possible.[164] The problem that many African constitutions have displayed are that they "establish terms of order that fail."[165] In the main they have not created structures that allow for the transformation of existing socioeconomic conditions.

There are a number of prerequisites that have to be met in order to transform African nations into more homogeneous units. First, there has to be institutionalized and uniform conditions of civil and political equality.[166] Democracy in terms of Western theory entails the periodic selection of political elites to whom decision making and implementation are entrusted. The experiences of African countries demonstrate the need to eliminate elite and ethnic privilege, something which liberal constitutions as they were introduced in Africa seem to promote. This means there has to be a new basis for formulating and implementing decisions.[167] Second, there have to be equal educational and occupational opportunities for all.[168] In analyzing the Nigerian experience, Melson and Wolpe argue that a lot of the communal conflict is conducted by "communities formed in the crucible of mobilization and competition."[169] It is the conflict that produces communalism and not communalism or tribalism that produces the conflict. Moreover, the communal groups are not static and can be changed over time.[170]

The constitutional framework adopted should help to eliminate sectional barriers. Moreover, it should be a constitution and form of state that allow the government to effect socioeconomic transformation and deal with differences in the population. The social and political structures should advance the entire population and operate on the principles of grassroots democracy and accountability of the delegates to the population as opposed to notions of minority or elite rule.[171] All the liberal constitutions introduced were dependent on the goodwill and integrity of the elite for success. Thus the federal or consociational model does not meet the requirement of promoting democracy and, arguably, may constitute the worst model of elite and minority rule.

In looking at the question of state structures in a future South Africa, the lessons of Africa have demonstrated that a constitutional framework should not merely outline the powers of government or limit the powers of government. The constitution of the country should foster national unity and help to restructure social life.[172] Nation building is the most important factor for the survival and stability of a future South African state.[173] It goes without saying that stability is crucial for the achievement of economic and development objectives. Stability and legitimacy in South Africa will include redistribution of the economic resources of the country, which the federal and consociational constitutional options will obstruct.

REFERENCES

1. Quoted in Ronald L. Watts, *New Federations: Experiments in the Commonwealth* (Oxford: Clarendon Press, 1966), 134.

2. M. Amoda, "The Relationship of History, Thought and Action With Respect to the Nigerian Situation," in Joseph Okpaku, ed., *Nigeria: Dilemma of Nationhood* (New York: Third World Press, 1972), 152.

3. Z. Motala, "Human Rights in Africa: A Cultural, Ideological And Legal Examination," *Hastings International and Comparative Law Review* 12 (1989): 384.

4. F. Gerster, *Federalism and Decentralization: Constitutional Problems of Territorial Decentralization in Federal and Centralized States*, (n.p., 1987), 414.

5. Ibid.

6. William H. Riker, *Federalism: Origin, Operation, Significance* (Boston: Little, Brown, 1964), 140, 142.

7. At that stage in history constituted in the plantation owners.

8. Ibid., 152.

9. Ibid., 142.

10. C. Tarlton, "Symmetry and Asymmetry as Elements of Federalism: A Theoretical Speculation," *The Journal of Politics* 27 (1978): 872.

11. Carl Friedrich states the relationship between federalism and nationalism is very complex. Carl J. Friedrich, *The Impact of American Constitutionalism Abroad* (Boston: Boston University Press, 1967), 201.

12. Tarlton, "Symmetry and Asymmetry," 872.

13. This study will argue that this has also been the case in Africa.

14. Friedrich, *American Constitutionalism*, 201.

15. Tarlton, "Symmetry and Asymmetry," 874.

16. Lord Russell, *The Tragedy of the Congo* (Lagos: Lagos Study Circle, 1964), 2; F. A. O. Schwarz, *Nigeria: The Tribes, the Nation, or the Race; The Politics of Independence* (Cambridge, Mass.: MIT Press, 1965), 194. The reasons for crisis and repression will be considered below.

17. S. A. de Smith, *The New Commonwealth and Its Constitution* (London: Stevens, 1964), 117.

18. Okpaku, *Nigeria*, 37.

19. John C. Hatch, *Nigeria; The Seeds of Disaster* (Chicago: H. Regnery, Co., 1970), 257.

20. Ibid.

21. F. A. O. Schwarz, *Nigeria*, 194.

22. M. Nziramsanga, "Secession, Federalism and African Unity" in Okpaku, *Nigeria*, 231.

23. B. O. Nwabueze, *Presidentialism in Commonwealth Africa* (New York: St. Martin's Press, 1974), 147.

24. Ibid., 146, 149.

25. Ibid., 148.

26. Crawford Young, *The Politics of Cultural Pluralism* (Madison, Wis.: University of Wisconsin Press, 1976), 42. The reason for insecurities goes to the heart of the question, in whose interest was the federal system? This question is considered below.

27. Christian P. Potholm, *The Theory and Practice of African Politics* (Englewood Cliffs, N.J.: Prentice Hall, 1979), 145.

28. de Smith, *The New Commonwealth*, 118.

29. The ruptures in each of these countries is considered below.

30. Michael Aletum Tabuwe, *The One-Party System and African Traditional Institutions* (Yaounde: n.p., 1980), 19.

31. Watts, *New Federations*, 128.

32. D. Rothchild, "Majimbo Schemes in Kenya and Uganda," in Butler and Castagno, *Boston University Papers on Africa*, 298–99.

33. F. A. O. Schwarz, *Nigeria*, 195.

34. Ibid. This is also consistent with developments in the field of human rights. Prior to World War II human rights arguments were seen as mainly the protection of individual rights, and were more concerned about preventing government encroachment. Today there is a recognition in international human rights thinking that there has to be advancement of what are termed second-generation human rights, such as social welfare, education, and creation of jobs and security for all. See International Covenant on Economic, Social, and Cultural Rights, 16 December 1966, 993 U.N.T.S., 3. Indeed, the right to second-generation human rights has been recognized in many European constitutions. See previous discussion of the welfare constitutions in chapter 5.

35. Almost all African countries at the end of colonial rule were characterized by social and economic problems. Asante, "Nation Building and Human Rights in Emergent African Nations," *Cornell International Law Review* 2 (1969): 100–101.

36. Henri Grimal, *Decolonization*, 300; and Rothchild in Butler & Castagno, *Boston University Papers in Africa*, 291.

37. Butler & Castagno, *Boston University Papers on Africa*, 311.

38. Grimal, *Decolonization*, 300.

39. M. Amoda, in Okpaku, *Nigeria*, 36.

40. Thomas R. Kanza, *Conflict in the Congo: The Rise and Fall of Lumumba* (Harmondsworth: Penguin Books, 1972), 80.

41. African Affairs Research Group, *Save the Congo, Save Africa!* (S.L.: African Affairs Research Group, 1965), 6.

42. M. Nziramasanga, in Okpaku, *Nigeria*, 232.

43. Kwame Nkrumah, *Challenge of the Congo* (London: Nelson, 1967), 68–69. Nkrumah goes so far as to attribute the secessionist attempt basically to colonialist machinations. Ibid., 19; Kanza, *Conflict in the Congo*, 131–34.

44. James O'Connell, "The Nigerian Case," in Arthur Hazelwood, *African Integration and Disintegration* (London: Oxford University Press, 1967), 182.

45. de Smith, *The New Commonwealth*, 210.

46. The South African experience of white minority rule can be characterized as colonialism of a different type. In this situation, instead of the country being subject to the rule of a distant country the colonialists have settled down in South Africa and continue to rule the country in a colonial fashion. For a discussion of the view that South Africa is a colonial country of a special kind, see chapter 10.

47. Boulle, *Constitutional Reform*, 51.

48. Leopold Marquard, *Federation of Southern Africa* (London: Oxford University Press, 1971), 142.

49. Theodor Hanf, et al., *South Africa, The Prospects for Peaceful Change: An Empirical Enquiry into the Possibility of Democratic Conflict Regulation*, trans. John Richardson (London: R. Collins, 1981), 384.

50. The government will need the approval of the minority groups to effect any changes. It is unlikely that the white population will accede to economic changes affecting their property interests.

51. D. Geldenhuys, "South Africa's Constitutional Alternatives," *South African International* (1981): 213.

52. The model hinges on the element of elite cooperation. The point is made by all theorists favoring the model that elite cooperation and deference to leadership is the most important requirement. Boulle, *Constitutional Reform*, 47.

53. No Sizwe, *One Azania, One Nation: The National Question in South Africa* (London: Zed, 1979), 92.

54. P. F. Gonidec, *African Politics* (Boston: M. Nijhoff, 1981), 173.

55. Leslie Rubin and Brian Weinstein, *Introduction to African Politics: A Continental Approach* (New York: Praeger, 1977), 170.

56. Hazelwood, *African Integration*, 181.

57. See the previous discussion about the Congo [Zaire] where the Katanga leadership saw tremendous benefits for both themselves and Belgian interests. See African Affairs Research Group, *Save the Congo*, 6; Rubin and Weinstein, *African Politics*, 173. Similar motives were at play in the attempt by Biafra to secede from the rest of Nigeria. The Igbo intelligentsia wanted a solution that would leave them in complete control of the oil reserves of the area. See V. P. Diejomaoh, "The Economics of the Nigerian Conflict," in Okpaku, *Nigeria*, 334; Hazelwood, *African Integration*, 182.

58. See discussion of Inkatha in chapter 10.

59. See, for example, Buthelezi Commission, *The Requirements for Stability and Development in KwaZulu and Natal* (Durban: H & H Publications, 1982). Also the trend in the recent Kwazulu-Natal Indaba was toward some form of federal arrangement with the protection of group rights. We will deal with the above constitutional proposals and the specific demands of Mangosuthu Buthelezi and Inkatha for regional solutions in chapter 10.

60. R. B. Neuberger, *Concepts of Nationhood in the Thought of Selected African Leaders* (n.p., 1975), 305.

61. Ibid., 120.

62. M. Amoda, in Okpaku, *Nigeria*, 36; and F. A. O. Schwarz, *Nigeria*, 193.

63. J. A. A. Ayoade, "Federalism in Africa, Some Chequered Fortunes" *Plural Societies* 9(1) (Spring 1978): 3.

64. de Smith, *The New Commonwealth*.

65. Y. P. Ghai, "Constitutions and the Political Order in East Africa," in *Dar es Salaam Inaugural Lecture Series* 10 (1970): 14. See previous discussion concerning Nigeria and Uganda.

66. There have been many criticisms of the entire notion of pluralism from the academic left. See, for example, Frederick A. Johnstone, *Class, Race, and Gold: A Study of Class Relations and Racial Discrimination in South Africa* (London: Routledge & Kegan Paul, 1976); and H. Wolpe, "Class, Race and the Occupational Structure," Institute of Commonwealth Studies (1967): 12. These criticisms are considered below. Johnstone and Wolpe's studies question the notion as a basis for understanding South African society. See note 121.

67. Pierre L. van den Berghe, *South Africa: A Study in Conflict* (Middletown, Conn.: Wesleyan University Press, 1965), 3.

68. Y. Barongo, "Alternative Approaches to African Polititics," *Political Science in Africa* (1983): 141.

69. van den Berghe, *South Africa*, 3.

70. Pierre L. van den Berghe, *The Liberal Dilemma in South Africa* (New York: St. Martin's Press, 1979).

71. Ibid.

72. Ibid.

73. Ibid., 59.

74. F. Van Zyl Slabbert and David J. Welsh, *South Africa's Options: Strategies for Sharing Power* (New York: St. Martin's Press, 1979), 17.

75. Ibid., 19.

76. Ibid.

77. Wolpe, "Class, Race," 100.

78. Ralph Miliband, *Marxism and Politics* (Oxford: Oxford University Press, 1977), 18.

79. Ibid.

80. Wolpe, "Class, Race," 102.

81. Hugh Collins, *Marxism and the Law* (Oxford: Clarendon Press, 1982), 19.

82. Y. Barongo, *Alternative Approaches*, 143–44.

83. Gonidec, *African Politics*.

84. Ibid., 31–32.

85. Such as laws and the apartheid institutions.

86. Wolpe, "Class, Race," 102.

87. Frank Parkin, *Marxism and Class Theory: A Bourgeois Critique* (New York: Columbia University Press, 1979), 3.

88. Ibid., 7.

89. Wolpe, "Class, Race," 102.

90. This is the approach that No Sizwe correctly argues for. Sizwe, *One Azania, One Nation*, 7.

91. H. Wolpe, "Industrialism and Race in South Africa," in Wilson Record, *Race and Radicalism* (Ithaca, N.Y.: Cornell University Press, 1964), 155.

92. William H. Hutt, *The Economics of the Color Bar* (London: A. Deutsch, 1964), 173.

93. Ibid., 175.

94. van den Berghe, *Study in Conflict*, 196–97.

95. Muriel Horrell, *A Survey of Race Relations in South Africa, 1951–1952* (Johannesburg: South African Institute of Race Relations, 1953), 208.

96. van den Berghe, *Study in Conflict*, 185.

97. Ibid., 191, 195.

98. Hutt, *Color Bar*, 178.

99. Ralph Horwitz, *The Political Economy of South Africa* (New York: Praeger, 1967), 11.

100. Ibid., 12.

101. Hutt, *Color Bar*, 177.

102. Wolpe, "Industrialism and Race," 168.

103. Johnstone, *Class, Race, and Gold*.

104. James Bryce, *Impressions of South Africa* (New York: Negro Universities Press, 1969), 23.

105. Bernard Magubane, *The Political Economy of Race and Class in South Africa* (New York: Monthly Review Press, 1979), 83.

106. Johnstone refers to the role of recruiters paid by the mine owners who engaged in credit schemes whereby Africans were indebted to the recruiters forcing them into the employment of the mine bosses. Johnstone, *Class, Race, and Gold*, 28.

107. Magubane, *Political Economy*, 71.

108. Ibid., 87.

109. Johnstone, *Class, Race, and Gold*, 26.

110. Ibid., 34.

111. Ibid., 47. This was because the gold was not easily accessible and would have needed heavy and costly mechanization to mine. The alternate and cheaper course was to exploit a large reservoir of labor at the cheapest possible cost.

112. See generally, ibid.

113. Ibid., 39.

114. J. Rex, "The Plural Society: The South African Case," *Race* 40 (1971): 404.

115. S. Trapido, "South Africa in a Comparative Study of Industrialization," *Journal of Development Studies* 7(4) (1971): 316.

116. Johnstone, *Class, Race, and Gold*, 126.

117. Wolpe, "Industrialism and Race," 166.

118. Ibid., 167.

119. Johnstone, *Class, Race, and Gold*, 130.

120. This does not mean that many features of apartheid are still attractive to the capital sector presently. The above analysis is based on the historical relation between apartheid and capital.

121. Act 30 of 1950.

122. See Rhoodie in D. J. van Vuuren, et al., eds., *Change in South Africa* (Durban: Butterworths, 1983), 483.

123. Native Land Act 27 of 1913 and Native Trust and Land Act 18 of 1936.

124. For example see Group Areas Act 36 of 1966.

125. See W. A. Robson, "The Transplanting of Political Institutions and Ideas," in *Political Quarterly* 35 (1964): 407ff.

126. Nwabueze, *Constitutionalism in the Emergent States*, 24.

127. Motala, "Human Rights in Africa," 384.

128. Jaramogi Oginga Odinga, *Not Yet Uhuru: The Autobiography of Oginga Odinga* (London: Heinemann, 1967), 13.

129. A. Gupta, "Political Systems and the One-Party State of Tropical Africa," *India Quarterly* 31(2) (1975): 160.

130. Watts, *New Federations*, 124.

131. de Smith, *The New Commonwealth*, 55.

132 Nwabueze, *Constitutionalism in the Emergent States*, 26; see also J. O'Connell in Hazelwood, *African Integration*, 181–82. O'Connell refers to the choice of state that favored interests of ethnic leaders under the federal system in Nigeria.

133. Nwabueze, *Constitutionalism in the Emergent States*, 24.

134. de Smith, *The New Commonwealth*, 216.

135. Young, *Cultural Pluralism*, 27.

136. Tabuwe, *One-Party System*, 9.

137. What this means is first the free market system was established and democracy in the sense of citizen participation in the elections and political process came later. See Crawford B. MacPherson, *The Life and Times of Liberal Democracy* (Oxford: Oxford University Press, 1977), 6.

138. Michael F. Lofchie, ed., *The State of the Nations: Constraints on Development in Independent Africa* (Berkeley and Los Angeles: University of California Press, 1971), 12.

139. M. F. Lofchie, "Representative Government, Bureaucracy, and Political Development: The African Case," *African Administrative Studies* 16 (1976): 131.

140. This sense of commonness applies even in respect to the federal system, which is cited as the best model for diversity in the population. See Watts, *New Federations*, 100.

141. K. Loewenstein, "Reflections on the Value of Constitutions in Our Revolutionary Age," in Harry Eckstein and David E. Apter, eds., *Comparative Politics: A Reader* (New York: Free Press of Glencoe, 1963), 151.

142. Lofchie, "Representative Government," 131.

143. Lofchie, *The State of the Nations*, 13–14.

144. See Lipset in Connolly, *Legitimacy and the State*, 88.

145. Loewenstein, "Reflections on the Value of Constitutions," 161.

146. Ibid.

147. Brian Kantor, et al., *South African Economic Issues* (Cape Town: Juta, 1982), 46.

148. South African Economic Research and Training Project, *Beyond Apartheid Working Papers, vol. 1, no. 1, Labor/Employment/Health Care after Apartheid* (1988), 42–44.

149. For statistics and information on the disparate amount of money spent on the "different population groups" see generally Roger Omond, *The Apartheid Handbook* (New York: Penguin Books, 1985). See also John Suckling and Landeg White, eds., *After Apartheid: Renewal of the South African Economy* (Trenton, N.J.: Africa World Press, 1988), x. See article of J. Cobbe, "Economic Policy Issues in the Education Sector," in Suckling and White, eds., *After Apartheid*, 146, 156.

150. Apart from the fact that more then 85 percent of the land has been set aside for the white group, even the little land that is set aside for blacks is barren and agriculturally unproductive. See generally Jill Nattrass, *The South African Economy: Its Growth and Change* (Cape Town: Oxford University Press, 1988), 99–100.

151. See R. Davies, "Nationalisation, Socialisation and the Freedom Charter," in Suckling and White, *After Apartheid*, 176, 178.

152. Ibid., 177.

153. Many of the uprisings in South Africa are organized around issues of inferior education, housing, health care, and other amenities.

154. No Sizwe argues that the theory of the nation "is itself a stake in the class struggle for national liberation." Sizwe, *One Azania, One Nation*, 90.

155. V. P. Diejimoh, "The Economics of the Nigerian Conflict" in Okpaku, *Nigeria*, 359–60.

156. Neuberger, *Concepts of Nationhood*, 32.

157. Onesimo Silveira, *Africa South of the Sahara: Party Systems and Ideologies of Socialism* (Stockholm: Raben and Sjogren, 1976), 36.

158. C. J. Mojekwe, "Nigerian Constitutionalism," in Pennock and Chapman, *Liberal Democracy*, 172.

159. The president had to receive at least one quarter of the votes cast in at least two-thirds of all the states in the federation. V. A. Olorunsola, "Questions on Constitutionalism and Democracy: Nigeria and Africa," in Dov Ronen, ed., *Democracy and Pluralism in Africa* (Sevenoaks, Kent: Hodder and Stoughton, 1986), 123.

160. See Barongo, *Alternative Approaches*, 205.

161. The checks and balances were provided in the form of twelve special bodies that share executive functions with the president. The president had to act with the advice of these commissions on many matters. See Pius Msekwa, *Towards Party Supremacy* (Kampala: East African Literature Bureau, 1977), 175.

162. Barongo, *Alternative Approaches*, 205.

163. See W. A. Robinson, "The Transplanting of Political Institutions and Ideas," *Political Science Quarterly* 35 (1964):413.

164. Irving L. Markowitz, *Power and Class in Africa: An Introduction to Change and Conflict in African Politics* (Englewood, N.J.: Prentice-Hall, 1985), 291.

165. David E. Apter, *Choice and the Politics of Allocation: A Developmental Theory* (New Haven: Yale University Press, 1971), 161.

166. M. G. Smith, "Institutional and Political Conditions of Pluralism," in Leo Kuper and M. G. Smith, eds., *Pluralism in Africa* (Berkeley: University of California Press, 1969), 60.

167. See the suggestions put forward in chapter 12.

168. Smith, "Institutional and Political Conditions," 60. This is in contrast to previous approaches of the elite where the better opportunities were only provided to group members.

169. Robert Melson and Howard Wolpe, eds., *Nigeria: Modernization and the Politics of Communalism* (East Lansing, Mich.: Michigan State University Press, 1971).

170. Ibid., 21.

171. See chapter 12.

172. See previous discussion of the crisis arising from inequalities in access to resources in South Africa.

173. This study does not investigate what constitutes a nation. For a discussion of the concept of nationhood, see Neuberger, *Concepts of Nationhood*, 6–23; Viktor S. Shevtsov, *The State and Nations in the USSR*, trans. Lenina Ilitskaya (Moscow: Progress Publishers, 1982). For a contrary view see D. Ronen, "Alternative Patterns of Integration in African States," *Journal of Modern African Studies* 14 (1976): 579. Ronen argues that it is not necessary to channel loyalties to a national center.

CHAPTER EIGHT

The Soviet Constitutional Model and African Marxist States

■ ■ ■

T HE DEMISE OF the Soviet Union and other Eastern European Communist nations since 1988 has radically altered the power of the state and the party in these states.[1] However, the Stalin/Brezhnev prototype was duplicated in some African Marxist regimes. The focus in this chapter will be on the Soviet constitution in the pre-glastnost and perestroika period. The model will be evaluated in terms of whether it offered an adequate framework to overcome the problems of African society. The main problems associated with the Soviet model will be highlighted by considering the experiences of the African Marxist countries that adopted it.

Constitutional Law and Legality
in Socialist Doctrine

In order to understand socialist thinking on constitution making, one has first to formulate a conception of the Marxist approach to law. Such a task is not without difficulties, since the founding fathers of Marxism, Karl Marx and Friedrich Engels, did not treat the law as a separate entity subject to specific analysis. It is therefore common for Marxist thinkers to maintain that there is no Marxist theory of law.[2] Not surprisingly, the Marxist approach to law does not consist of a single theoretical perspective. According to Ralph Miliband, the corpus of Marxism provides no "smooth, harmonious, consistent and unproblematic Marxist political theory."[3] On the other hand, other writers assert that there is enough substance in the works of Marx and Engels to develop and put forward a theory of law.[4]

Marxist writers allude to the two polar versions of Marxism.[5] The first is a theory that sees all law as an instrument of class rule.[6] The second sees the law as an extension of liberalism and seeks to introduce the rule of law, separation of powers, and the other liberal tenets into a socialist order.[7]

MARXIST THEORY AGAINST ALL LAW

The first version is premised to a great extent on the Marxist metaphor of base and superstructure and the apparent conclusions drawn from it. A much-quoted passage in Marxist literature is the statement:

> In the social production of their life, men enter into definite relations that are indispensable and independent of their will, relations of production which correspond to a definite stage of development of their material productive forces. The sum total of these relations of production constitutes the economic structure of society, the real foundation on which rises a legal and political superstructure and to which correspond definite forms of social consciousness. The mode of production of material life conditions the social, political and intellectual life process in general. It is not the consciousness of men that determines their being, but, on the contrary, their social being that determines their consciousness.[8]

The core interpretation drawn from the above statement and other writings of Marx and Engels has been to emphasize the primacy of the economic base. Accordingly, all social institutions and political structures are seen to originate from and adapt themselves to the nature of the relations of production. Similarly, the law is determined in content and form by the relations of production and the material base.[9] Overall, the material base is determinative of all ideas, values, beliefs, superstitions, and the law. The law is therefore an epiphenomenon and part of the superstructure.[10] This approach to law in fact turns into a theory against law, and the "principal aim of Marxist jurisprudence" then becomes "to criticize the centerpiece of liberal political philosophy, the ideal called the rule of law."[11]

This classical Marxist approach to law deserves consideration, as it has certain important consequences. The first is the notion that all law is an instrument of class oppression and that the existence of law is necessary for the maintenance of capitalist society: "The executive of the modern state is but a committee for managing the common affairs of the whole bourgeoisie."[12] Law is viewed as the equivalent of terror and violence, and the presence of law is associated with control.[13] The police and courts are similarly viewed as instruments of coercion to protect the interests of the dominant class.[14] This view is a negation of liberalism and sees liberal notions such as parliamentary democracy, equality before the law, the rule of law, and so on as mere fraud disguising the brute realities of oppression and exploitation. The task of the socialist theorist therefore is to demystify the law and expose its harsh realities. Communist society envisages no state and no law—"the withering away of the state"; social relations would change so much that there would be no need for law, and work would be performed in a cooperative manner by a population living in harmony.[15] Thus societies having a plethora of laws and regulations cannot correctly be labeled Communist societies.[16] The presence of law in such countries is attributed to a need to maintain a repressive system.

Several twentieth-century Marxist theorists aim to attribute the presence of law specifically to capitalist societies. The first is E. Pashukanis,[17] whose views are based on the writings of Marx and Engels claiming the decay of law. Pashukanis sees law as a manifestation of capitalism, reflecting the fetish for commodities. A socialist order can have no socialist law because commodity relations would be abolished.[18] For Pashukanis law is defined in terms of "subject" and "right," and essentially amounts to a recognition of the rights of subjects concerning possessions. Law is necessary to the system of production, and it is through law that the system of production is regulated.[19] In this scheme of things, law is conceived as property rights and capitalist social relations.

The popular liberal view sees the presence of law in society as a neutral institutional arrangement whereby conflict can be resolved, as opposed to the imposition of any ideology. Hence, law (influenced by natural rights) is equated with justice and not influenced by any material forces. The Marxist view of law rejects the autonomy of legal reasoning and the notion of law as having an inherent logic of its own. Drawing on the base and superstructure metaphor, law is seen to be materially in the first instance determined by the relations of production.[20] Hence, the law as part of the superstructure cannot be an independent influence on social behavior. The rejection of law as an autonomous entity has profound consequences. According to this view, it is the relations of production that require primary consideration, with legal considerations taking a secondary role as their outgrowth.

MARXIST THEORY IN FAVOR OF LEGALITY

The second polar version of Marxist theory shares several similarities with liberalism, namely, its commitment to the rule of law. The leading Marxist proponent in favor of the rule of law is the English writer E. Thompson,[21] who asserts that the rule of law is "an unqualified human good" in the sense that it "imposes effective inhibitions upon power."[22] For Thompson the rule of law is opposite to arbitrary power and is a value worth preserving. In a sense law is looked at as *defining* the relations of production,[23] which is a major point of departure from the classical Marxist approach.

This approach applauds the achievements of liberal thought such as the rule of law and the maintenance of civil liberties and sees a democratic character in law and state power. The argument has been expressed more forcefully—that all states having public functions need to have public law. In a socialist system where there is greater state involvement in the public sphere, there is a greater need for a legal framework of public law. Constitutional restraints on state authority are seen as essential and the notion of the withering away of the state is viewed as unattainable.[24] Many countries claim the socialist mantle and do have state constitutions. The problem with these states and their constitutions (according to these theorists) is the absence of a framework that limits the power of state agencies.[25]

MARXISM IN PRACTICE

In classical Marxism, the presence of law is inconsistent with the ultimate stage of society where the state would wither away. Marx saw the necessity for the retention of liberal rights only in the transition period,[26] yet liberal rights were important principles in the transformation of society.[27] The polar versions of Marxist attitudes to law to a certain extent reflect this paradox, with each side basing its tenets on apparently conflicting interpretations. The reality is that Communist countries have greater state involvement in the activities of people and hence greater need for legal regulation.[28] In terms of orthodox theory the state and law are only temporary phenomena,[29] yet the Communist state in the Soviet Union was in existence for some sixty years.[30] The continued existence of the state has called for rationalization and justification for the presence of law in these societies.

According to modern theorists of Marxism, the answer to the paradox was to be found in the content and form of law in a new social context. The form of law was related to the relations of production, and the changing relations of production are interconnected to the forms of law.[31] Any social arrangement needs rules to coordinate people's behavior. This was particularly true in a country that believed in central planning and central direction of economic and social affairs. However, according to latter-day theorists, these rules have to be distinguished from rules that exist to inhibit freedom. In the political sense, the state was still preserved, but the Communist order argued the state was not a "coercive" state imposed on society.[32] In a Communist society the state was merged with society,[33] and state functions became social functions,[34] as opposed to the liberal society's striving to separate state and individual. Law was seen as more a form of social regulation operating in a context where there were no antagonistic interests, and not an entity separated from the society.[35] This new Marxist interpretation questioned the notion of the withering away of the state[36] though of course these rationalizations all came ex post facto. There will always be a need to perform public functions and there will also be a need for the division of labor. In this sense, there was a recognition of the organizing functions of law in a constitution.[37] As long as these needs persist, the Marxist criticism of all laws or legal systems per se is without basis.[38]

SEPARATION OF POWERS

AND THE RULE OF LAW

The Soviet constitutional system did not fathom any notion of constitutionalism and separation of powers to act as a brake on government or the party.[39] The general spirit was that there should be unity of state authority from top to bottom.[40] Since the people were seen as the source of all power and the elected representatives (to the legislature) were chosen by the people, there was no need for a separation of powers. As the people were the source of all power, there could be no limitation on the power of the people as represented by their legislature, the Supreme Soviet. In terms of orthodox theory, the notion of separation of powers was an insufficient compromise between the legislature and the bureaucracy, which had the effect of freeing the executive from popular control.[41] An independent judiciary with the ability to question an act of the legislature would negate the principle of the sovereignty of the people.[42] Accordingly, the legislature had to be supreme at all times, and giving the courts a testing power was viewed as bringing the courts into the political process.[43]

Since the central government owned all land there was no demarcation of power between different agencies. Moreover, the ideology of Soviet socialism saw the unity of economic and political systems as an important aspect of the authority of the state; there could be no different "centers" of power. Central direction of economic affairs was a fundamental tenet of Soviet socialism.

There may have been division of tasks and functions, but these had to be performed in terms of fixed mandates given by the elected representatives. This was a significant point of departure from Western constitutional systems, and we saw the delegation of power by the Supreme Soviet (the Soviet legislature) to the Presidium (the collective head of state), and the further delegation from the latter to the Council of Ministers (the equivalent of the cabinet).[44] Under the Soviet system, there were no such popularly elected officials as mayors, governors, or a president. All matters were conducted in committee or assembly, where decisions could be arrived at collectively.[45] Those with titles were in fact spokespersons for the respec-

112

tive assemblies or communes chosen by the various forums under party supervision.[46] In terms of Marxist ideology, the representatives of the people were not to be full-time or professional representatives, but were to come from the ordinary ranks of working people,[47] thus the legislature did not sit for long periods of time. For this reason there had to be a permanent organ of state power that would function in the periods when the legislature was not sitting. This resulted in the delegation of power (as opposed to separation) by the legislature to the Presidium, with the latter having all the powers the Supreme Soviet had while not in session.[48]

The Soviet system did, however, have a system of courts, and the judges of the courts were popularly elected.[49] The purpose of the court was to decide on matters in a flexible way, with emphasis on political affairs in the spirit of a "socialist conscience"[50] rather than adopting a "legal" approach, as is the case under Western systems. However, the judges were not free to interpret the law in terms of their own conceptions. In acting, the judges should merely interpret the intention of the legislature.[51] Invariably, most judges were members of the Communist Party. In keeping with the communal orientation of Soviet ideology, cases were held collegially with lay assessors (who were essentially ordinary people) sitting with the judges.

The rule of law, particularly the need for certainty in the law (the cornerstone of Western constitutional systems), had no place in Soviet constitutional doctrine. The contrary principle of flexibility in the law was the operative notion.[52] The idea of law as representing eternal justice was rejected—law was seen as something that could and should constantly change to achieve the goals of society. It was integral to the society, and in a society where there was central direction, the purpose of legislation was to transform the political programs into legal processes.[53] The constitution could not be a rigid document if it was to serve as a framework for social change. The constitutions of Western systems were interpreted as being designed to protect certain interests as opposed to being a vehicle for socioeconomic change. Consequently, the prevailing notion of constitutions in Soviet-bloc countries was that every time there was a change in the state, constitutional amendments or changes to take account of the transformation had to occur.[54] But altering the constitution every time social values changed involved a great deal of legislative activity and social instability. So the Soviet system provided the higher organs of state power, namely, the cabinet represented in the Council of Ministers, with the discretionary power to adopt plans of regulation.[55]

THE ROLE OF A CONSTITUTION
IN A SOCIALIST ORDER

A constitution can contain two primary sets of provisions—the main offices of state, that is, the machinery of government, and the ideological basis of the political system. The first must be present in all systems.[56] Against the background of the Marxist approach to law and the general conclusion that a legal system is necessary, we pose the question, What function did the constitution serve in the Soviet order? The discussion here has parallels with the differences between a constitution and the notion of constitutionalism in liberal systems, formulated in terms of a preference for "state law" or "constitutional law."[57] According to the former, the constitution is meant only to reflect "the structure of state power" and merely performs "a codification function, recording and legitimating the changes in state structure as they occur."[58] The constitutional law school argues against the reduction of a constitution to a mere outline of an institutional structure, and argues for a normative content. The constitution is viewed as a legal instrument that should define the social order,[59] incorporating ideological goals and policies.[60] The preference in the socialist order was to consider the constitution explicitly as a political charter with details of the objectives the government should work toward. There had to be unity between the constitution and party program, with the party enforcing its changes through the constitution.[61] In this sense the constitution was more overtly a political as opposed to a legal document.[62] This line of reasoning is consistent with the overall socialist notion of unity of economic and political systems as an aspect of the state.

The Soviet Constitutional Model

The Soviet constitution identified the Soviet Union as a federal state.[63] This federation was differentiated from Western federal states in light of socialist ideology, which played an important role in the legal structure and institutional arrangements of Communist states whether they were classified as federal or unitary. The Communist ideology subscribed to by the Soviet Union and most of Eastern Europe provided a degree of commonality in the way institutions operated, particularly in regard to the role of the party. The Communist Party was overwhelmingly the dominant actor in the Soviet government.[64] The agents of the state historically had been mere appendages of the party. Some commentators have argued that the federal and unitary dichotomy was superfluous under Soviet Communist ideology. This is erroneous because the Soviet state was a federation and must be viewed in the context of Communist ideology and as such should be discussed as a federation of a new type.[65] The institutional arrangements and the actors that occupied positions in these institutions did make important decisions and were important to the overall functioning of the system.[66]

FEDERALISM IN THE SOVIET UNION

From a historical vantage, Communist ideology was opposed to a federal or fragmented state because it was not conducive to central planning.[67] Classical Marxism considered problems of ethnicity or nationality as deriving from the underlying social class system.[68] Once the class problem was solved, ethnic, religious, and national problems would dissipate.[69] However, under certain circumstances, the founders of Marxism were prepared to accept a federal state.[70] At the time of the Russian Revolution, the state was facing a serious problem of national revolts by myriad ethnic groups.[71] The federal structure was adopted as a compromise measure to accommodate the nationality problem, allowing each a measure of self-determination.[72] Some theorists have expressed the view that the adoption of a federal form of state saved the Russian Revolution and the Communist state in the USSR.[73] Without the linguistic and cultural concessions made to the states, many theorists argue that the Soviet Union would have disintegrated under the strain of national tensions.[74] A federal state was also the preference for other Communist countries that had diverse national and religious groups, such as Yugoslavia and Czechoslovakia.[75]

In terms of the Soviet Union's constitution, the country was identified as a federal entity made up of several sovereign states.[76] The major sovereign states were the fifteen constituent republics. Sovereignty was highlighted by provisions that gave each of the union republics the right to enter into direct relations with foreign states and to exchange consular and diplomatic relations with them.[77] Moreover, the right of secession was also given formal expression as a fundamental tenet.[78] Taking this right seriously meant that any of the units in the federation could if it wished secede from the Soviet Union in favor of separate independence. The constitutional expression allowing the right to secede from the union was a fundamental point of departure from Western federalism, particularly as expressed in the United States.[79]

There was, however, no strict demarcation of power between the regions and the central government as is the case in most Western federal systems, since the central government owned all land.[80] Moreover, the ideology of Soviet socialism saw the unity of economic and political systems as an important aspect of the authority of the state. Central direction of economic affairs was a fundamental tenet of Soviet socialism. In terms of section 73 of the Soviet constitution, it was the jurisdiction of the highest organ, meaning the central legislature, to establish general principles "for the organization and functioning of republic and local organs of state power and administration."[81] There had to be a unified economic policy and a centrally directed budget.[82] Actions taken by the units had to be in harmony with the rules enacted by the central government.[83] General rules were laid down by the central government and the various republics only enacted legislation to put into effect decisions taken at the center in the light of the peculiarities of the republic or unit.[84] Consequently, the units did not enjoy any separate jurisdiction such as an independent taxing power. The term *sovereignty* had a limited meaning in that the only distinct powers conferred on the units concerned language and cultural rights.

According to the Soviet conception of federalism the various units came together for their common good; the constitution expressed the notion of equality between the various units in the form of equal representation in the organs of the USSR government, which was the essential component of Soviet federalism. Federalism in the West is a device that disperses power and limits the central government.[85] In the Soviet system with the exception of language and cultural rights there were no powers that were considered outside the purview of the central government. The essential component of Soviet federalism was to allow all the units in the federation to participate as equals in the central legislature[86] and executive, and to allow expression of the cultures and peculiarities of the myriad groups within the context of Communist ideology. In practice what this entailed was that the units had the right to conduct matters in their own languages, and to have respect and recognition for the practice of their different traditions and cultures. The units did not have sufficient autonomy to take fundamental decisions in such areas as transport, commerce, education, criminal law, etc. (which under many western systems would be considered as local affairs), without the overall guidance from the center. The units however had the right to participate equally at the center in the formulation of the above decisions.[87] In the event of a dispute between the legislation of the Union and the USSR, the laws of the center prevailed.[88]

ORGANS OF THE SOVIET STATE

The organs of government were designed to express the equality of the various units. In terms of the constitution, the legislature of the Soviet Union—the Supreme Soviet—was the highest body of state power and it had the greatest legislative power.[89] The Supreme Soviet, like most federal systems, was bicameral, with one house called the Soviet of Nationalities and the second, the Soviet of the Union. The Soviet of Nationalities comprised delegates elected by the various units of unequal size and population, and was designed to protect the interests of the units. The Soviet of the Union comprised delegates elected directly by the people from equally populated districts.[90] The delegates to both houses of the Supreme Soviet were not full-time legislators but came from a variety of fields where they held full-time jobs.[91]

116

To be passed, legislation required a majority of both houses of the legislature. Decisions of the Supreme Soviet were made by majority vote. The Supreme Soviet was an extremely large body in comparison with most legislatures. It was required by the constitution to meet at least twice a year, but the sessions were very short. Owing to time constraints on the legislators, at its first session (after a national election), the Supreme Soviet elected a smaller body called the Presidium to carry out the functions of the Supreme Soviet while the latter was not in session.[92]

The tenure of the Presidium was the same as that of the Supreme Soviet. The Presidium could exercise all powers of the Supreme Soviet when the Supreme Soviet was not in session.[93] The chairman of the Presidium was internationally recognized as the head of state of the Soviet Union, although the Presidium in actual fact operated as a collective head of state.[94] In terms of Soviet federalism, all fifteen of the union republics were guaranteed representation on the Presidium in the form of fifteen vice-chairmen. This meant that at all times there was permanent representation of the union republics in the Presidium.[95]

The Presidium selected a smaller body termed the Council of Ministers for the implementation of policy. The Council of Ministers was the equivalent of a cabinet and was therefore the executive branch of the government.[96] It had wide-ranging powers to issue decrees and orders that had the effect of legislation and were binding on the entire country unless annulled by the Supreme Soviet or the Presidium, although decisions of the Council of Ministers were never annulled by the Supreme Soviet or the Presidium. Most of the legislation in the Soviet Union was issued by the Council of Ministers, which in itself was not a legislative body.[97] For the first time legislative power was delegated by the legislature to another body, which in turn subdelegated it to a third body.

The Soviet constitution was a very flexible document, and (for reasons that will become apparent) flexibility in the law was seen as an important aspect for the realization of its goals. Unlike most Western federations, the constitution of the USSR could be amended easily with a two-thirds majority of both houses of the Supreme Soviet and did not require the separate consent of the units.[98]

THE ROLE OF THE PARTY

How institutions of the Soviet Union in terms of the old constitution operated cannot be understood without considering the Communist Party and its role in Soviet society. The Communist Party was above all the most powerful institution of government. The functions of the state organs have to be seen against the background of what the party considered the best interest of the country. The constitution gave the Communist Party the single most important role as "the leading and guiding force of Soviet society and the nucleus of its political system and of all state and social organizations."[99] Political decisions were monopolized by the party. No other body could challenge its decisions or what it considered correct for the country. Control of the party ensured control of the state. The institutions of state existed to execute the decisions and policies taken by the party.[100] The party was highly centralized and therefore well suited to exert uniformity throughout the country. Despite recognition of the sovereignty of the units, the party constituted "the single thread that weaved together the entire union into a compact, highly centralized system."[101]

There was considerable overlap between the party and all the important state organs. For example, the members of the Council of Ministers were all members of the party. Constitutionally, the Council of Ministers was responsible to the Soviet legislature just as cabinet ministers are responsible to the legislature in liberal parliamentary systems. Members of the council were responsible to their party in the same way a prime minister in Britain is responsible to his party, except that in the USSR there was only one party.[102] The party imposed strict discipline on its members. Not surprisingly, the head of the party was recognized as the single most powerful person in the country. The one-party monopoly was the core feature in the maintenance of most Communist countries.

DEMOCRATIC CENTRALISM

Apart from the strict discipline the party imposed on its members, another centralizing feature and one that had serious implications for democracy was the Soviet notion of democratic centralism. All organs of the party were elected by the people at the base, be it at the workplace or the residence. The delegates elected at the primary level in turn elected representatives to the next level, for example, the region, who in turn elected delegates to the next higher level, and so the process went until one reached the central or highest organs of the party, the central committee, politburo, and secretariat. The higher organs comprised the elected representatives of the lower units. Each one of the higher organs represented a greater number of people and the highest organ represented the greatest number of people. An important principle in the whole process of decision making was the notion that the minority had to succumb to the majority. The effect was that decisions taken by upper organs had to be followed by the lower organs.[103] Although this structure contained a democratic element in theory, in practice most decisions were made by the top leadership of the party and were executed centrally through state institutions.[104]

THE SOVIET COURT SYSTEM

The Soviet system had a functioning system of courts. The lowest courts were termed People's Courts, and judges were elected by the ordinary people for a period of three years.[105] In keeping with the communal orientation of Soviet ideology, cases were held collegially with lay assessors (who were essentially ordinary people) sitting with the judges. The origin of lay participation dates back to the Russian Revolution and the Marxist notion that the courts were an instrument of class oppression.

Above the local courts were district courts whose members were elected by the local soviets. Above the lowest-level courts were provincial or union courts, which heard appeals from the lower courts.[106] At the apex of each republic was a supreme court. At the apex of the entire judicial system was the Supreme Court of the USSR. The judges of the USSR Supreme Court were elected by the legislature for a period of five years. With the exception of matters involving disputes between the constituent units of the USSR, the latter body had only appellate jurisdiction over cases heard in the lower tribunals.[107]

The judges were not free to interpret the law in terms of their own conceptions of what was right or wrong but were to give effect to the intention of the legislature.[108] The purpose of the court in this system was to decide on matters in a flexible way with greater emphasis on political affairs in the spirit of a "socialist conscience"[109] rather than adopting a "legal" approach, as is the case under Western systems.[110] The judge's role was seen not only to rule on disputes but also to propagate ideology in terms of what members of the top party echelons felt was correct for society. Invariably most judges were members of the Communist Party. Through a variety of ways the party exercised general supervision over judicial activity. The form this took included direct instructions about how a case should be adjudicated.[111]

Soviet history, particularly during the reign of Stalin, has demonstrated that the judicial system does not offer protection of fundamental liberties. What constituted justice was often determined by the single party's conception of what were the best interests of the state. This practice is not necessarily in harmony with the views of Karl Marx. While Marx attacked the doctrine of separation of powers because it freed the executive of popular control, both Marx and Engels supported the independence of the legislature and judiciary over the executive.[112] According to Fine, Marx supported the independence of the judiciary to ensure the maintenance of civil liberties such as freedom of speech, press, and assembly.[113] This would seem to suggest that Marx supported the rule of law, equal rights, and the independence of the judiciary but rejected the separation of powers.[114]

THE SOVIET SYSTEM AND DEMOCRACY

Policy decisions in the Soviet constitutional order were not determined by the society at large but instead by the single Communist Party,[115] an elite party to which membership was restricted to a small section of the population. All state officeholders had to be approved by the party. This meant that a great number of people were denied the right to participate in the affairs of the state because of the monopoly of the single party. Socialism conceived as an ideology striving for equality was a fiction in the Soviet order. The rewards of the system were not uniform: party members received better jobs, bonuses, houses, health care, and education.[116]

But then the theoretical notion of collective leadership had on many occasions been a fiction. In terms of the practice of democratic centralism, the party and state structure operated like an army command with major decisions taken by the upper echelons of the party and in the reign of Stalin by a single person.[117] The legislature historically had been more of a rubber stamp body fulfilling an ornamental role. The Supreme Soviet sat for such short periods that it was not possible for the delegates to the legislature to influence the course of political decisions.[118]

The Soviet system departed fundamentally from democratic principles as enunciated by Marx and Rousseau. For Marx, "democracy was a constitutional principle."[119] The Soviet system did not provide for participatory democracy but resorted to directed rule under a single centralized party. Some Soviet theorists have gone so far as to assert that coercion was legal and acceptable if enforced by the working class.[120] At the level of reality, the dictatorship of the proletariat was an elite party largely detached from the rest of the population and imposing its ironlike will from above. In terms of Lenin's doctrine, there had to be a transitory period where the state made despotic inroads into private property and made use of dictatorial forms of government.[121] The reality is that no Communist system moved beyond what was considered a transitory period; and this despotism and dictatorial form of government seemed to be an enduring legacy.

Soviet Constitutions
and Law in African Marxist Countries

In most African countries the constitutions introduced at independence were modeled after constitutions of the departing colonial power.[122] In previous chapters we have compared the jurisprudence of state law and the institutions of the state in Africa,[123] questioning the appropriateness and success of constitutionalism and the transfer of Western institutions into African society.[124] The general consensus among constitutional lawyers and political scientists is that the record of institutional transfer from Western societies to African countries has been a failure for various reasons, among them inappropriateness to tradition and needs and a lack of legitimacy.[125] Unfortunately, no studies (from the constitutional law perspective) have been conducted on African countries that at independence were committed to pursuing the ideals of Marxism.[126]

It is imperative for comparative scholars to conduct such an investigation in light of the strength of "left leaning" political organizations in South Africa such as the South African Communist Party and the Azanian People's Organization. The enquiry in this section will be limited to an investigation of African countries that followed the ideology of Marxist-Leninism at the stage of independence.[127] The only three countries that fit into this category are Mozambique, Angola, and Guinea-Bissau.[128] The first two countries are South Africa's neighbors. The liberation movements, namely, the African National Congress and the South African Communist Party operated from the African front line states (notably Mozambique) prior to their unbanning in February 1990. The focus of this ensuing section is to consider the constitutions and state institutions of the African Marxist regimes in Africa. Extensive reference will be made to their respective constitutions.[129] In 1992, both Angola and Mozambique made considerable revisions to their constitutions as part of the peace initiatives with the rebel movements in both countries. Consequently, Angola held its first multiparty elections in November 1992 and Mozambique and the RENAMO [Mozambique National Resistance] rebel group have agreed to hold multiparty elections in 1994. The discussion in this chapter will be limited to the constitutions in the African Marxist states prior to the peace initiatives when the countries essentially followed the Soviet state structure. The similarities and differences between African Marxist forms of government and the Soviet model of government and state will be investigated. Moreover, institutions in the African Marxist states will be evaluated in terms of their capacity to overcome the problems of subnationalism, underdevelopment, absence of mass participation, and the overall legitimacy crisis so crucial for the survival of any constitutional system.

IDEOLOGICAL ORIENTATION
OF AFRICAN MARXIST GOVERNMENTS

Many states in Africa profess to pursue a socialist path of reconstruction and proclaim socialism as the ideology of the state.[130] Indeed, socialism is embedded in the constitutions of some of the states.[131] This notion of socialism is premised on the practices of traditional African societies as opposed to the principles of scientific socialism on which the Soviet and Chinese models of state were based. On the ideological level, countries such as Mozambique, Angola, and Guinea-Bissau were committed to the

121

principles of scientific socialism and the notion of a "class struggle," which sets them apart from the many one-party states in Africa that adhere to the notion of African socialism.[132]

For the ruling Movement for the Liberation of Angola (MPLA) in Angola, the only socialism was that enunciated by Marx, Engels, and Lenin.[133] For the ruling party in Mozambique, Frento de Libertacao de Mocambique (FRELIMO), the belief (just as in Russia at the time of the Revolution) was that the country did not have to wait for a transition from feudalism to capitalism but could proceed directly to socialism.[134] In keeping with the principles of scientific socialism, all three countries followed an active policy of nationalization at independence. The constitutions of all three states embodied the idea that land and all natural resources belong to the state or cooperatives.[135] Moreover, the idea that economic and social objectives will be achieved through the process of central planning was given expression in the constitution.[136] In this regard the African Marxist governments followed the Soviet constitutional model of being both an overt political-ideological document as well as a legal document embodying the institutions of the state.

BACKGROUND TO AFRICAN MARXIST CONSTITUTIONS

The above were the only three countries in Africa to introduce models of government at independence committed to pursuing the ideals of Marxism-Leninism.[137] It seems the most "radical" constitutional departures (from that which existed under colonial power) were introduced in African countries where independence was won by a bloody violent struggle. For example Mozambique, Angola, and Guinea-Bissau each won independence after a protracted liberation war. In the process of the struggle the liberation movements introduced their own forms of government.[138] In Mozambique the FRELIMO Party introduced cooperative endeavors with their own separate institutions in those parts of the country they had liberated.[139] A similar feature existed in Guinea-Bissau, where the idea of an egalitarian state was introduced in the process of the struggle against the colonial power.[140] In instances where a state came into existence in a relatively peaceful manner, the colonial structures were to a greater extent replicated in the independence constitutions.[141] In the few instances where independence was won through a protracted armed struggle, a break with the past[142] and the introduction of new structures were more likely.[143]

INSTITUTIONS OF STATE AND PARTY

The structure of the state in all three countries had many similarities with the Soviet model. The distinction between party and state, for one, was blurred. The ruling PAIGC (African Party for the Independence of Guinea and Cape Verde) in Guinea-Bissau ruled large parts of the country at independence, and up to 1973 the central organs of the party and the state were the same.[144] In Angola as well, in the period after independence the executive functions of the state were performed by the Council of Revolution, which consisted of members of the party central committee.[145] Subsequently, separate legislatures and state structures were introduced and a theoretical separation was made between party and state. There was, however, considerable overlap between party leaders and prominent state officials in all three countries and it was not always easy to identify the boundaries between the two.[146] The blurring of the boundaries was more explicit in terms of the Angolan and Mozambique constitutions where the head of the party was automatically the head of state.[147] The feature of the head of the party being the head of the state was the de facto situation that had mostly prevailed in the former Soviet Union.[148]

At the level of practice, just as in the Soviet model,[149] the single party was supreme in respect to all decisions. The late Mozambique President Samora Machel summed up the role of the party as being "to lead, organize, guide and educate the masses."[150] In Angola, the ruling party defined its role by stating that it was the leading organ of state power responsible for deciding how power should be exercised.[151] No other parties or independent areas of political power were allowed. Similarly, in Guinea-Bissau "the power to define, discuss, and approve political, judicial, economic, social, and cultural policies" remained in the hands of the party.[152] The preeminence of the single party was enshrined in the constitutions of all three states. In Guinea-Bissau the PAIGC was defined as the society's and state's ruling political force.[153] The Mozambique constitution specified that FRELIMO was the leading force of the state and society.[154] Similarly, in Angola the MPLA Workers Party as the Marxist-Leninist party was entrusted with the economic and social leadership of the state.[155] Clearly, national policies and goals were set by the party and not the legislature. Moreover, the party controlled all major aspects of life including communications, the media, and the press.[156]

The legislature was designated a role in these countries similar to that of the Soviet model. The theoretical separation between party and state did not confer on the legislature independent decision-making powers. At first glance this may be difficult to comprehend as all three constitutions designated the national legislatures as being the supreme organs of the state.[157] These provisions have to be read against the background of the earlier provisions that made the party supreme. This was consistent with the overall tenor of Marxist-Leninist ideology. Moreover, the constitutions specified that the institutions of the state were responsible for carrying out the goals and objectives as defined by the party.[158] The function of the legislature was therefore not to initiate programs and policies but primarily to implement decisions taken by the party.[159] The observation has been made that the legislature was more of a rubber stamp to legitimize party decisions.[160] In this sense it was an administrative arm of the party. Its primary power derived from its ability to control the application of policy. Beyond that it fulfilled a symbolic function.

ELECTIONS AND COMPOSITION OF LEGISLATURE

In the Soviet experience, the legislature was a bicameral body designed to reflect the federal character of the Soviet state. In all three African Marxist models, despite "diversity" in the population, the preference was for a unitary state. The constitutions of Angola and Guinea-Bissau explicitly stated that the form of state would be unitary.[161] Consequently, no separate representation was accorded to any region or group, the professed aim being to fight any manifestation of ethnocentrism.[162] The constitution of Guinea-Bissau further specified that no change could be made affecting the unitary character of the constitution.[163] Similarly, the Angolan constitution specified any attempt to erode the unitary nature of the state would be resisted.[164] As in all unitary states the constitutions of the three states did permit decentralization into regions for purposes of administrative efficiency.[165]

In the Soviet model, elections to the popular chamber the Soviet of the Union were done directly. None of the three African Marxist models adopted the Soviet approach of allowing the population to elect representatives directly to the legislature. Mozambique, Guinea-Bissau, and Angola all instead adopted the Soviet party method of electing officials of the state in the pyramidal fashion. In practice, the way members of the legislature were elected in all three instances show great similarity.

In Mozambique elections first took place at the local level, where the population selected delegates to the assemblies of the towns, villages, and cooperatives.[166] The members at the local levels in turn selected members to the Provincial Assembly. The latter in consultation with FRELIMO nominated members to the national legislature called the People's Assembly.[167] In Guinea-Bissau the population chose representatives at the local or regional level through universal and direct franchise.[168] The delegates at the local level in turn chose the representatives to serve in the National Assembly.[169] In terms of its constitution, the MPLA envisaged a similar pyramidal setup for Angola,[170] but was hampered in implementing it by the civil war.[171] Consequently, elections in Angola were held only in those areas where the ruling MPLA was organizationally and ideologically strong.[172] The practice, however, led to a complete merging of the state and party. In those areas where elections were conducted, delegates to the legislature in the People's Assembly were also selected in the pyramidal fashion. The population first selected an electoral college, which in turn elected a Provincial Assembly. The delegates to the Provincial Assembly in turn elected the delegates to the People's Assembly.[173]

The legislature was not a permanent or professional body, nor did it sit throughout the year. This was in keeping with the Marxist maxim that members of the legislature should come from the ordinary ranks of the people and should not be a professional body. Like the Soviet experience, many of the deputies came from the ranks of peasants and workers.[174] The effect was that the national legislatures sat for very short periods in regular session. In Guinea-Bissau the National People's Assembly was supposed to meet only once a year,[175] and in Angola and Mozambique it was supposed to meet twice a year.[176] However, provisions were made for the legislature to meet in extraordinary session.[177] Sometimes the assembly failed to meet the ordinary obligation.[178]

The absence of a permanently sitting legislature like the Soviet model resulted in the delegation of power to a smaller body (in the Soviet Union the Presidium) that met more frequently. In Guinea-Bissau the People's Assembly elected from among its members a State Council,[179] which assumed all the powers of the assembly while the latter was not in session.[180] The People's Assembly also elected a president of the State Council as chief of state.[181] The State Council in turn selected a smaller body called the Government, which was the equivalent of a cabinet. In terms of the old constitution, the latter body was termed the Council of State Commissars and it was responsible for drawing up political and economic state programs and coordinating the activities of all state agencies.[182] The later updated constitution gave it the same role.[183]

Similarly, in Mozambique the People's Assembly elected a smaller body called the Permanent Commission to take over the functions of the legislature when the latter was not in session.[184] The Permanent Commission elected a smaller body termed the Council of Ministers, which was presided over by the president.[185] The Council of Ministers fulfilled the role of a cabinet and it was entrusted with the responsibility of drawing up and implementing state programs.[186] In Angola the central legislature elected a Permanent Commission to conduct the business of the legislature when it was not sitting.[187] The latter in turn selected a smaller Council of Ministers who collectively acted as the government of Angola.[188]

Theoretically, in all three countries the delegated bodies elected by the national assembly were accountable to the central legislature for all their actions.[189] Like the Soviet model the delegated bodies were meant to take over the functions of the central legislature and they enjoyed all the powers of the central legislature when the latter was not in session.[190] In Mozambique and Guinea-Bissau the lawmaking powers were limited to the Permanent Commission[191] and State Council[192] respectively, whereas the Angolan constitution resembled the Soviet constitution by extending decree-making powers to the cabinet in the form of the Council of Ministers.[193] This meant in all instances that respective delegated bodies could issue orders and decrees that had the force of law. This accorded with the overall Soviet view that law and state structures should not be rigid or they would obstruct dynamic development. According to Mozambique's late President Machel, state structures should be flexible to meet changing conditions.[194] In reality, just as in the Soviet experience, none of the delegated bodies' decisions was overturned by the legislature, which meant the delegated bodies were the greater source of power.[195] The Mozambique and Guinea-Bissau constitutions followed the Soviet model by precluding the delegated bodies from altering the constitution, which was the only real limit to their lawmaking powers.[196]

THE ROLE AND ORGANIZATION OF THE PARTY

The constitutions of all three countries proclaimed the equality of all citizens and the right of all citizens to vote and be elected to political office.[197] The point has been previously made that the party was supreme over and above all bodies and institutions. But, as far as elections to the legislature were concerned, in all instances delegates either at the local or national level had to be approved by the party. For example, the party would screen a set of candidates and put a single candidate to the electorate for approval or rejection.[198] According to Samora Machel, the elections had to turn out in such a way that the masses chose those who had internalized the party line.[199] In Angola the MPLA maintained that the party must lead to achieve political domination and the exercise of "People's Power."[200] The reality was that an individual could not be elected to political office, particularly if he or she did not find favor with the party elite.

Being elected to office was difficult, as the party in all three instances was a vanguard party. According to the Guinean leadership, only a revolutionary minority would be aware of what is in the best interests of the masses.[201] In practical terms the onus of determining what was in the best interests of all fell on the shoulders of a select few. The vanguard were referred to as cadres, dynamizing groups, or party committees. It was these "best" elements who were charged with leading the state and directing and organizing the people.[202] Membership of the party was restricted to the few who could demonstrate fidelity to the party line. In Angola, the MPLA policy was that the party would "be composed of the best elements of the working class and other revolutionary groups."[203] In Angola and Mozambique, to become a party member a person had to be nominated by two present members of the party in the district and serve a one-year period of probationary membership.[204] Those who did not toe the party line could be stripped of their party membership.[205] The constitutional provisions "all citizens shall be equal before the law and enjoy the same rights,"[206] "all citizens enjoy the same rights and are subject to the same duties,"[207] and the notion that the rights and liberties concerning the constitution "don't exclude any other" were subject to qualification, namely, party supervision and approval.

DEMOCRATIC CENTRALISM

The operative principle with respect to party and state activities was the notion of democratic centralism. In theory this called for full participation in and discussion by all segments of society at the base of ideas communicated to the top. The leadership at the top would in turn make a decision based on the wishes of all, which would be binding on all lower organs.[208] In the words of the MPLA, democratic centralism entailed broad democracy at the bottom, and "the existence of a centralized leadership which faithfully interprets the thinking of all members of the organization and directs and coordinates all its activity."[209] All lower organs had to accede to the decisions of the higher organs.[210]

The notion of democratic centralism was reinforced in the constitution and translated into government structures. The Angolan constitution specified that the organs of the state shall be organized and function according to the principles of unity of power and of democratic centralism.[211] In terms of the former Mozambique constitution, the "Peoples's Assemblies practice a unity of decision-making, implementation and control at each appropriate level."[212] Both the Mozambique and Guinea-Bissau constitutions proclaimed each People's Assembly at a lower level was bound by the decision of the People's Assembly at the higher level.[213]

The party structures revealed the same hierarchal arrangement as the Soviet Communist Party. However, not all the parties were as functional in terms of spreading parties' hierarchal wings across the country. In the Angolan situation the civil war was in great part responsible for this. As previously alluded to, in Angola elections for legislative bodies were only held in those areas where the party had stronghold. State and party thus became synonymous. The institutions of the state merged with the party were meant to operate according to the principles of democratic centralism.[214] The PAIG in Guinea-Bissau was accused of becoming moribund, but nevertheless maintained a formal structure resembling the Soviet prototype. Theoretically, the Party Congress was the main organ of power. The Party Congress in turn selected a Central Committee from which a smaller body, the Political Bureau, was formed.[215] In the Mozambique instance where the party was active, there was more of a separation and separate existence (albeit in the manner of the Soviet state and Soviet Communist Party) between state and party structures. The party structure revealed the prototype Communist Party organization with the FRELIMO Congress being the supreme organ. At the Party Congress a Central Committee was elected. The Central Committee was responsible for formulating policies,[216] and could break up into various subgroups responsible for various departments.[217]

In Mozambique and Guinea-Bissau villagization programs had an important political objective of bringing people together and allowing them to take control of political and economic decisions.[218] These villages in Mozambique characteristically consisted of populations of five hundred to seven thousand inhabitants.[219] The villages had to develop their own institutions, and administrative and governing bodies. The aim was to make them self-sufficient in terms of food. Clinics and school systems were established.[220] A similar program existed in Guinea-Bissau. These village structures have been described as "the most democratic institutions within the party structure where peasants have the opportunity to engage in local decision-making."[221]

An additional feature of the Mozambique system was the election of production councils at the factory levels. These production councils were elected by the workers; together with the state-appointed administrative councils they were responsible for the operation of the factory.[222] The workers' councils were more than trade unions and had a significant influence on decision making at the workplace and on levels of output.[223] With the administrative councils the production councils also had input into matters pertaining to salaries and promotion, and social issues such as alcoholism and absenteeism.[224]

JUDICIAL SYSTEMS

The constitutions of all three countries made provisions for a system of courts. In all three there was a system of popular justice at the lowest levels, based on the principles of the Soviet system. The courts functioned in a collegial manner with the participation of ordinary people as judges.[225] The persons elected to serve as judges came from within the ranks of the ordinary people and included factory workers, peasants, professional people, and farmers.[226] The notion of popular justice meant that the values applied should be those of the community and applied by members of the community as opposed to the values of a detached judiciary.[227] The persons elected to serve as judges were given paid leave to serve on the courts.[228]

In Guinea-Bissau the people's court served between four and seven villages. At the local level the courts consisted of three elected members with the village teacher acting as the clerk recording all the proceedings.[229]

In Angola the local people's court was presided over by a professional judge together with two lay judges elected by the population of the area.[230] All three judges had equal powers.[231] In Mozambique, there were local people's tribunals or neighborhood people's tribunals consisting of elected judges.[232] However, the judges of these forums were elected by the local assemblies if they were in existence. If the local legislative assembly had not been established, then the judges were elected by the community at large.[233] In addition to the local tribunals there were district courts to serve a particular area. In Mozambique the district court was presided over by a qualified professional magistrate or district administrator.[234] The jurisdiction of the lower courts, be it the people's or district court, was restricted to minor crimes and disputes.

Above the people's court were zone courts in Guinea-Bissau or provincial courts in Mozambique and Angola, which acted as courts of appeal and also exercised greater jurisdiction.[235] At the apex of all three judicial systems was a supreme court, the members of which were selected by the president in Guinea-Bissau,[236] and by the People's Assembly in Angola.[237] Members of the supreme court in Mozambique (referred to as the Supreme People's Tribunal) were elected by the legislature.[238]

In theory the constitutions of all three states proclaimed the independence of judges.[239] In practice, the position of judges had to be considered against the background of the ruling parties' seeing themselves as the leading organs of the society. Not surprisingly, the party determined the selection of judges.[240] The Mozambique constitution specified that all courts of law were subordinate to the legislature.[241] Similarly, in Angola the constitution specified the supreme court must answer to the legislature and present reports of its activities to the latter.[242] The subordinate position of the judiciary to the legislature and the selection of judges by the party are features modeled on Soviet practice.

Marxist Models of State and Government in Africa

At independence the former Portuguese colonies were left in an impoverished and underdeveloped state, perhaps in a worse situation than any other former colonies. For example, in Mozambique there were fewer than fifty doctors to serve a population of over nine million people.[243] Illiteracy ran at over 95 percent of the population because the colonial government had provided very few schools.[244] White settlers followed a scorched earth policy, leaving behind a path of destruction and sabotage. They destroyed cattle and industries.[245] After having wrecked much of the industry, most of the skilled (white) personnel left the country.[246]

Commentators have alluded to the difficulty of clearly judging the record and success of the forms of government in Angola and Mozambique because of the profound destabilization the two countries have been subjected to from outside forces. Angola has been involved in a civil war—albeit greatly aided and abetted by outside forces—ever since independence. The war has continued despite multiparty elections at the end of 1992. Likewise, Mozambique since independence has been subject to savage aggression, initially from Ian Smith's regime in former Rhodesia (now Zimbabwe). Since the independence of Zimbabwe, the destabilization policies were taken over by South Africa, which had also been actively engaged in a war against Angola.[247] The results have been great human loss and destruction of infrastructure.[248] The South African destabilization policies came about through direct military intervention in these two countries as well as aid to mercenary forces.[249] The destabilization policies were aimed at both economic and civilian targets and have resulted in great financial strain.[250] Foreign intervention has been less a factor in the case of Guinea-Bissau.[251]

The successes and failures in Angola and Mozambique must be measured in light of the destabilization policies. Serious attempts were apparently made to solve problems such as a lack of basic services, underdevelopment, ethnocentrism, and racism. Determined efforts were made to conduct literacy programs, establish schools, inoculate the population, provide clinics and health services, develop projects, and provide food.[252] There is evidence of the ruling party instituting similar reforms in Guinea-Bissau.[253]

In the period before and after independence, the MPLA in Angola made it a priority to eradicate all manifestations of tribalism or calls to parochial loyalty, and pursued a policy of recruiting membership from across the country.[254] In Mozambique FRELIMO opened a school to teach ideology in order to combat racism, and further instructed its cadres to help instill in the population a national ethic to fight racism and tribalism.[255] Recruitment was conducted across all groups in the country. Since independence several whites were appointed to senior positions in the government.[256] The government in Mozambique has resorted to severe punishment of persons arousing ethnic sentiments.[257] In Angola today ethnicity is still a factor in the politics of the country owing to the rebel National Union for the Total Independence of Angola (UNITA) movement which (prior to liberation and presently) conducts much of its activities on the basis of ethnic sentiments. However, in Mozambique ethnicity is not a significant factor in the politics of the country, which shows the country has gone a long way toward resolving the problem.[258]

Both Angola and Mozambique understood the potential for an indigenous elite to step into the shoes of the departing colonial power and continue the oppression of the people. Unlike most other African countries, Angola and Mozambique eschewed the Africanization method of replacing white power with black power in the economic, political, and administrative spheres.[259] This in itself has ramifications for the nationalist problem.[260] Both preferred merit to ethnicity or race and accepted all groups as part of the new nation. Socioeconomic change to benefit the entire population, as opposed to Africanization to benefit a few, was the operative principle. Socioeconomic equality has been accorded one of the highest priority.[261]

Alongside their attempts to solve the serious problems a new nation faces, the leadership in Angola and Mozambique tried to prevent the rise of a powerful civil service and black bourgeoisie. The salaries and conduct of the civil servants and government officials in both countries were regulated to prevent them from using public office for personal aggrandizement.[262] This is not to say all three former African Marxist governments have been spared the corrupt practices endemic to so many African countries.[263] In the case of Guinea-Bissau there is evidence of widespread corruption committed by senior party and government officials.[264] To a lesser extent there is also evidence of corruption in Mozambique.[265] However, in the latter instance the leadership has made serious efforts to punish and eradicate such practices.[266]

Notable in Mozambique was widespread participation by ordinary people in political and civil institutions.[267] The first instance of participation was at the state level with the election of delegates to the local legislatures. All Mozambican citizens had the right to vote in the elections. The second and more direct method of participation was that of workers at the level of the workplace through production councils. These councils had a great influence on decision making with regard to production output and worker conditions.[268] Similarly, participation in the village councils in both Mozambique and Guinea-Bissau was a novel institution in democracy widely suited to an underdeveloped region.[269] In Mozambique an attempt was made to anchor the movement symbolized in the party among the population.[270]

At the level of performance, the economy of Mozambique continues to be in complete shambles largely on account of the war,[271] though the perception is that the government did represent the aspirations of the majority despite economic failures. This arguably can be attributed to the participatory devices the ruling party had introduced, which go a long way toward resolving the legitimacy problem so many African governments face. The FRELIMO Party was a functioning party that attempted to link the government to the masses and create a sense of trust.[272] The party was not a one-man government but collegial.[273] And the system allowed for criticism of mistakes in government policies—a departure from most African governments.[274] The perception that the existing form of government represented the interests of the population flows from

131

FRELIMO discussing most of the issues in community organizations, the party, and the media. This allowed the leadership to be in touch with the people and respond appropriately to their demands.[275] For example, in the early 1980s there were accusations of detentions, brutality, and torture on the part of government troops. Instead of suppressing news of these atrocities (as occurs in so many parts of the continent), the government went on a major offensive and repudiated the actions as a violation of Mozambique's legality.[276] The issue was debated publicly and the abuses criticized.[277]

THE MARXIST-LENINIST MODEL AND
THE PROBLEM OF DEMOCRACY

The major problem with all three states arises from the fundamental contradiction in all Marxist states following the Leninist line between on the one hand espousing political mobilization and the participation of all and on the other preferring a vanguard party operating under the principles of democratic centralism. In both Mozambique and Angola participation was kept to limits defined by the party. In the election process the party was responsible for screening candidates elected to the legislature at each level. This approach is inconsistent and amounts to saying to the people, we take our instructions from you, while at the same time the single party places itself in the leading role as the sole decision maker. Moreover, membership of the party was restricted to a few who met the predetermined standards set by the leadership.[278] Clearly, these two approaches are not compatible. Evidence has shown that it is only a matter of time before one view gives in to the other. Unfortunately, the tendency has been to strengthen the role of the party in terms of decision-making powers at the expense of the people.[279]

A second problem arises from the basic notion of democratic centralism and the idea (in theory) that higher organs are elected by the lower organs and take their mandate from the lower units. In practice it appears that most major state decisions are taken at the center by the higher organs of power and then enforced through the lower organs. The democratic element of participation from the bottom is a fiction. The result is that the upper echelons of the party override the people's will and submerge their voices to enhance the interests of party elites. There is evidence of such practices in all the African Marxist states.[280] At its worst, the danger is that the institutions replicated in Africa could lead to the absence of accountability and tyrannical one-person dictatorship that characterized Stalinist rule in the USSR.[281] Examples of such practices have already occurred in Guinea-Bissau.[282]

In all three countries the delegates to the local legislatures were the only candidates approved by the population. However, the extent to which

132

they could influence the central decision-making processes was limited as they did not serve in the central legislature. The policy of having local delegates select regional delegates who in turn select the delegates to the central legislature has to be critically examined in terms of the extent to which local people can have input into the central decision-making process. There is no connection between the delegates to the legislature and the population in the various districts. Moreover, the practice of the legislature sitting for such short durations in the year questions the effectiveness of such a body as a representative institution. It is not possible for a legislature to deliberate seriously on national policies and programs in a few days.[283]

The way the entire legislative framework was designed was suited to elite decision making in that power was delegated to a smaller body that had the power to make laws and issue decrees binding on all. The legislature served merely a symbolic role of rubber stamping the decisions taken by the elite whose decisions were never overruled. The indirect method of elections to the central legislature was a further limitation on the participation of the people. The absence of a more involved and vigorous legislature in favor of a permanent delegated body had the consequence of promoting elite decision making.[284]

The absence of more direct methods of participation and greater institutional controls in the three African Marxist systems was a severe deficiency, and it is not surprising to find them slipping into repression. In the case of Mozambique the country was spared the widespread repression and despotic rule characteristic of so many governments of this kind.[285] This was primarily due to the caliber of the leadership, which was committed to the welfare and uplifting of the nation as a whole. But even in Mozambique, the system has suffered lapses into tyranny,[286] the correction of which was dependent on committed leadership.[287] Because so much depends on the conceptions of the leadership, as well as their desire not to be entirely out of touch with the demands of the people, we would classify the primary state structures in such systems under Marxist constitutions as having offered a mild form of democracy that did not have sufficient institutional safeguards to ensure grassroots participation, prevention of tyranny, or corruption.

The single deficiency of these systems was their reliance on the caliber of leadership. Where the leadership's commitment to the general welfare is weak, it would be only a matter of time before decisions are taken by an elite in their own interests. Evidence of such developments can be seen particularly in the case of Guinea-Bissau, which has not been subjected to the same counterinsurgencies that Mozambique and Angola have experienced. The ruling PAIG in Guinea-Bissau was the only legal party in the country. Many of the leaders of the party have used their eminent positions to enrich themselves.[288] Resources earmarked for the needy have been concentrated in the hands of party officials.[289] Without the commitment to the nation's welfare, mild or partial participation will most certainly erode. Regional participation and the notion that it allowed the people the opportunity to take control of their destinies has been characterized as an illusion.[290] Regional bodies did not have the ability to select their own representatives. Instead the representatives were appointed by the central government.[291] The party at times often resorted to manipulation to get its approved candidates elected at lower levels to prevent dissent from below against its programs.[292]

This kind of conflict often results in coercion, a problem all three Marxist-Leninist models of state have encountered. For example, in Mozambique there is evidence of the villagization program being instituted by force when some people were reluctant to move to the village areas.[293] The forced removals caused others to take up arms against the government by joining the opposition RENAMO (Resistencia Nacional de Mocambicana [Mozambique National Resistance]) forces.[294] There were few or no economic benefits achieved where coercion was employed.[295]

In Angola it is understandable that many measures were taken and constitutional reforms delayed because of the continuing war. However, it is difficult to accept the purging and detention of elements in the ruling party who showed mild dissent or indulged in jest against party officials.[296] Criticism and accountability are essential requisites for democracy to thrive. Brummel argues that in Angola the limitation of participation and the strong hold that an inner core of the party exercised in respect to decision making have contributed to a general political demobilization.[297] This undermines development policies, as the government needs the support of the masses in its development effort.[298]

In Guinea-Bissau peasants were coerced and penalized when they acted in ways that conflicted with party interests.[299] The lack of participation combined with coercion, manipulation, and corruption exercised by the leadership[300] was a major factor in eroding the legitimacy of the government. Lack of participation and consensus in decision making leads to erosion of national unity and the seizure of power by the "strongman." Guinea-Bissau has experienced two coups since independence.[301] The alienation of the majority resulted in lack of cooperation with government officials.[302]

POSITIVE LESSONS FROM THE AFRICAN MARXIST MODEL

Although African Marxist models of state did not provide an appropriate constitutional framework, there are positive lessons to be drawn. The first concerns their experiment with production councils at the level of the workplace. Production councils allowed workers significant democracy in matters relating to the operation of the workplace. Similarly, the village councils allowed ordinary people real opportunities to participate in important decisions. The latter was an important participatory feature well suited to development objectives of the rural and underdeveloped areas. Finally, the model has demonstrated (particularly in the case of Mozambique) that overcoming ethnocentric tendencies is best possible in a unitary state. However, in order to achieve national unity there is also a need to prevent the growth of bureaucratic and middle-class elites in government who utilize the institutions and powers of the state to further their own interests.

REFERENCES

1. This chapter will not deal with the Soviet constitution in the Gorbachev "reform" era.

2. Ralph Miliband, *Marxism and Politics* (Oxford: Oxford University Press, 1977), 2–5; George D. Cameron, *The Soviet Lawyer and His System: A Historical and Bibliographic Study* (Ann Arbor, Mich.: Division of Research, Graduate School of Business Administration, University of Michigan, 1978), 19.

3. Miliband, *Marxism and Politics*, 5.

4. Maureen Cain and Alan Hunt, eds., *Marx and Engels on Law* (London: Academic Press, 1979), xiv.

5. Bob Fine, *Democracy and the Rule of Law: Liberal Ideals and Marxist Critiques* (London: Pluto Press, 1984), 1.

6. Hugh Collins, *Marxism and Law* (Oxford: Clarendon Press, 1982), chap. 1.

7. See the last ten pages of Edward P. Thompson, *Whigs and Hunters: The Origin of the Black Act* (Harmondsworth: Penguin, 1977).

8. K. Marx, Preface to "A Contribution to the Critique of Political Economy," quoted in Miliband, *Marxism and Politics*, 15.

9. Collins, *Marxism and Law*, 19.

10. K. A. Mollnau, "The Dynamics of The Object of Legal Regulation and Legality Under Socialism," in Zoltan Peteri, ed., *Legal Theory, Comparative Law: Studies in Honor of Professor Imre Szabo* (Budapest: Akademiai Kiado, 1984), 227.

11. Collins, *Marxism and Law*, 1, 12. The interpretation that Collins and most Marxist writers give to the rule of law is in terms of the legality principle, that is, that power should be exercised according to preannounced rules, which should be known to all. The law applies to all alike and there need be no particular content to the law.

12. Karl Marx and Friedrich Engels, *The Communist Manifesto*, trans. Samuel Moore, II (New York: New York Labor News, 1948).

13. Nicos Poulantzas, *L'Etat, le pouvoir, le socialisme* [State, Power, Socialism], trans. Patrick Camiller (London: NLB, 1978), 76–92.

14. M. Gordon, "Class and Economics of Crime," *Review of Radical Political Economics* 3(3) (1971): 52–70.

15. V. I. Lenin, *L'Etat et la Revolution* [The State and Revolution] (Paris: Librairie de l'Humanite, 1925), chap. 5.

16. Collins, *Marxism and Law*, 2; Poulantzas, *L'Etat, le pouvoir, le socialisme*.

17. The following discussion of Pashukanis's views is taken from his work "The General Theory of Law and Marxism," reprinted in Evgenii B. Pashukanis, *Pashukanis, Selected Writings on Marxism and Law*, ed. Piers Beirne and Robert Sharlet (London: Academic Press, 1980).

18. Ibid., 273–74.

19. Ibid.

20. Collins, *Marxism and Law*, 68–69.

21. His views are best expressed in the last ten pages of his work *Whigs and Hunters*.

22. Thompson, *Whigs and Hunters*, 266.

23. Thompson states that law "is deeply imbricated within the very basis of productive relations." Ibid., 261.

24. Paul Q. Hirst, *Law, Socialism, and Democracy* (London: Allen & Unwin, 1986), 85.

25. Ibid., 86.

26. It seems Marx's views were that liberal rights were so ingrained in the society that there would have to be a temporary period during which these rights would have to be maintained. William G. Andrews and Franz D. Scholz, *Soviet Institutions and Policies: Inside Views* (Princeton, N.J.: Van Nostrand, 1966), 32.

27. Fine, *Democracy and the Rule of Law*, 125.

28. In terms of orthodox Marxist theory, it is inconsistent to have a state and law in a Communist order.

29. V. I. Lenin, *State and Revolution*, especially chap. 5. The relevant part of Lenin's views are also quoted in W. G. Andrews and Scholz, *Soviet Institutions*, 28, 33.

30. The state was to exist only until the new Communist society was established.

31. Fine, *Capitalism and the Rule of Law*, 44.

32. Radoslav Selucky, *Marxism, Socialism, Freedom: Towards a General Democratic Theory of Labor-Managed Systems* (New York: St. Martin's Press, 1979), 110.

33. The new arguments contend that in liberal society law is seen as abstract and eternal, whereas in the socialist order law is part of social and economic conditions and plays a role in the social development of the community. See V. Chirkin, *Fundamentals of the Socialist Theory of the State and Law* (n.p., 1987), 226.

34. Andrews and Scholz, *Soviet Institutions*, 53.

35. Alessandro Pizzorusso, et al., *Law in the Making: A Comparative Study* (Berlin: Springer-Verlag, 1988), 309.

36. Lenin, *State and Revolution*.

37. Istvan Kovacs, *New Elements in the Evolution of Socialist Constitution*, trans. J. Decsenyi (Budapest: Akademiai Kiado, 1968), 17.

38. Collins, *Marxism and Law*, 122.

39. The role of the party in Soviet society is beyond this jurisprudential enquiry.

40. Andrey Y. Vyshinsky, *The Law of the Soviet State*, trans. Hugh W. Babb (Westport, Conn.: Greenwood Press, 1979), 300.

41. Fine, *Capitalism and the Rule of Law*, 123.

42. John N. Hazard, *Communists and Their Law: A Search for the Common Core of the Legal Systems of the Marxian Socialist States* (Chicago: University of Chicago Press, 1969), 42.

43. Osakwe, "Equal Protection of Law in Soviet Constitutional Law and Theory—A Comparative Analysis," *Tulane Law Review* 59 (1985): 981. 555

44. Ibid., 975.

45. L. Slepov, *Pravda*, 16 April 1953, 2. Translated and republished in Andrews and Scholz, *Soviet Institutions*, 113.

46. Hazard, *Communists and Their Law*, 43.

47. The majority of deputies came from within the ranks of workers and peasants. See Jerry F. Hough and Merle Fainsod, *How the Soviet Union is Governed* (Cambridge, Mass.: Harvard University Press, 1979), 364–65.

48. Peteri, in Pizzorusso, *Law in the Making*, 319.

49. The Soviet court system and its ideological underpinnings is investigated in chapter 9.

50. Hazard, *Communists and Their Law*, 90–91.

51. In this regard the party exerted considerable control. See F. J. M. Feldbrugge, "Law and Political Dissent in the Soviet Union," in Donald D. Barry and William E. Butler, *Contemporary Soviet Law* (The Hague: M. Nijhoff, 1974), 55–68; Cameron, *The Soviet Lawyer*, 38.

52. Hazard, *Communists and Their Law*, 81.

53. Peteri in Pizzorusso, *Law in the Making*, 314.

54. Aspaturian, "The Theory and Practice of Soviet Federalism," *Journal of Politics* 12 (1950): 41–42.

55. Mollnau, *Dynamics*, 282.

56. S. K. Panter Brick, "Four African Constitutions: Two Models," *Government and Opposition* 14:3 (Summer 1979): 340.

57. R. Sharlet, *The New Soviet Constitution of 1977: Analysis and Text* (n.p., 1978): 8.

58. Ibid., 8–9.

59. Kovacs, *New Elements*, 71–72.

60. Otto Bihari, *The Constitutional Models of Socialist State Organization* (Budapest: Akademiai Kiado, 1979), 125; Sharlet, *Soviet Constitution of 1977*, 8.

61. G. Schuster, "Politics and Law in the Period of Progressing towards an Advanced Socialist Society," in Peteri, *Legal Theory, Comparative Law*, 390–91.

62. Osakwe, "Equal Protection," 978.

63. Soviet Constitution, art. 70.

64. On 13 March 1990 the Soviet Legislature voted to abolish Article 6 of the Soviet Constitution, which guaranteed the Communist Party's monopoly of power. See *Chicago Tribune*, 14 March 1990, 1.

65. Viktor S. Shevtsov, *The State and Nations in the USSR*, trans. Lenina Ilitskaya (Moscow: Progress Publishers, 1982), 52.

66. Jerry F. Hough and Merle Fainsod, *How the Soviet Union is Governed* (Cambridge, Mass.: Harvard University Press, 1979), 362–63.

67. Shevtsov, *State and Nations*, 37.

68. Frederick C. Barghoorn and Thomas F. Remington, *Politics in the USSR*, 3d ed. (Boston: Little, Brown, 1986), 143–44; P. F. Gonidec, *African Politics* (Boston: M. Nijhoff, 1981), 29.

69. Ibid.

70. H. A. I. Sugg, "Soviet Concepts of Federalism," in *Politics 72: Trends in Federalism* (1972): 97.

71. Aspaturian, "Theory and Practice," 20.

72. Sugg, *Soviet Concepts*, 99.

73. Aspaturian, "Theory and Practice," 21.

74. Ibid.

75. Ivo D. Duchacek, *Power Maps: Comparative Politics of Constitutions* (Santa Barbara, Calif.: ABC-Clio, 1973), 116.

76. Soviet Constitution, art. 70.

77. Ibid., art. 80.

78. Ibid., art. 72.

79. Ibid., art. 4. This raises interesting questions whether the Soviet Union was in fact a federation or confederation in light of the provision allowing the units the right to secede. If it was a confederation this would mean that the states who voluntarily joined the union of their own will could leave the union. In other words, there is no permanence to the union. In the past—in the pre-Gorbachev era—the reality was that no unit actively spoke about seceding, nor would they have been allowed to secede from the union. However, on 11 March 1990 the Republic of Lithuania voted to secede from the Soviet Union while the Soviet Union was still in existence.

80. On 13 March 1990 the Soviet legislature voted to permit ownership of certain private property, such as small businesses and factories in certain instances. See *Chicago Tribune*, 14 March 1990, 14.

81. Soviet Constitution, art. 73, sec. 3.

82. Ibid., subsec. 5 and 6.

83. See Soviet Constitution, art. 77, which calls on the various territories to implement the decisions of the central organs of the Soviet state.

84. Shevtsov, *State and Nations*, 124; M. Faizliev in A. Beloken and I. Vail, *The Development of Soviet Law and Jurisprudence*, (n.p., 1978), 48.

85. Soviet Constitution, art. 83 and 74.

86. Ibid., art. 3 and 108.

87. Ibid., art. 110.

88. The constitution stipulates that a deputy must not leave work while serving as a deputy. Ibid., art. 104.

89. Ibid., art. 119.

90. Roy C. Macridis, *The Study of Comparative Government* (Garden City, N.Y.: Doubleday, 1955), 368. Soviet Constitution, art. 121 enumerates the powers of the Presidium.

91. Joseph H. Price, *Comparative Government: Four Modern Constitutions*, 2d ed. (London: Hutchinson, 1975), 361.

92. Soviet Constitution, art. 120. See Sugg, *Soviet Concepts*, 108.

93. In keeping with the Soviet concept of federalism, the council has representatives (in the form of the chairman of the council of ministers of each of the Union republics) from each of the Union republics. Soviet Constitution, art. 129.

94. Macridis, *Comparative Government*, 368.

95. Soviet Constitution, art. 174.

96. Ibid., art. 6. The article was abolished on 13 March 1990.

97. Andrews and Scholz, *Soviet Institutions*, 118.

98. Aspaturian, "Theory and Practice," 48.

99. Macridis, *Modern Political Systems*, 369.

100. Sugg, *Soviet Concepts*, 104.

101. Vyshinsky, *Law of the Soviet State*, 300; Shevtsev, *State and Nations*, 114.

102. Soviet Constitution, art. 3.

103. Joseph H. Price, *Comparative Government: Four Modern Constitutions* (London: Hutchinson, 1975), 363.

104. Frederick C. Barghorn and Thomas F. Remington, *Politics in the USSR*, 3d ed. (Boston: Little, Brown, 1986), 360.

105. In this regard the party exerts considerable control. See Feldbrugge, "Law and Political Dissent," 55–68; Cameron, *The Soviet Lawyer*, 38.

106. Hazard, *Communists and Their Law*, 90–91.

107. This is not to say that there is no ideological bias on the part of Western judiciary. However, in the Western systems, this is not openly advocated, and therefore not as overt as in the Soviet model. Second, the ideological orientation is not fixed by a single party in the Western systems.

108. Barghorn and Remington, *Politics in the USSR*, 361.

109. Fine, *Democracy and the Rule of Law*, 122.

110. Ibid.

111. Ibid., 123, 125. The rejection of the separation of powers and the rejection of any special powers for the executive are consistent with Marx's idea of democracy, namely that the executive should not be a detached part of society but should be a committee from the legislature accountable to the legislature. See Marx's views on the Paris Commune in chapter 3.

112. Bernard A. Ramundo, *The Soviet Legal System: A Primer* (Chicago: ABA, 1971), 12.

113. Barghorn and Remington, *Politics in the USSR*, 125.

114. Andrews and Scholz, *Soviet Institutions*, 80–81.

115. Hough and Fainsod, *Soviet Union*, 368; Andrews and Scholz, *Soviet Institutions*, 170.

116. G. Schussler, "Politics and Law in the Period of Progressing Towards an Advanced Socialist Society," in Peteri, *Legal Theory, Comparative Law*, 392.

117. Ibid., 385.

118. Selucky, *Marxism, Socialism, and Freedom*, 110.

119. Pius Msekwe, *Towards Party Supremacy* (Kampala: East African Literature Bureau, 1977), 1–8; J. J. Okumu, "Party and Party-State Relations," in Joel D. Barkan and John J. Okumu, eds., *Politics and Public Policy in Kenya and Tanzania* (New York: Praeger, 1979), 44–45.

120. See Michael Aletum Tabuwe, *The One-Party System and the African Traditional Institutions* (Yaounde, n.p., 1980), 9; de Smith, *The New Commonwealth*; Christian P. Potholm, *The Theory and Practice of African Politics* (Englewood Cliffs, N.J.: Prentice-Hall, 1979); F. Olisa Awogu, *Political Institutions and Thought in Africa: An Introduction* (New York: Vantage Press, 1975).

121. See the studies in Barkan and Okumu, *Politics and Public Policy*; and note 1.

122. R. Emerson, "The Erosion of Democracy in the New States," in Harry Eckstein and David E. Apter, *Comparative Politics, a Reader* (New York: Free Press of Glencoe, 1963), 642.

123. Nwabueze, *Constitutionalism in the Emergent States*, 24, 55.

124. Yash P. Ghai, *Constitutions and the Political Order in East Africa* (Dar es Salaam: University College, 1970), 14.

125. See Seymour M. Lipset, "Social Conflict, Legitimacy, and Democracy," in William E. Connolly, *Legitimacy and the State* (New York: New York University Press, 1984), 88.

126. Blaustein and Flanz, *Constitutions of the Countries of the World*, make the point that much has been written from the view of international politics but nothing has been written about the constitution and political system in Angola. The present author has searched and reached the same conclusion with respect to research (in English) concerning the constitutions of Mozambique and Angola.

127. There is particular merit in considering Mozambique and Angola because of their proximity to South Africa. Guinea-Bissau is included in the discussion to show the problems associated with the African Marxist models despite the "unique" problems Mozambique and Angola experienced.

128. Subsequent to independence or the overthrow of monarchies several African countries have purported to follow the Marxist-Leninist ideology. See C. V. Scott, "Political Development of Afro-Marxist Regimes: An Analysis of Mozambique and Angola," Ph.D. diss., Emory University, 1986, 1.

129. The constitutions to be considered include the *Constitution of the People's Republic of Mozambique* issued in 1975; *The Constitution of the People's Republic of Angola* issued in 1978; and the *Constitution of the Republic of Guinea-Bissau* adopted in 1984. For an English copy of the texts of all three constitutions see Blaustein and Flanz, *Constitutions of the Countries of the World*.

130. For examples see the constitutions of Algeria, Egypt, Tanzania and Guinea. J. N. Hazard, "Socialist Legal Models for Africa," Peteri, *Legal Theory, Comparative Law*, 91.

131. Ibid.

132. Luis B. Serapiao and Mohamed A. El-Khawas, *Mozambique in the Twentieth Century: From Colonialism to Independence* (Washington: University Press, 1979), 138; Angola MPLA, *First Congress Central Committee Report and Thesis on Education* (trans. by Mozambique, Angola & Guinea Information Centre 1977), 10–13.

133. Keith Somerville, *Angola: Politics, Economics and Society* (London: F. Pinter Publishers, 1986), 80–81.

134. Serapiao, *Mozambique*, 140.

135. Mozambique Constitution, art. 8; Angola Constitution, art. 9; Guinea-Bissau Constitution, art. 12.

136. Mozambique Constitution, art. 9; Angola Constitution, art. 11; Guinea-Bissau Constitution, art. 13(1).

137. Subsequent to their independence, additional countries such as Ethiopia and Somalia have also adopted the Marxist-Leninist approach. For a discussion of the constitutions and models of government in these countries see Fisseha-Tsion, "Highlights of the Constitution of the People's Republic of Ethiopia (PDRE): A Critical Review of the Main Issues," *Review of Socialist Law* 14 (1988): 129–79; Ajani, "The 1979 Somali Constitution: The Socialist and African Patterns and The European Style," *Review of Socialist Law 8 (1982): 259–79.*

138. In Guinea-Bissau the ruling PAIGC set up village committees for local self-government in the liberated areas. See Basil Davidson, *Growing from Grass Roots: The State of Guinea-Bissau* (London: Committee for Freedom in Mozambique, Angola and Guinea, 1974), 7.

139. T. H. Henriksen, *Some Aspects of Mozambique's Emerging Marxism* (n.p., n.d.), 6.

140. John S. Saul, *The State and Revolution in Eastern Africa: Essays* (New York: Monthly Review Press, 1979), 11.

141. This was the case in almost all former British and French territories with the exception of Algeria.

142. Zimbabwe would constitute a notable exception here. However, one can debate the point whether independence was achieved primarily through the armed struggle or more as a compromise between the various parties at the Lancaster House agreements.

143. S. Washington, "Some Aspects of Post-War Reconstruction in Guinea-Bissau," Ph.D. diss. Howard University, 1978, 98.

144. Lars Rudebeck, *Guinea-Bissau: A Study of Political Mobilization* (Uppsala: Almquist & Wiksell, 1974), 109.

145. Somerville, *Angola*, 106–7.

146. Joseph Hanlon, *Mozambique: The Revolution Under Fire* (London: Zed, 1984), 140.

147. Angola Constitution, art. 52; Mozambique Constitution, art. 5.

148. Lenin, Stalin, Brezhnev, and Gorbachev were all heads of the party as well as the state.

149. The Communist Party's monopoly of leadership was constitutionally entrenched in all East European countries. Brenner, "The Functions of Communist Constitutions: An Analysis of Recent Constitutional Developments," *Review of Socialist Law* 3 (1977): 127.

150. Samora Machel, *Establishing People's Power to Serve the Masses* (Toronto: Toronto Committee for the Liberation of Southern Africa, 1976), 126.

151. Angola MPLA, *First Congress*, 15.

152. A. Cabral, "Return to the Source," 89, quoted by Washington, "Post-War Reconstruction," 104.

153. Guinea-Bissau Constitution, art. 4(1).

154. Mozambique Constitution, art. 3

155. Angola Constitution, art. 2.

156. J. A. Marcum, "The People's Republic of Angola: A Radical Vision Frustrated," in Edmond J. Keller and Donald Rothchild, eds., *Afro-Marxist Regimes: Ideology and Public Policy* (Boulder, Colo.: Lynne Reinner Publishers, 1987), 72–73.

157. Mozambique Constitution, art. 37; Angola Constitution, art. 37; Guinea-Bissau Constitution, art. 48.

158. Mozambique Constitution, art. 3; Angola Constitution, art. 37; Guinea-Bissau Constitution, art. 48.

159. Machel, *People's Power*, 27.

160. Washington, "Post-War Reconstruction," 107.

161. Angola Constitution, art. 4; Guinea-Bissau Constitution, art. 1; Although not defined explicitly in the Mozambique constitution no provision is made for separate power to be exercised by a region independent of the center.

162. Angola Constitution, art. 4; Mozambique Constitution, art. 26.

163. Guinea-Bissau Constitution, art. 102.

164. Angola Constitution, art. 4.

165. Mozambique Constitution, art. 66–67; Angola Constitution, art. 66; Guinea-Bissau Constitution, art. 78.

166. Mozambique Constitution, art. 40 and 63; A. Isaacman's Report in U.S. Congress, House of Representatives, Committee on International Relations, Subcommittee on Africa, *Perspectives on Mozambique: Hearing Before the Subcommittee on Africa of the Committee on International Relations, House of Representatives, Ninety-Fifth Congress, Second Session, May 16, 1978* (Washington: U.S. GPO, 1978), 41 (hereinafter referred to as *Subcommittee on Africa Report*).

167. Ibid., 43.

168. Guinea-Bissau Constitution, art. 47(1).

169. Guinea-Bissau Constitution, art. 47(2).

170. Angola Constitution, art. 32.

171. Ole Gjerstad, *The People in Power* (Oakland, Calif.: LSM, 1976), 106.

172. Angola MPLA, *First Congress*, 16.

173. Somerville, *Angola*, 59, 107–8.

174. Isaacman, *Subcommittee on Africa Report*, 44.

175. Guinea-Bissau Constitution, art. 58.

176. Mozambique Constitution, art. 47; Angola Constitution, art. 42.

177. Ibid.

178. Hanlon, *Mozambique*, 144.

179. Guinea-Bissau Constitution, art. 62(1).

180. Ibid.

181. Guinea-Bissau Constitution, art. 63 and 65.

182. Washington, Post-War Reconstruction, 142.

183. Guinea-Bissau Constitution, art. 72.

184. Mozambique Constitution, art. 50 and 51.

185. Mozambique Constitution, art. 59.

186. Mozambique Constitution, art. 60.

187. Angola Constitution, art. 49.

188. Angola Constitution, art. 56.

189. Mozambique Constitution, art. 52 and 61; Angola Constitution, art. 51 and 60; Guinea-Bissau Constitution, art. 62(1) and 75.

190. Mozambique Constitution, art. 51; Angola Constitution, art. 57; Guinea-Bissau Constitution, art. 64(1)(m).

191. Mozambique Constitution, art. 51.

192. Guinea-Bissau Constitution, art. 64(2).

193. Angola Constitution, art. 54 and 59.

194. See Machel, *People's Power*, 24 and 36.

195. Washington, "Post-War Reconstruction," 138.

196. Mozambique Constitution, art. 48; Guinea-Bissau Constitution, art. 101.

197. Mozambique Constitution, art. 26 and 28; Angola Constitution, art. 20; Guinea-Bissau Constitution, art. 28.

198. Hanlon, *Mozambique*, 137–38.

199. Machel, *People's Power*, 26.

200. Angola MPLA, *First Congress*, 15.

201. Cabral quoted in Rosemary Galli and Jocelyn Jones, *Guinea-Bissau: Politics, Economics, and Society* (Boulder, Colo.: Lynne Rienner Press, 1987), 60.

202. Henriksen, *Emerging Marxism*, 27.

203. Angola MPLA, *First Congress*, 11.

204. Serapiao, *Mozambique*, 148.

205. Blaustein and Flanz allude to rectification campaigns against persons seen to have joined the party to serve personal interests. Blaustein and Flanz, *Constitutions of the Countries of the World*, vol. 2, *Angola*.

206. Angola Constitution, art. 18.

207. Mozambique Constitution, art. 26.

208. Galli, *Ginnea-Bissau*, 61.

209. Angola MPLA, *First Congress*, 12.

210. Ibid.; Hanlon, *Mozambique*, 137–38.

211. Angola Constitution, art. 21.

212. Mozambique Constitution, art. 37.

213. Ibid.; Guinea-Bissau Constitution, art. 48.

214. Gjerstad, *People in Power*, 105–6.

215. Galli, *Ginnea-Bissau*, 61–62.

216. Henriksen, *Emerging Marxism*, 27.

217. Ibid.

218. Hanlon, *Mozambique*, 122.

219. Henriksen, *Emerging Marxism*, 17. Serapiao, *Mozambique*, 155.

220. Serapiao, *Mozambique*, 155.

221. Galli, *Ginnea-Bissau*, 65.

222. Isaacman, *Report of Subcommittee on Africa*, 50.

223. Saul, *State and Revolution*, 441.

224. Isaacman, *Report of Subcommittee on Africa*, 50.

225. Angola Constitution, art. 75; Guinea-Bissau Constitution, art. 91(2).

226. A. Sachs, "Changing the Terms of the Debate: A Visit to a Popular Tribunal in Mozambique," *Journal of African Law* 28 (1984): 99.

227. Ibid., 101.

228. H. Klug, "The South African Judicial Order and the Future," *Hastings International and Comparative Law Review* 12 (1988): 223.

229. Rudebeck, *Guinea-Bissau*, 139.

230. Somerville, *Angola*, 111.

231. Angola Constitution, art. 75.

232. Klug, "South African Judicial Order," 220.

233. Ibid.

234. Charles S. Rhyne, ed., *Law and Judicial Systems of Nations* (Washington: W.P.T.L.C., 1978), 500–501.

235. For example in Guinea Bissau, it adjudicates on crimes that carry a penalty of imprisonment of up to four years. See Rudebeck, *Guinea-Bissau*, 140; Rhyne, *Law and Judicial Systems*, 501.

236. Guinea-Bissau Constitution, art. 92.

237. Angola Constitution, art. 78.

238. Mozambique Constitution, art. 72.

239. Mozambique Constitution, art. 73; Angola Constitution, art. 76; Guinea-Bissau Constitution, art. 95(2).

240. Somerville, *Angola*, 111.

241. Mozambique Constitution, art. 27.

242. Angola Constitution, art. 78.

243. Isaacman, *Hearing of Subcommittee on Africa*, 45.

244. Ibid., 1.

245. Hanlon, *Mozambique*, 46.

246. Ibid., 49.

247. Jan Marsh, *Stop the War Against Angola and Mozambique: Chronological Account of Acts of Aggression Against the Front Line States by Apartheid South Africa, 1975–1981* (London: Campaign to Stop the War Against Angola and Mozambique, 1981), 5. The destabilization policies have to a greater extent been conducted by the South African government as an attempt to coerce these countries not to provide bases for South African freedom fighters.

248. Saul, *State and Revolution*, 431.

249. Marsh, *Stop the War*, 5.

250. The problems have also been compounded by severe natural disasters, in the case of Mozambique, such as flood and famine. See R. M. Moose, in *Report of Subcommittee on Africa*, 24–27.

251. Guinea-Bissau does not share a common border with South Africa.

252. See generally, *Report of Subcommittee on Africa*, especially 10 and 46.

253. Galli, *Guinea-Bissau*, 67–68.

254. Irving Kaplan, ed., *Angola, A Country Study* (Washington: American University, 1979), 96–97.

255. Serapiao, *Mozambique*, 161.

256. Isaacman, *Report of Subcommittee on Africa*, 35.

257. Serapiao, *Mozambique*, 162.

258. Isaacman, *Report of Subcommittee on Africa*, 38.

259. Machel, *People's Power*, 16.

260. At the constitutional level, they all adopted the unitary state with the express purpose of fighting all manifestations of tribalism or ethnicity. See previous discussion.

261. Serapiao, *Mozambique*, 161.

262. Somerville, *Angola*, 75; Henriksen, *Emerging Marxism*, 8.

263. Richard Sklar, "The Nature of Class Domination in Africa," *Journal of Modern African Studies* 17 (1979): 551–52. Sklar charges the Angolan and Mozambique governments with behaving in an authoritarian fashion and preventing freedom of speech and political association.

264. Galli, *Guinea-Bissau*, 69.

265. Blaustein and Franz, *Constitutions of the Countries of the World, vol.1, Mozambique*, 5. The author has been unsuccessful in obtaining any information on corruption in Angola.

266. Ibid.

267. Henriksen, *Emerging Marxism*, 28.

268. Saul, *State and Revolution*, 441.

269. Serapiao, *Mozambique*, 155; Galli, *Guinea-Bissau*, 65.

270. Henriksen, *Emerging Marxism*, 28.

271. See transcript of "20/20," an ABC News production of 1 March 1990.

272. H. Howe and M. Ottaway, "State Power Consolidation in Mozambique," in Keller and Rothchild, *Afro-Marxist Regimes*, 43.

273. Ibid., 50.

274. Hanlon, *Mozambique*, 3.

275. Ibid., 137.

276. Machel, *People's Power*, 9–10.

277. Ibid., 5–6.

278. One of the arguments for such an approach has been to present candidates to the population to prevent them from resorting to choices based on ethnicity and race. See Hanlon, *Mozambique*, 138.

279. There is evidence of this in all three African Marxist states. See the discussion below.

280. Howe, in Keller and Rothchild, *Afro-Marxist Regimes*, 48; Blaustein and Franz, *Constitutions of the Countries of the World, vol. 11, Guinea-Bissau*, 6–7.

281. Brummel, *Angola*, 130.

282. See generally Galli, *Guinea-Bissau*, especially 76 and 90, and her general accounts of events in Guinea-Bissau.

283. See previous discussion of the legislature only sitting for a few days in a year. The above two limitations have been recognized by the Soviet reformers in their recent restructuring of the Soviet legislature.

284. Washington, "Post-War Reconstruction," 149.

285. For example the USSR under Stalin.

286. Amnesty International has reported incidents of human rights abuses in Mozambique. See Blaustein and Franz, *Constitutions of the Countries of the World, vol. 1, Mozambique*, 6.

287. See previous accounts of detentions and torture on the part of certain government troops. The President subjected the issue to public debate and investigation. See Machel, *People's Power,* 5–10.

288. Galli, *Guinea-Bissau*, 69.

289. Ibid.

290. Washington, "Post-War Reconstruction," 169.

291. Galli, *Guinea-Bissau*, 76 and 90. If the local people cannot elect their own representatives, it is not possible for the people in the region to ensure that decisions are taken in terms of their wishes.

292. Ibid., 71.

293. Hanlon, *Mozambique*, 129.

294. Howe, "State Power," 48.

295. The government needed the cooperation of the people in its economic and resettlement programs and without their cooperation there was less chance of success. Ibid., 47–48.

296. For example a group of people in a party performed a play that poked some fun at the party leadership only to find that they were removed from the party. Somerville, *Angola*, 61.

297. Jurgen Brummel, *Angola: Development Opportunities and Policy Options in the Southern African Area of Conflict* (Bonn: Research Institute of the Friedrich-Ebert-Stiftung, 1984), 16–17.

298. Ibid., 17.

299. Galli, *Guinea-Bissau*, 71.

300. For accounts of government manipulation and coercion in elections, see Ibid., 71.

301. Blaustein and Franz, *Constitutions of the Countries of the World, vol. 11, Guinea Bissau,* 6–7.

302. Galli, *Guinea-Bissau*, 108.

CHAPTER NINE

African Socialism and One-Party States

■ ■ ■

A NEW FRAMEWORK OF government emerged in many African countries shortly after independence. This was one-party government operating on the concept of African socialism. The new framework was presented by the leadership as the most efficient structure for both nation building and economic development, two primary concerns of all the new states.[1] Moreover, it was presented as a democratic model that was an outgrowth of traditional African society[2] and allowed expression of the African personality.[3]

The new model characterized a swing in the pendulum from constitutionalism and limited government to a strong centralized authority. The leadership saw strong government as necessary for a developing country, given the crisis the new nation was facing was similar to an emergency situation.[4] According to African leaders, the one-party state offered a model to unite the population politically beyond traditional, regional, or ethnic boundaries and would achieve rapidly expanding social services.[5] This chapter will investigate the notion of African socialism and examine problems associated with it. It will consider the institutions associated with African one-party states that African governments claim to be *the* model for implementing African socialism. And most important, it will evaluate the features that have come to characterize African one-party states and relate them to democratic theory.

The One-Party State and the Ideology of African Socialism

African socialism has been put forward by various African leaders as the proper basis for the organization of African society. Exactly what African socialism means is not always consistent since different African leaders have provided their own meaning. It is therefore important to appreciate at the outset that African socialism is a particularly vague notion and that it is difficult to define it as a coherent theory. Before considering the interpretations given to the notion by different African leaders, it is worthwhile to consider the few common features articulated by them.

The first claim made by all African leaders is that African socialism is based on the traditions of African society. For example Léopold Senghor of Senegal claims the concept is based on traditional political and cultural values that are rooted in precolonial times.[6] According to former Tanzanian President Julius Nyerere, the foundation and objective of African socialism is drawn from the traditional heritage.[7] The Kenya government under Jomo Kenyatta claimed African socialism belongs to traditional African society.[8] Similarly, Abbe Kanouté of Mali and Muammar al-Qadaffi of Libya speak about African socialism as returning to the original values of past society.[9] It follows without exception that they all projected the solidarity of traditional African society and collective working together as the best basis for the organization and creation of the new order.[10]

The second common feature in all ideas of African socialism is the rejection of the Marxist notion of class struggle.[11] According to most African leaders there is no equivalent of classes or class antagonism in African society.[12] As far as African leaders were concerned, the problem of class was a particularly Western phenomenon. As class conflict did not exist in African society, the problem of government was not to combat it but to prevent it from occurring.[13] Since they saw no social differentiation or stratification in their society, African leaders projected it as one unit. For this reason, the leaders argued, the political organization of society must be effected in terms of a single party that represents the will of all the people united and organized as one.[14] In terms of their vision, political pluralism represented in different political parties amounted to giving credibility to the idea that society was compartmentalized.

African leaders posited the one-party state operating in terms of African socialism as the third path or model for the organization of society.[15] Their thoughts show some departures from liberal and Marxist thought. The rejection of class struggle is the single most important factor differentiating the notion of African socialism from the "scientific" socialism of Marx. In the Marxist idea of class warfare, the dominant party must represent the interests of the working class, whereas the African leaders projected their one party as the party of the nation at large. The emphasis on the group as opposed to the individual as the unit of society is the most important factor differentiating many African leaders' ideas of African socialism from liberal thought. This would suggest that there is an alternate program and theory on which a society could be organized. The difficulty is to categorize African socialism as a coherent ideology because of differences in the leaders' conception of society and the way it should be organized.[16] For example, even though they speak about the community spirit of traditional African society there are considerable differences with respect to the way they interpret the aspect of working together. For the independence leader of Guinea, President Sekou Toure, the party was of absolute importance over the state and the individual. A person did not enjoy any individual rights outside the society of which he or she was a part.[17] For Léopold Senghor, on the other hand, the human being as an individual was more important than a human being as part of a larger entity such as a nation. Individual spiritual and aesthetic values were extremely important and there should be diversity in human aspirations and interests.[18] For Julius Nyerere on the other hand democracy is an ethic which is rooted in society and cannot be separated into just a spiritual or social part.[19]

The vagueness of African socialism[20] is most vividly illustrated in the economic and social visions the leaders offer for the organization of their respective societies. For some socialism meant unqualified emphasis on the public ownership of the means of production, especially land. This was the position particularly of Julius Nyerere.[21] The resources of the country had to be put at the benefit of the entire society. Moreover, the government should operate as a centralized organization. This policy contrasts with the approach of Senghor and Jomo Kenyatta of Kenya who believed that the development of society would be better promoted by private enterprise. Senghor and Kenyatta rejected capitalism and Marxism but still conceptualized human beings in individualistic terms. They claimed private enterprise and the growth of the middle class had a place in African socialism.[22]

The One-Party System and Democracy

The test of democracy is ultimately the extent to which the people participate in the decision-making processes that affect their lives. A one-party state could be compatible with democracy providing the requisite of participation is realized.[23] This conception was popular with many African leaders, whose notion of the single party was a party representing and uniting all sectors of the population.[24] In order for democratic prerequisites to be met, party membership has to be open to the entire population regardless of the leadership's political views or orientation. The party must be a party of the masses as opposed to a vanguard party and synonymous with the nation as opposed to a particular interest.[25] Such practice is in contrast with the Soviet variety of one-party states, which

147

assumed an elitist character with only a fraction of the population being members of the party.

The party must be the expression of the people as opposed to the expression of the leadership. If the party is synonymous with the nation, then nothing can be done without the consent of the people.[26] The institutional arrangements should be of a nature that allows the people to have decisions changed should they disagree with the position of the leadership.[27] The role of leadership and intellectuals must be to educate people and help them understand issues. The decisions, however have to be taken by the people, and the leadership have to act in terms of these decisions. Moreover, there must be mechanisms to remove the leadership from office should the electorate feel they are not carrying out their tasks satisfactorily.

Full intraparty democracy means all members have to be free to contribute input and criticize decisions taken by the leadership.[28] The population must be allowed constant contact with the party leadership (as opposed to the top being a separate and detached part). Indeed, the one-party state in Africa has often been described as a mass party encompassing all sections of the population and allowing the population to exercise a meaningful influence upon the governmental process.[29] It has also been described as the stimulator of projects; the educator of the population; and a vehicle for emancipation.[30]

Thus theoretically one-party states are compatible with democracy providing the institutional arrangements that allow for mass participation.[31] The crucial question is: How does the reality of one-party states in Africa square with the idealized model? And if the idealized model is not present in any country, is it a model that can be achieved and is it worthwhile to strive toward such a model of government?

Different Strategies of One-Party States

THE "LIBERAL" PATH TO DEVELOPMENT:
THE CASE OF KENYA

In the struggle against colonialism almost all the African leaders were critical of socioeconomic inequities, particularly vis à vis colonial settlers. Their rhetoric espoused social justice, equality, and egalitarianism.[32] One would think that the overall orientation of the new constitution and order would be designed to allow for a redress of the vast problems and injustices, but Kenya,[33] for example, introduced a one-party state in a system that overall did not seek to alter the economic structure of the society. Although the party was supreme, there was little state interference in economic affairs.[34] The emphasis instead was on achieving high rates of economic growth through the private sector with the assistance of international capital.[35] Kenya also attempted rapid "Africanization" by replacing white and Asian personnel with Africans.[36]

INSTITUTIONS OF STATE
PRIOR TO MULTIPARTY ELECTIONS[37]

Kenya previously had a set of state institutions including a legislature whose members were elected by the population. All members of the legislature were members of the single party. There was electoral competition in that citizens had a choice of electing different candidates from the party. In this sense Kenyans participated in the election process insofar as they were able to elect representatives to the legislature.[38] The more important enquiry is the nature of the party, its relationship to the legislature, and the relationship between the different levels of government and the population at large.

The party did not in any way serve as a vehicle to stimulate participation. Both the character of the party and the practice of government departed in significant ways from the idealized model. The party had no ideology and for all practical purposes as an organization was nonexistent.[39] Over the years power had swung from the legislature to the executive, particularly the president. Little attention was given to the views of the legislature.[40] The power of the president was more like that of a king with nepotism and the dispensing of favors to family and friends rife.[41] The leaders did not see participation in the party and government as an end in itself, necessary for freedom to thrive. Neither the citizens nor the delegates elected to the legislature participated in formulating goals and objectives. Policy matters were rarely debated, and the president exercised decision-making powers on his own.[42] Hopkins asserts that in many instances executive actions were taken impulsively or even capriciously.[43] As the party was nonfunctional, there was no way to obtain accountability of the executive to the party or to the legislature. The legislature was more an ornamental body to provide legitimacy to the system.[44]

The consequence of the decline in the power of the legislature was that (discretionary) power shifted to civil servants and the bureaucracy. The state could be characterized as an administrative state as opposed to a representative state. Being part of the administrative machinery of the state conferred status as well as the power to distribute resources and patronage.[45] Being dismissed from one's job from the state machinery meant the loss not only of power to dispense favors, but also loss of a car, house, medical benefits, and various other allowances not obtainable in other employment.[46] Consequently, those who obtained coveted jobs were indebted to the state and would work to hold on to the jobs for as

149

long as possible. In many instances the obtaining of rewards and jobs was along ethnic lines and patronage.[47]

Not surprisingly, electoral competition was also conducted along ethnic lines.[48] This had the consequence of increasing ethnocentrism and polarization.[49] While the Kenyan system provided for electoral competition, like all one-party states the candidates needed the approval of the party, which entailed the approval of the top party leadership.[50] The electoral competition was between competing elites, and invariably those elected to office were those with the greatest resources. Once elected, a patron-client relationship between those at the top and those at the bottom prevailed with representatives trying to get the maximum from the system for their own clients.[51] In effect, the elections amounted to the individual making a choice about which candidate to elect as the patron. The electoral competition might be very intense.[52] It was in such circumstances that ethnicity became more salient in the elections. At the same time, there was no emphasis on reducing class disparities in the society. Studies have shown that class inequality in Kenya has increased since independence.[53]

A dictatorial pattern of leadership is characteristic of most African one-party states that have adopted the "liberal" path to development.[54] All of them show a tendency to limit democratic participation. Since there is a lack of democratic procedures, there is no way for the majority to check corruption or to achieve a redress of socioeconomic inequalities. Several one-party states such as Kenya and Malawi have moved toward a multi-party system recently.

THE "SOCIALIST" RECORD IN AFRICA

Other one-party states such as Algeria, Ghana, Mali, and Guinea claimed to have adopted the socialist option. In many instances, the leadership spoke about nonexploitation and equality. But all "socialist" one-party states in Africa have suffered the same criticisms of not having a democratic party through which the masses can make decisions.[55] The result is the familiar pattern of civil servants who occupy the top positions and became a social class of their own.[56] Rule by civil servants is characterized by corruption, nepotism, and oppression.[57]

The denial of democratic participation was often implicit in the program of the leadership. For example, both Sekou Toure[58] in Guinea and Kwame Nkrumah[59] in Ghana spoke about the general society being directed and controlled by the center through the single party. The single party was to be the guide of the nation and should permeate all aspects of life, be it trade unions or state administrations.[60] In both instances the principle of democratic centralism was supposed to be the guiding principle in the conduct of affairs.[61] In principle, all party officials were elected by members at the local level, and all members of the party at the local level were free to discuss all projects openly and freely. The views of the local party members were in turn communicated to the upper level of the party,[62] which took decisions based on the wishes of the rank-and-file members. As soon as a decision was made, all members had to abide by it without dissent. Like the Soviet model, the democratic element of inner party discussion was never practiced, as most decisions were taken at the top and handed down to the lower levels for implementation.[63] The reality was little participation from the people, and freedom of expression was often viewed as counterrevolutionary.[64]

An overview of most one-party states in Africa that proclaimed themselves socialist reveals a party that resembled the Soviet Stalinist model of organization. It is a model theoretically premised on mass participation. At the level of reality all important decisions were made at the top by the party bosses or one boss. The system acted to curtail participation with the assumption that the leadership was endowed with superior intellect and foresight in the best interest of the people.[65]

The most distinctive and committed attempt to introduce grassroots participation and economic restructuring was the Tanzanian experiment under Julius Nyerere. Nyerere saw his path to development as an outgrowth of traditional African society, which he called *ujaama*, derived from Swahili and meaning familyhood. There were several aspects to Nyerere's philosophy that merit consideration.

Tanzania conceived the role of government in positive terms and called on it to be active in the affairs of the community.[66] The function of the state was to work toward the realization of socioeconomic goals such as trade, agriculture, education, and health services.[67] Since the state was given responsibility to achieve these goals, central planning was essential.[68]

The Tanzanian system was ideologically committed to social and economic equality. Accordingly, all property, particularly land, belongs to the community and could not be owned for private purposes. Individuals had the right to use the land and derive benefits from it, but the right did not extend beyond this.[69] Flowing from the ideological commitment to economic and social equality, great emphasis was placed on the elimination of social and economic disparities.[70] To give practical effect to this equality, no person could have a surplus (in material aspects) if another individual was lacking in material needs.[71]

Nyerere emphasized the worth of the individual and the importance of individual participation. The right of the individual to take part in the affairs of the community and to voice opinions, the security of the individual's person, and the absence of hunger, disease, and poverty were collectively considered freedom.[72] For Nyerere there could be no freedom if any one of these elements was missing.[73] Nyerere saw the participation of people in decision-making processes as an element of development,[74] which cannot be measured in material terms such as an increase in output.[75] There could only be development if the people were developing, which for Nyerere was measured in terms of the people making decisions for themselves.[76]

The Tanzanian system contrasted with Kenya's (and all other African socialist one-party states) in significant ways. First, there was a leadership commitment to people's participation and equality. Second, the institutions created provided for greater accountability of the leadership, thus preventing a burgeoning administrative state prone to corruption. Third, the Tanzanian model had a strict leadership code, which regulated party and state leaders. Finally, the system showed an absence of subnationalist and other centrifugal tendencies that have erupted in so many other parts of the continent. Many practical lessons can be drawn from the Tanzanian experience.[77]

Eschewing the path of elevating a single and glorified cult personality over and beyond all other institutions was another important lesson. Undoubtedly, independence leader Julius Nyerere commanded a tremendous amount of respect among his people. However, he refused to have himself proclaimed president for life, and was one of the few African leaders who voluntarily stepped down from office. Moreover, he instituted constitutional reforms limiting the tenure of presidential office to only two terms.

The Tanzanian one-party system was an exception with certain unique variables absent in the South African political landscape, which adds to the unattractiveness of the one-party model. First, unlike Tanzania, there is no single nationalist movement in South Africa. With manifold political tendencies, a one-party state in South Africa would compromise democracy, as it would entail many parties having to compromise their positions to the views of the dominant faction. The experiences of Africa have shown that in the absence of voluntary compliance the only way this can be done is by coercion. Indeed, there is evidence of coercion employed by officials of the Tanzanian state when they encountered resistance to their resettlement policies.[78] Second, Tanzanian development was more a product of the leadership of Nyerere and his commitment to certain ideals. This factor always has to be borne in mind. The Tanzanian experience could have been very different. It is therefore not sufficient to rely on a benevolent leader to act in the best interests of the country. Although the quality of leadership is important for the success of most orders, it is essential to establish proper institutions to promote mass participation and control of leadership. To their credit, the leadership in Tanzania also recognized the limitations in their model and abolished the one party-state, replacing it in 1990 with a constitution that provides for multiparty elections and contains a bill of rights.

African One-Party States and Social Transformation

One party-states were generally characterized by one-man rule and a swollen bureaucracy that became the de facto machinery responsible for implementation of state decisions. The overall scenario was a lack of democracy or democratic institutions, economic corruption, and stagnation.

In many instances power was de facto or de jure centralized on an individual.[79] Almost every restriction on the ability of the leader to act was done away with. The party leader reveled in becoming a cult personality,[80] the legitimacy of such action being ostensibly based on traditional practices.[81] Under such systems the bureaucracy often came to exert a greater influence (in comparison with the legislature and the party) in the lives of the ordinary people.

In other instances a functioning party acted together with strong personal leadership. The party, however, operated more like a machine from top to bottom.[82] Power resided in the upper echelons of the leadership and the party became the controlling agent in the state. The expression of the party being the supreme organ in the state was found in many African one-party constitutions.[83] The institutions of the state became secondary to those of the party. Accompanying subordination of the state to the party was the practice of a few people at the top levels of the party controlling everyone else. The people at the top stultify all criticism to protect their positions. Thus, intraparty democracy declined and became nonexistent.[84] Moreover, party membership was restricted to a selected group of people. General political participation was reduced.

One-party states in Africa have been a deliberate policy by the elite to keep participation in the affairs of the party and state as low as possible. The decline in participation occurs regardless of the ideological nature of the system, that is, regardless of whether the system professes a socialist or liberal capitalist philosophical orientation.[85] In many instances the policy of limited participation is defended on the grounds that what the people need is not democracy but guidance from the top.[86] The above justification is a departure from the original reasons given for the adoption of the one-party state as a vehicle to achieve the consensus found in traditional settings. The likening of the one-party state to custom by many African leaders is erroneous in conception and practice.[87] Where a society is organized around a family, clan, or small group, communal consensus could be achieved in the context of the group by discussing things. However, in the context of a large society, particularly a nation-state, a single party is more likely to institutionalize elite domination.[88]

153

One of the primary arguments presented for the abolition of Western constitutions inherited at independence was that they placed too many limitations on the government of a new nation. The institutions of the one-party state sought to do away with the restrictions to "release the brakes" so the country could achieve vital socioeconomic programs. While the colonial institutions may have been inappropriate for the new nation, the new institutions have in most instances resulted in the personal accumulation of power in the hands of a single individual[89] or a small group of people.[90] The party has become subordinate to the elite.[91] Where power is concentrated in an individual, the single leader becomes like a demigod, portraying himself as the symbol of the state and wishing to cling to power for life.[92] The pattern in independent Africa rarely allows for a peaceful transition of power from one leader to the next.[93] The leader who "led" the country into independence is still in power or remains in power until his death. In other instances, power changes by virtue of a military coup.[94]

With the elevation of the party over the state, the role of the legislature is ornamental. Members of the legislature generally have to be approved by the party leader and for the most part the "representatives" are selected in secrecy.[95] Since the choice of party candidates is made by the leadership at the top, elections are merely a ritual.[96]

BUREAUCRACY, WASTE, AND CORRUPTION

The ministries or the bureaucracy collectively preside over a situation of great corruption. Vast amounts of money are spent on prestige projects such as monuments, hotels, and mansions for the leaders.[97] Being a member of one of the ministries or bureaucracies presents the opportunity to get rich. It is the entry to obtain fancy cars, robes, and other forms of ostentation.[98] At times corruption is so great that necessary services such as medical care or access to jobs can only be obtained by a bribe or knowing someone in high office.[99] Those jobs that are available reward workers disproportionately to their services, with the ministers and bureaucrats taking the lion's share.[100] The situation that most of Africa under one-party government finds itself in is a far cry from the social values and equality that the nationalist leaders espoused during the struggle for liberation.

THE ONE-PARTY STATE AND SOCIOECONOMIC CHANGE

Despite a professed capitalist or socialist orientation one-party states have not achieved socioeconomic restructuring of their respective societies. Almost all are poverty stricken and ridden with corruption.[101] African societies presently rank among the most unequal in the world.[102] The maldistribution of wealth is most marked between the bureaucracy and political elite and the rest of the population.[103] The elite invariably utilize the institution of the one-party state to enhance their own political and economic interests. The original argument of most African socialist leaders was that African societies were not characterized by different classes. And, in fact, given the low level of development in most of Africa, it is possible to argue that African society did not have the class divisions known to European society.[104] However, contrary to the classical Marxist idea of economic power conferring political power, in the African situation political power is utilized by the elite to further their enrichment.[105] Simultaneously, the gap between those in power and the rest of the people increases.[106]

THE ONE-PARTY STATE AND NATIONAL UNITY

The task of nation building is clearly a priority in African countries, though admittedly, the forms of state and constitution at independence in many instances were not conducive to the process. There are countries where there is now less national strife with the advent of the one-party state.[107] However, in most instances traditional symbols and the single party have been used to cement the rule of a cult personality. In the process, force and authoritarianism were employed to stamp out any manifestations of dissent, which included subnationalist tendencies.[108] In such a situation it cannot be said that the national problem has in any way been solved. The situation was merely held in check through authoritarian rule. The above situation is analogous to the practice in the Soviet Union where for many decades subnationalism was suppressed by the single party.[109]

The African one-party state in practice has not been the answer for nation building. The aspect of nation building and the maintenance of the one-party become blurred and the argument for unity invariably is a call for conformity.[110] National unity is elusive in a situation where one has political elites who are more like patrons dispensing favors to their own family, lineage, or ethnic group.[111] It is conceivable that a lessening of the stranglehold of the party could result in ethnic ruptures similar to those that occurred in the Soviet Union.

INDEPENDENCE OF THE JUDICIARY
AND PROTECTION OF INDIVIDUAL RIGHTS

An independent judiciary is popular in Western constitutional systems because of the belief that there is a need for an independent agency to arbitrate between the executive and legislative branches. In societies subject to a bill of rights, the judiciary fulfills the role of protecting the rights of individual citizens. In this respect the judiciary is the instrument that ensures both the division and limitation of government power central to the principles of constitutionalism. We saw that many of the independence constitutions attempted to provide an independent judiciary to arbitrate between the different branches of government as well as to protect individual rights. In African one-party states, however, with the blurring of the distinctions between the single party and the government there is less likelihood of a conflict between the executive and legislative branches of government. In such a situation the judiciary does not really have the problem of mediating conflicts between the two branches of government, which brings us to the second function of the judiciary, namely, to act as a bulwark for the protection of important individual rights.

Protecting individual rights requires both the judicial system and the powers of the judiciary to be of a nature to allow the judiciary to perform this task. For example, under the former Soviet system the judiciary was by and large an extension of the party and its function was to dispense justice in terms of the ideological orientation of the party. Group rights were seen as more important than individual rights. The judiciary did not have the power to defend individual rights against the party or its conception of what constitutes the common good for society.

African one-party states showed considerable variation regarding judicial independence. Some states saw the role of the judiciary in terms identical to the Soviet model and called on the judiciary to dispense justice in terms of the ruling (single) party's conception of justice. This was the practice in Algeria, Mali, Guinea, Benin, and Togo.[112] Some even went so far as to abolish any notion of an independent judiciary and considered the judiciary as ordinary civil servants.[113] Judges were expected to be militant in their support of state policies. Thus the judiciary was not seen as a limit on government power but more as an agent to carry out the programs and policies of the government.[114]

Other African one-party states encouraged an independent judiciary. Such was the case in Tanzania, Kenya, and Botswana. Once appointed the judiciary had security of tenure and were independent in their decision-making powers. The government sometimes call on the judiciary to exercise their powers in "terms of the assumptions and aspirations of the society in which they live."[115] This should be seen as a call on the judiciary to free themselves from the previous order and consider the realities and aspirations of a society free from colonial rule. However, in the main the judges are still free to decide matters independently of the government or party.

Despite the security of tenure and noninterference by the state in the decisions of the judiciary in some states, the judiciary in most African states have not been made the bulwark for the protection of individual rights. In no African one-party state does the judiciary's ambit of powers extend to protecting fundamental rights as an absolute value. The judicial role in most instances is seen in positivistic terms. Independence of the judiciary operates in the main in the British tradition in that the courts although independent cannot question an act of the legislature. The result is an independent judiciary existing alongside abuses and torture, which in many instances is sanctioned by the law. Consequently, many one-party states have been characterized by coercion, torture, detention, and other gross violations of human rights.[116] A few African one-party states have a bill of rights embodied in the constitution,[117] and where it exists it can act as a bulwark against arbitrary government and prevent torture and ensure the right to life and liberty. However, within the context of a one-party state, certain freedoms such as freedom of association, expression, and assembly would be limited.

CONSTITUTIONALISM AND SOCIALIST IDEOLOGY

The one-party state was postulated by African leaders as an alternative state framework to solve their nations' problems. Its ideological underpinnings in most instances rejected the principles of Western constitutionalism,[118] as well as the Marxist notion of class conflict. It is arguable that a division of power and an acknowledgment of the class conflict in African countries are both inimical to the concerns of the present rulers.[119]

In practice African one-party states manifest the worst from both Western and former Soviet models. In the first instance, the model is geared toward enhancing the interests of an elite in the economic atmosphere of laissez-faire.[120] However, without the economic infrastructure and basis of the Western system, the interests of the elite are served by having access to political power and the distribution of favors by controlling the bureaucracy. And African one-party states depart from Western models in another very fundamental way: Western legal institutions allow for political pluralism and the possibility of removal or rotation of elites.

The way the elite cling to power, their repression of all opposition and dissent, and their belief in the supremacy of the party (although in the African context this is a greater fiction) is a lesson from the former Soviet model. In African countries where the party is functional, its structure is more typical of the Soviet example of a vanguard party despite the claim that the party represents all sections of the population. The restriction of party membership to a select group of individuals is also based on the Soviet pattern. Like the Soviet model, the party in most one-party African states has been given prominence over all state institutions.[121] The personalization of power and its concentration in the hands of a single individual are akin to the Soviet model under Stalin.

ADEQUACY OF THE FRAMEWORK

African socialism as an ideology was not a discovery of the past but has proved to be eclectic; in the final analysis it amounts to a rationalization for holding on to power. The point has been made that there are many important values in traditional African society (such as humanism and community spirit). However, the notion of African socialism is not a coherent idea and in effect has shown to be just what different leaders feel is best for the interests of the leaders.

There is a fundamental error in the one common assumption that all the strands of African socialism share, namely, their rejection of the class nature of their society. Even if African leaders believed that their societies were free of class divisions at independence, their ideology and institutions allowed for the creation of a minority middle class constituted in the party and bureaucracy. Moreover, ignoring the nature of the class divisions in different African countries, it is clearly erroneous to classify South African society as being free of class divisions. It is important to recognize and accept the class divisions in African societies as something that must be remedied. Addressing class divisions goes beyond the constitutional debate, yet it is still part of it. The point has been repeatedly made in this study that institutions are important in enhancing the values people hold important.

The arguments for a one-party state may have an element of common sense to them, namely, the need for Africans to put their energy and resources together into a solid unit to work for the collective interests. In a situation of "perfect" goodwill and good leadership, it is possible that it may be the best framework. At this stage, however, it is necessary to distinguish between abstract thought and political reality. At the level of practice the lessons of independent African countries have demonstrated that the institutions of one-party states are weak or nonexistent and rely too much on the leadership, with no mechanism of control. The potential for corruption and waste of energy is present in all forms of political structures, but the one-party framework seems universally prone to such practices.[122]

The one-party state has proved incapable of meeting the socioeconomic challenges of African society, regardless of whether the country has followed a "socialist" or "capitalist" path to development. If socialism is conceived as an ideology of economic equality, this equality cannot be attained by dictatorial means from above. Most of the constitutions drafted at independence did not enjoy legitimacy, as the people did not participate in drawing them up.[123] With the exception of Tanzania, not a single one-party state in Africa was voted into office with the consent of the majority.[124] In some instances where there have been referendums, as in Nkrumah's Ghana, the results were rigged.[125]

Options for a future South Africa will have to take into account the relationship between structures and tasks. The problems of Africa and those that a future South African government will have to face have been identified. Reliance should not be placed on leaders and parties as the avenue to achieve the goals of the society.[126] Admittedly, caliber of leadership is crucial to any country, particularly a new nation. However, the dilemma in independent Africa has been a failure to create boundaries between the leadership and the party on the one hand, and the state on the other.[127] The institutions of the state are made secondary to that of the party. The one-party state degenerates into a situation of unqualified power where a small segment controls all aspects of life be it political, economic, education, or the media.[128] Centralizing authority with concentration of power in the long run leads to instability.[129] It is almost inevitable that there will be instability with so many sections of the population having no access to political and economic power. There is no democratic way for citizens to make their needs felt, or to change the government.[130] The only avenue is the overthrow of the existing government. The most powerful institution has been the military, which in many countries across Africa has intervened and overthrown existing powers,[131] although this has not necessarily been for the betterment of the people.

There is a need for a future South Africa to erect an appropriate institutional framework that goes beyond entrusting power to political elites.[132] This is not to posit the notion of autonomy of the state, the idea that the state can exist as some neutral body detached from society, because the government must be the representative and agent of the people. What South Africa needs are institutions that protect democratic decision making and a system based on voluntarism as opposed to coercion.

REFERENCES

1. Arnold Rivkin, *Nation-building in Africa: Problems and Prospects*, ed. John H. Morrow (New Brunswick, N.J.: Rutgers University Press, 1969), 48.

2. Denis V. Cowen, *The Foundations of Freedom, with Special Reference to Southern Africa* (Cape Town: Oxford University Press, 1961), 11.

3. Rita Hinden, *Africa and Democracy* (London: Encounter, 1962), 3.

4. Nwabueze, *Presidentialism*, 234.

5. See Basil Davidson, *Crossroads in Africa* (Nottingham: Spokesman Books, 1980), 131; Also see Nwabueze, *Presidentialism*, 89.

6. Onesimo Silveira, *Africa South of the Sahara: Party Systems and Ideologies of Socialism* (Stockholm: Raben & Sjogren, 1976), 112.

7. J. Nyerere, "Ujaama: The Basis of African Socialism," in Robert I. Rotberg and John Barratt, eds., *Conflict and Compromise in South Africa* (Lexington, Mass.: Lexington Books, 1980), 246.

8. This claim was made in a government paper put out just after independence. See paragraphs 7–11 of Republic of Kenya, *Sessional Paper Number 10* (1963): 5.

9. P. F. Gonidec, *African Politics* (Boston: M. Nijhoff, 1981), 132–33.

10. At the level of reality, working together and consensual spirit are lacking in most African one-party states. In the later section we will show that the practices of African one-party states depart from the idealistic model of traditional African society.

11. Leslie Rubin and Brian Weinstein, *Introduction to African Politics: A Continental Approach* (New York: Praeger, 1977), 199.

12. See Tanzanian former President Julius Nyerere, *Ujaama: Essays in Socialism*, 11. See also views of Sekou Touré of Guinea and Léopold Senghor of Senegal, in Gonidec, *African Politics*, 129, 144.

13. Busia, *Africa in Search of Democracy*, 78.

14. Silveira, *South of the Sahara*, 100.

15. Gonidec, *African Politics*, 129.

16. See Silveira, *South of the Sahara*, chap. 6–8 for the different thoughts of Touré, Senghor, and Nyerere.

17. Ibid., 99, 121.

18. Ibid., 111–12.

19. Ibid., 123–24.

20. Simmons R. Leigh, "Tanzanian Socialism: A Critical Assessment," Ph.D. diss., Howard University, 1985, 5; Ivan I. Potekhin, *African Problems: Analysis of Eminent Soviet Scientist* (Moscow: Nauka Publishing, 1968), 108.

21. J. Nyerere, *Freedom and Unity* (London: Oxford University Press, 1967), 167.

22. Silveira, *South of the Sahara*, 118, 142.

23. Breytenbach, "One Party Regimes and Majority Rule," *Bulletin of the Africa Institute* 15 (1977): 18.

24. Davidson, *Which Way Africa*, 131.

25. Cowen, *Foundations of Freedom*, 8.

26. Sekou Touré quoted in Gonidec, *African Politics*, 156.

27. Ibid.

28. Irving L. Markovitz, *Power and Class in Africa: An Introduction to Change and Conflict in African Politics* (Englewood Cliffs, N.J.: Prentice-Hall, 1977), 296.

29. Immanuel M. Wallerstein, *Africa, The Politics of Independence: An Interpretation of Modern African History* (New York: Vintage Books, 1961), 96.

30. Gwendolen M. Carter, *African One-Party States* (Ithaca, N.Y.: Cornell University Press, 1962), 9.

31. In the discussion below it is argued that there are problems with the ideal model that make it difficult if not impossible to achieve democracy within its framework.

32. See Jaramogi Oginga Odinga, *Not Yet Uhuru: The Autobiography of Oginga Odinga* (London: Heinemann, 1967), 362–63; Markovitz, *Power and Class*, 200.

33. To this list can be added the Côte d'Ivoire, Malawi, and Zaire.

34. A. Gupta, "Political System and the One-Party States of Tropical Africa," *India Quarterly* 31:2 (1975): 182.

35. Henry Bienen, *Kenya: The Politics of Participation and Control* (Princeton, N.J.: Princeton University Press, 1974), 3; Joel D. Barkan and John J. Okumu, *Politics and Public Policy in Kenya and Tanzania* (New York: Praeger, 1979), 10.

36. R. F. Hopkins, "The Influence of the Legislature on Development Strategy: The Case of Kenya and Tanzania," in Joel Smith and Lloyd D. Musolf, eds., *Legislatures in Development: Dynamics of Change in New and Old States* (Durham, N.C.: Duke University Press, 1979), 159.

37. Kenya had multiparty elections for the first time in over a decade in December 1992.

38. Barkan and Okumu, *Politics and Public Policy*, 29.

39. There is no framework to link the population to the party. Dirk Berg-Schlosser, *The Social and Economic Basis of Politics in Kenya: A Structural and Cultural Analysis* (Ann Arbor, Mich.: University of Michigan Microfilm, 1979), 654.

40. Cherry J. Gertzel, *The Politics of Independent Kenya, 1963–1968* (Evanston, Ill.: Northwestern University Press, 1970), 150.

41. Bienen, *Kenya*, 77–78.

42. Journal of African Marxists, *Independent Kenya* (London: Zed Press, 1982), 15.

43. Hopkins, "Development Strategies," 168.

44. Bienen, *Kenya*, 77–78.

45. Susanne D. Mueller, *Government Opposition in Kenya, 1966–1969* (Boston: African Studies Center, Boston University, 1983), 16.

46. Ibid.

47. Berg-Schlosser, *Politics in Kenya*, 655.

48. Bienen, *Kenya*, 107.

49. Ibid., 99.

50. Gertzel, *Independent Kenya*, 155.

51. See Barkan and Okumu, *Politics and Public Policy*, 28.

52. Berg-Schlosser, *Politics in Kenya*, 662.

53. Barkan and Okumu, *Politics and Public Policy*, 21. In our discussion below the argument will be made that the increase in inequalities is largely due to corruption and an inefficient bureaucracy, both of which are greatly attributable to the lack of viable state structures that make officials of the state accountable to the population. Being elected to political office is an opportunity to get rich.

54. For example, Malawi under Hastings K. Banda, Zaire under Mobuto Seso Seke, and Tunisia under Habib Bourguiba. In not all the one-party states that have adopted the liberal path to development does the leader behave like a dictator. Houphouët-Boigny is a case in point. See Davidson, *Which Way Africa*, 111.

55. Ibid., 181, 197.

56. For examples of these patterns particularly in Ghana and Mali, see generally C. Meillasoux, "A Class Analysis of the Bureaucratic Process in Mali," *Journal of Development Studies* 6:2 (1970). Hinden, "Africa and Democracy," 96.

57. For example, in Guinea there was great emphasis on non-exploitation and equality. However, the element of democracy and accountability was never a characteristic feature in the implementation of these ideals. Ibid.

58. C. Andrain, "The Political Thought of Sekou Touré" in W. A. E. Skurnik, ed., *African Political Thought: Lumumba, Nkrumah, Touré* (Denver: University of Denver, 1968), 121–22.

59. Kwame Nkrumah, *Africa Must Unite* (New York: Praeger, 1963), 129.

60. Kaba, "Guinean Politics: A Critical Overview," *The Journal of Modern African Studies* 15:1 (1977): 31.

61. Ibid.

62. See, "Party and State Relations in Guinea" in Butler and Castagno, *BU Papers on Africa*, 330.

63. W. Grundy, "The Political Ideology of Kwame Nkrumah," in Skurnik, *African Political Thought*, 81.

64. Butler and Castagno, *BU Papers on Africa*, 330.

65. Andrain, "Political Thought," 123.

66. Julius K. Nyerere, *Man and Development* (Dar es Salaam: Oxford University Press, 1974), 14.

67. Ibid.

68. Robert I. Rotberg and John Barratt, eds., *Conflict and Compromise in South Africa* (Lexington, Mass.: Lexington Books, 1980), 10.

69. Potholm, *Theory and Practice*, 74.

70. J. D. Barkan, "Comparing Politics and Public Policy in Kenya and Tanzania," in Barkan & Okumu, *Politics and Public Policy*, 10.

71. R. F. Hopkins, "The Influence of the Legislature on Development Strategy: The Case of Kenya and Tanzania," in Smith and Musolf, *Legislatures in Development*, 158. The reality is all property and major industry are owned by the state and officials of the state are responsible for distributing excess resources.

72. Nyerere, *Man and Development*, 25.

73. Ibid.

74. Barkan, "Comparing Politics," 27–28.

75. Nyerere, *Freedom and Unity,* 26.

76. Ibid., 27.

77. This is not to suggest replicating the model in South Africa. See discussion why the model should not be replicated below.

78. J. Boesen, *Tanzania: From Ujaama to Villagisation,* Institute for Development Research Papers A.76.7 (1976); D. E. McHenry, Jr., *Tanzania's Ujaama Villages: The Implementation of a Rural Development Strategy* (Berkeley and Los Angeles: University of California Press, 1979), 115.

79. For example, as in Kenya, Ethiopia under Selassie, Côte d'Ivoire. See Bienen, *Kenya,* 75–76. To this list can be added Malawi and Zaire.

80. Nwabueze, *Constitutionalism,* 159.

81. Nwabueze, *Presidentialism,* 105. See previous discussion in chapter 3 where such arguments are refuted. In the traditional setting a leader could not act in an autocratic manner, or if he did it was contrary to traditional norms.

82. Ibid. Countries like Guinea, Mali under Keita, and Ghana under Nkrumah can be added to this category.

83. Gonidec, *African Politics,* 143, provides the examples of Algeria, and formerly Sudan. To this list can be added Tanzania, Tunisia, Kenya, and Malawi.

84. Rubin and Weinstein, *Introduction to African Politics,* 187.

85. See generally Potholm, *Theory and Practice,* for a detailed country-by-country commentary on the practices of various African one-party states. See also Markovitz, *Power and Class in Africa,* 298.

86. Gupta, "One-Party States," 167.

87. Busia, *Africa in Search of Democracy,* 27.

88. B. Davidson, "Pluralism in Colonial African Societies" in Leo Kuper and M. G. Smith, eds., *Pluralism in Africa* (Berkeley: University of California Press, 1969), 236.

89. L. Gray Cowen, *The Dilemmas of African Independence* (New York: Walker, 1968), 16.

90. Brun-Otto Bryde, *The Politics and Sociology of African Legal Development* (Frankfurt am Main: Metzner, 1976), 27.

91. Ibid.

92. Nwabueze, *Constitutionalism,* 222.

93. The transition in Tanzania is a noticeable exception.

94. Bryde, *African Legal Development,* 23.

95. Gonidec, *African Politics,* 142–43, 175–76.

96. Nwabueze, *Presidentialism,* 243.

97. Rivkin, *Nation-Building in Africa,* 58.

98. Ronald E. Wraith and Edgar Simpkins, *Corruption in Developing Countries* (New York: Norton, 1964), 15.

99. Ibid., 17.

100. For example, the top 5 percent of the population in Cote d'Ivoire obtained 29 percent of the national income, 64 percent of the national income went to 20 percent of the population in Sierra Leone, and the bottom 40 percent of the population in Gabon received only 8 percent of the national income, while the bottom 40 percent of the population received only 14 percent of the income in Nigeria. See studies reported in Markovitz, *Power and Class in Africa,* 206–209. See also, Davidson, *Which Way Africa,* 135.

101. Davidson, *Which Way Africa,* 116–17.

102. J. D. Barkan, "On Comparing East African Political Systems," in Barkan and Okumu, *Politics and Public Policy,* 20.

103. Ibid.

104. See R. Miliband, *Marxism and Politics,* 108.

105. Ibid., 108–9.

106. Davidson, *Which Way Africa*, 148.

107. For example, in both Kenya and Zaire. In the latter instance (in terms of the independence constitution) there was greater ethnic strife, which led to civil war in the former Congo.

108. A good example of this is found in the use of symbolism in what the Zairean leader Mobuto calls "authenticite," which in the final analysis amounts to a call for compliance. See Ronen, *Democracy and Pluralism*, 587–88.

109. See our discussion of the Soviet Union in chapter 8.

110. Rivkin, *Nation-building in Africa*, 50.

111. See Aloo Ojuka and William Ochieng, eds., *Politics and Leadership in Africa* (Kampala: East African Literature Bureau, 1975), 267–68. The authors argue that the concept of tribalism is a mental concept used by leaders to point to the problems of the country that have their source elsewhere. The problem of tribalism lingers on for so long because of an absence of egalitarian policies and lack of will to effect equality in the economic sphere, which is the major source of the problem.

112. Gonidec, *African Politics*, 215–17.

113. This is the practice in Togo. Ibid., 217.

114. Austin Amissah, *The Contribution of the Courts to Government: A West African View* (Oxford: Clarendon Press, 1981), 35.

115. Nyerere, "Freedom and Unity," 112.

116. See previous discussions of Kenya. See also Amnesty International, *Amnesty International Report* (1979): 12–13, 24–25; Amnesty International, *Political Killings by Government* (1983): 44–50; F. Ajami, "The Fate of Non-Alignment," *Foreign Affairs* 59 (1980–81): 366, 379.

117. For example of Zambia, Sierra Leone, and Tanzania, see F. Moderne, "Human Rights and Postcolonial Constitutions in Sub-Saharan Africa" in Louis Henkin and Albert J. Rosenthal, eds., *Constitutionalism and Rights: The Influence of the United States Constitution Abroad* (New York: Columbia University Press, 1990), 330, 334.

118. Silveira, *South of the Sahara*, 16.

119. Ibid.

120. However, modern Western industrial systems do not experience the same magnitude of socioeconomic problems, as their productive capacities enable them simultaneously to fulfill the distributive or social welfare function to alleviate the severest problems.

121. For example, Gonidec refers to the constitutions of Angola (Article 31) and Algeria (Article 94). To this list can be added Côte d'Ivoire, Tanzania, and a host of other countries including Zaire, Chad, Mali, Gabon, Malawi, Mozambique, and Guinea-Bissau.

122. Rivkin, *Nation-building in Africa*, 57.

123. See Nwabueze, *Presidentialism*, esp. chap. 8, 221–25.

124. Busia, *Africa in Search of Democracy*, 123–25, 134.

125. Ibid., 126.

126. The one-party states that have been most successful in terms of providing for mild forms of participation are those where the leaders had a commitment to the welfare of the population, such as Tanzania under Julius Nyerere. However, even the Tanzanians changed their form of government from a one-party state to a multiparty state in 1990.

127. Rivkin, *Nations by Design*, 16.

128. Ibid., 18.

129. R. Charlton, "Political Science and the Problem of Post-Independence Institutional Change," *Civilizations* 28:1/2 (1978), 113.

130. Tanzania is the notable exception which perhaps accounts for the greater stability alluded to.

131. Silveira, *South of the Sahara*, 82.

132. Rivkin makes the point that what is missing in Africa is an adequate institutional framework. See Rivkin, *Nations by Design*, 6.

CHAPTER TEN

South African Political Organizations

■ ■ ■

I N THIS CHAPTER we analyze and compare the constitutional options and scenarios of the various political organizations and movements in South Africa. Significant developments have taken place in the Congress for a Democratic South Africa (CODESA) and no doubt will continue to take place since the holding of the 27 April 1994 elections. We will relate the historical evolution of constitutional thought and notions of democracy of the various political organizations and evaluate the way the respective parties have historically looked at the national problem, the socioeconomic structure, and democracy, and their perspectives on how to deal with these issues. The discussion will be limited to constitutional scenarios of political organizations/movements (or their visions for a future society) as opposed to programs of individuals. Moreover, the discussion will be limited to the programs of organizations historically opposed to apartheid and politically left of the present government.

CODESA

In December 1991, nineteen political organizations met in a historic conference called Congress for a Democratic South Africa to lay the groundwork for drawing up a new constitution. At the end of the conference, sixteen of the nineteen organizations signed a declaration to work for a free and open society based on democratic values, equal opportunities, and social justice. The organizations also agreed that a new constitution should provide for a multiparty democracy, universal adult suffrage, and an independent judiciary. The delegates established five working groups to debate the details of transferring power. The CODESA talks have seen highs and lows since the beginning as the various groups continue to debate the transition from white minority rule. The African National Congress (ANC) and the National Party have for some time been divided over the questions of veto powers to minority parties and the setting up of an interim government and a constituent assembly to draw up a new constitution. The government, the ANC, and other organizations agreed to hold the country's first nonracial elections for an interim government on 27 April 1994. We will devote less attention to the actual talks in CODESA than to the positions of the various organizations with respect to CODESA and the negotiations. The final agreement, embodied in the Interim Constitution, is discussed in the Epilogue.

White Liberal Political Organizations

THE DEMOCRATIC PARTY

The main parliamentary liberal political organization in the white house of the legislature was constituted in the Democratic Party (DP) formed in April 1989. The Democratic Party was formed by a merger of principally white liberal political parties opposed to apartheid and the Nationalist government.[1] Its primary short-term purpose[2] was directed at gaining the maximum number of parliamentary seats in the legislature in order to force the government to negotiate with the black majority.[3] The common themes of the leadership are a nonracial dispensation, acceptance of cultural diversity, an independent judiciary, adherence to the rule of law, and a commitment to negotiation.[4]

The DP called for the release of all political prisoners, the unbanning of all political organizations, and the repeal of all apartheid legislation.[5] The party historically has been committed to preventing majority rule and calls for the protection of various languages, cultures, and religions. It is opposed to a unitary state and favors a federal system, the units of which should enjoy a high degree of autonomy with respect to the own affairs of the units.[6] The jurisdiction of the national government should be limited to matters of common concern such as foreign affairs and finance. The DP favors a bill of rights to protect the individual and group rights of the units. Moreover, it calls for the independence of the judiciary and the rule of law to be entrenched in the constitution.[7]

The DP believed in the principle of proportionality, arguing that all parties who receive at least 10 percent of the vote should be represented at all levels of government including the cabinet. A better understanding of the DP can be gained from a consideration of the programs of the two principal parties, the Progressive Federal Party (PFP) and the New Republic Party (NRP) which disbanded to form the DP.

The DP favors free enterprise and private ownership while containing government spending. Historically, it has not addressed itself to the poverty of the black majority or to the gross inequalities in the distribution of wealth and resources between the white minority and the black majority. Its program was directed at removing all apartheid and discriminatory legislation. Its primary emphasis has been on extending liberal democratic rights to all people while ignoring the socioeconomic reality of the black majority. In the CODESA talks, the DP clung to the view that the best constitutional dispensation is one that devolves power to the regions.

THE PROGRESSIVE FEDERAL PARTY

For many years the Progressive Federal Party was the main white liberal opposition party in the legislature. In some quarters, the DP is seen as the PFP in disguise, attempting to bring together all the liberal elements opposed to the Nationalist government.[8]

The PFP constitutional proposals contained two parts.[9] The first related to the actual drawing up of a new constitution. The PFP called for a national convention attended by all significant political groupings that are against violence. The national convention should be presided over by the government of the day. During this process of negotiation the government would do away with discriminatory practices and create institutions for the implementation of the new constitution. Hence, the white government would initiate the national convention and would ultimately be responsible for bringing about a new dispensation. The national convention once convened would elect an advisory council to assist the government in working out a new constitution.[10]

The second part of the PFP proposals contained its model of state and government. The PFP rejected the unitary nature of the South African state and called for a federal constitution. The unitary state was associated with a winner-take-all political system and was therefore not suited to a plural society.[11] The essential features of the PFP's constitutional proposals were a decentralization of power to the various units on a geographical basis in a federal framework. The units should be defined in terms of groups by taking into account the wishes of the people in the area. The number of states in the federation and the boundaries of the states should be decided by an impartial commission appointed by the national convention. The terms of reference for the commission include community of interests of the people in the area and a desire to make the units homogeneous.[12] With respect to the "independent" homelands, the PFP said their

166

participation would depend on the wishes of both the delegates to the national convention as well as the homeland governments.

The PFP called for separation of powers between the legislature, executive, and the judiciary. It advocated a bill of rights to protect both individual and group rights.[13] The PFP saw the principle of equal rights and full citizenship as nonnegotiable. However, it also saw the aspect of group rights as a nonnegotiable principle—the presence of population groups and their "separate" rights—were to be a permanent feature in a new constitution. The groups should not be predetermined but should be allowed to emerge in a voluntary manner.[14]

With respect to the agencies of government, they envisaged a federal parliament and a federal executive council with authority over a defined set of matters that included finance, foreign affairs, and defense. The remainder of the powers, including health, social welfare, and community development would reside with the states.[15] The states should be free to raise and spend taxes as they please without interference from the central government. They advocated the representation of all significant political groupings in the central government, which they argued would not be possible in a one-person, one-vote unitary state. The representation of all groups in the legislature and executive would be achieved through a process of proportional representation.[16] Moreover, there should be a right of veto accorded to each group providing they represent 10 to 15 percent of the population.[17] The only exception where there would be no veto power would be bills relating to money matters and the election of the prime minister.

The PFP advocated a parliament consisting of two houses. One house would consist of representatives of the political parties elected on a proportional basis within each state. The number of votes accorded to each state would depend on the proportion of voters in each state.[18] The second chamber would consist of equal representatives from the various states. Moreover, it would also include senators representing the various cultural councils.

A cultural council would be established where a cultural group could organize itself and register with the federal constitutional court to help protect and maintain its cultural interests.[19] No legislation affecting the interests of the state or cultural interests of the cultural group represented in the Senate would be passed unless it was referred to and approved by the state legislature and the cultural council concerned.[20]

The executive would be constituted in the Federal Executive Council. The chairman of the latter body would be the prime minister elected by the federal legislature. The prime minister would select the members of his cabinet (executive council) in proportion to the strength of the various political parties in the legislature. The members of the executive, although selected by the legislature, would not continue to maintain membership of the legislature if they elect to serve on the executive.

The PFP called for an independent judiciary, the members of which should be appointed by an independent judicial appointments committee. Moreover, they advocated a federal supreme court divided into two divisions. One division would hear cases on constitutional issues while the second would hear matters of a nonconstitutional nature.[21] Finally, the PFP advocated a bill of rights entrenched in the constitution.

NEW REPUBLIC PARTY

The New Republic Party also subscribed to the view that South Africa consists of different groups and races and the best model is one that allows each of the groups to run their own affairs. The NRP advocated the coming together of representatives of the different groups on matters of common concern. It operated from the assumption that there are two elements in the South African situation that must be accommodated in a new constitution. The first is a common area inhabited by different groups, and the second is the homelands inhabited by blacks.[22] The NRP's constitutional proposals thus contain elements of a federal-confederal constitutional framework.[23] For the NRP, South Africa consists of four main groups, namely, whites, Indians, coloreds, and blacks.[24] It makes a further distinction between homeland and nonhomeland blacks. The institutions created would not include homeland blacks, who the NRP argue should enjoy political rights in the homelands. The NRP envisaged the creation of separate legislative, executive, and administrative authorities for the four groups residing in "South Africa."[25] The separate institutions would be responsible for legislating and administering the affairs of each of the groups. With respect to matters of common concern, the NRP advocated the creation of federal institutions.

The federal legislature would consist of two chambers. The lower house would consist of representatives of the four groups appointed by the group parliament in proportion to the number of votes each party obtained in the respective parliament.[26] The upper house would consist of an equal number of representatives of the units in the federation.[27] The federal executive would be elected by the legislature in a proportional manner representing all four groups. The members of the executive could not belong to the legislature. Like the Swiss system, the NRP advocated a rotating head of state.[28]

With respect to the "independent" homelands, the NRP advocated the creation of a confederal body with a set of institutions to deal with matters of common concern between the homelands and the federal South African republic.[29] However, the NRP did not provide complete blueprints for the composition and institutions of the confederal relationship.

OVERVIEW OF LIBERAL OPTIONS

There is considerable overlap among the programs of the liberal white political parties, although the institutions they propose may differ. All liberal options for a post-apartheid South Africa operate within the plural paradigm. Their constitutional options aim to entrench group rights and individual rights. The former is constituted in the veto power accorded to the groups or units, while the latter is secured in a bill of rights. The liberal vision rejects majority rule and favors a decentralized and asymmetrical federal system. There is some flexibility on the latter point, where some are prepared to accept decentralized corporate groups. The constitutions and institutions they promote are of the federal-consociational variety.[30] They share all the trappings and weaknesses of the plural paradigm:[31] First, their assumptions do not explain the basis of the plural nature of South African society; second, they essentially attempt to promote a weak central government; third, their models allow for a continuation of the status quo. The protection and entrenchment of group rights permit presently privileged white interests to hang on to their economic power.

THE NATIONAL PARTY'S PROPOSALS IN CODESA

The National Party's constitutional program for power sharing was first outlined in the 1983 constitution. However, in recent years we have witnessed such developments as the unbanning of political movements and the release of prominent political leaders. In his speech to Parliament in February 1990, the South African president spoke about the introduction of a new constitutional dispensation that would bring all South Africans into the constitutional process. The president has spoken about the government's commitment to achieve votes for all. However, because of the "diversity" in the population there must be protection of minority group rights.[32] Initially, there were suggestions for bringing Africans into the central decision-making process by "accommodating" them in the legislature.[33] However, this would be done within the framework of group rights and the notion of consensus politics. A separate legislature would be created to represent Africans.[34] An additional separate legislature would be created to decide on matters of common interest. Moreover, the institutions of the central government such as the election of the state president and the cabinet would be done with the participation of all political groups. These proposals envisage a constitution of the federal variety comprising corporate groups and therefore of the consociational form. The National Party has consistently rejected any measures of redistribution, higher taxes, or nationalization of property and argues that black advancement must be achieved by higher levels of growth.[35] The National

169

Party leader F. W. de Klerk said Africans could be "accommodated" in a new constitution and could very well be a major part in a future government. However, there would be no threat to the economic and social interests of whites by virtue of the protection of group rights and veto power.

The National Party government further articulated its position on minority and veto rights in the CODESA talks, which originally led to an impasse in negotiations. In the second round of talks in May 1992, the ANC-led alliance broke off talks with the government because of the government's insistence on a 75 percent consensus before a new constitution can be agreed on and the government's insistence on a two-tier legislative chamber with veto power given to the upper house.[36] The National Party has insisted on a federal system with a rigid constitution, protection of minority rights with a bill of rights, and giving minorities a special role in the adoption of the constitution and future legislation by a new legislature.[37] The National Party has insisted on a legislative body with checks and balances and a bicameral parliament, the lower house to be chosen by proportional representation and an upper chamber where white representatives could exercise veto power.[38] The upper chamber would represent regional interests. In addition, the National Party wants a bill of rights with protection for individual rights and property rights.[39] The veto power will conceivably allow a minority to prevent political changes from being effected at the central level. In effect, even though the National Party or any other political party might lose a general election, the losing parties would still be able to block decision making because of the veto powers envisaged in the party's proposals. Much of the conflict at the CODESA talks revolved around the National Party's insisting that regional powers, private property rights, and a bicameral parliament have to be agreed upon before any national elections can proceed. The National Party wanted these principles to be binding on the subsequently democratically elected constituent assembly.[40] These issues will continue to be debated after the 27 April 1994 elections.

With respect to form of government, the National Party has proposed a collegial executive as well as proportional representation in the other key organs of government.[41] Under the guise of self-determination, the party has also proposed devolution of power to metropolitan areas and has spoken about introduction of franchise for local elections based on property ownership. Since blacks do not own much property, this would in effect ensure whites control over their "sensitive" interests.

The National Party stance is consistent with liberal notions of democratic pluralism. Its position also indicates that, apart from the rightist parties, the programs of white political parties are not really opposed to each other but are mere variations on the same theme. They include provisions for power sharing with the black majority, but they envisage a constitutional situation in which a great amount of power will reside with the segments. The segments would be able to veto decisions taken at the central level, particularly if the decisions affect the vital interests of the segments. It is thus conceivable that the white minority could make themselves into a separate segment and obstruct any measure that erodes their economic and property interests.

Inkatha/Buthelezi and the Regional Option

The Inkatha Freedom Party was founded by the KwaZulu leader Mangosuthu Buthelezi. There is considerable debate over whether the movement is a black political organization or more an ethnic movement to promote the interests of the "Zulu" people and Buthelezi. Its most dominant personality is Buthelezi, who has come to symbolize the movement and everything it stands for.

Over the years Inkatha has come out in favor of consociational constitutional options as a regional solution for the KwaZulu-Natal area. Two dominant themes emerge from the constitutional vocabulary of Inkatha. First is the familiar notion that any constitutional option must take account of South Africa being a plural society, however, with a single economy.[42] The second theme is the desire to seek a regional constitutional solution in the specific province and region of KwaZulu-Natal.[43] Inkatha asserted the regional option can in turn be used as a basis for constitutional planning for the whole of South Africa.[44] Inkatha has approved specific and detailed constitutional options, the two most famous being embodied in the Buthelezi Commission Report and the report of the KwaZulu-Natal Indaba.

THE BUTHELEZI COMMISSION REPORT

The Buthelezi Commission was organized at the behest of Buthelezi "to add a new dimension to the political evolution of South Africa."[45] However, the report was limited to providing proposals for the future of KwaZulu-Natal. The recommendations of the commission were subsequently adopted as part of the policy of Inkatha. The commission's report consists of several reports dealing with a host of matters. The important report dealing with constitutional options was presented in the Main Report of the Constitutional and Political Committee.

The Main Report of the Constitutional and Political Committee recommended a consociational form of government[46] and called for elite cooperation of leaders of various groups that do not necessarily have to be racially defined.[47] The executive would be drawn from the legislature.

The KwaZulu-Natal area would be divided into a number of regional areas based on "community of interests" with a regional structure of government. The legislature would consist of representatives of the various "community of interest regional areas on a proportional basis."[48] Over and above the proportionality principle, there would be guaranteed representation in the legislature of all groups in the region. The legislative assembly would be limited in terms of its competence to a defined list of matters. The overall constitutional system would be subject to a bill of rights and to judicial scrutiny. Moreover, a right of veto would be available to any minority group that felt its interests threatened.[49]

The recommendations of the Buthelezi Commission are federal in orientation and more specifically consociational. They seek to protect the interests of all the groups and allow them to maintain their identity. They envisage a legislature made up of representatives of all the units and an executive made up of representatives of the different groups on the basis of proportionality.

THE KWAZULU-NATAL INDABA

The KwaZulu Natal Indaba was a meeting of some forty organizations representing various political, economic, cultural, and religious organizations to discuss a new form of government for the KwaZulu-Natal region.[50] The idea of the Indaba was initiated by Mangosuthu Buthelezi and Frank Martin, a member of the Natal Provincial Executive. They conceived the Indaba as a continuation of the discussions of the earlier Buthelezi Commission Report. The meeting took place in the Durban City Hall from 3 April to 5 December 1986. The meetings of the Indaba were closed to the public.

From the start the participants agreed on several principles that would guide them in subsequent formulations, namely, the indivisibility of KwaZulu-Natal, the region's inseparability from the rest of South Africa, full political rights for all, an end to discrimination, protection of group and individual rights, a free economic system, and maximum devolution of power.[51] Eight months of discussions culminated in the formulation of detailed constitutional proposals. To the supporters of the Indaba, the proposals have the merit of recognizing the rights of all people including minorities to participate in government.

The constitutional proposals envisaged the creation of a two-chamber provincial legislature. The first chamber will consist of 100 elected members using a system of multimember constituency based on proportional representation.[52] The proportional representation will ensure the representation of all parties proportional to their electoral strength. The second chamber will consist of 50 members composed of representatives of the African, Afrikaans, Asian, English, and South African[53] background groups. Except for the last category, voters can only vote for the category to which they belong. Elections for the second chamber are also conducted on a proportional basis. To become law legislation must be passed by a majority of both chambers of the legislature. However, if a bill affects the cultural, religious, or language group of a particular background group then it requires the support of the majority of representatives of that group as well.

The prime minister will come from the majority party in the first chamber. The prime minister chooses half the executive; the other half will be chosen by the minority parties in the first and second chambers. Moreover, at least one member of each background group must be represented in the executive. In this sense, the executive is a cartel of elite leaders from the various parties and groups.

The system envisaged additional checks and balances in the form of standing committees and cultural councils. It envisages the creation of standing committees for each portfolio (department) of government. All laws have to be approved by at least two-thirds of the members of the relevant standing committee. This is an additional feature designed to promote a government based on consensus. The members of the standing committees must come from every party represented in the legislature. Second, no party can have more than 60 percent of the members of a standing committee.

The cultural councils are intended for "the protection, maintenance and promotion of the religious, language and cultural rights and interests of groups representing the principal segments of the population of the Province."[54] A cultural council has the right to receive all copies of draft legislation and to make representations to all branches of the government with respect to matters affecting the rights of the group it represents. The cultural council has the locus standi to appeal to the Supreme Court to set aside any prospective law the cultural council considers will affect the interests of the group it represents.

Over and above all the checks and balances provided, the system will be subject to a bill of rights protecting both individual and group rights. Any individual has the right to apply to the Supreme Court for the enforcement of the rights embodied in the bill of rights. The bill of rights and the constitution will be rigid and difficult to amend. First, a two-thirds majority of both chambers is required to pass a bill aimed at amending the constitution. Second, if the bill affects a language, religious, or cultural group of a community, it requires the support of the majority of that group in the second chamber. If the second requisite cannot be met, then the bill can be submitted to the electorate via a referendum. In order for the bill to be passed by the electorate, a majority of four of the five groups in the second chamber have to approve the amendment.

At the head of the entire system will be a titular governor. As the proposals are for the Natal-KwaZulu region, the latter will be appointed by the state president. The governor will be responsible for assenting and promulgating all legislation.[55]

The constitutional proposals that came out of the Indaba have received the official acceptance of Inkatha and the KwaZulu government. Moreover, they have been accepted by a host of business and parliamentary groups.[56] A Joint Executive Authority (JEA) has been created as a first step toward the creation of a single legislature for the region.[57]

INKATHA'S ECONOMIC POLICY

Inkatha is committed to the principles of a free economic system.[58] The Indaba proposals did not address the disparate economic positions of the black majority vis à vis the white population. Nor did they have anything to say about alleviating the socioeconomic problems of the black majority such as lack of adequate housing, education, infrastructure, health, and shortage of social and welfare facilities. On the contrary, they seek to secure and entrench the present situation by devolving a great measure of autonomy to the segments, which could be defined in terms of color. Not only are the institutions designed to protect the interests of the groups, but they are designed in a watertight fashion with a host of mechanisms to protect the interests and positions of the dominant group.[59] In real terms what this means is the white group does not have to surrender or compromise the dominant economic position they have attained over the years. The corollary is the government of the day will not be able to effect socioeconomic changes, as the constitution allows the groups considerable veto power. Not surprisingly, most of the participants in the Indaba were from the business sector.

INKATHA, THE INDABA, AND DEMOCRACY

There are serious questions about Inkatha's commitment to democracy as well as the way in which the Indaba proposals and the Buthelezi Commission Report were arrived at. With respect to the Buthelezi Commission Report, the proposals were formulated by a number of academics and funded by the business sector with little or no community involvement. The proposals were clearly presented from the top. Letters of invitation were sent out to a host of political and community organizations. But extraparliamentary groups such as the United Democratic Front (UDF) and the Azanian Peoples Organization (AZAPO), independent trade union movements, and the then-exiled movements including the ANC, Pan Africanist Congress (PAC), all declined. The primary reasons for the refusal to attend can be attributed to the latter movements' positions of noncollaboration and their rejection of Inkatha's and the other attendees participation in government-created structures. From a practical standpoint it would have been impossible for the largest liberation movement—the ANC—to attend, as it together with the PAC were banned from operating in South Africa at the time the Indaba was held.[60]

As the Indaba progressed it was apparent that there were other differences that would have made it difficult for most of the extraparliamentary groups to participate in the negotiations. First, the Indaba discussions took place in complete secrecy, with no discussion between the participants and their constituencies. Nor were the discussions of the Indaba open to public debate and criticism. The organizers felt it was essential to create an atmosphere of confidentiality and trust, which could not be done if the delegates were playing to an audience.[61] As far as the participants of the Indaba were concerned, the proposals would be put to the people for their approval in a referendum.[62] But the lack of community participation and consultation is a serious deficiency.[63]

At the second level, Inkatha as an organization and the style of its political leader have been subjected to various criticisms. Buthelezi asserts that Inkatha is a functioning political party that operates on the principle of democracy.[64] He further asserts that all his actions are a reflection of the position of the organization and are endorsed by the general membership of the organization. Moreover, he maintains that no black political leader enjoys the same degree of support he enjoys.[65] On the other hand, he claims his leadership position is something that he inherited and is therefore determined by history.

But democracy and the election of leaders to represent the people cannot be compatible with any notion of "divine" right to lead. While Inkatha claims to have the greatest support in South Africa, there is widespread evidence that many people are coerced to join the organization.[66] For example, journalists report members joining the organization under threats of assault, murder, or denial of houses, jobs, and pensions.[67] Inkatha members are coerced to pay membership fees and make contributions to the organization.[68] In the light of the history of coercion and brutality, many groups have criticized Buthelezi as being primarily concerned with his own political fortunes and accuse him of creating a political base for himself.[69] These are indeed very serious criticisms of the organization, and they parallel the experiences of moribund parties and elite leaders gone wrong in so many parts of Africa.[70]

Buthelezi is considered in many antiapartheid circles as an apologist for the apartheid order. He uses whatever platform is available to further his own political ambitions.[71] He has used his position in the KwaZulu government to consolidate his base and penetrate all aspects of life that affect the community to exercise the greatest measure of control over the population. This is best illustrated in the link between Inkatha, the South

African police, and the KwaZulu police.[72] Although Buthelezi denies it, stories of Inkatha and the South African police working jointly in harassing, detaining, and interrogating residents and beating up people opposed to the government or to Buthelezi's participation in the Bantustan government have been documented by journalists.[73] The Goldstone Commission confirmed this collaboration. There is evidence that Buthelezi cannot tolerate criticism, particularly of his role in the Bantustan government. While Buthelezi claims his organization is nonviolent, he and his organization have been accused of beating and killing people opposed to his policies and role in the KwaZulu government.[74] In pursuit of his personal interests, Buthelezi is accused of trying to become a cult personality beyond reproach and on whom much praise and adulation are showered.[75] He stands as a figure above the organization and institutions he purports to represent, and in many regards is considered to be a one-man show.[76]

Many of Buthelezi's activities and statements cast doubt on his commitment to democracy. He and his supporters are given to personalizing the struggle as a leadership battle between him and some other leader. For example, he claims in his book to be the incontestable voice of black political leadership.[77] Similarly, he claims that he is the leader with the greatest political support in the country.[78] It is erroneous and dangerous for anyone to characterize the struggle as being one for the elevation of one or another leader. The task is to create institutions that promote democracy. The purpose of the leader regardless of who he or she is, is to serve the people in terms of the people's wishes within a democratic framework.

INKATHA AND CODESA

Inkatha participated in the first CODESA meeting in December 1991. However, together with the leaders of Ciskei and Bophuthatswana, Inkatha refused to sign the Declaration of Intent agreed to by all other participants because Inkatha felt the declaration did not guarantee a federal form of state. In October 1992 Inkatha withdrew from constitutional negotiations because, according to Buthelezi, the National Party and the ANC were moving in a direction that would wipe out the role of regional leaders like himself.[79] Many people see Buthelezi's actions as flowing from a fear that his homeland power base will be eroded under a majority government. He has since become fiercer in his appeals to Zulu cultural and ethnic sentiments. He has spoken about the situation in South Africa turning into a civil war along the lines of the former Yugoslavia.[80]

Buthelezi has on several occasions threatened the country with secession. In December 1992 he announced a plan to combine KwaZulu with the province of Natal in an autonomous state within the framework of a federal South Africa.[81] The measure was passed by the KwaZulu legislative assembly. According to Buthelezi, the plan would have to be ratified by the electorate of Natal and KwaZulu and once this was done the new regional constitution would govern the entire area regardless of any decision taken at the CODESA talks.[82] The draft constitution provides for an elected governor, a two-chamber legislative assembly, and an independent judiciary.[83] The proposed state would also have its own militia and would not pay any taxes to any other authority.

Buthelezi's latest initiative is consistent with his previous moves seeking a regional solution to the South African problem. It reflects a desperate act of a regional leader who has been marginalized and who is, with a limited constituency, attempting to play the tribal and regional card in order to maintain a political base. In this sense, it shares similarities with the Biafran and Katanga secessionist movements in other parts of the continent, which does not bode well for southern Africa. Many feel that the initiative will be supported by the business community in the area,[84] who would rather have a collaborative effort with Buthelezi than face "redistributive" measures under a popularly elected majority government. This again is a rerun of the Katanga and Biafran crises, where minority elite and commercial interests historically have supported irredentist tendencies in other parts of the continent to gain possible financial rewards. Buthelezi withheld his participation in the 27 April 1994 elections until one week before the elections.

Black and Extraparliamentary Perspectives

This section investigates the constitutional perspectives and visions for a future South Africa of the liberation movements and the predominantly black political organizations that historically have operated outside government-created platforms or as liberation movements in exile (prior to 1990). The questions to be addressed include not only constitutional options, but also the different historical perspectives and evolution in thought with regard to the different conceptions of democracy and the national question.

THE AFRICAN NATIONAL CONGRESS

Any consideration of black politics in South Africa has to proceed with an examination of the programs and policies of the ANC, the oldest and arguably most popular political movement in South Africa. The ANC was formed in 1912 as a political movement to represent the grievances of the African majority. For a very long period the ANC was a predominantly

African organization and until recently leadership positions were restricted to Africans only.[85]

The early ANC leadership were essentially liberal in their political outlook and sought equal rights for Africans within the existing constitutional structures.[86] The movement was influenced by natural law reasoning particularly owing to a leadership who in the main consisted of the clergy or were heavily influenced by the Christian church.[87] The primary objective of the early leadership was the winning of political and civil rights within the Westminster parliamentary constitutional system.[88] The movement accepted the precepts of the existing constitution in terms of the "civilization" test requiring a certain degree of education and wealth as qualification for the franchise.[89]

The ANC's position in regard to other "groups" in South Africa from a historical perspective was one of multiracialism. Although the ANC was an African organization whose membership was restricted to African people,[90] it was prepared to come together with other groups to embark on a common strategy for fighting apartheid.[91] This policy was changed first to allow open membership to all persons regardless of race. In the early 1980s the ANC adopted a fully nonracial approach and opened its leadership positions to all "groups."[92] From a historical point of view the ANC emerged from an Africanist tradition fused with liberal values.

The Freedom Charter. The political manifesto of the ANC for many years was embodied in the Freedom Charter adopted by the Congress of the People in 1955. According to the late ANC leader Oliver Tambo, the Freedom Charter is a blueprint for a political, economic, and social structure.[93] The Freedom Charter was the political document of several significant political groupings, notably the African National Congress, the United Democratic Front (UDF), and the South African Communist Party (SACP). An investigation of the Freedom Charter is therefore crucial to an understanding of the programs and blueprints of all these organizations. Before going into a discussion of the charter, it is important to make the preliminary point that the UDF, which since 1983 was the leading anti-apartheid umbrella organization for all practical purposes, was considered as a front of the ANC. Its policies were, with the exception of the use of violence, the same as the ANC's. Since the ANC has been unbanned, and the UDF has since disbanded, no separate mention will be made of the UDF.

Background to the Freedom Charter. In August 1953 the President of the African National Congress, Z. K. Matthews, suggested that a congress of the people be convened to draw up a Freedom Charter for the democratic South Africa of the future.[94] The idea of a congress of the people was a campaign to go out to the people and collect their demands with respect to a future South Africa. These demands would be collected and put into a single document.[95] The Congress of the People was held in Kliptown on 25 and 26 June 1955, and was attended by approximately three thousand delegates from various groups.[96]

The African National Congress was the major sponsor of the Congress of the People. However, the Congress of the People was a racially based alliance of various political groupings representing the African, Indian, white, and colored populations.[97] Policy making had to be coordinated by the joint executives of the four sponsoring organizations, which represented the four "population groups."[98] In this sense the policy making of the Congress of the People had consociational features attached to it.

The Freedom Charter and Democracy. There is considerable debate concerning the drawing up of the Freedom Charter and how democratic the document is. For supporters of the charter, the document is the voice of "the people." The Congress of the People was a process that allowed the people to speak for themselves. Every demand, no matter how small, was collected by the volunteers and considered.[99] Hence, the Freedom Charter is posited as the charter of the people, originating from them and expressing their desires and aspirations.[100] In some quarters the Congress of the People and the meeting at Kliptown are equated with a people's parliament.[101]

Critics, however, question the way the Freedom Charter was drawn up and its democratic content. For example, the historian Tom Lodge questions whether the charter was the expression of the "general will" or more the perceptions and beliefs of those responsible for drafting the charter.[102] A small drafting committee was responsible for the final production,[103] but who the members of the committee were and how they worked is unknown.[104] Lodge makes the point that there had to have been an ordering of priorities and interpretation performed by the drafters from all the lists of demands. Then ANC President Albert Luthuli stated that the draft charter was not circulated among all members of the committee.[105] The chairman of the meeting at Kliptown, Wilson Conco, claimed he saw the Freedom Charter for the first time at the Kliptown meeting.[106] At the meeting there was no discussion on the demands of the charter nor were alternate programs presented. Instead all the provisions of the charter were adopted by acclamation.

In light of the above unanswered questions, it is legitimate to question the authencity of the Freedom Charter as the democratic expression of the wishes of the ordinary people of South Africa.[107] However, by South African standards and from a historical point of view one has to accept that the Congress of the People and the drawing up of the Freedom Charter in 1955 were the most democratic acts in the history of modern South Africa.[108] The document has been adopted by many of the major political movements and enjoys the greatest support among the black majority.[109] It should not, however, be held as a sacred document but rather as an expression of some of the people at a particular stage in the struggle against the apartheid order, because democracy is an ongoing experience that allows people to express their wishes, which may change over the years.[110]

Interpreting the Freedom Charter. The questions of what vision the Freedom Charter offers for a future South Africa and how one interprets the provisions of the Freedom Charter are vexing. Although the charter is not a constitutional blueprint, many of its provisions are contained in a classical bill of rights. For example, the charter calls for the right to vote, equal rights, the right to a fair trial, and impartiality of the judiciary. Moreover, it speaks about freedom of speech, organization, worship, travel, and education. But the charter also goes beyond a classical bill of rights (which essentially calls for an impartial and passive government) and calls for the nationalization of certain sectors of the economy and the division of the land among those who work it. Unlike a classical bill of rights, the charter calls for the provision by the state of housing, health care, and education. These are very important goals, which we have identified as crucial to the legitimacy and stability of a future South African order. Today, a wider debate is being waged over whether the Freedom Charter is a liberal or socialist document.

Many contend that the Freedom Charter essentially reflects socialist aspirations and is therefore a socialist document.[111] Similarly, many liberals, while acknowledging that the charter has many liberal political demands, see the economic provisions of the charter calling for state intervention in the economy as incompatible with a capitalist system.[112] For many activists, the Freedom Charter is socialist in orientation because it addresses demands such as "work and security," the freedom "to form trade unions," restoration of "the national wealth of the country . . . to the people," and the right to housing.[113] Moreover, the demands for nationalization, public control, and redivision of lands are specifically socialist demands.[114] Hence, the charter is projected as seeking to address the class problem in South African society. In a similar vein, the argument is presented that national liberation and economic liberation are interlinked and part of the same process. In this light the charter is seen not just as a list of democratic reforms but as a revolutionary document that foresees the breaking up of the present economic and social system.[115] The nationalization of banks, mines, and land is seen as a logical step in this direction.[116]

Counter to the view that the charter seeks to promote a black middle class, the socialist interpretation is that the charter wishes to introduce a socialist order and speaks first to the worker and then to the small trader, peasant, and manufacturer. The latter groups would be permitted a degree of independence to carry on their activities independently of the state in the interests of efficiency.[117] The activities of the small trader and farmer would be controlled by the state to prevent them from becoming big capitalists.[118]

There are other people who assert that the Freedom Charter as it stands is too vague to be construed as a socialist document. Some categorically reject the equation of the Freedom Charter and socialism and assert the charter envisages a mixed economy that falls within the purview of a capitalist order. If the charter is placed in historical context, one would have no problem in rejecting its link to socialist ideals. For example, Nelson Mandela has strongly denied that the charter was a blueprint for a socialist state; rather it envisaged the prosperity of the nonwhite middle class.[119] It was a document that would enable the nonwhite middle class to flourish as never before.[120] In Mandela's view the charter did not envisage the transfer of power to any single social class, but was to benefit all the people of the country.

This interpretation sees the charter not as anticapitalist but as antimonopoly capitalist, as opposed to being socialist. Thus the charter is neither a revolutionary document nor a socialist blueprint but is instead a "popular document" meant to achieve the maximum unity of all groups in South African society.[121] In this sense the charter is projected as the people's document. It seeks to give all a share in the wealth of the country, which can only be achieved by smashing the power and control of the few monopolies that largely control that wealth.[122] According to this view, black majority rule will not in itself solve the problems of the country. The inequalities of wealth, dire housing problems, and lack of education in the black community all have to be dealt with. To this end nationalization of key industries does not in itself amount to socialism. In many capitalist countries such as Britain and France key industries are owned by the state and function alongside private industries. The charter envisaged a similar scenario for South Africa.[123]

Others see the charter not in terms of any single group or idea be it capitalism or socialism but as a reflection of the interests of all oppressed people in South Africa and those who support an end to apartheid.[124] The economic clauses in the charter are not socialist but are derived from the "historical basis of South African society where nearly all the country's land has been seized from the original inhabitants."[125] The wealth has been concentrated in the hands of a few, today represented by the monopolies. Most strata of society are seen as having an interest in the smashing of the monopolies, again a strategy that is neither socialist nor capitalist but is based on the interests of all the people.[126] According to this conception, the charter is "a national democratic document."[127] It is a people's charter, and not a class charter, aimed at promoting rule by all the people and not by the bourgeoisie or by the working class alone. Its emphasis is on national unity.

On yet another level the charter is seen to take its inspiration from African socialism.[128] The rejection of capitalism and socialism based on class analyses together with the notion of some sort of redistribution of resources is consistent with the idea of African socialism. The reality is that the charter cannot be exclusively equated with liberalism or socialism. While it speaks about nationalization of industries and the provision of many social amenities, these provisions are not, as we have pointed out, inconsistent with capitalism. It is therefore possible that many of the charter's provisions are vague and open to conflicting interpretation.

The Freedom Charter and the National Question. It cannot be overemphasized that one of the greatest problems in independent Africa is the failure to overcome the national problem. Many African countries came to independence with the view that their societies were plural in nature and required constitutional protection for the different ethnic groups or nationalities. The record has shown that this was an unfortunate position.[129] The constitutions, forms of state, and programs should have been directed at promoting national unity[130] and a single national identity. To promote an attitude that South Africa consists of different national groups each requiring protection of its culture and identity is to proceed along the path mistakenly followed by so many independent African countries. From a historical vantage the sponsors of the Congress of the People met as four principal and distinct political groups representing what in 1955 were perceived as the different population groups.[131] As a matter of fact, two of the political organizations SACPO (South African Colored People's Organization) and COD (Congress of Democrats) were formed to represent the colored and white communities respectively.[132] At the time it appears it was common currency among the congress movement that South Africa consisted of different nations. Policymaking of the Congress of the People had to be coordinated by a meeting of the joint executives of the four racially oriented sponsoring organizations.[133] In a sense the organization of the Congress of the People had some consociational features based on consent of the "different groups" as represented by distinct organizations.

Today, some proponents of the Freedom Charter reject the interpretation of the "different groups" as meaning the creation of different nations. They interpret the provision as a call for the respect of different languages and cultures, which presently is not the case in South Africa.[134] This demand is legitimate and correct.[135] Similarly, the ANC publication *SECH-ABA* states that it has worked out the theory of the nation and has come to the conclusion that presently South Africa consists of two nations, the oppressed and oppressor. The defeat of the oppressor nation will lead to the creation of a single nation.[136] This interpretation also calls for the creation of new loyalties to a single South African nation. However, other supporters of the charter say one cannot be utopian and one has to accept that the South Africa of the future must recognize the "birthmarks" of the present, which include the categorization of race and color.[137] Similarly, the ANC publication *SECHABA* speaks about the "equality of all ethnic groups—large or small, black or white."[138] This language is unfortunate and symptomatic of the categorization of the white government. Again, the inconsistencies show the need for clear guidelines that do away with ambiguities, misconceptions, and conflicting interpretations. In this context it is difficult to accept the assertion that the charter fights racial compartmentalization.[139]

Overview of the Charter's Provisions. The Freedom Charter elaborates many important goals essential to the legitimacy of any future order in South Africa such as the right of the people to govern, equality before the law, sharing in the wealth of the country, enjoyment of human rights, and the provision of work, security, and education. However, ambiguities and lack of detail in many vital provisions in the charter make it difficult to resolve interpretations. One major criticism of the charter is that it does not adequately spell out whether it is a socialist or capitalist document. This criticism is without merit. The lessons of the past decade show the failures of rigid, doctrinaire programs. The primary concern for a future South Africa is not that constitutions be labeled capitalist or socialist but that an unequivocal commitment be made to set the country on a path of socioeconomic transformation.[140] In addition, the needs of society must be articulated not by a minority (regardless of whether it is represented by a group or governing elite) but by the majority population. It is in this context that we will evaluate the charter.

Insofar as the charter speaks about equal rights, the rights to education, work, security, and sharing in the wealth of the country, it goes a long way toward addressing the important goals of a future society. A major criticism can be leveled against the charter for its ambiguities and incompleteness with respect to other important provisions. For example, the charter does not define what it means by democracy and whether it is to be one-party or multiparty. It does not tell us how it will reconcile the class aspirations of the different groups.[141] It is also silent on the relationship between the electorate and those elected.[142]

To be fair, the Freedom Charter was not envisaged as a constitutional blueprint. The vagueness in its provisions was initially a strength in that it allowed many different groups opposed to apartheid to come together. However, the charter by 1980 had become the seminal document in the political and constitutional debate in South Africa—almost all political organizations are called to define their positions in regard to it.[143] Much will depend on the human factor and the caliber of leadership. But it is important to orient the new order in a direction that promotes democratic participation, thus ensuring that the people will have control over the leadership. This necessitates the creation of viable institutional structures that link the leadership to the people.

Some people dismiss the lack of clarity in the charter by saying paper demands are irrelevant, and what is important is the movement and the support for it,[144] a view that is shortsighted. Many independence movements in Africa came into power with widespread mass support against the colonial power. Prior to independence the party rhetoric contained many slogans calling for equality, redistribution, and democracy. Unfortunately, after independence many of the parties deteriorated into elite clubs primarily concerned with the interests of the leadership. It is shortsighted to leave everything to a movement or the leadership. Clearly there is a need to create viable constitutional structures and institutions whereby the people will be able to exercise control over the leadership. In the light of the experiences of so many constitutions and independence movements gone wrong in Africa it is imperative that any blueprint spell out not only what it is against but also what it is in favor of. The charter fails to do this in that many of its provisions are vague and open to conflicting interpretations, which takes us to the constitutional proposals of the ANC and its position in CODESA.

Constitutional Proposals of the ANC. In 1988 the African National Congress produced its own "Constitutional Guidelines for a Democratic South Africa."[145] These guidelines have been further elaborated upon and refined since the unbanning of the ANC, and the ANC has pushed its proposals in the CODESA talks.

The 1988 proposals are extremely important not only because they revealed the constitutional policies of the organization with the largest support in the country, but also because they were the first ever constitutional proposals presented by the nationalist movement. The guidelines were prepared over a period of two years. According to the ANC, the guidelines were just that—guidelines and not concrete constitutional proposals that would be drawn up by elected representatives of the people.[146] Moreover, the ANC attitude was there should be no separation between the guidelines and the Freedom Charter.[147] In other words, the proposals should not be viewed as contradicting anything contained in the Freedom Charter. The guidelines made attempts to resolve some of the ambiguities in the Freedom Charter, at least in terms of how the ANC interprets it.

The ANC guidelines suggest a unitary state with a single legislature, executive, judiciary, and administration. They unequivocally promote a "single national identity and loyalty binding on all South Africans,"[148] addressing the problem of ethnic chauvinism that so many African countries have experienced. At the same time, the guidelines respect the linguistic and cultural diversity of the people. The commitment to a unitary state and a single national identity is without a doubt a positive feature and suggests a move away from any notion of multinationalism, which the charter leaves ambiguous. The promotion of a single national identity is not inconsistent with respecting the linguistic, cultural, or religious affiliation of all people. Since the CODESA talks, the ANC has acceded to the creation of various regions—however, within the structure of a strong unitary state.[149] It has rejected Inkatha's proposal for a constitution to encompass a federal state in the KwaZulu-Natal area, which it likens to the balkanization of South Africa.[150] The ANC has committed itself to a government of national unity to "share power" with other political parties under the Interim Constitution.[151]

The guidelines and other recent ANC pronouncements at the CODESA talks affirm the right of every individual to vote and be elected under a system of universal suffrage. Interestingly, the guidelines call for a constitution that includes a bill of rights (based on the Freedom Charter) guaranteeing fundamental human rights such as equality before the law, the right to work and to organize, free education, travel, housing, and health care. This suggests a departure from a traditional bill of rights, which basically calls for a passive government guaranteeing individual human rights. The ANC's proposals see the role of government in positive terms and the function of the bill of rights not only to guarantee individual rights but also to achieve second and third generation rights. This governmental duty is stated in positive terms: "The State and all social institutions shall be under a constitutional duty to take active steps to eradicate, speedily, the economic and social inequalities produced by racial discrimination."[152] Moreover, the state has the duty to provide social security and land reform. The ANC's different conception of rights beyond classical individual rights can also be seen in the provisions that seek to protect worker's rights to strike and to bargain collectively.[153] The guidelines show a concern for the material conditions of society and call for constitutional norms to eradicate economic and social inequalities.

The guidelines unequivocally commit to a mixed economy with the operation of both a private and public sector.[154] The type of economy envisaged is neither the "classical" laissez-faire capitalist economy nor the Soviet variety of central control, but a social democratic or welfare state with massive state involvement in the economic and social spheres. There is no rigid doctrine and there is a cautiousness toward massive nationalization in the light of the experiences of Mozambique and other African countries.[155] The present policy also favors the growth of a black business sector. The ANC does not appear to see itself as a workers' party.[156] Its present commitment is to equalize life opportunities for all as opposed to achieving factual equality or worker control over the means of production, as socialist doctrine would claim.[157] This means the ANC does not necessarily desire to transfer resources to the underprivileged but instead seeks to introduce policies that will allow the present under-privileged equal access to whatever facilities are available.

Historically some ANC theorists have adhered to the position that there are two stages in the struggle. The above goals constitute the objectives of the first stage, which constitutes the national revolution.[158] All black people are united in freeing themselves from racism and colonial domination.[159] It is only after the first stage is attained that they can proceed to the second stage of introducing a fully fledged socialist order.[160]

The ANC and Other Groups. From a historical vantage the ANC's tolerance of other liberation movements and tendencies has been somewhat contro-versial. To be fair, the same also applies to the other black nationalist movements, which have been less than tolerant of the ANC. It has been an unfortunate tendency among the nationalist movements to consider themselves as the "authentic" voice of the people.[161] The ANC considered the Pan-Africanist Congress as disruptive adventurers funded and abet-ted by foreign interests,[162] a treacherous countermovement representing the interests of imperialism.[163] The ANC attitude to the Black Conscious-ness movement was (to paraphrase their leader) to prevent them from becoming a parallel movement to the ANC or allow them any opportunity to compete with the ANC.[164] The growth of another political movement was likened to the creation of a "third force."[165] Similarly, the formulation of the Azanian Manifesto, another program or blueprint for a future South Africa is viewed as divisive.[166]

Clearly, divide-and-rule tactics is an old colonial strategy and the attempt to create divisions within the popular movements is a prime objective of the South African government. However, it is an extremely dangerous attitude to view any political movement whose ideology is different from one's own as a danger to the interests of the people.[167] Democracy entails the acceptance of different ideas, and this does not have to be within the confines of a single movement. Under the guise of promotion of national unity much ill will and oppression have been generated in Africa. However, national unity is an essential prerequisite for South Africa. Any manifestation of ethnic chauvinism must be discour-aged. Norms have to be laid down and structures created to deal with any tendency to propagate national divisions.[168]

Since the unbanning of political organizations in 1990, and the subse-quent CODESA talks, the ANC embarked on a program to launch a Patriotic Front with the PAC, AZAPO, and other organizations to present a united front in talks with the government. Unfortunately, the Patriotic Front broke down before the CODESA talks began because of mistrust on the part of the other organizations that the ANC was carrying out secret talks with the National Party.

THE SOUTH AFRICAN COMMUNIST PARTY

The Communist Party of South Africa was formed in 1921 by members of the white working class with the express purpose of uniting white workers.[169] In its initial stages the party regarded nationalism as a reactionary ideology, and propagated class struggle with the aim of uniting all races on a class basis against capitalism.[170] In 1950 the party ceased to operate as a legal organization following the passing of the Suppression of Communism Act. It later regrouped itself as an underground organization called the South African Communist Party (SACP).[171]

After the passing of the Suppression of Communism Act, many members of the SACP began working within the Congress Alliance headed by the ANC. Following the banning of the ANC in 1960, the SACP and ANC leaders jointly formed the military unit Umkhonto we Sizwe, translated "Spear of the Nation."[172] The SACP later accepted the Freedom Charter as a political blueprint for a future South Africa.

SACP's Program. The early program of the South African Communist Party was embodied in a document put out in 1963 entitled "The Road to South African Freedom."[173] In this document the SACP categorically stated its preference for the Soviet-type Communist system based on the principles of Marxism-Leninism.[174] It sought to do away with the capitalist system and place the means of production under public ownership. It also proposed destroying the present state structures and creating new institutions in their place. The state and economy would operate under conditions of central planning and all land would be subject to public ownership. The state would provide full social, welfare, and educational facilities to all citizens.[175] The party favored a unitary form of state with universal adult suffrage. Early statements advocated representatives of the state elected at the local and regional levels and subject to recall,[176] and guarantees of freedom of speech, thought, movement, and religion.[177] However, they also spoke about the gains of the revolution being preserved by the dictatorship of the people against the "former dominating and exploiting classes."[178] The party historically subscribed to the notion of democratic centralism and the idea that lower party organs must adhere to the higher organs of government.[179] The new society would be led by a vanguard Marxist-Leninist party consisting of the best[180] members of the society, who would lead the working class.[181]

Recently with the changes in the Soviet Union there have been several policy changes in the SACP. The SACP General Secretary Joe Slovo now speaks about the ravaging effects of both the untramelled free market and pervasive central planning and direction, and about a search for a mix between the two polar options.[182] This would seem to suggest that the SACP has abandoned the Soviet doctrinaire approach of nationalization of all resources and central direction of all affairs of the state and society. In its place they favor a balancing and coexisting of private and public enterprises.[183] Similarly, the collapse of East European regimes has resulted in the party moving away from the rhetoric of the Stalinist party organization and acknowledging that such a party leads to tyranny. The membership must be able to criticize and change leadership if they lose confidence in it.[184] The party leader has repudiated the approach of the past and in its official organ speaks out against bureaucratic authoritarian leadership and the concentration of power in the hands of a small clique.[185] More importantly, the party has now repudiated the doctrine of a one-party state saying that it is impossible to achieve democracy in a one-party state.[186] However, the party has not abandoned restricting its membership to select members.[187] Under the present constitution the top officials (as has been characteristic of all European Communist parties) continue to exercise the greatest power in respect to decision making.[188]

SACP and the Two-Stage Theory. The question arises, How could the SACP, which was historically committed to a Communist order on the Soviet model, support the Freedom Charter, whose commitment to socialism is unclear? The answer is to be found in the SACP's analysis of South African society. The SACP characterized South African society as colonialism of a special type in which a white race occupied the same territory and oppressed the "non-White majority."[189] The white sector shows all the features of an advanced capitalist state, while the indigenous people are subject to the most extreme national oppression. For the SACP there are thus two stages to the struggle for liberation. The first is what they term the national democratic stage, which seeks to put an end to all forms of racial domination and the achievement of democratic rights as outlined in the Freedom Charter.[190] The rights outlined in the charter are not a program for socialism but a list of common demands around which socialist and nonsocialist can rally.[191] Interestingly, although the party does not consider the charter a socialist document, neither does it advance the view that it is a capitalist document. The aims of the charter "are proposals for what it calls the building of a national democratic state."[192] The SACP considers the achievement of the aims of the charter an important step in the advance along a noncapitalist path toward the Communist future.[193] This first stage will see both state and private ownership of the means of production, since to aim for socialism in the first stage would be counterproductive.[194] Use of violence is legitimate to achieve the national democratic state. The SACP does not spell out how it seeks to move from the national democratic state to the socialist or Communist state. With the recent change in thinking of the leadership with respect to nationalization, it is unclear what the second stage of liberation would entail.[195]

Nation and State. Although the party speaks about a unitary state with protection of individual rights, historically the party has conceived South

Africa as a plural society. In this regard, the SACP speaks about protecting and upholding the culture of all national groups, as well as protecting and safeguarding the rights of minority groups such as Europeans, coloreds, and Indians.[196] But the SACP also promotes internationalism and fights against all manifestations of isolationism "and the glorification and perpetuation of reactionary traditions, which have their roots in capitalist, tribal and feudalist outlooks."[197] The SACP and the ANC historically worked together as part of the congress alliance to achieve the goals of the Freedom Charter. It is estimated that almost half of the executive of the ANC hold membership of the SACP as well.[198] Since the alliance between the ANC and the SACP was an alliance in exile, the exact degree of tension between the liberal and Marxist tendencies in the alliance has been subject to a great deal of debate. It is still to be seen how this tension plays itself out in the South African reality with the recent unbanning of the two movements. The alliance has endured through the CODESA talks.

At the CODESA talks the SACP also announced its proposals for a new constitution. The SACP favors a multiparty system based on proportional representation. Regions would not be permitted to secede from the united South Africa.[199] It calls for entrenchment of cultural, language, and religious rights of all individuals, though regions would enjoy autonomy guaranteed in the constitution. However, the regions would not elect representatives to the central organs of government.[200] The SACP also favors a bill of rights subject to judicial review. However, nothing in the constitution should prevent a future government from addressing the ills of racial discrimination. The SACP leader Joe Slovo recently caused a stir when he announced that the government and the nationalist movements should agree to a government of national unity in terms of which smaller parties would be guaranteed representation in a future government for a limited period. This position has also been accepted by the ANC as the main basis on which the interim government would operate after the 27 April 1994 elections.[201]

PAN-AFRICANIST CONGRESS

The Pan-Africanist Congress's (PAC) ideology has contained strong currents of African nationalism and ideas of African socialism. The PAC was formed as a result of a split from the ANC in 1959 by a group opposed to the ANC's adoption of the Freedom Charter and alliance with other organizations. They split from the ANC because they believed the ANC leadership was being influenced by Communism and other foreign ideologies and in the process was sacrificing the interests of the African majority.[202] The PAC leadership consisted of so-called Africanists in the ANC.

The Africanists believed that the nationalist movement should consist only of Africans who were the oppressed and downtrodden, and were the only people who had an interest in the overthrow of the racist system.[203] The involvement of other groups results in compromises (checks and guarantees) that stultify the movement and aspirations of the Africans. The Africanists believed that the thrust of the movement should be directed at the restoration of the land and the natural resources to the indigenous people. At the political level, the PAC stands for a "government of the Africans for the Africans, by the Africans."[204] An African is anybody who accepts the rule by an African majority and owes their loyalty to Africa.[205]

The PAC rejects the protection of minority rights because it perceives the problem in South Africa historically has been the protection of minority rights. Moreover, it rejects the categorization of racial groups and subscribes to the view that there is only one race, namely, the human race.[206] Its orignial manifesto does not tolerate the existence of other national groups "within the confines of one nation."[207] The PAC was the first organization to reject any concession to caste or group prejudice and to commit to the idea of a single nation.[208]

However, the PAC does favor the protection of individual rights that apply to all people and not to defined groups.[209] The PAC has favored a unitary state. It views a federation as a compromise that would destroy national unity. It envisages a strong central government elected by universal suffrage.[210]

The PAC's economic policies are based on the idea of African socialism[211]—"an Africanist Socialist Democratic order of society which recognizes the primacy of the vital, material, intellectual and spiritual interests of the individual." This is consistent with most notions of African socialism and the idea that an individual enjoys individual rights through the group of which the individual is a part.

The PAC's economic program called for a planned economy with a redistribution of wealth. Land belongs to the indigenous people;[212] one cannot treat "foreign settlers" and indigenous people as equals, because "land robbery" took place in Africa.[213] The task of a future government is to restore the land to the indigenous people.

Needless to say, the PAC took exception to many of the provisions of the Freedom Charter: that South Africa belongs to all who live in it;[214] that South Africa consists of many national groups;[215] that minority rights should be protected (everyone is welcome to stay in South Africa but only on the terms of the African majority). The PAC considered many of the provisions in the charter to be the work of white Communists and considered Communism an alien ideology that did not represent the aspirations of the African majority.[216]

The PAC is the second liberation movement that enjoyed international recognition. Like the ANC, the PAC was banned in 1960 following the Sharpville uprisings. Prior to its unbanning in February 1990, its supporters tried to regroup internally and formed the Pan-Africanist Movement (PAM) in December 1989.[217] The PAC's program and constitutional vision for a future South Africa are not adequately spelled out. It does not explain what it understands democracy to mean. For much of its existence it has attacked the policies of the rival ANC and the Freedom Charter, accusing the ANC of selling out the African majority.[218] It adopts the view that it alone has the correct message for the oppressed,[219] an unfortunate and dangerous position and an ill omen for democracy.

The PAC stayed out for a long time of the CODESA talks because it felt CODESA was a prepackaged forum of the National Party and the ANC and their affiliates, together with representatives of homeland governments.[220] The PAC also accused the ANC of colluding with the National Party behind closed doors.[221] The PAC position was that talks for a new constitution should not proceed in CODESA but should take place in the context of a democratically elected constituent assembly. On a number of occasions the PAC has threatened to use force to derail any agreement between the ANC and the National Party with respect to a new constitution,[222] but it finally decided to contest the 27 April 1994 elections.

BLACK CONSCIOUSNESS MOVEMENTS

The term *Black Consciousness* (BC) was applied to the movement that emerged in the early 1970s under the leadership of Steve Biko and other student activists. The movement started with the formation of the South African Students Organization (SASO) in 1969. The movement later spread into the community with the formation of the Black People's Convention (BPC) in 1972. SASO was formed as a response to perceived paternalism from the dominant white liberal student organization, the National Union of South African Students (NUSAS).[223] The BC movement historically (particularly the policies of SASO and BPC) shares many similarities with the PAC. However, there are important points of departure as well, as will become evident in the class analysis of the present BC umbrella organization, AZAPO.

Ideology of BC, SASO/BPC, and AZAPO. The BC movement attempted to bring black people together around their common experiences. The term *black* was used to include all oppressed peoples—Africans, coloreds, and Indians. It thus shared similarities with the PAC, though its conception of the oppressed was larger than the Africanism of the PAC.[224] However, this did not mean that anyone who was not white was automatically black. From its inception there was a class element in the ideology in that the black was defined to include all those who by law or tradition were politically, socially, or economically exploited against as a group in South African society and who identified themselves as a unit in the struggle for

191

liberation.[225] The definition was meant to take into account the condition of people and also called on those people to identify and show solidarity with their oppressed fellows. This still constitutes the definition of *black* accepted by the present Black Consciousness movement, The Azanian People's Organization (AZAPO).

The central tenet of the BC movement was to work toward the psychological liberation of blacks from Eurocentric values. In the words of Steve Biko, the BC movement was not interested in integration and assimilation of blacks into an existing system of values and norms that a settler minority imposed on an indigenous majority.[226] Instead it sought to make black people proud of their identity and their history and to define themselves in terms of their own identity as opposed to white or European standards.[227] Psychological liberation was seen as an essential prerequisite for physical liberation. An interrelated aspect in cultivating this self-belief was the BC idea that in matters relating to the struggle, blacks as the oppressed had to go it alone without interference from whites.[228] The BC approach resembled that of African nationalism, but differing in its use of the more inclusive term *black*.[229] However, the early movement made a point of African culture and the communal way of life as the central basis for the organization of society.[230] Whites would be free to continue residing in South Africa on the terms and conditions of the black majority.[231] These arguments have a lot in common with notions of rediscovering the African personality or reconstructing the majority's concepts of life, politics, and economics.[232] The values of a future South African society should be based on the traditions of black society.[233]

Economic Policy of the BC Movement: From SASO to AZAPO. From its early days the BC movement (like the PAC) lay great emphasis on the right of the indigenous people to repossess the land. Early visions with regard to the future society were not altogether coherent and contained both elements of African socialism and the idea of promoting a black capitalist class. The movement always had the idea of restructuring the values, politics, and economics of South African society, which in the early years (SASO/BPC era) was done in terms of the notions of African socialism.[234] Clearly, the notion of African socialism differed from Marxism. This was evident in the programs and emphasis of the early movement. For example, the early leadership emphasized the establishing of black business cooperatives and banks.[235] The early economic policy was one of a mixed economy with state regulation of economic activity existing alongside private enterprise.[236]

In the middle 1970s the government was implementing its homeland policy and there was a greater effort on the part of the state and business sector to create a black middle class. These events caused a change in BC thinking toward a greater emphasis on the class issue as opposed to just looking at matters in terms of race.[237] The movement began to recognize that it was possible for the state to co-opt sectors of the black population and use them in the interests of white supremacy.[238] By the end of 1977, all the BC organizations were banned and almost all their leaders were in detention[239] or serving prison sentences, and the class analysis was not developed to any great extent. The theoretical development took place with the formation of AZAPO in 1978.

In AZAPO's "aims and objectives,"[240] the BC movement for the first time speaks about black workers as being responsible for creating the wealth of the country, about developing BC as a philosophy for workers, and about the black working class as the vanguard of the struggle for liberation. The first aim of the organization is listed as the conscientization and politicization of workers through the philosophy of BC.[241] AZAPO's characterization of what constitutes the "revolutionary" working class is a fusion of traditional BC and Marxism. According to AZAPO, in the South African formation race is a class determinant.

Since the formation of AZAPO, the organization has taken a distinct anticapitalist approach. Subsequent programs and congresses of the movement have emphasized that their opposition is not only against racism but capitalism as well.[242] Racial oppression is seen as working side by side with capitalist oppression in the impoverishment and dispossession of the black majority.[243] In this regard the BC movement merges the social question and the national question, which is an important point of departure from the South African Communist Party's position.[244]

AZAPO sees mere independence like the rest of Africa or majority rule in itself as insufficient. Democracy can only be achieved with a socialist revolution.[245] In the words of AZAPO's official publication *Frank Talk*, AZAPO has moved beyond the "the nebulous Black Communalism" of the former BC days and sharpened its definition of a future society.[246] AZAPO's program for a future South Africa is embodied in the Manifesto of the Azanian People formulated by the National Forum in June 1983.

The National Forum and the Manifesto of the Azanian People. The National Forum was a meeting of some two hundred black community, political, cultural, church, and sporting organizations held at Hammanskraal on 11–12 June 1983 to discuss the future direction of the struggle in South Africa. The forum was organized by a committee consisting of personalities from various community, civic, cultural, sports and political organizations.

At the first meeting the National Forum split into four commissions that presented different reports on a host of subjects. At the end of the meeting delegates to the forum adopted seven resolutions and the Manifesto of the Azanian People. The manifesto was produced by the heads and reporters of the four commissions who met and consolidated their reports.[247] It was amended at the second National Forum meeting held in Edendale in April 1984. The Manifesto was finally adopted by the National Forum at a meeting in Lenasia outside Johannesburg in July 1984.

In a key paper delivered by Neville Alexander, one of the principal conveners, the forum was told the goal of national liberation was the destruction of racial capitalism and that opposition to apartheid was the starting point in this struggle.[248] This view is embodied in the preamble to the manifesto. The divisions in the South African population such as Xhosa, Indian, Zulu, colored, and so on are attributed to a divide-and-rule strategy aimed at fragmenting the working class. The ideology of racism and the notion that South Africa consists of many nations or races was developed in order to justify the policies of the white government.[249]

The manifesto sees antiracism as a principle in the struggle.[250] This has to be contrasted with nonracialism, which many of the liberation movements espouse as the basis of a future society. Nonracialism in the view of many delegates to the forum meant the rejection of the concept of race as a basis for discrimination against people. Antiracism, on the other hand, posits the rejection of the concept of race as having any validity in distinguishing between people. Delegates to the forum were very critical of some of the constituents in the UDF (such as the Transvaal Indian Congress and the Natal Indian Congress), which organized along ethnic lines and accepted the labels of different ethnic groups as self-evident.[251] According to Alexander, if one accepts the notion of different racial or national groups as self-evident, then it is logical that one espouses a separatist or federal constitutional order. The notion of antiracism and its embodiment in the manifesto is the furthest the liberation movements have gone toward rejecting any notion of pluralism and the idea that South Africa consists of different groups. It is also the clearest conception of a single national identity. The manifesto does not speak about the nature of the future state, but the tenor of its antiracist sentiments makes it certain that it rejects any notion of pluralism. AZAPO has followed on the sentiments expressed at the forum and in the manifesto. In its official publication, AZAPO acknowledges that the phenomenon of racism has shaped social forces, but it rejects the concept of race as a biological entity.[252]

The manifesto does not provide any blueprint for the organization of the future society. However, it is socialist in orientation. The manifesto proclaims its goals to be the "establishment of an anti-racist worker Republic in Azania where the interests of the workers shall be paramount through worker control of the means of production, distribution and exchange." Moreover, unlike the previous BC approach, which sought to repossess the land and wealth for the black majority, the manifesto proclaims that the land "and all that belongs to it will be wholly owned and controlled by the Azanian people."[253] It does not define who will constitute the future Azanian nation. The National Forum rejected any notion of pluralism, ethnicity, or national groups in favor of a single nation.[254] However, the BC element is still reflected in the Manifesto in that the black working class is seen as the "vanguard" and "driving force" of the struggle.

The National Forum and Democracy. The manifesto was an important document in the fight of the oppressed to develop a framework for a future society. However, it should be viewed as a further step in the ongoing debate and not as a blueprint for a future society. The manifesto was drawn up at the National Forum where a host of political organizations and groupings were represented. It is democratic insofar as the participants to the forum as delegates of their respective constituencies participated in its formulation and took it back to their constituencies for approval. However, most of the UDF and pro-ANC affiliates did not participate in the forum. Thus a significantly large section of the black population and its organizations were absent. In this sense the manifesto cannot claim to be representative of the wishes of the people at large.

The manifesto is socialist in rhetoric. It seeks to entrench the interests of the working class as the primary concern of the future society. The third commission report eschewed the institution of private property saying that the land shall be held by the state for the benefit of all. Moreover, it spoke about the land being for the benefit of all Africa and international trade. Both these provisions are problematic. The experiences of state socialism rife with corruption and inefficiency in Eastern Europe and Africa should be a lesson architects for a future South Africa should not ignore. And to talk about the use of the land for the benefit of other nations or international trade smacks of imperialism and is symptomatic of so many countries in Africa gone wrong.

The manifesto does not discuss the basis of the future state or how power is to be organized and exercised. The first commission report of the National Forum accepted the right of different political tendencies to propagate their programs. However, the forum accepted the view that once a decision is taken by a majority after discussion it must be accepted by all,[255] though the resolution is vague and could conceivably mean a call for decisions to be taken on the basis of the principle of democratic centralism. In the light of the experiences of democratic centralism and its inevitable decline to authoritarianism from the top to bottom in Communist and African socialist states, the provision sets a dangerous precedent. The manifesto has been adopted by AZAPO and together with the organization's aims and policies can be considered as the political blueprint of the organization.

AZAPO/National Forum on the National Convention. Although neither the National Forum nor AZAPO addresses the organizational structure of a future society, both have come out vociferously against any attempt to have a national convention to resolve the problems of South African society.[256] At the National Forum summit meeting in Edendale on 21-22 April 1984, the forum resolved there can never be a transference of power via a national convention because power is wrested and not transferred.[257] The government of the day is seen as too strong and would impose its will on the majority at a national convention.[258] Moreover, a national convention is seen as an exercise where the present rulers compromise with an indigenous elite to share the spoils of the system while the majority are left in a debilitating condition.[259] The forum resolved to do everything in its power to ensure there would be no national convention, and called instead for a constituent assembly along the lines of one called at the time of the French Revolution to be responsible for drawing up a new constitution.[260] For a long time neither AZAPO nor the National Forum elaborated on what was meant by a constituent assembly. Recently, the idea has been expressed more coherently as involving the resignation of the ruling party, who would then play a role identical with all other political organizations in drawing up a new constitution.[261] All the political organizations would send their representatives to draw up a new constitution and decide on a formula as to who should rule.[262]

Similarly, AZAPO has refused to participate in CODESA, insisting instead that the government should resign and that there should be elections for a constituent assembly that would be entrusted with drawing up a new constitution.[263]

AZAPO's Position on the Future State, Democracy, and Other Movements. The manifesto does not define the basis for the organization of a future state, and AZAPO's position is if not inconsistent at least ambiguous. While the manifesto maintains the right of different tendencies to exist, AZAPO's *Frank Talk* goes back to the Marxist cliche of the state and all its institutions being part of the machinery to keep down the oppressed and exploited.[264] It asserts the future state will take the form of a revolutionary dictatorship of the black proletariat. In this state all classes will be eliminated and power will reside with the black working class.[265] In terms of the classical Marxist interpretation, this cannot be achieved in a multiparty political setting. Not surprisingly, the vanguard party will lead the revolution, the state being merely an administrative body in a classless society.[266] The rhetoric and sentiments (apart from the element of black consciousness) expressed are almost identical with those of Communist parties in other parts of the world. Single-party states under vanguard leadership are experiencing legitimacy problems almost everywhere. In the light of the atrocities, lack of accountability, and degeneration into autocratic and elite one-party rule which so many Communist countries have experienced, the AZAPO sentiments in this regard are problematic.

At an organizational level, since its inception AZAPO has actively kept away from promoting the image of a single personality as a leader over and above others in the organization. It has committed the organization to collective leadership, as opposed to promoting a leadership cult. In this regard, the organization continually rotates its leadership positions.[267] The experiences of Africa have shown the inherent dangers in cult personalities and power revolving around a single personality; AZAPO's maturity at this level is a positive development.

AZAPO's tolerance for other organizations and political tendencies has been less favorable. Many AZAPO attacks have been directed toward what it considers to be "liberalism."[268] On many occasions the leaders have claimed they are the only liberation movement operating in South Africa.[269] AZAPO has been particularly critical of the Freedom Charter as being a bourgeois democratic and civil rights document that does not address the real needs of the people.[270] AZAPO members and former UDF activists were involved in bitter ideological and territorial feuds that at times have taken on civil-war proportions.[271] Conceptions of democracy and liberation may differ across different movements. However, like other organizations, the claim by certain AZAPO leaders that they are the only liberation movement is a lofty and dangerous claim.

REFERENCES

1. See *Weekly Mail*, 14–20 April 1989.
2. Before the February 1990 unbanning of the major organizations.
3. See *Weekly Mail*, 7–13 April 1989.
4. *Weekly Mail*, 14–20 April 1989.
5. The Democratic Party, *A Government in the Making* (Cape Town: Pioneer Press, n.d.).
6. Ibid.
7. Ibid.
8. *Weekly Mail*, 13–19 October 1989, 8.
9. The proposals of the Progressive Federal Party are embodied in the *Report of the Constitutional Committee of the Progressive Federal Party and Policy Decisions Made by the Federal Congress of the P.F.P at its Federal Congress held in Durban on 17th and 18th November, 1978* (Cape Town: P.F.P., 1979).
10. Ibid., 9.
11. Ibid., 15.
12. Ibid., 35.
13. Ibid., 4.
14. Ibid., 12, 30.
15. Ibid., 27.
16. Ibid., 29–30.
17. Ibid., 30.
18. Ibid., 33.
19. Ibid., 34.
20. Ibid.

21. Ibid., 37.

22. D. J. van Vuuren and D. J. Kriek, *Political Alternatives for Southern Africa* (Durban: Butterworth's, 1983), 565.

23. F. Venter, *South African Constitutional Law in Flux* (n.p., n.d.), 135.

24. Boulle, *Constitutional Reform*, 112.

25. D. Geldenhuys, "South Africa's Constitutional Alternatives," *South African International* (1981): 205.

26. Ibid., 205.

27. Venter, *Constitutional Law in Flux*, 135.

28. Boulle, *South Africa's Constitutional Options*, 112.

29. Geldenhuys, "Constitutional Alternatives," 206.

30. The federal-consociational arrangements designed to protect the interests of "different groups" in South African society. For a fuller discussion of the federal-consociational arrangement see chapter 4.

31. For a fuller discussion and criticisms of the plural paradigm see chapter 7.

32. See the transcript of the interview conducted by Ted Koppel of Nightline with South African President De Klerk on 13 February 1990.

33. *Weekly Mail*, 12–18 May 1989.

34. Ibid.

35. See De Klerk, interview on Nightline.

36. Inter Press Service, 1 June 1992.

37. PR Newswire, 19 May 1992.

38. *Nikkei Weekly*, 19 October 1992.

39. *Washington Post*, 13 October 1992.

40. Agence France Presse, 12 October 1992.

41. H. Giliomee, "The Last Trek? Afrikaaners in the Transition to Democracy," *South Africa International* (January 1992): 117.

42. Buthelezi Commission, *The Requirements for Stability and Development in KwaZulu and Natal*, Vol. 1 (1985), 105.

43. Ibid.

44. Munger Africana Library Notes Issue no. 56, *The Buthelezi Commission* (1980), 7. However, the movement does not spell out how its proposals can be used in other parts of the country.

45. Boulle, *Constitutional Reform*, 137.

46. Buthelezi Commission Report, 112.

47. However, for an initial period (before the region was divided and the other structures set up) the commission called for an executive made up of equal number of whites and representatives from the KwaZulu government together with representatives of the Indian and colored communities.

48. Ibid., 114.

49. Ibid.

50. Indaba, *A Leadership Publication* (n.p.: 1987): 45.

51. Ibid., 46.

52. For details about the actual institutions see *KwaZulu Natal Indaba Constitutional Proposals Agreed to on 28 November 1986*.

53. This group includes people who do not wish to be classified in terms of any ethnic label.

54. Indaba, *Constitutional Proposals*, item K.1.

55. In this sense the State President will still have a veto power over decisions in the region.

56. For a list of the participants and their attitudes to the Indaba see Indaba, *Constitutional Proposals*, particularly 48.

57. *Indaba News*, 8 November 1987, 7.

58. Mangosuthu Gatsha Buthelezi, *South Africa: Anatomy of Black-White Power Sharing* (Lagos: Emmcom Books, 1986), xxii.

59. More specifically achieved through the rigid nature of the constitution and the veto power accorded to the groups.

60. Like its internal affiliates it is most unlikely that the ANC would have participated in the Indaba. Similarly, the PAC adheres to the principle of noncollaboration and would not have participated in a program that included organizations.

61. Indaba, *Constitutional Proposals*, 47, 77.

62. See the Indaba, *Constitutional Proposals*. See also L. Schlemmer in *Indaba News*, 9 December 87/January 1988, 6.

63. See previous discussion about the legitimacy problem that many constitutional dispensations experience when the majority are not involved in the formulation of the constitutional proposals (chapters 2, 7 and 9).

64. Buthelezi, *South Africa*, 7.

65. Ibid., 7–8.

66. *Weekly Mail*, 14–20 July 1989, 7.

67. Ibid. The reality is Buthelezi is the head of the government-created homeland of KwaZulu. The government provides him with large sums of money for providing education, housing, and infrastructure. Moreover, the KwaZulu government has its own civil service.

68. Ibid., 8.

69. Oliver Tambo, *Preparing for Power* (New York: G. Braziller, 1988), 146.

70. More recently the *Weekly Mail* has documented a leader of the Inkatha Youth Brigade being responsible for leading assaults on hostel workers who are opposed to Inkatha. See *Weekly Mail* 7 September 1990, 1.

71. See view of Maylam and Wright in Indaba, *Constitutional Proposals*, 18.

72. Inkatha has a policy of signing all members of the police force into the organization and sees the police's allegiance to the organization as being more important than their duty as policemen. See *Weekly Mail*, 29 September to 5 October 1989, 12.

73. *Weekly Mail*, 23–30 March 1989, 1–2.

74. See Buthelezi's response to these criticisms in Buthelezi, *South Africa*, 43. See also *Weekly Mail*, 23–30 March 1989, 1–2.

75. *Weekly Mail*, 21–27 July 1989, 13.

76. There are no structures which link Inkatha to the community or vice versa. See *Weekly Mail*, 21–27 July 1989, 13.

77. Buthelezi, *South Africa*, 14, 20.

78. Ibid., 83. In the South African climate and given the strongarm tactics that he and his supporters use over the local population it is difficult to gauge the precise nature of Buthelezi's support.

79. *New York Times*, 1 October 1992, sec. A, 6.

80. *Reuters Library Report*, 6 October 1992.

81. *Reuters Library Report*, 1 December 1992.

82. *United Press International*, 1 December 1992.

83. Ibid.

84. Agence France Presse, 3 December 1992.

85. Tambo, *Preparing for Power*, 211.

86. Gail M. Gerhard, *Black Power in South Africa: The Evolution of an Ideology* (Berkeley: University of California Press, 1978), 12–13.

87. Thomas K. Ranuga, "Marxism and Black Nationalism in South Africa: A Comparative and Critical Analysis of the Ideological Conflict and Consensus Between Marxism and Nationalism in the ANC, the PAC, and the BCM: 1920–1980." Ph.D. diss., Brandeis University, 1983, 1.

88. Gerhard, *Black Power*, 94.

89. Robert Fatton, *Black Consciousness in South Africa: The Dialectics of Ideological Resistance to White Supremacy* (Albany, N.Y.: State University of New York Press, 1986), 8.

90. African National Congress, *Selected Writings on the Freedom Charter 1955–1985, A Sechaba Commemorative Publication* (London: ANC, 1985), 104.

91. Fatton, *Black Consciousness*, 3.

92. ANC, *Freedom Charter*, 105.

93. Tambo, *Preparing for Power*, 33.

94. Zachariah K. Matthews, *Freedom for My People* (London: R. Collings, 1981), 173.

95. Raymond Suttner, et al., *30 Years of the Freedom Charter* (Johannesburg: Ravan Press, 1985), 12–19.

96. B. Fine, "The Freedom Charter: A Critical Appreciation," *South African Labour Bulletin* 11(3) (1984) 38.

97. R. T. Kono, "Marxism and Black Nationalism." Ph.D. diss. Brandeis University, 1982, 174.

98. Gilbert Marcus, *The Freedom Charter: A Blueprint for a Democratic South Africa* (Johannesburg: University of the Witwatersrand, 1985), 6.

99. ANC, *Freedom Charter*, 80.

100. Ibid.

101. Suttner, *30 Years*, 86.

102. T. Lodge, "Remembering the Freedom Charter," *SALB*.

103. Marcus, *Freedom Charter*, 15.

104. Unfortunately, the ANC leadership have not been forthcoming on this vital issue of how the process took place and who did the ordering of values.

105. Albert J. Luthuli, *Let My People Go: An Autobiography* (Johannesburg: Collins, 1962), 158.

106. *Weekly Mail*, 26 June 1985.

107. D. M. Davis, "30 Years of the Freedom Charter," *South African Journal on Human Rights* 2 (1986): 368.

108. No other gathering to date has represented so wide a cross-section of the population in a single place to voice demands for a post-apartheid South Africa.

109. M. Swilling, "The Freedom Charter and the Economy," in James A. Polley, ed., *The Freedom Charter and the Future: Proceedings of the National Conference on the Freedom Charter and the Future* (Johannesburg: Ad. Donker, 1988), 38.

110. Fine, *The Freedom Charter*, 40.

111. H. MacLean, "Capitalism, Socialism, and the Freedom Charter," *SALB* (May 1986): 8.

112. Swilling, "Freedom Charter," 39.

113. Suttner, *30 Years*, 143–44.

114. MacLean, "Capitalism," 8.

115. Sechaba, *Selected Writings on the Freedom Charter, 1955–1985* (London: ANC, 1985), 76.

116. Ibid.

117. Suttner, *30 Years*, 178–79.

118. See Billy Nair, in Suttner, *30 years*, 180.

119. N. Mandela, in Thomas Karis and Gwendolen M. Carter, eds., *From Protest to Challenge; A Documentary History of African Politics in South Africa, 1882–1964* (Stanford, Calif.: Hoover Inst. Press, 1972), 245. Most of text also printed in Sechaba, *Selected Writings*.

120. Ibid.

121. Fatton, *Black Consciousness*, 18.

122. Mandela, in Sechaba, *Selected Writings*, 24.

123. Sechaba, *Selected Writings*, 30–31.

124. Suttner, *30 Years*, 128.

125. Ibid., 129.

126. Ibid., 129–30.

127. Sechaba, *Selected Writings*, 84.

128. Tshetwe, in Suttner, *30 Years*, 210–13.

129. For the results of a constitution based on ethnic mobilization, see chapter 7.

130. Together with the other urgent goals of economic redistribution and democracy to be discussed.

131. ANC, SAIC, COD, and SACPO to represent the African, Indian, white, and colored people respectively.

132. Marcus, *Freedom Charter*, 4.

133. Ibid., 6.

134. Suttner, *30 Years*, 136–37.

135. See chapter 12, where it is argued that there should be recognition of equality of languages and beliefs, but this is not the same as institutionalized fragmentation.

136. Mzala, in Sechaba, *Selected Writings*, 98.

137. Tshetwe in Suttner, *30 Years*, 218.

138. Sechaba, *Selected Writings*, 65.

139. James A. Polley, ed., *The Freedom Charter and the Future: Proceedings of the National Conference on the Freedom Charter and the Future* (Johannesburg: Ad. Donker, 1988), 33–34.

140. Indeed, the goals and objectives (which have constantly been emphasized) have to be defined. We will deal with the question of how the constitution could do this in chapter 13.

141. Davis, *30 Years*, 369; Fine, *The Freedom Charter*, 40.

142. Fine, *The Freedom Charter*, 40.

143. P. Hudson, "The Freedom Charter and Socialist Strategy in South Africa," *Politikon* 13(1) (1986): 75.

144. MacLean, "Capitalism," 14.

145. For a copy of the guidelines see A. Sachs, "Towards a Bill of Rights for a Democratic South Africa," *Hastings International and Comparative Law Review* 12 (1989): 322.

146. Z. Skweyiya of ANC Constitutional Committee, in Sechaba, *Selected Writings*, 6.

147. Ibid.

148. ANC constitutional guidelines, clause (G); ibid.

149. *Economist*, 5 December 1992.

150. Agence France Presse, 3 December 1992.

151. *Daily Telegraph*, 26 November 1992.

152. Clause (J), ibid.

153. Clause (V), ibid.

154. Clause (Q), ibid; See also *Weekly Mail*, 7–13 July 1989, 6.

155. *Weekly Mail*, ibid. Nationalization in almost all African countries resulted in the transfer of wealth to agents of the state and over a period of time resulted in corruption, inefficiency, and economic slowdown. See especially chapter 9.

156. Jack Simons, in Sechaba, *Selected Writings*, 103.

157. Ibid.

158. Sechaba, *Selected Writings*, 87.

159. Ibid.

160. Ibid., 92–93. Clearly, the two-stage theory of revolution is the policy of the South African Communist Party. There is an overlap of membership between the SACP and the ANC, and it is uncertain whether the two-stage theory is a dominant view within the ANC leadership as well.

161. Sechaba, *Selected Writings*, 86.

162. African National Congress, *The Pan Africanist Congress of South Africa: Whom Does it Serve* (n.p., 1968).

163. Ibid., 1, 4.

164. Tambo, *Preparing for Power*, 116–17, 126.

165. Ibid.

166. Sechaba, *Selected Writings*, 82.

167. The attitude of the writer in the ANC publication *Sechaba* is that anyone who opposes the charter is a counterrevolutionary and a tool of imperialism.

168. In chapter 12, we suggest the creation of a constitutional court along the lines of the German model with similar power to outlaw political parties that endanger the principles vital to the existence of the new nation.

169. Robert H. Davies, et al., *The Struggle for South Africa: A Reference Guide to Movements, Organizations, and Institutions* (London: Zed, 1984), 292.

170. Ranuga, "Marxism and Black Nationalism," 2.

171. Davies, *Struggle for South Africa*, 293.

172. Ibid., 293.

173. See "The Road to South African Freedom," *African Communist*, First Quarter (1963).

174. Ibid., 27, 37.

175. "The Road to South African Freedom," 66–67.

176. Ibid., 64.

177. These provisions are not inconsistent with what was found in the Stalin and Brezhnev constitutions.

178. Ibid., 65.

179. Ibid., 59.

180. Meaning the cadres of the party.

181. "The Road to South African Freedom," 34.

182. Joe Slovo, quoted in Supplement to *Weekly Mail*, 30 March–4 April 1990, 4.

183. Ibid.

184. South African Communist Party, *Umsebenzi* 6(1) (1990): 3.

185. J. Slovo, "General Secretary of SACP," *Umsebenzi* 6(1) (1990): 4.

186. Ibid., 5, 8.

187. See views of Govan Mbeki, quoted in *Weekly Mail*, 9–15 February 1990, 10.

188. See the various criticisms levelled by trade union and black consciousness leaders against the SACP in *Weekly Mail*, 11–17 May 1990, 9.

189. "The Road to South African Freedom," 43. This view was echoed in the recent 7th Congress of the party. See SACP, *Umsebenzi* 5(2) (1989): 7.

190. Ibid., 9.

191. "The Road to South African Freedom," 62.

192. Ibid., 64.

193. Ibid.

194. Extracts from SACP's 7th Congress, *Umsebenzi* 5(2) (1989): 10.

195. See discussion above where the SACP have accepted the existence of a mixed economy.

196. "The Road to South African Freedom," 68–69.

197. Ibid., 39.

198. Hudson, "Freedom Charter," 87.

199. British Broadcasting Corporation, 13 Febrary 1992.

200. Ibid.

201. *Weekly Mail*, 27 November 1992, 4

202. Ranuga, *Marxism and Black Nationalism*, 5.

203. Pan-African Congress, *One Azania, One Nation, One People! Speeches and Documents of the Pan-African Congress* (1977), 2.

204. Ibid.

205. More recently the leadership have said that this loyalty does not depend on a person's color.

206. See Pan African Congress, *The Manifesto of the P.A.C, Adopted by the Inaugural Conference in April 1959.*

207. Ibid., art. (K).

208. No Sizwe, *One Azania, One Nation* (London: Zed, 1979), 117.

209. Pan African Congress, *Time for Azania* (Toronto: Norman Bethune Institute, 1976), 16.

210. Their idea of a unitary state encompasses the whole of Africana. See PAC, *Time for Azania*, 3.

211. PAC Manifesto, art. (N) and (l).

212. Ibid., art. (M) and (I).

213. Ibid., art. (B).

214. Gerhard, *Black Power*, 147.

215. Ranuga, "Marxism and Black Nationalism," 227.

216. Ibid., 5.

217. See *Weekly Mail*, 17–23 November 1989, 12.

218. See PAC Manifesto, art. (I).

219. Ibid., art. (O).

220. British Broadcasting Corporation, 21 December 1991.

221. Agence France Press, 2 December 1991.

222. The PAC military wing APLA has claimed responsibility for a wave of armed attacks on whites. *The Independent*, 16 December 1992, 12.

223. Davies, *Struggle for South Africa*, 303.

224. Fatton, *Black Consciousness*, 32.

225. See SASO manifesto.

226. Steve Biko, *I Write What I Like* (San Francisco: Harper & Row, 1986), 25.

227. Ibid., 30.

228. According to Biko, if blacks were to transform the system they had to believe in themselves; a process which could not develop in an artificial alliance between whites and blacks. Ibid., 24, 49.

229. The term black encompasses Africans, coloreds, and Indians.

230. Ibid., 41.

231. See *Frank Talk*, 1(2/3) (July/August 1984): 10.

232. See Fatton, *Black Consciousness*, 57.

233. Sometimes there was a blurring of concepts; Biko spoke about traditional African society, while members of the BC movement spoke about black values. While one can talk about a core African culture among the indigenous population, it is questionable whether there is a core black culture. See *Frank Talk*, 1(2/3) (July/August 1984): 10.

234. The Mafikeng Manifesto of the Black People's Convention, adopted in 1975.

235. Biko, *I Write What I Like*, 97.

236. Davies, *Struggle for South Africa*, 306.

237. Sizwe, *One Azania, One Nation*, 124–25.

238. For example the homeland and separate development "leaders."

239. The most prominent, Steve Biko, was killed in detention in September 1977.

240. Official Aims and Objectives of AZAPO.

241. Ibid.

242. *Frank Talk*, 1(6) (February/March 1985): 11, 21.

243. See paper presented by AZAPO President Mabasa at the National Forum meeting held in June 1984, in the booklet produced by the National Forum (1984).

244. *Frank Talk*, 2(3) (September 1987): 17.

245. *Frank Talk*, 1(2/3) (July/August 1984) 8, 10.

246. *Frank Talk*, 2(3) (September 1987), 14.

247. In terms of Resolution 6 of the National Forum meeting.

248. Alexander, in *National Forum*, 19.

249. Ibid., 21.

250. See preamble of the Manifesto.

251. See Alexander in *National Forum*, 23.

252. *Frank Talk*, 2(3) (September 1987), 17.

253. Mafikeng Manifesto, resolution 2.

254. *National Forum*, 30.

255. Resolution 1, *National Forum*, 65.

256. *Frank Talk*, 1(2/3) (July/August 1984): 11.

257. *National Forum*, 15.

258. *Frank Talk*, 1(6) (February/March 1985): 6.

259. Ibid., 3.

260. Ibid., 16.

261. *Weekly Mail*, 4–10 August 1989, 15.

262. Ibid.

263. Xianhua General Overseas News Service, 23 August 1992.

264. *Frank Talk*, 2(3) (September 1987): 20.

265. Ibid., 21.

266. Ibid.

267. *Frank Talk*, 1(6) (February/March 1985): 13. The pattern of elections of officeholders at AZAPO's national congresses indicates rotation on a continual basis.

268. *Frank Talk*, 2(3) (September 1987): 22.

269. This sentiment was expressed by many of the leaders at the AZAPO Congress held in Edendale in January 1983.

270. *Weekly Mail*, 21–28 June 1985.

271. *Frank Talk*, 2(3) (September 1987): 3.

CHAPTER ELEVEN

The Constitution and Judicial Review

■ ■ ■

T HE TENDENCY IN ALMOST all constitutional discussion for a post-apartheid South Africa is to accord the judiciary a central position in the constitution along the lines of the U. S. constitutional system. In this chapter we investigate the notion and practice of judicial review in Anglo-American constitutional systems[1] and its potential and possible pitfalls in a new South African order. The problem for a future South Africa is not merely to replace the present judiciary (appointed by the apartheid order) with a new set of judges, but to devise an alternative judicial structure that is more democratic[2] as well as suited to the realities of the South African situation.[3]

Judicial Review, the Separation of Powers, and the Rule of Law

Independence of the judiciary is an important principle in Western constitutional systems.[4] Judicial review is essential to the U.S. system, related to concepts of separation of powers and the rule of law. The separation of powers doctrine comprises the idea of checks and balances[5] and the idea of dispersing power among the different agencies of government.[6] The prevention of the concentration of power in a single agency is considered pivotal for the guarantee and protection of individual rights.[7] In the event of a dispute between the agencies of government in regard to their respective authority, or the interpretation of the constitution, the popular liberal view is that neither the legislature nor the executive should have the final word. The dispute-resolution function is the duty of the judiciary.[8] Moreover, in terms of the strict notion of the separation of powers the personnel responsible for interpreting the constitution must be separate from the other branches of government.[9] The philosophical arguments for the separation of powers can be found in the writings of Locke, Montesquieu, and Rousseau.[10]

The idea of government acting in terms of the rule of law is accepted in all Western constitutional systems. In terms of liberal theory,[11] that means the state must act in accordance with law and be limited by law,[12] a control is exercised by the judiciary. Judicialism is the backbone of constitutionalism, the "practical instrument whereby constitutionalism may be transformed into an active idea of government; it is our best guarantee of the rule of law and our liberty."[13] Although Western constitutional systems accept the notion that the state must act in terms of law and within the law, there are different limits to which the individual systems are prepared to permit the judiciary to protect the rule of law.

The Scope of Judicial Review

Although judicial review is an accepted principle in almost all Western political systems,[14] there is considerable variation in the nature and ambit of the judicial function. The most crucial variation is seen in the British and U.S. constitutions. In the former instance the judiciary's role is seen as primarily performing an adjudicating function to rule on disputes between parties. The role of the judiciary in the British system is constrained by the dominant constitutional principle of legislative supremacy. This means no court of law can pronounce on the validity of any act of the legislature. The judicial function in this instance does not extend to an active policy-making power.[15]

The British view is that judges are unelected officials and should not be responsible for shaping the law in terms of what they consider desirable.[16] In terms of this view, judges merely state the law as it is as opposed to fashioning it in terms of what it ought to be. Judges are considered spokespersons for the community and their judgment represents the values and consensus of the community.[17] Judges are entitled to personal opinions, but these opinions should not be reflected in their decisions. The members of the judiciary are appointed in recognition of their skills as legal experts. Once appointed to the bench, the popular view holds that with their security of tenure they are transformed into a liberating voice untouchable by public opinion.[18] The judiciary is elevated to a "majestic" institution and insulated from public opinion. Any attempt to cast aspersions on this institution or to influence its decisions is punishable by contempt-of-court proceedings.[19]

In the United States, on the other hand, the Constitution includes a Bill of Rights and all acts of the legislature have to be measured against the Bill of Rights. Thus the courts exercise active policy-making powers. The courts have the ability to look into the validity of acts of the legislature and the executive against the values embodied in the Bill of Rights. In the United States system the courts are the guardians of the Constitution and the protector of individual rights. Not surprisingly, it has become an established principle that the determination of what the law is, is left to the courts.[20] This means the courts exercise substantive judicial review. However, the meaning of the Constitution and Bill of Rights has not been static throughout the years. The courts in the United States find it their duty to reinterpret the Constitution in response to the changing social climate.[21]

Judicial Review in African Constitutions

In traditional African society there was no concept of judicial review performed by a separate or specialized body. By and large authority was centralized, and the judicial function was performed by the governing chief in council.[22] The type of justice dispensed, although simple, was democratic and popular.[23] The chiefs were assisted in their law-making powers by the senior people of the group.[24] Important decisions were referred to a general meeting of all the people. There was thus no tripartite division of authority, but the people participated in the judicial system and controlled the courts.[25]

The growth of constitutional review from a worldwide perspective was exacerbated in the post-World War II period in an attempt to prevent constitutional failures and the accumulation of power in a single person or group.[26] The U.S. Bill of Rights was an important source of inspiration to many constitutions. Africa was not immune to these developments, and the independence constitutions of most African countries contained provisions guaranteeing the independence of the judiciary and in some instances included a bill of rights.[27] An independent judiciary with judicial review was a mechanism to prevent arbitrary government and ensure the rule of law and protection of individual rights.

The types of constitutions introduced into African countries and the nature of the judiciary contained many of the features found in the constitutions of the former colonial powers. In countries subject to French rule, the French model was introduced, and in countries subject to British rule by and large the practices of the British model were reproduced.[28]

The British attempted to introduce a form of government along the British tradition,[29] though the constitutional order departed from the British model in two significant ways. First, the type of state introduced in many instances was federal. Second, many of the independence African constitutions contained a bill of rights that like the U.S. model would bring the judiciary into the active policy-making process. However, the British ignored the political nature of many judicial decisions, and they took steps to isolate the judiciary from the political process.

Not only did it become an article of faith that the judiciary must be isolated from politics, but many African constitutions went further than the Anglo-American model in incorporating extraordinary measures to create a nonpolitical appointing process and noninvolvement in politics of the judiciary.[30] They attempted to do this by creating judicial service commissions made up of lawyers not involved in politics.[31] The judicial service commissions were entrusted with the responsibility of judicial appointments.[32] This marked a departure from the Anglo-American model where judicial appointments are essentially an executive decision and arguably performed in recognition of a judge's political services and social views.

Similarly, one of the conclusions of the African Conference of the Rule of Law held in Nigeria in 1961 was that ways and means should be found to ensure an absolute independence of the judiciary and control of the judiciary by the legal profession.[33] Liberal political parties in South Africa have also advocated an independent judicial appointments committee with exclusive powers for the appointment of members of the judiciary.[34] More recent proposals ask that the committee consist of the chief justice, minister of justice, secretary for justice, two members of the bar (advocates' professional organization), and two members of the side bar (attorneys' professional organization).[35] The Interim Constitution stipulates that seven of the eleven judges to the South African Constitutional Court be nominated by an impartial Judicial Service Commission.

Attempts to isolate the judiciary from politics are impractical and short-sighted, and symptomatic of notions of the law operating in some neutral autonomous fashion. They ignore the reality that many judicial decisions entail political judgment. In the exercise of this judgment, the political outlook of the judges is extremely important, particularly to a new nation on the threshold of major social and economic changes. The political views of the judges assume greater importance when the constitution of the country is of a federal nature and subject to a bill of rights. If the judiciary is entrusted with policy-making powers, it should be aware of the political realities of the society and the fact that its judgments will affect the new society. The failure to recognize or accept the political role of judiciary decisions was to pose serious problems to many independent African countries.

Judicial Review in South Africa: The Historical Model

The South African parliamentary system has been influenced by British constitutional doctrines, the most important of which is the principle of parliamentary supremacy. Historically, the South African judiciary sees its role in terms identical to that of the British judiciary. According to the former chief justice of South Africa, the task of the courts in interpreting a statute is to ascertain the intention of Parliament.[36] The traditional view is that the judiciary has to stand aloof from the public, politics, and the media and not indulge in questioning the morality or justness of a law. The judge's role when confronted with a statute is not to interpret the law in terms of what he thinks the law ought to be but to express the law in terms of the intent of the legislature.[37] Such a view subscribes to the fiction that the judiciary does not have any law-making powers.

Since the role of the courts is a mechanical function, in the context of the apartheid order the judiciary is regarded in some quarters as the servant of the legislature.[38] But then why in the South African situation have a judiciary at all? Some characterize the role of the courts as providing legitimacy for the existing order. The government was comfortable with an independent judiciary because it was sure that by and large the judiciary would uphold its policies.[39] Independence in this context meant the judiciary would not examine the substance of law or rule on the government's policy issues. Some "radical" theorists assert that not only do the courts play a role in the system of domination, but they also provide a sense of "orderliness and regularity to domination," that the paraphernalia of the court helps to calm people.[40] The courts thus served as a vehicle that accommodated "the dominated to the dominators."[41]

Despite these criticisms, many South African ideologues consistently assert that the South African judiciary was independent and consists of the finest judges to be found anywhere in the world,[42] even the most eminent in the world,[43] contributing to an aura of infallibility about the judiciary.[44] Criticism of the South African judiciary and examination of its background and judgments are not looked upon favorably. For example, it is not usual to scrutinize the pattern of judicial appointments or to publicly comment on them.[45] Comments that question the integrity of the judiciary and the administration of justice are punishable by contempt-of-court proceedings.[46] But the impartiality of the present South African judiciary and its ability to mediate between the interests of different sectors cannot just be assumed and protected. The judicial role has to be subjected to honest investigation. Important questions such as how the present judiciary has been appointed, what its background is, how it arrives at its decisions, and how it has historically fulfilled its functions need to be addressed.

Demystifying the Judiciary

While there may be debate about the role of the judiciary, there is no question about the faith Western political systems have in the judiciary as a neutral institution mediating between the interests of all sectors of society. The South African system is not immune from this line of thought. Not surprisingly, almost all constitutional disucssions in South Africa thrust the existing judiciary into the center of constitutional scenarios, making the judiciary the custodian of the constitution. The ensuing discussion will show that this faith in the independence of the South African judiciary is misplaced.

RECOGNITION OF LAWMAKING POWERS

As alluded to, there is an ongoing debate in Anglo-American constitutional systems as to what constitutes the proper role of the judiciary. No matter how much British, South African, or other judges say they reach decisions on technical or legal grounds, there will inevitably be a personal value judgment or political element in many policy decisions.[47] A constitution or statute is very often phrased in vague and general terms, as is the U.S. Constitution. Because of the lack of specificity, the judges are often called on to give meaning to the phrases and provisions in the statute or constitution, and various canons of interpretation serve to guide them in arriving at a decision. Needless to say, the individual philosophies of the judges also play an important role in shaping decisions. The overall process entails a judge filling in the gaps, which inevitably involves the creation of law.[48] However, this creative element is different from the U.S. position that constitutional law is to be determined by the judiciary; in the British and South African traditions the creative process is less active and confined to statutes. Nevertheless, there is a creative function in the interpretation of statutes.

A second way the courts exercise a limited testing right in South Africa is to demand compliance with the procedure elaborated in the constitution or statute. In other words, the courts cannot declare that an act of the legislature is invalid because it is morally repugnant, but they can declare an act invalid on the grounds that the legislature did not enact the statute in terms of the prescribed constitutional procedure.[49] This principle is embodied in the South Africa Constitution Act of 1983.[50]

POLITICAL CONSIDERATIONS
IN THE APPOINTMENT PROCESS

According to the former chief justice of Tanzania, Telford Georges, political considerations always play a part in the appointment of judges, and this is inevitable.[51] In the Anglo-American model the executive is entrusted with the responsibility of choosing the members of the judiciary. For example, in England the executive has complete discretion in the appointment process. In the United States the Senate must approve all presidential nominations to the Supreme Court.[52] The appointments in many instances are made in recognition of political services,[53] which have led many to question the meaning of judiciary independence. They argue the courts are creatures of the political process,[54] since it is unlikely that the executive would appoint to the bench a person whose political views are in opposition to those of the government. To an extent, the U.S. system in giving the Senate a role in the approval of the Supreme Court justices contributes to the maintenance of judicial standards and will prevent the president from nominating a candidate who is completely unqualified. Although the Senate may prevent the appointment of a candidate because of the individual candidate's political and social values, the executive will always prevail in getting a candidate whose views he believes are similar to the president's.[55]

The appointment of judges in South Africa under the apartheid constitution was done by the state president.[56] In most instances the appointments were made from within the ranks of senior advocates. There is a shortsighted assumption that a lawyer's training and experience at the bar will produce an independent frame of mind and a quest for justice.[57] But the government was unlikely to appoint a large number of judges opposed to its policies. A number of eminent jurists have alluded to the government appointing judges in terms of political preferences both during and in the pre-National Party rule era.[58] Complaints have been made that political factors have been given greater priority than merit, with better-qualified persons being passed over in favor of candidates who share the government's views. Sydney Kentridge asserts most lawyers knew about these appointments but refrained from discussing them because to do so would impair the dignity and reputation of the Supreme Court.[59] There have been allegations of relatively unknown and progovernment Afrikaaner advocates being appointed as judges.[60] A well-known and most controversial judicial incident was the elevation of L. C. Steyn to the position of chief justice over persons considered more senior and deserving than he.[61] It is possible that to raise many of these issues would entail a person being faced with contempt-of-court proceedings. This is not to say there are no judges who are opposed to the philosophies of the government; but the point is the majority of appointees to the bench are proestablishment and arguably hold political views and attitudes not dissimilar to the government's.[62]

The events surrounding the packing of the court following the constitutional crisis in the 1950s confirm the extent to which the government can and indeed did go to manipulate the courts to suit its purposes. Following the Appellate Division ruling that the government's attempts to remove coloreds from the common voters roll was invalid because the correct constitutional procedure was not adhered to, the government increased the number of judges to the division from five to eleven.[63] More significantly, they increased the quorum of judges from five to eleven with respect to disputes pertaining to the interpretation of the constitution. It is arguable that the obvious intent was to pack the highest court in the land with government appointees to ensure the success of the government's impending constitutional amendments.[64] Moreover, there was considerable room for government manipulation of the judiciary as was shown in the constitutional crisis. At a more serious level, studies question the selection of judges in cases involving political controversies. This would seem to suggest that there was some leverage on the part of the executive to directly influence the outcome of decisions, particularly when the case pertains to persons fighting against the present order. For example Dugard asserts that in his study over a five-year period he found that in the Transvaal provincial division 17 percent of the judges heard 84 percent of the cases.[65]

SOCIALIZATION/BACKGROUND OF JUDGES

A second argument for the assumption of the independence of the judiciary relates to security of tenure once appointed to the bench. The Anglo-American model provides judges security of tenure unless forced retirement obtains.[66] Security of tenure is also guaranteed in the South African order.[67] So although a judge may be appointed by the executive because of his or her prior political views, once appointed to the bench there is no way the executive can ensure the judge will act in terms of those political views. The crucial question is how the judges balance and weigh competing interests and claims in exercising their discretionary law-making powers.[68]

Studies have shown that judges are drawn from a small section (invariably the wealthy) of society.[69] It cannot be said that the values and experiences of these people are reflective of the society at large. Indeed, there is the wider argument that the judiciary in Western society has been the conservative wing of government and historically the protector of the propertied class.[70] For example, in France ever since the French Revolution, the courts have been prevented from pronouncing on the validity of the acts of the legislature because of a perception that judges come from the upper strata of society.[71]

In the United States there are clear examples in history where the courts were closely associated with the conservative wing and the wealthy class in society. For example, in the post-1880 period, the court distinctly assumed a position sympathetic to big business.[72] The Supreme Court became the protector of property interests. Elementary economic regulations of every sort were held unconstitutional on the grounds that they interfered with freedom of contract and amounted to the taking of liberty and property without due process of law. The rights to form trade unions and to minimum wages and stipulated maximum working hours were set aside.[73] Business was protected from state regulation, labor rights were denied, federal income tax was outlawed, and antitrust laws were watered down.[74] The perception that the courts were under the control of the bankers, railroads, and manufacturers resulted in a movement to introduce measures to recall judges or have their decisions subject to recall.[75] Even today there are arguments that the decisions of the courts essentially favor big business.[76]

In South Africa as a rule race and class tend to converge. The judiciary in South Africa is an almost all-white preserve.[77] It is difficult to convince the black majority that a judiciary appointed by an unrepresentative government will be able to arbitrate disputes and dispense justice in an impartial manner. The one point that is incessantly emphasized (in South Africa media, schools, and society at large) is the superiority of whites over blacks and a need for the separation of the races. John Dugard asks whether judges being human can be influenced by subconscious stimuli. He answers that the major inarticulate premise (of judges drawn from a small section of the white population), namely, loyalty to the status quo, will inevitably manifest itself in a number of ways.[78] The opinions of the judges in cases pertaining to challenges to the status quo will inevitably not be any different from those of the privileged white executive.[79] The argument here is different from judges being appointed in recognition of their political views. Here the assertion is even if judges were appointed on merit, they are still subconsciously influenced. Clearly, it is impossible to ignore the position of the present South African judiciary and their social and class composition.[80] Any discussion of the neutrality of the present judiciary becomes lopsided if its social and class composition are ignored.[81]

THE SOUTH AFRICAN JUDICIARY AND LAWMAKING POWERS

A number of studies on the decisions of the South African judiciary have focused on the exercise of creative functions (with respect to interpretation of vague statutes), particularly in the areas of race relations and individual liberties.[82] The broad consensus is that there is a predominant tendency on the part of the judiciary to favor the political status quo.[83] For example, Dugard alludes to the Appellate Division's decision in *Goldberg v. Minister of Prisons* whereby the division denied a convicted political prisoner the right to receive news of a political nature. He argues the court could easily have arrived at a different decision favoring individual liberties.[84] Similarly, in a string of decisions pertaining to implementation of the Group Areas Act, the judiciary in interpreting the statute could have invoked liberal principles to curtail discrimination.[85] In many instances the courts have filled in the gaps in favor of the status quo and imputed things against the individual even though the statute does not expressly authorize this erosion of rights. For example, in the case of *Minister of Interior v. Lockhat*,[86] even though the Group Areas Act did not expressly authorize inequities the Appellate Division held Parliament must have envisaged the hardships caused by the compulsory moving of people.[87] Similarly, there are a litany of other cases where the judiciary could have come out in favor of individual liberties, for example, in cases pertaining to detention without trial, but instead sought to invoke reasoning favoring the executive.[88] In the case of *Adams*,[89] the defendant argued that he contravened the Group Areas Act because of necessity; as a person of color he had no other accommodation. The court held that necessity was not a defense to prosecution under the Group Areas Act. The court could very well have come to the opposite result—that the black defendant had no other place to live. Similarly, in many decisions where there was a supposed tension between national security and individual liberty, justice could have ruled in favor of the individual. In the case of *R V. Sachs*[90] the judge could have ruled that giving a detainee reading material in prison would not endanger state interests. Instead, the judge gave police officials the discretion to provide the detainee the material.

SOCIALIZATION AND BACKGROUND
OF JUDGES IN AFRICA AT INDEPENDENCE

By and large the judiciary in African countries in the period before independence was essentially an extension of the colonial administration. The judicial system and administration of justice existed primarily for the colonists.[91] As far as the indigenous people were concerned, justice often meant inhuman and discriminatory practices against them. The judges consisted of an elitist body of European judicial administrators, aloof from the local population, and appointed by the colonial government. Once appointed to the bench there was little interference by the government, since the judiciary generally met the expectations of the government.[92] It is difficult to imagine a judiciary trained and socialized in the colonial tradition suddenly being able to dispense justice to the local people. Not surprisingly, the African people did not believe the judiciary were independent or impartial even in the period just before independence.[93] The perception of the judiciary in African countries subject to colonial rule arguably was no different from the perception that blacks have of the judiciary in South Africa.[94]

In the period after independence, most African countries followed a policy of Africanization. Africans were propelled into positions of authority and control over the expatriate or settler population. The perception was that the bench would achieve greater legitimacy with an African judiciary, though experience has shown that this is not necessarily true. The nature of the legal training and the social background of lawyers in African countries in many ways mirrors the experiences of their counterparts in the Western systems. To a great extent the majority of judges in Africa are members of a small elite who have high incomes and education levels.[95] The legal education they receive both confers on them a privileged position and socializes them toward Western models and thinking.[96] The legal curriculum and training do not generate innovators or social engineers.[97] Amissah makes the point that the African judiciaries' attitudes to legal problems in many instances have been the same as the expatriate judges'.[98]

Theorists allude to a legitimacy crisis in the South African judicial system because the bench is an all-white preserve.[99] This view also presupposes that Africanization or the promotion of a black judiciary will surmount the legitimacy crisis. In a sense, the change from a colonial situation to independence marks an alteration in the starting point of the legal system or *grundnorm*.[100] It is possible that a government in a new order will be able to appoint judges who were opposed to the old order. However, the important question is whether these judges have the skills and training to meet the challenges of a radically different system. Arguably, the judiciary—white or black—in the immediate period after independence is not equipped to fashion the law to the new reality or to meet changing needs.

A new South African order will inevitably entail major ideological changes. Moreover, and more difficult, there will have to be ideological consensus with regard to the course the new nation is going to pursue. It is inconceivable to allow the present unelected and unaccountable judiciary to interpret the ideological orientation and values of the new order.[101] McWhinney raises the question whether judges trained in the old order can intervene and mediate conflicts between rival forces.[102] In the light of the history of judicial review in Western systems, more specifically the role of the judiciary in the United States after the abolition of slavery and during the Roosevelt New Deal era, it is not inconceivable that judges may rule in terms of values consistent with their own social backgrounds and training.

A course of action open to the government of a future South Africa is the example followed by the Allied forces after their victory over Germany. In the immediate period after World War II, judges appointed by the Nazi Party posed a potentially grave problem by providing judgments that "belonged" to the disgraced order.[103] The Allied forces resorted to closing down all the German courts and firing all the judges and prosecutors.

For a while they contemplated keeping the courts closed for a period of ten years during which they hoped to reeducate an entire new generation of judges.[104] They encouraged old retired judges (who sat on the bench before the Nazi era) to return to the bench. But firing all the old judges would have caused a rupture throughout the judicial system. Subsequently, the Allied powers allowed the former judges back after conducting individual background checks on them and their role in the Nazi era.[105] Such a course of action in South Africa would necessitate an investigation and profile of each and every judge sitting on the bench and would present enormous logistical difficulties.

A variation would be to allow judges appointed by the previous order to sit on the bench at the discretion of the new government. This was the course of action followed in some African countries, particularly, Tanzania at independence.[106] Expatriate judges served on a temporary basis and could be terminated with six months' notice.[107] A drawback to this arrangement is that it gives the government of the day the power to dismiss judges whom the government feels uncomfortable with. It is not possible for judges to fulfill their duty fearlessly because there is always a danger that their services will be terminated.

And one has still to contend with a judiciary trained and appointed by the old order. The history of judicial review in independent Africa has demonstrated its problems. For example, Nwabueze recounts an incident in Uganda where a white mercenary who illegally entered the country was sentenced to a prison term of one year by an African magistrate who identified with the objectives of consolidating African independence and unity by fighting mercenary forces.[108] A white judge on appeal quashed the conviction and asserted that the real problem was not that the white person was a mercenary but that he was an illegal alien.[109] A similar incident took place in Zambia, where two colonial Portuguese soldiers were convicted and sentenced to two years' imprisonment by an African magistrate for entering the country illegally. The sentence was quashed on appeal by a white judge.[110] The decision met with widespread public protests and criticisms from the government, which accused the judiciary of ignoring the hostile activities of the Portuguese government against the new nation.[111]

The disputes in these cases did not involve interpretation of the constitution per se but pertained to other statutes. Legal purists could argue that legal rules and not ideology should be the guiding force in the decisions of judges.[112] From a legal point of view it is conceivable that decisions of both the lower court and the higher court could be supported, but the cases highlight the problems associated with decisions made by a judiciary from an old order applying standards from that era. Whereas the countries had been freed from colonial rule, the judges in the higher courts had failed to decolonize. Zambia was facing a serious problem of mercenaries from outside its borders trying to destabilize the government. The country enacted a law to deal with the threat. The judges appointed by the old order did not take the threat seriously and instead viewed the intrusion of the mercenaries as an entry into the country by two illegal aliens.

The importance of these decisions has to be appreciated in the context of the myriad liberal constitutional options for a post-apartheid South Africa, almost all of which call for a bill of rights and judicial review exercised by the existing judiciary. A vague constitution (such as the United States) with such provisions as "due process," and "equality before the law" would open up conflicts between the judiciary and the executive and legislative branches of government. Typically in providing an interpretation to vague clauses the judge will weigh various priorities and interests, which could include factors such as the national interest, individual liberty, property interests, and the welfare of the community. In a new order it is hoped that the legislature would be elected on democratic principles by the entire population. However, the present judiciary being a product of the apartheid order, the lessons of history have demonstrated that it could very well become an obstructionist force leaning toward priorities that are not in the interests of the majority in the new order. It is therefore questionable whether it is appropriate to introduce judicial review in terms of the American model into newly emergent nations or more importantly to allow the existing judiciary policy-making powers or authority to rule on the policy-making powers of the legislature. It is possible that these are transitional problems that would be resolved with a turnover of judges. But for reasons that will be explored in the ensuing sections, it is necessary that constitution makers look beyond the Anglo-American model of judicial review toward a more responsive model of judicial review that allows for greater democracy.

Judicial Review and Democracy

Strictly speaking the conclusion that judges make law goes against a popular strain in Western political theory that sees law being made by the elected representatives of the people. The type of lawmaking engaged in by the judiciary is not identical to that of the legislature.[113] However, the important point to realize is that the judiciary is engaged in the process of lawmaking. This leads to the very crucial question: Is the lawmaking exercise legitimate, and on what basis can an unelected and unaccountable judiciary exercise discretionary lawmaking power? The question is very serious since the judiciary is not always reflective of the wider society. With their security of tenure an unelected judiciary can impose its view on the rest of society. In some instances the members of the court sit so long on the bench that their views belong to a different age. This was particularly evident in the United States in President Roosevelt's New Deal era, when the justices of the Supreme Court continually frustrated urgent economic reforms.[114] All other branches of government are accountable for their actions and have to present themselves for periodic reelection. It is arguably inconsistent with democracy that an unelected body can frustrate the wishes of a popularly elected legislature on matters of economic and social affairs.[115]

Various reasons are put forward for judicial review. Some theorists assert that majority rule is only one element of democracy.[116] The other and more important element is the protection of individual rights, which cannot be infringed upon even by the majority,[117] who "have no right to abridge or defeat the rights of individuals."[118] Some liberal theorists are even prepared to concede that the judiciary is an elitist body, and judicial review in its present form is inconsistent with democracy. But while democracy may be promoted in the short run by abolishing judicial review, in the long run basic rights and freedoms would be eroded.[119] In terms of "pure" democratic theory there is a tension between constitutionalism and democracy, as the constitution aims to tie the community's hands in regard to certain decisions.[120]

Judicial review is posited by some theorists as particularly important in a plural[121] society to reconcile ethnic and other cleavages. South African history is characterized as one of conflict between various "tribes"[122] and between blacks and whites.[123] It is a society seen as having a multitude of different groups with extreme cultural heterogeneity influenced from three continents.[124] According to De Silva, judges enjoy a unique status in having a secure tenure; the detached position away from the hurly-burly of political pressures together with their legal training (to consider matters on principle rather than expediency) make them better equipped to deal with ethnic strife.[125] It is the purpose of the legislature to attend to social and welfare functions. However, in fulfilling its functions the legislature is seen as subject to various influences of lobby and pressure groups act.[126] It is for this reason the judiciary is seen as the best protector of individual and minority rights.[127] Unfortunately, the above view does not take into account the social position or background of the judge and just assumes that the position of the judge on the bench together with their legal training makes him/her the best institution to reconcile differences.

The right to life, liberty, freedom against abuse, torture, and so on are very important rights. However, the way these rights are conceptualized may vary across different societies. Traditional African society was social in orientation and generally catered to the social and welfare needs of its members. Similarly, the scope of what constitutes fundamental rights whether static (encompassing merely important civil liberties) or enlarged to encompass economic and social rights is a political decision. In the United States judicial review has extended beyond mere protection of "fundamental" rights toward the determination of economic and social policies.[128] This negates any notion that sovereignty resides with the people. The United States Justice Felix Frankfurter summed up the situation best by stating that democracy does not need an oligarchic and irresponsible body for its preservation.[129] According to Frankfurter, history has shown that the judiciary can misconceive what is in the public good; the best protector of democracy is the people and their vigilance over their representatives.[130]

Although the nature of the judicial process in Western constitutional systems inevitably entails the judiciary making law, a judiciary being able to pronounce on social and economic policies is a practice that is more specific to countries with constitutions containing a bill of rights. Most liberal constitutional proposals for a post-apartheid South Africa put forward a bill of rights to protect individual and property rights along the lines of the U. S. Constitution.[131] Theorists advocating a bill of rights make the erroneous assumption that an entrenched bill of rights in the South African system would do away with the status quo-mindedness approach of the judiciary.[132] Undoubtedly, this would remove judges from the ambit of legislative supremacy. With a historically conservative judiciary, judicial review in this situation often amounts to the elite being able to prevent social and economic change from taking place and maintaining certain privileges of the status quo.

The most desirable constitutional system is one that institutionalizes an order that ensures democracy and control by the people over their representatives.[133] Many governments have used the ideology of African socialism and Marxism to argue for a fusion of government power—the institutions of state represented in the legislature are supreme as they represent the wishes of the people. In the modern era no constitutional system has yet been designed to ensure popular control over the agents of the state, and African socialist systems in practice, to say the least, leave much to be desired. The judicial system in most African one-party and Marxist states serves as an instrument of state domination to effect the programs of the state or party elite. In many societies, an unfettered executive or government has trod roughshod over fundamental rights and liberties, and indeed the African continent is rife with torture, brutality, and other abuses of fundamental rights. It does seem that judicial review and an independent judiciary[134] enhance the protection of rights such as freedom of person, speech, assembly, conscience, and freedom from torture and arbitrary detention. But herein lies the crux of the problem. On the one hand, one has a judiciary in South Africa tainted by the previous order and with the potential of being an obstructionist element in a new order, an unaccountable judiciary that might prove undemocratic and work against the wishes of the majority. On the other hand, in societies where there is no independent judiciary, there is a tendency for gross violation of fundamental rights.[135] We suggest a better model.

An Alternate Model of Judicial Review

In the British and United States system, judicial review is exercised by the ordinary courts of the land. In other words, the courts under these systems are courts with authority to rule on all disputes in the private or public realm. In most instances judges have security of tenure. The court system in South Africa is like the Anglo-American model and exercises general jurisdiction. The role of the judiciary (in terms of all constitutional options presented for a future South Africa) is invariably seen as a debate or choice between the British system and the U.S. model. In terms of liberal options, the pendulum has swung toward a preference for the U.S. system with a bill of rights with substantive judicial review.

After World War II many countries introduced novel court structures (departing fundamentally from the Anglo-American model) entrusted with specific jurisdiction. The most notable development was the creation of special constitutional courts in many European countries to adjudicate on constitutional disputes only, which gave rise to the classification of centralized and noncentralized or decentralized judicial review.[136] The former applies to a system where judicial review is exercised by a single or special judicial organ, while the latter applies to a system where judicial review is exercised by all the judicial organs in the legal system.[137]

The most important difference in these Continental tribunals is that they are specialized agencies with jurisdiction limited to constitutional issues only. A system of ordinary courts exists separately from the specialized constitutional tribunals and fulfill all the functions of courts in any system except disputes that involve constitutional issues. Members of the ordinary courts (as opposed to the constitutional courts) enjoy security of tenure much like their counterparts in the Anglo-American model.

Second and more important, the assumptions underlying these specialized constitutional court structures recognize the political nature of the judicial function. This recognition is most vividly reflected in the composition and method of election of members of the constitutional courts. We will not consider all the specialized constitutional courts but instead will only focus on the German Federal Constitutional Court and the French Conseil constitutionnel to highlight the attributes of the specialized constitutional courts.

Judges to the German Federal Constitutional Court are selected by the two houses of the legislature with each house choosing half the judges of the Constitutional Court.[138] The lower house, the Bundestag, selects an electoral college of twelve members who represent the political parties in proportion to their strength in the lower house.[139] The upper house, the Bundesrat, selects its half of the members of the Constitutional Court by a two-thirds vote. The actual appointment is made by the federal president.[140] The judicial tenure of members of the Constitutional Court is limited to a single term of twelve years.

Although the French Conseil constitutionnel exercises its power in a manner different from other judicial tribunals, the important aspect for our purposes is the recognition of its political function and its composition. The Conseil constitutionnel consists of nine appointed judges, three of whom are appointed by the president of the republic, three by the president of the senate, and three by the president of the National Assembly. In addition, all former presidents of France are ex-officio members of the Conseil. The appointed members of the Conseil are limited to a term of office of nine years.

OVERVIEW OF THE SPECIALIZED TRIBUNALS

The important difference in the specialized tribunals from the Anglo-American model is the recognition of the political nature of judicial review, particularly as it pertains to constitutional issues. This is seen in the way members of the constitutional courts are appointed. Invariably, the members of a constitutional court consist of members of all the major political parties.[141] This marks a recognition that many functions considered judicial are in fact political. The members of the court do not have to be career judges, or even lawyers or legally trained persons, which again shows the political nature of their appointment and functions. Once appointed, judges are independent and free from political pressures. However, the second striking difference is the tendency in the Continental systems to limit the tenure of judicial appointees, allowing elected representatives a measure of political control through periodic renewal of the bench.

In the light of the questions surrounding the present judiciary in South Africa, the creation of a special constitutional court to interpret the provisions of a new constitution is an extremely attractive option. The members of this court could be elected in such a way as to represent different interests. While the German system like most Continental systems entrusts the selection of members of the Constitutional Court to the political parties in the legislature, the South African system could expand the number of organizations responsible for the selection of judges to give real effect to the notion that the judiciary represents all sectors of the population. For example, trade unions, women's organizations, and business organizations could be accorded the right to elect representatives to the constitutional court.[142] There is considerable variation in terms of how the election of the judges could take place. Depending on the composition of the future legislature, it is possible that these organizations would be directly represented in the legislature. The second option is to allow the different sectors a direct vote in the selection of the judges.

A constitutional court representing the entire population would enjoy greater legitimacy than a judiciary appointed by the old and disgraced order. It is also more likely to represent the interests of all sectors of the population. Moreover, a constitutional court whose membership can be renewed at periodic intervals is more likely to be sensitive to the realities of the society. This is not to say that a specialized constitution court operating on its own is a panacea for harmony. Several African countries have at one stage or another at independence introduced a specialized constitutional court along the lines of the French Conseil constitutionnel.[143] Its success depends on establishing democratic political structures that link society with other organs of government. The important point is that a representative and accountable judiciary together with a democratic constitutional structure would ensure that the judicial function would be performed in terms of the values of the larger society.

AMBIT OF JUDICIAL REVIEW

In the U.S. tradition the judiciary has taken it upon itself to make important policy choices, something historically considered as part of the legislative domain.[144] The constitution in South Africa must strive toward an order where the legislature is the only body responsible for lawmaking and determining policies.[145] In other words, the legal system should be associated with precise rules and certainty. This is the model generally found in civil law countries.[146] While a bill of rights in Germany protects many fundamental freedoms, there is still a greater reliance on the formal text of the constitution to influence decisions.[147] The German system aims at achieving a correspondence between norms and reality (between the text and polity) to preserve a "secure" way of life.[148] In such a system there is less ambiguity in the law and fewer possibilities of judge made law. In the United States, on the other hand, law is generally viewed as provisional until contested and altered.[149] This does not mean that the legislature can violate fundamental rights because of any notion of legislative supremacy. The constitution should outline the protection of fundamental human rights that neither the executive nor the legislature should be able to override. However, the judiciary should not have the power to enlarge the scope of the constitution by giving it interpretations beyond what it specifies, as the U.S. Supreme Court has continually done, for example, in interpreting rights to privacy in abortion cases or extending the First Amendment rights beyond what the Constitution specifies as it did in the *Buckley v. Valeo*[150] judgment.[151] In the words of Justice Holmes, the judiciary should not be permitted to substitute their judgments for that of the body whose business it is in the first place to decide such questions.[152]

The Rest of the Judicial System

The discussion thus far has concerned itself primarily with judicial review as it pertains to constitutional issues. There is still the question of the court structure and the role of the judiciary in regard to nonconstitutional issues, for example, criminal law or private disputes between parties. The following section will provide some thoughts with respect to the rest of the judicial system.[153]

Some maintain the dual nature of South African law consists of both repressive law and formal law.[154] The first pertains to the area of public law, and the judiciary in terms of the doctrine of parliamentary supremacy is essentially an agent of the sovereign in exercising and enforcing public control. In matters of private law, however, there is little government involvement, and the judiciary essentially fulfills its role of mediating disputes between parties in an impartial fashion. In terms of this conception it is the rule of law as opposed to the rule of man that is operative in the guiding and judging of actions.[155] If one accepts this view of South African law, then the assumption would be that in the area of private disputes both the judiciary and law are untainted and can be maintained intact in any new order.

But this view is clearly erroneous. It ignores the reality that what constitutes law in South Africa is not rules created in an impartial manner based on the consent of the majority. The assumptions of South African law operate in terms of Western principles derived from Roman, Dutch, and English traditions. The indigenous majority had little input into shaping South African legal development. Moreover, there is at present little recognition of indigenous customary law. The conception of rights in the present order involves the individual while the conception of rights in the traditional African setting involved the group or unit.[156] In traditional African society the institution of private property (which is central to the conception of private rights in the present South African order) was nonexistent.[157] Many rules, even in the area of private law, must be redefined. In traditional society the right to life included an obligation by the society to provide subsistence to needy members of the community. It is questionable whether the present judiciary, trained and socialized in terms of status quo concepts of rights, can move beyond its background. Even the judicial institutions are primarily for the service of the wealthy class. Present court structures are inaccessible to the majority of the population who do not have the resources to use them, and the way the legal profession is organized makes it difficult for many blacks to break into it.[158] A restructuring not only of the court system but also the legal profession is in order.

Important lessons can be drawn from the popular court structures at the lower levels of the community in Mozambique and the other former Portuguese colonies in Africa.[159] The system of popular courts that exists in Mozambique allows for lay participation in the judicial system. The type of justice to be dispensed in such an order will be in terms of the values of the community as opposed to the values of a "detached" judiciary appointed by the racist order or an elite single party. However, it is imperative that the judicial structure in contrast to the practice of the African Marxist countries be freed of control by a party. The structure of the people's courts could be organized at a local, regional, and provincial level with a supreme court at the very apex of the system. At the local level the procedure must be simplified as much as possible, and the site of the court should be where it is accessible to the people, be it in a rural or urban area. This is more likely to make the participation of people at the local level a reality. In this way the courts can enter into a direct relationship with the people. In this environment "free from the influence of the laws and formalism of the colonial system," the cultural values of the people and their popular sense of justice can be expressed.[160]

More complex matters can be deferred to higher organs such as district or provincial courts. In the African Marxist models, judges of the higher court are professional judges with judicial training. There is no reason why the same system cannot be followed in South Africa as well. Except that instead of having the judges elected by the legislature, it is better to follow the example of many states in the United States and have the judges popularly elected by the population in the district or province.[161]

The traditional posture of the judiciary being aloof from society and clouded in mysticism must be done away with. The judicial officer, particularly at the higher forums, must explain the reasons for judgments so that the people subject to the law understand it. The judicial role must be open to public criticism as is the case in the United States. It is incompatible with democracy to require the people to unquestioningly accept the authority of a body that in many instances is unelected.[162]

REFERENCES

1. Although Britain does not have a bill of rights like the United States system, the common denominator in the Anglo-American system is a decentralized system of courts. For a distinction between decentralized systems versus centralized systems see below.

2. One of the arguments of this chapter is that there is great potential for the judiciary, particularly in the American model, to subvert the ends of democracy and to work as a reactionary tendency to protect elite interests.

3. The realities include devising a structure that allows for economic redistribution.

4. It is an essential principle in constitutionalism. See chapter 2.

5. For the difference between separation of powers and the rule of law, and the different theories of separation of powers and the rule of law see chapter 2.

6. John Agresto, *The Supreme Court and Constitutional Democracy* (New York: Cornell University Press, 1985), 142.

7. G. Kateb in Pennock and Chapman, *Constitutionalism*, 146.

8. This is the popular view of judicial review in the Anglo-American model, which has been accepted in most Western models. The French system, however, takes a different view: that one should not be able to appeal against an act of the legislature or executive just as one cannot appeal a decision of the judiciary to the legislature or to the executive. A constitutional court thus previews legislation as opposed to reviewing it. See W. A. Robson, "The Transplanting of Political Institutions and Ideas," in *Political Science Quarterly* 35 (1964): 412.

9. Nwabueze, *Constitutionalism*, 15.

10. Alan R. Brewer-Carias and Donald F. Bur, *Judicial Review in Comparative Law* (Cambridge: Cambridge University Press, 1989), 10–14.

11. For the expansive notion of the rule of law as a doctrine that seeks to protect social and economic rights (which goes beyond the liberal notion), see chapter 2.

12. Brewer-Carias and Bur, *Judicial Review*, 7.

13. Benjamin O. Nwabueze, *Judicialism in Commonwealth Africa: The Role of the Courts in Government* (London: Hurst, 1977), preface.

14. The exception is the French system.

15. The term *active* is used because—as will be shown below—the courts in the British system still do make laws in exercising their powers of interpretation.

16. Ibid., 60.

17. J. Bell, in Rajeev Dhavan, et al., eds., *Judges and the Judicial Power: Essays in Honour of Justice V. R. Krishna Iyer* (London: Sweet and Maxwell, 1985), 58–59.

18. Louis L. Jaffe, *English and American Judges as Lawmakers* (Oxford: Clarendon Press, 1969), 67.

19. Ibid., 64.

20. This principle was enunciated very early in U.S constitutional history in the case of *Marbury v. Madison*, 5 U.S. (1 Cranch) 137; 2 L. Ed. 60 (1803).

21. See the seminal Supreme Court decision of *Brown v. Board of Education of Topeka*, 347 U.S. 483. The Supreme Court's attitude was the court ought to consider public education in the light of present-day knowledge and developments, and went on to overturn the hitherto doctrine of separate-but-equal education.

22. Austin Amissah, *The Contribution of the Courts to Government: A West African View* (Oxford: Clarendon Press, 1981), 1.

23. South African Communist Party, "The Road to South African Freedom," *African Communist* (1963): 41.

24. For the role of elders in traditional African society, see discussion on democracy in traditional African setting in chapter 3.

25. G. I. Welch, "Pluralism, Colonialism and the Law," in Neelan Tiruchelvam and Radhika Coomaraswamy, eds., *The Role of the Judiciary in Plural Societies* (London: F. Pinter, 1987), 163.

26. Edward McWhinney, *Supreme Courts and Judicial Law-making: Constitutional Tribunals and Constitutional Review* (Dordrecht: M. Nijhoff, 1986), 1. All the defeated countries in World War II including Italy, West Germany, and Japan introduced judicial review into their

constitutions as mechanisms to prevent autocratic government. See Cappeletti and Cohen, *Comparative Constitutional Law*, 14.

27. This was embodied in the constitutions of countries subject to British or French rule. See Kofi Busia, *Africa in Search of Democracy*, 104–5.

28. Brun-Otto Bryde. *The Politics and Sociology of African Legal Development* (Frankfurt am Main: Metzner, 1976), 71.

29. See discussion of influence of British constitution on African countries in chapter 5.

30. Amissah, *Contribution of the Courts*, 98.

31. Ibid., 105–6. Various rules and qualification criteria were imposed pertaining to previous office and eligibility to serve on the bench.

32. The countries included Kenya, Zambia, Lesotho, Swaziland, Gambia, and Ghana. See Amissah, *Contribution of the Courts*, 102. There were variations in the composition of the Judicial Service Commission with members being appointed by the professional societies as well as the ministry of Justice or a combination of both. See also recommendations for Judicial Service Commission in South Africa below.

33. International Commission of Jurists, *African Conference on the Rule of Law: A Report of the Proceedings, Lagos 1961* (Geneva: ICJ, 1961), 19–20.

34. This was the constitutional policy of the former White liberal parliamentary opposition party (the Progressive Federal Party) as elaborated in *Report of the Constitutional Committee of the Progressive Federal Party* (Cape Town: P.F.P., 1979), 34, 37.

35. Ibid.

36. Chief Justice Steyn quoted in Hugh Corder, *Judges at Work: The Role and Attitudes of the South African Appellate Judiciary*, 1910–50 (Cape Town: Juta, 1984), 12.

37. This follows the lines of the United States model for statutory construction except that in the United States the judge can rule a statute invalid if it does not conform to a "higher law" as laid out in the Bill of Rights. In South Africa the judiciary have no power to rule a legislative invalid against any higher law.

38. A. Cowling, "Judges and the Protection of Human Rights in South Africa: Articulating the Inarticulate Premise," *South African Journal of Human Rights* 3 (1987): 181.

39. John Hund and Henrik W. Van der Merwe, *Legal Ideology and Politics in South Africa: A Social Science Approach* (Lanham, Md.: University Press of America, 1986), 23–24.

40. Albie Sachs, *Justice in South Africa* (London: Sussex University Press, 1973), 261.

41. Ibid., 262.

42. See the views of Judge C. S. Margo in Ellison Kahn, ed., *Fiat Iustitia: Essays in Memory of Oliver Deneys Schreiner* (Cape Town: Juta, 1983), 283; G. Cameron, "Nude Monarchy: The Case of South African Judges," *South African Journal of Human Rights* 3 (1987): 339.

43. See the views of Judge C. J. Claassen, "Retain the Bar and Side-Bar," *South African Law Journal* 87 (1970): 25.

44. See Hugh Corder, *Judges at Work: The Role and Attitudes of the South African Appellate Judiciary, 1910–50* (Cape Town: Juta, 1984), 2.

45. See views of S. Kentridge, "Telling the Truth About Law," *South African Law Journal* 99 (1982): 652.

46. See the contempt proceedings against the late Professor Barend Van Niekerk, *S v. Van Niekerk* 1970 (3) SA 654 (T); *S v. Van Niekerk*, 1972 (3) 711 (AD).

47. J. A. G. Griffith, *The Politics of the Judiciary* (Manchester: Manchester University Press, 1977).

48. J. Dugard, "The Judicial Process, Positivism and Civil Liberty," *South African Law Journal* 88 (1971): 183.

49. See the various court decisions dealing with the constitutional crisis in the 1950s: *Harris v. Minister of Interior* 1952 (2) SA 428 (A); *Minister of Interior v. Harris* 1954 (4) SA 769 (A).

50. Section 34 (2) of the act empowers the court to determine whether the provisions of the constitution have been followed, while Section 34 (3) declares that no court of law has the power to pronounce on the validity of an act of the legislature.

51. See T. Georges, in G. F. A. Sawyer, ed., *East African Law and Social Change* (Nairobi: East African Publishing House, 1967), esp. chap. 2.

52. U.S. Constitution, art. II, sec. 2(2). All federal judges are appointed by the president and their appointments have to be approved by the Senate.

53. Amissah, *The Contribution of the Courts,* 107.

54. R. J. Steamer, "Judicial Leadership: English and American Experience," in John R. Schmidhauser, ed., *Comparative Judicial Systems: Challenging Frontiers in Conceptual and Empirical Analysis* (London: Butterworth's, 1987), 167.

55. For example, President Reagan was unsuccessful in getting his first choice, Robert Bork, appointed to the Supreme Court. However, he was still successful in getting a candidate (Justice Anthony Kennedy) whose political views were broadly consistent with his own. Recent Supreme Court judgments in abortion and civil rights cases bear this out.

56. In terms of the Supreme Court Act 59 of 1959, sec. 10.

57. Cameron, "Nude Monarchy," 430.

58. Kentridge, "Telling the Truth," 652.

59. Ibid.

60. John D. Jackson, *Justice in South Africa* (London: Secker & Warburg, 1980), 24–25.

61. Criticisms of South African judiciary are rare in South African publications. For a criticism of Steyn's appointment see G. Cameron, "Legal Chauvinism, Executive-Mindedness, and Justice L.C. Steyn's Impact on South African Law," *South African Law Journal* 99 (1982): 42. Cameron charges that Steyn's appointment defied all conventions. For example, unlike other judges he was not a practicing member of the Bar. Moreover, his years of service at the provincial level were far fewer than is usually the case for appointment to the Appellate Division. Ibid.

62. This point will be elaborated upon when considering the executive-mindedness of many of the decisions.

63. In terms of the Appellate Division Quorum Act 27 of 1955.

64. C. F. Forsyth, *In Danger for their Talents: A Study of the Appellate Division of the Supreme Court of South Africa from 1950–1980* (Cape Town: Juta, 1985), 15. Some of the judges it seems had accepted their appointments on the basis that the vote case would not be questioned. See ibid., 24.

65. J. Dugard, "The Judiciary and National Security," *South African Law Journal* 99 (1982): 657–58.

66. Subject to good behavior. See U.S. Constitution, art. III sec. 1.

67. Section 10(7) of the Supreme Court Act of 1959 above.

68. This is not to posit that there at all times will be a harmony of political and social values between the judge and the executive responsible for appointing the particular member of the judiciary. For example, Chief Justice Earl Warren of the United States Supreme Court was appointed by a conservative Republican President Eisenhower and proved to be a great social engineer. It was during Warren's era on the bench that most of the historic decisions striking down racial segregation (such as *Brown v. Board of Education*) were delivered. Overall, however, it is impossible to ignore the history, socialization, training, and background of the judiciary.

69. See Henry Cecil, *The English Judge* (London: Stevens, 1970). In South Africa they are drawn exclusively from the white sector of the population.

70. D. G. Smith, "Liberalism and Judicial Review," in Pennock & Chapman, *Constitutionalism,* 209.

71. John H. Merryman and David S. Clark, *Comparative Law, Western European and Latin American Legal Systems: Cases and Materials* (Indianapolis, Ind.: Bobbs-Merrill, 1978), 187.

72. Derrick A. Bell, *Race, Racism, and American Law,* 2d ed. (Boston: Little, Brown, 1980), 36–37.

73. *Lochner v. New York,* 198 U.S. 45, 25 S. Ct. 539; 49 L. Ed. 937 (1905).

74. *United States v. E.C. Knight, Co.,* 156 U.S. 1 (1895). See the views of D. Bell, *Race, Racism, and American Law,* 36–37.

75. Jaffe, *Judges as Lawmakers,* 87. Most of the judges who obstructed Roosevelt's New Deal programs later changed their stance and accepted the measures. Roosevelt had threatened to pack the Supreme Court with his nominees, and the change in the attitude of the Supreme Court justices is described by some as "a switch in time which saved nine."

76. See the criticisms of the Supreme Court justices by A. S. Miller, "On Politics, Democracy, and The First Amendment: A Commentary on *First National Bank v. Bellotti,*" *Washington and Lee Law Review* 25 (1981): 38–40.

77. To date there has been only one black judge appointed to the South African courts, Judge Ismail Mohamed in the Transvaal Provincial Division.

78. J. Dugard, "The Judicial Process, Positivism and Civil Liberty," *South African Law Journal* 88 (1971): 190–91.

79. Ibid., 191.

80. See decisions below where the South African judges in a number of cases had the opportunity to come out in favor of individual liberty but instead resorted to ruling in favor of the executive.

81. All the judges are white. Although there have been no polls on the political affiliation of the judges in South Africa, it is fair to say that the majority are National Party supporters.

82. There have been studies of judgments of individual judges as well as general trends. See, Cameron's study of L. C. Steyn, "Nude Monarchy," 38–75. Also in same issue see Study of Dyzenhaus, "L. C. Steyn in Perspective," 380–91.

83. See the conclusion of Corder, *Judges at Work,* 242. Also Dyzenhaus previous note; and Cameron, previous note. For a contrary view see Forsyth, *In Danger for Their Talents,* 225.

84. J. Dugard, "Some Realism About The Judicial Process and Positivism—A Reply," *South African Law Journal* 98 (1981): 385.

85. Ibid., 385–86. In the case of *S v. Adams* and *S v. Werner* Dugard argues the Appellate Division could have limited the injustice of the Group Areas Act by calling on common law basic rights and internationally protected human rights.

86. 1961 (2) SA 587 (A).

87. See the note of Cameron, "Nude Monarchy," 57.

88. Cowling, "Protection of Human Rights," 190; Sachs, "Toward a Bill of Rights," 252–53.

89. Ibid.

90. Nwabueze, *Judicialism in Commonwealth Africa,* 265–68.

91. See ibid. See also G. I. Welch, in Tirucheluam, *The Role of the Judiciary,* 159.

92. Amissah, *The Contribution of the Courts,* 68.

93. Ibid., 96–97.

94. To my knowledge no surveys have been conducted with respect to the black population's perception of the judiciary. It is unlikely that the South African government would allow one to be conducted. But see the views of D. Mokgatle, "The Exclusion of Blacks from the South African Judicial System," *South African Journal of Human Rights* 3 (1987): 48.

95. In a society where there are high shortages of skilled personnel, it is not surprising that those people who are professionals or have access to needed skills would achieve greater incomes.

96. Not the least of which is the protection of their individual interests. See Bryde, *African Legal Developments,* 75–76.

97. Where a constitution with a vague bill of rights (like the United States') is subject to judicial scrutiny, there is a greater likelihood of the judiciary imposing its will on other social bodies. Questions considered political, economic, or moral would tend to be subject to legal reasoning. Although undesirable, if introduced such an order would require a judiciary that is responsive and capable of social engineering. See J. M. Brokeman, "Legal Subjectivity as a Precondition for the Intertwinement of Law and the Welfare State," in Gunther Teubner, ed., *Dilemmas of Law in the Welfare State* (Berlin: Walter de Gruyter, 1986), 76–77.

98. Amissah, *The Contribution of the Courts*, 83.

99. Mokgatle, "Exclusion of Blacks," 44–51.

100. For a view of the *grundnorm* and what it means in a legal system see, McWhinney, *Supreme Courts*, 114–15.

101. One option is to replace the entire bench (in a new order) with a new set of appointees. This option is evaluated below.

102. McWhinney, *Supreme Courts*, 125.

103. Ingo Müller, *Furchtbare Juristen: die unbewaltigte Vergangenheit unserer Justiz* [Horrible Jurists: The Unexamined History of the Judiciary], trans. P. Van Randow (Munich: Kindler, 1987), 196. See the judgment of Hans Karl Filbinger, where the judge after the war sentenced a soldier to six months' imprisonment because the soldier refused to obey his commander who ordered the soldier to wear the Swastika and other Nazi symbols on his uniform. Ibid.

104. Ibid., 204.

105. Ibid.

106. Telford Georges, *Law and Its Administration in a One-Party State: Selected Speeches*, ed. R. W. James and F. M. Kassam (Nairobi: East African Literature Bureau, 1973), 25.

107. Ibid.

108. Nwabueze, *Judicialism in Commonwealth Africa*, 142.

109. Ibid., 142.

110. *People v. Silva and Freitas H.C.Z.* July 1969.

111. Nwabueze, *Judicialism in Commonwealth Africa*, 278.

112. See the views in the journal *Transition* quoted in Nwabueze, *Presidentialism*, 143.

113. Some categorize it as secondary lawmaking or interstitial lawmaking. For a view on the different models of the role of the judge, see J. Bell, "Three Models of The Judicial Function," in Dhavan, *Judges and the Judicial Power*, 55–75.

114. McWhinney, *Supreme Courts*, 275–76. See the Supreme Court decisions in *United States v. Butler*, 297 U.S. 1 (1936) and *A.L.A. Schecter Poultry Corp. v. United States*, 295 U.S. 495 (1935).

115. See Jerold L. Waltman and Kenneth M. Holland, *The Political Role of Law Courts in Modern Democracies* (New York: St. Martin's Press, 1988), 1.

116. P. Railton, in Pennock and Chapman, *Constitutionalism*, vol. 25, 156.

117. Nwabueze, *Constitutionalism*, 230–31.

118. G. Kateb in Pennock and Chapman, *Constitutionalism*, Vol. 25, 148.

119. Railton, , 158.

120. S. Holmes, "Precommitment and the Paradox of Democracy," in Jon Elster and Rune Slagstad, *Constitutionalism and Democracy* (Cambridge: Cambridge University Press, 1988), 196–97.

121. Theodor Hanf, et al., *South Africa, The Prospects for Peaceful Change: An Empirical Enquiry into the Possibility of Democratic Conflict Regulation*, trans. John Richardson (London: R. Collings, 1981), 3; J. Rex, "The Plural Society: The South African Case," *Race* 40 (1971).

122. Leopold Marquard, *The Peoples and Policies of South Africa*, 4th ed. (London: Oxford University Press, 1971), 28.

123. Ibid.

124. van den Berghe, *South Africa*, 38. For a full discussion of the plural paradigm see chapters 4 and 7.

125. H. L. De Silva, "Pluralism and the Judiciary in Sri Lanka," in Neelan Tirucheluam and Radhika Coomaraswamy, eds., *The Role of the Judiciary in Plural Societies* (London: F. Pinter, 1987), 81.

126. Jaffe, *Judges as Lawmakers*, 33.

127. Ibid., 34–35. See also Agresto, *The Supreme Court*, 142.

128. The U.S. Supreme Court determines the scope of abortion and education. See *Roe v. Wade*, 410 U.S. 113; *Brown v. Board of Education*, above.

129. *A. F. of L. v. American Sash & Door Co.*, 335 U.S. 538, 555–56 (1948).

130. Ibid. Frankfurter accepts that the courts have the power to rule on the validity of legislation, but he asserts that the courts have to keep the implications of that right in mind. Frankfurter rightly asserts that the courts have to leave policy judgments to the legislative body, which is chosen by the people.

131. For example, see The Democratic Party, *A Government in the Making*.

132. Cowling, "Protection of Human Rights," 196.

133. See F. Sejersted, "Liberal Constitutionalism to Corporate Pluralism," in Elster, *Constitutionalism and Democracy*, 299.

134. Independence in this context is used to denote a judiciary free of political manipulation by the government or any other state agency.

135. See the events surrounding the dismissal of judges of the Supreme Court of Ghana by President Nkrumah and the subsequent actions by the executive reported in Busia, *Africa in Search of Democracy*, esp. chap 6.

136. For this classification see Mauro Cappelletti and William Cohen, *Comparative Constitutional Law: Cases and Materials* (Indianapolis, Ind.: Bobbs-Merrill, 1979), 73–75.

137. Ibid., 73.

138. West German Basic Law, art. 94(1).

139. Waltman and Holland, *Political Role of Law Courts*, 93.

140. Ibid.

141. Cappelletti and Cohen, *Comparative Constitutional Law*, 77.

142. See the views in this regard of H. Klug, "The South African Judicial Order and the Future: A Comprehensive Analysis of the South African Judicial System and Judicial Transitions in Zimbabwe, Mozambique, and Nicaragua," *Host Intertech Complete Law Review* (1989): 233. This is not to suggest that only the above organizations should be represented. Exactly which organization is given a say in the selection of judges and what role the organization plays in the selection process will depend on the nature of the legislature and other institutions of state.

143. Countries such as Mali, Gabon, Togo, Burundi, Rwanda, Zaire, Côte d'Ivoire, and Comoros have at one stage or another had specialized constitutional courts modeled primarily on the French system. See F. Moderne, "Postcolonial Constitutions in Sub-Saharan Africa," in Louis Henkin and Albert J. Rosenthal, eds., *Constitutionalism and Rights: The Influence of the United States Constitution Abroad* (New York: Columbia University Press, 1990), 337.

144. In a host of matters the courts have intervened to read into the constitution and impose its interpretation overriding both state and federal legislation. For example see *Roe v. Wade* above where the Supreme Court upheld a woman's right to abortion on the grounds that it was a privacy issue. See also *Buckley v. Valeo*, 424 U.S. 1 (1976) where the Supreme Court invalidated sections of the Federal Election Campaign Act Amendments of 1974 and limited the amount of money individuals and groups could spend from their own funds or other parties could spend on their behalf in a federal election campaign. Congress made a policy choice when it passed the act as an endeavor to prevent the legislature from being dominated by wealthy interests. (See H.R. Report 93–1239, 93d Cong., 2d Sess.). The Supreme Court imposed its own views above that of Congress and invalidated various provisions

of the act on the grounds that it contravened the First Amendment, freedom of speech. For a criticism of the Supreme Court actions see D. Alfange Jr., "Freedom of Speech, Judicial Review and Public Policy Making in The United States," in Eidlin, *Constitutional Democracy*, 81–82.

145. However, this does not mean that the organs of state can ride roughshod over fundamental human rights. The constitution of a future South Africa should attempt to entrench these rights in terms of the civil law model. Also, there will always be instances where the judiciary will create law when they interpret vague provisions in the constitution or statute. However, this is not the same as saying that what constitutes the law is the province of the court to determine.

146. See A. G. Peters, "Law as Critical Discussion," in Teubner, *Dilemmas of Law*, 250.

147. This is because of the civil law influence and the idea that law should be based on codes as opposed to decisions of judges.

148. Donald P. Kommers, *The Constitutional Jurisprudence of the Federal Republic of Germany* (Durham, N.C.: Duke University Press, 1989), 44–45.

149. Peters, "Law as Critical Discussion," 251.

150. In other words if the Constitution is to protect abortion, the Constitution must include an express provision to this effect rather than the courts reading into provisions of the Constitution.

151. See *Roe v. Wade* above, and *Buckley v. Valeo* above.

152. Quoted by William R. Brock, *Welfare, Democracy and the New Deal* (Cambridge: Cambridge University Press, 1988), 13.

153. The discussion offered in this section is tentative since the structure of the lower-level courts will go beyond the constitution. However, it is a topic that needs attention since the rest of the judicial system must also be organized in a democratic and responsive manner if the system is to achieve legitimacy.

154. Hund and Van der Merwe, *Legal Ideology*, 10.

155. Ibid., 12.

156. For a discussion of the different conception of rights, see Z. Motala, "Human Rights in Africa: A Cultural, Ideological, and Legal Examination," *Hastings International and Comparative Law Review* 12 (1989): 373–410.

157. Ibid., 382–83.

158. Mokgatle, "Exclusion of Blacks," 47.

159. For a full discussion of the court structure, see chapter 8.

160. G. I. Welch, "Pluralism, Colonialism and the Law," in Tirucheluam and Coomaraswamy, *The Role of the Judiciary*, 163.

161. This is more consistent with our theme of emphasizing democracy.

162. See T. Georges, *Law and its Administration*, 78. In the United States court proceedings and judicial decisions are subject to widespread discussion in the media and in the public, unlike the present strong doctrine of sub judice in South Africa which prevents the media or public from discussing pending trials.

CHAPTER TWELVE

Conclusion: Constitutional Options for South Africa

■ ■ ■

I N THE MODERN AGE it is necessary to erect a constitution to structure social relations and provide regularity in the way the affairs of the state are conducted. The main focus of this study was not to provide a constitutional blueprint but instead to outline the boundaries of constitutional choice and the direction in which a future South African constitution should develop. A constitution can be (and historically in the South African context has been) a tool to legitimize oppression.[1] However, a constitution can also provide an effective framework for the participation of people in the decision-making process and the control of arbitrary government. We have seen how a society with weak political institutions would be incapable of curbing "the excesses of personal and parochial desires."[2] The error in many independent African countries has been the assumption that the departure of the colonial power and its replacement with an indigenous government would result in peace and prosperity. Too often what resulted was a mere changing of authoritarian leaders with the majority of people still living under abusive conditions and poverty. In South Africa there was greater unity of the majority against the oppressive system of apartheid. Like many parts of Africa (in the fight against colonialism) there was great mobilization against the disgraced order. There is, however, less unity with regard to the type of political system to be introduced in the post-apartheid era. Viable state structures must be created to allow the people to articulate their demands and preferences in a democratic way, to avoid reproducing the worse features of the present order in the "new" South Africa or allowing the authoritarian practices that prevail in so many African countries to be introduced.

The stability and legitimacy of any constitution can only be achieved if the new order is democratic and responsive to the urgent concerns of the majority of South Africans. The urgent concerns are primarily the ills which apartheid has created. Some of these problems include the achievement of a sense of national identity, socioeconomic restructuring to redress the vast imbalances in wealth and land distribution, provision of housing, education, healthcare, infrastructure, employment, and other social services.

We provide below proposals and guidelines to illustrate mechanisms for introducing democratic structures for widespread participation in a future South African constitution. The proposals relating to the choice of institutions are not in any way final or sacred, as this study has repeatedly suggested that there are many procedural ways for achieving certain goals. Moreover, procedures adopted to achieve these goals would depend on the actual dynamics and exigencies of the situation. We hope these suggestions will spur the debate with respect to the introduction of democratic structures that move beyond the plural constitutional models.

Constitutional Guidelines: Absolute Boundaries

UNITARY FORM OF STATE

The constitutional system should aim at integrating the country and promoting national identity. No geographical area should be accorded any special protection or jurisdiction. There are compelling reasons to centralize such aspects of the economy as education, land reform, property distribution, healthcare, and social welfare and deal with them in an organized fashion in a unitary state. The federal and consociational models of state, which seek to institutionalize ethnic differences, are inappropriate solutions to South Africa's national problem as well as its socioeconomic challenges. The constitutional models of the federalist variety in particular aim to institutionalize differences in the population, in this case, differences that have their roots in the apartheid order. They aim to preserve the economic power of the dominant white sector of the population by devolving a large measure of autonomy to the racial and ethnic groups (to be entrenched in the constitution), which in effect will retard the process of economic and social restructuring.

To achieve the unitary state, the so-called independent homelands will have to be reabsorbed into greater South Africa. This does not mean that the country cannot be later divided into smaller units for administrative purposes (though in so doing as far as possible the division should cut across racial and ethnic boundaries as opposed to reinforcing them). Over a period of time the political system has to evolve toward the creation of viable local governments within the context of the unitary state. The local units should enjoy greater autonomy in regard to economic, social, and educational matters. However, in the immediate period after apartheid there should not be much devolution of authority to the local units. Many areas require central planning and direction of resources, particularly in the areas of housing, education, social welfare, and the building of infrastructure. In the immediate period many of these concerns will have to be dealt with and coordinated by the central government.

SPECIFIC PROVISIONS FOR INDIVIDUAL AND WELFARE RIGHTS

1. The constitution should guarantee important individual rights, especially: (a)freedom of speech, (b)freedom of assembly, (c)freedom of conscience, (d)freedom of person, (e)freedom of movement, (f)freedom of association, including a multiparty political system and the right to form independent trade unions, (g)freedom against torture, (h)the right to participate and be elected to political office, (i) freedom of religion and culture.

The rights accorded above would apply to all regardless of religious, ethnic, linguistic, or other affiliation. There is no need to protect the interests of groups, because the major problem of apartheid in South Africa has been precisely the protection of group rights. The granting of special rights to groups is a sophisticated device for allowing the present dominant group to hang on to its privileges.

2. The state must be responsible for providing a decent standard of living for all its citizens, which includes: (a)free and compulsory education, (b)free and adequate healthcare, (c)social welfare, including disability grants and pensions, and (d)housing. These rights should be entrenched in the constitution either as separate provisions or in the form of a bill of rights. At one level this is antimajoritarian. However, at the level of reality there are certain human rights that are universal and binding on all societies.[3]

SPECIFIC PROHIBITIONS

Any calls on ethnic chauvinism, or promotion of racism, or inciting of tribalism should be outlawed. Provisions relating to freedom of speech and assembly must be limited with respect to this provision. This is not inconsistent with the protection of fundamental human rights. The German Basic Law, which entrenches (in perpetuity) certain basic rights, limits these rights against persons who seek to use them against the constitutional order. In the context of Germany, the German Constitutional Court outlawed political parties that promote Nazism or fascism. This limitation of freedom of speech and organization in Germany has to be seen in the context of the German experience of authoritarianism and national chauvinism, which resulted in persecution of other groups. Similarly, apartheid was a major curse and is primarily responsible for the divisions in South African society. It is only appropriate that the new order should aim at combating the worst feature of the old order.

Democratic Conduct of Affairs

REGULATION OF POLITICAL PARTIES

The constitution should make it compulsory for all political parties seeking representation in the legislature to have a democratic internal structure. This is along the lines of the German Constitution, which prescribes a democratic internal structure for all political parties in the legislature. This provision would prevent elite or vanguard parties that have characterized so many African countries.

REPRESENTATION OF STATE ENTERPRISES

Enterprises nationalized and put under state control should provide for worker control or participation. The experiences in Africa and other places show that state ownership of the means of production more often then not means enterprises run for the benefit of the state elite as opposed to workers or the population at large. If it is deemed necessary to take over any sector of the economy, it is necessary to grant the workers a say in the decision-making processes.

PREVENTING ELITE OR "STRONGMAN" RULE

While there is great flexibility in the procedure for instituting democracy, the institutions adopted must provide for substantive participation by the people in decisions that affect their lives. Apart from the idealistic argument that widespread democracy is the best constitutional scenario, the experience of African countries has demonstrated that constitutions based on elite decision making establish terms of order that are not appropriate to African countries. Those in positions of power in the state institutions have invariably used the state to enhance their own economic power, leading to greater economic and social abuse. We cannot overemphasize this point; there has been a tendency for elite leaders to resort to any means available to hang on to power, including arousing ethnic sentiments to obtain the support of their constituencies.[4] The popular constitutional models put forward in South Africa based on the consociational and federal systems are primarily based on elite cooperation and are designed to cement ethnic and racial differences.

The alternate scenario followed in many African states has been to impose iron government based either on the former Soviet Communist model or some fictitious notion of the working of traditional African society. Neither of the above "alternatives" provides for viable state structures to resolve the problems of African society. The strongman option leads to a blurring between the state and party leadership, leading almost universally to a situation of authoritarianism, decay, and corruption.

Given the failure of both the elite and strongman options, the alternative model of government is one that promotes accountability by the officials of the state to their constituency in ways that move beyond the limited elite model of periodic election and rotation of officials of the state. Admittedly, such a model has not been introduced in any African country, but we maintain it cannot be dismissed as impractical simply because it has not been applied.

INDEPENDENCE OF THE LEGISLATURE

The legislature must be the supreme organ of law and policy making; lawmaking power must not be divided between the legislature and the executive, or between the legislature or any other unit in the state. The legislature must be completely independent of the executive or any political party.

LIMITATIONS OF TERMS

The members of the legislature as well as the head of state (if the constitutional order provides for a single popular head of state) must be limited to a maximum period of say two five-year terms. The rationale is to prevent the rise of the strongman or cult leader around whom power is concentrated. The lessons of Africa show many examples of the popular independence leader being swept into office with widespread support. With time, authority was centralized and concentrated around a single person or a group of people, which in most cases led to despotism and greater instability. If the constitutional order provides for a collective and rotating presidency as is found in Switzerland there will be less need to limit the tenure of the executive head.

Institutions: Suggestions to Spur the Debate

COMPOSITION OF THE LEGISLATURE

The reality of the modern state requires long-term planning, particularly in regard to economic and social projects. Revisionist or modern-day theorists of democracy allude to a possibility that substantive democracy poses a problem in that decisions can be undone at any time by the whims and fancies of the majority, thus eroding long- and medium-term planning, resulting in great instability. Grassroots participation in decision making is certainly not uncomplicated, particularly in the infant stages where participation and democracy are new to a society. But merely erecting a mechanism for electing political elites entrusted with decision-making powers (as the revisionists demand) has led to great abuse and corruption in Africa and the violent overthrow of governments. What is needed is a legislative structure that provides for grassroots democracy and control (over decision making) as well as stability.

The following suggestions proceed by combining what David Apter calls the radical-liberal structural solution.[5] A lower house (first chamber) would represent populist interests. The first chamber would consist of members elected directly from the population in single-member districts. A hazard in South Africa is that single member constituencies might convert an election into an ethnic or racial contest.[6] Therefore, electoral districts must be drawn up to cut across ethnic and racial affiliations.

The delegates to the first chamber must be accountable to their constituency, which might necessitate mechanisms to break the electoral districts into further subunits. The subunits could appoint their own delegates, who in turn could meet and communicate the wishes of the subconstituency to the central delegate with respect to matters to be decided in the central legislature. Elections to the lower house would be short-term, say two years. Moreover, it should be possible to remove a delegate who is not acting in accord with the mandates of the constituency. Such a lower house would link the population in a direct way to the legislature. Moreover, it would give citizens a direct measure of input and control into decisions taken at the central government level.

An upper house (second chamber) would represent functional elites or the professional core.[7] The members of the second chamber would comprise representatives from the various political parties in terms of proportional representation based on the number of votes cast for the different political parties at the general election. However, the selection of the professional core or functional elites referred to as the executive must be made by the political parties represented in the second chamber of the legislature. It is likely that political parties would have more coherent and well-thought-out programs and policies than individual delegates from the various constituencies. In the context of the nation-state, programs have to be adopted and implemented at the national level while still allowing the local units a say in the decision-making process. The initiating of law and policy making should be entrusted to the second chamber. However, the passing of all laws would require the consent of both houses of the legislature. This does not mean that the political parties are organs detached from society. In terms of our previous proposal, the political parties themselves must have a democratic structure and be linked to the population.

The second chamber would be totally party based. To prevent the spawning of a multitude of small fringe parties, representation in the legislature should be limited to parties receiving at least 10 percent support from the population. Parties should also receive a minimum level of support from each province or administrative unit in order to prevent tribal and ethnic banding.

Some theorists would like to see workers represented in the central organs of the state, particularly the legislature. The only problem with this is workers would have double representation both at the level of the workplace as well as at the level of residence, while housewives, the unemployed, the disabled, or the elderly would receive only a single vote. Many community needs would thus be underrepresented.[8] A better solution for workers who seek special representation would be to form a political party and seek representation through the ordinary electoral process.

APPOINTMENT OF THE EXECUTIVE BY THE LEGISLATURE

There is flexibility as to whether the executive would originate from the legislature or not, but the executive must in all instances be elected by the legislature and be accountable to the legislature. An unaccountable executive in the context of the experience of many independent African countries often leads to a situation of a state bureaucracy, corruption, and erosion of civil and human rights.

ADJUDICATION OF CONSTITUTIONAL MATTERS

A special constitutional court must be set up and entrusted with the responsibility to ensure that the constitution is adhered to at all times. The members of the constitutional court should be elected by the legislature for a single and nonrenewable term of, say, seven years. Once elected to office, the members of the court should be completely independent and free from influence or pressure from any outside source.

Although it should be the duty of the judiciary to ensure that the constitution is adhered to at all times, the judiciary must not take it upon themselves to exercise policy-making powers. In other words, there must be greater reliance on the formal text of the constitution, and insofar as possible the judiciary must seek to achieve congruity between the text of the constitution and the polity. This is consistent with democratic theory that it is the duty of the elected representatives to exercise law and policy-making powers. This is not to say that the judiciary will be an appendage of the executive or legislature; the German experience shows that an elected judiciary can work as an important bulwark for the protection of fundamental human rights.

The Constitution in Jurisprudential Perspective

The two polar models for the choice of values underlying a constitution are liberal constitutionalism and Soviet Communism. In between these two polar versions are the welfare constitutions of Europe and various models based on theories of African socialism. It is undesirable for a future South African constitution to define the socioeconomic and political order in terms of a single philosophy. Nor is it appropriate to adopt the eclectic approach followed by many African countries of introducing a form of government purportedly based on traditional African society. Democracy entails the making of decisions based on the wishes of the majority, and the constitution should provide appropriate mechanisms to ensure that this is done. To rigidly define the socioeconomic and political order in the constitution in terms of narrow beliefs risks committing future generations to dogma. However, we suggest that certain fundamental human rights such as the right to life, right against torture, and freedom of person are fundamental human rights that should be entrenched in the new constitution. No society condones the arbitrary deprivation of these rights, whatever its practice.[9] Similarly, developments in the human rights field, most notably the drawing up by the United Nations of the International Covenant on Economic, Social, and Cultural Rights,[10] recognize the fundamental importance of social and economic rights to the well-being of society. From a historical standpoint socialist constitutions have been more concerned about social and economic rights, and this study has defined the achievement of these rights as crucial to the stability of any future South African order.

The central purpose of liberal constitutionalism has been to provide institutions to protect the individual against the state and to protect the institution of private property. The first purpose is achieved primarily by limiting government power from interfering with individual rights. These limitations apply regardless of whether the primary officials of the state (the legislature and executive) and the majority of the citizens are united in their intent of a certain course of action.[11] Certain individual rights are inviolable. Liberal constitutions guarantee such rights and freedoms as life, free speech, assembly and conscience, and protection against torture. These values should be enshrined in the future South African constitution as well.

However, with regard to the aspect of protection of private property, the historical liberal tradition of absolute guarantee of private property is not a viable option for a future South African constitution. In many instances protection of private property is explicitly spelled out in liberal constitutions.[12] From the radical perspective, the liberal protection of private property is aimed at preventing any redistribution of wealth. Over the last few decades the absolute protection of private property has been considerably watered down in liberal societies.[13] In many instances the agencies of the state are permitted to encroach on private property for public use by providing compensation to the aggrieved party. The welfare constitutions in the European countries take this development further by imposing duties on the owners of the property as opposed to the classical liberal position of merely conferring rights on the owners of property.[14]

Although the right against encroachment of private property is no longer inviolable, protection of private property is still one of the most important aspects in liberal constitutionalism. In chapter 2 we saw that in the clash between equality and liberty the latter is seen as more important. Traditional liberal theory sees an unequal distribution of property as the result of people employing their different and unequal faculties.[15] In other words, although liberty may bring about inequality, this inequality is the result of people freely using their unequal faculties.

Marxist theory sees property owners and the wealthy strata of society as having acquired their dominant position through exploitation of the working class. Without going into the merits of liberal or Marxist theory of wealth accumulation in a global context, it is historically inaccurate to assert that in South Africa those people who are better endowed financially and materially (namely the white sector) have acquired their wealth based on better utilization of their talents. In chapter 7 we detailed the historical nature of the process of capital accumulation in South Africa, which entailed deliberately driving the indigenous population off the land and concentrating wealth in the hands of the white settlers. The entire history of apartheid has been the deliberate oppression, exploitation, and impoverishment of the black majority.

Consequently, protection of present property relationships is open to serious debate given the record of South Africa's political and economic history, a record of widespread inequalities in access to wealth and education. More than 80 percent of the land is under white ownership, and it is inevitable that there will have to be measures aimed at remedying the gross disparities. Liberal constitutional theory largely sees resolution of such problems determined by the marketplace, a view that if implemented would provide for a limited and restricted kind of government. The notion that everyone would benefit from the present status quo (represented mostly by the white minority) keeping what property they have is far-fetched and unrealistic. The experience of other countries, particularly

Western Europe, in the post-World War II period, indicates the importance of state intervention in the economy to overcome problems that arose after the ravages of the war.[16] The position that the majority of black South Africans find themselves in can be compared to a postwar situation. Socioeconomic disparities in the population cannot be ignored. The legitimacy and success of a new order in the long run will be determined by the extent to which the people believe institutions are appropriate for meeting the challenges and needs of the society. These needs include the provision of land, education, health care, and social services to the majority. The future South African constitution should follow the model of the welfare and socialist constitutions and constitutionally enshrine the duty of the state to provide education, welfare, health care, and housing for the entire population.

Constitutional models have to be evaluated in terms of whether they offer an adequate framework for dealing with the problems of South African society. The plural paradigm does not provide a viable framework, because its constitutional prescriptions would mean freezing the economic and social disparities in the population. Democracy in a new South African order cannot be determined by constitutional guarantees of property rights for the rich. Nor should a minority exercise veto power over important economic and social programs. A future constitution should provide for a strong government equipped and mandated to tackle urgent economic and social problems.

The major dilemma of existing socialist states and their structures are their authoritarian practices. Fundamental human rights such as freedom of speech, assembly, and conscience have been transgressed by state authorities for the supposed benefit of the majority. The economic and social records of former East European and African-Marxist states show that important goals such as national unity and economic progress cannot be achieved with coercion and authoritarian practices. The demand for a strong government in a new South African order is not synonymous with unrestricted government.

The approach adopted in this comparative study is to draw from the strengths of major traditions while rejecting what is not appropriate to the new South African order. In this regard the values of liberalism, socialism, and traditional African society all have a contribution to make. Unbridled capitalism is unsuited to the South African reality, which requires major redistribution and economic restructuring and reforms. However, state socialism, where the state appropriates all the resources in the supposed interest of the majority, has proved to be impractical. It often leads to stagnation and bureaucratic rule. The effecting of economic and social changes should not be equated with nationalization of all property and assets.[17] Today many political organizations and trade unions have correctly come to the position that South Africa's economic problems are neither capitalist or socialist but a mix of the two.[18] The experience of Europe has shown that redistribution can be effected in many ways, of which nationalization or public ownership is only one. For example, the social welfare models in Germany and Sweden seek to protect the spirit of innovation associated with private initiative while achieving social equality.[19] It is inappropriate for the South African constitution to define a specific economic system. The legislature should enjoy a large measure of discretion and be free to pursue any economic policy necessary for the country provided decisions are reached through a democratic process that guarantees the protection of fundamental human rights.

REFERENCES

1. As the orthodox Marxist doctrine posits.

2. Samuel P. Huntington, *Political Order in Changing Societies* (New Haven: Yale University Press, 1968), 24.

3. Z. Motala, "Human Rights in Africa; A Cultural, Ideological and Legal Examination," *Hastings International Comparative Law Review* 12 (1989): 379. See also Berger, "Are Human Rights Universal?" *Commentary* (September 1977): 62.

4. See Aloo Ojuka and William Ochieng, eds., *Politics and Leadership in Africa* (Kampala: East African Literature Bureau, 1975), 267–68.

5. For this particular approach see David E. Apter, *Choice and the Politics of Allocation: A Developmental Theory* (New Haven: Yale University Press, 1971), 160.

6. Ali Al'Amin Mazrui, *Cultural Engineering and Nation-Building in East Africa* (Evanston, Ill.: Northwestern University Press, 1972), 120–21.

7. See Apter, *Developmental Theory*, 165.

8. See Radoslav Selucky, *Marxism, Socialism, Freedom: Towards a General Democratic Theory of Labor-Managed Systems* (New York: St. Martin's Press, 1979), 115.

9. Berger, "Are Human Rights Universal?," 62; Motala, "Human Rights in Africa," 379.

10. Adopted on 16 December 1966, 993 U.N.T.S., 3.

11. The Bill of Rights in the U.S. Constitution is the classic example.

12. For example many of the individual rights provisions such as the contract clause, the due process clause, and the clause requiring just compensation for the taking of property in the U.S. Constitution are designed to protect private property.

13. In the United States the watering down process has been performed by the courts. See J. Nedelsky, "American Constitutionalism and Private Rights," in Jon Elster and Rune Slagstad, *Constitutionalism and Democracy* (Cambridge: Cambridge University Press), 247. Nedelsky makes the point that today (unlike the pre-1937 period) the courts rarely overrule legislative interference with property rights.

14. The German Basic Law specifies that there is a social duty associated with the ownership of property and that property may be expropriated in the public interest. See German Basic Law, art. 14, 19. See also comments of Donald P. Kommers, *The Constitutional Jurisprudence of the Federal Republic of Germany* (Durham, N.C.: Duke University Press, 1989), 257–58.

15. Nedelsky, *American Constitutionalism*, 244.

16. The German government after the war intervened in the economy to aid weaker sectors of the economy. For the German experience see Kurt Sontheimer, *Deutschland zwischen Demokratie und Antidemokratie* [The Government and Politics of West Germany], trans. Fleur Donecker (London: Hutchinson, 1972), 40–42.

17. See E. V. Kohak, "Possessing, Owning, Belonging," in Irving Howe, ed., *Beyond the Welfare State* (New York: Schocken Books, 1982), 155.

18. See views of the different political tendencies in "Focus: The Great Economic Debate," in Special Supplement to the *Weekly Mail*, 30 March-4 April 1990.

19. The Swedish approach is to prefer higher rates of taxation as opposed to government ownership of the means of production. See Jorgen Dalberg-Larsen, *The Welfare State and Its Law* (Berlin: Tesdorpf, 1987), 52.

''

EPILOGUE

■ ■ ■

In July 1993, the South African government, the African National Congress, and various other political organizations agreed to hold South Africa's first nonracial elections on 26–28 April 1994. In December 1993, the white-controlled South African parliament adopted an Interim Constitution for South Africa that ended three hundred years of white minority rule. The Interim Constitution will be in effect for five years, during which period a permanent constitution will be negotiated after the April 1994 elections.

The agreement also provided for creation of a Transitional Executive Council (TEC) entrusted with responsibility for monitoring the runup to South Africa's first elections and for ensuring a level playing field for all political parties. All twenty-one political parties that negotiated the Interim Constitution had representation in the TEC. During the runup to the election, the TEC was empowered to order the government to follow a course of action that would contribute to a free and fair election. The TEC did not constitute an end to white minority rule, because the cabinet under former President F. W. De Klerk still remained in charge of day-to-day affairs. However, special subcouncils on matters such as defense, law and order, finance, and foreign affairs were created to supervise the work of the white cabinet until the elections.

Under the terms of the Interim Constitution, the government installed after the elections will be one of national unity comprising all political parties that received over 5 percent of the national vote. Decisions taken in the cabinet will be decided by majority vote. Within two years after the first election, the new legislature, comprising both the national assembly and the senate, must agree on a permanent constitution. In effect, the legislature sitting jointly will constitute a constituent assembly. In the drawing up of the final constitution, the constituent assembly will be guided by constitutional principles that guarantee fundamental human rights and democracy.

The Interim Constitution stipulates that a 66 percent majority is required in the legislature for the adoption of the final constitution. If this majority is not achieved, then the final draft must be presented to the population in a referendum, in which case it will be adopted if 60 percent of the voters approve the new constitution. If the constitution is rejected in the referendum, elections for a new legislature will be held. The next time round a 60 percent majority is required for approval of the new constitution. However, before the constitution can take effect, or be put to the population in a referendum, a Constitutional Court will have to certify that the final constitution incorporates the fundamental principles and guidelines contained in schedule 4 of the Interim Constitution. In other words, the Constitutional Court has an effective veto over the final constitution. Regardless of how soon the final constitution is approved, the government of national unity will serve a full five-year term.

With respect to the interim legislature, there is a two-chamber legislature, comprising a 400-member, popularly elected national assembly and a 90-member senate. The 400 seats in the National Assembly are filled as follows: First, 200 seats are filled through election from a regional list with a fixed number allocated to each region. The remaining 200 seats are filled from a national list compiled by the various political parties. Each party receives an allocation of seats from both the national list and the regional list based on proportional representation. The senate comprises 10 senators from each of the nine provinces. Senators are nominated by the provincial/state legislature by the various political parties based on proportional representation.

Executive power shall rest in the president. Mr. Nelson Mandela was elected South Africa's first black president in nonracial elections by the National Assembly at its first sitting on 9 May 1994 in Cape Town and was sworn in on 10 May 1994 in Pretoria. The Interim Constitution makes provision for every party that has 20 percent of the vote in the National Assembly to designate a deputy president, or the party with the second highest vote to designate a deputy president.

The cabinet consists of 27 cabinet positions. All parties with at least 20 seats in the National Assembly are given a right to cabinet positions based on proportional representation. The president makes the determination on the distribution of portfolios among the various parties.

The Interim Constitution created nine defined provinces, the borders of which can be changed in post-election referenda. These new provinces will replace the existing four provinces as well as the ten former homelands or bantustans.

A new Constitutional Court was created to adjudicate constitutional disputes and to enforce the bill of rights. The only time there can be derogation from the bill of rights is in a state of emergency.

In the drawing up of the final constitution, the constitutional assembly is guided by a set of constitutional principles contained in schedule 4 of the Interim Constitution. These constitutional principles cannot be amended at all in terms of the Interim Constitution. It is possible for the Constitutional Court to reach the conclusion that these provisions are binding on the South African population in perpetuity.

There are important parts of schedule 4 that merit serious consideration. The schedule makes reference to fundamental rights, freedom, and liberties, which are contained in chapter 3 of the Interim Constitution. These rights in terms of article II of schedule 4 should be protected and entrenched in the final constitution and made justiciable. What this means is that the constitutional principles have to be given expression in the final constitution, and the Constitutional Court has to certify to this effect. Judicial review by the Constitutional Court of the final constitution is also made an unamendable part of the Interim Constitution.

Three questions arise in the context of schedule 4. First, what are the provisions of schedule 4 that have to be entrenched? Second, what is the composition of the Constitutional Court? Third, taken together, are there principles contained in schedule 4 that could prevent real economic and social change, and could the Constitutional Court act as a reactionary force to perform a rearguard action by protecting the interests of the status quo?

The idea of the Interim Constitution was to allow for democratic elections and the democratically elected representatives to draw up the final constitution. Having elections before the drawing up of a constitution makes tremendous sense. It is imperative that those entrusted with the responsibility of drawing up the final constitution have a democratic mandate. However, when we look at the Interim Constitution and schedule 4, it is arguable that certain aspects of the final constitution are already written, for example, the protection of "fundamental rights." Liberal constitutionalism seeks to protect the individual against the state and to protect the institution of private property. In pursuing the first purpose, the state is limited to certain prescribed limits that cannot transgress individual rights. These limitations apply regardless of whether the primary officials of the state (the legislature and executive) and the majority of the citizens are united in their intent on a certain course of action. Certain individual rights are inviolable. The Interim Constitution in chapter 3 seeks to protect certain very important fundamental rights such as the right to life, protection against torture, free speech, assembly, and conscience. These are important values that society ought to protect and should be enshrined in the final South African constitution. However, the Interim Constitution in article 28 protects property rights that if interpreted by the Constitutional Court to mean the spoils of the apartheid legacy can be preserved would be very problematic. This study has repeatedly suggested that the present property relationship should not be frozen in a future South African constitution.

The Interim Constitution provides for affirmative action as a constitutional principle as well as makes provision for restitution of land to any community or person who has been dispossessed subject to certain conditions. First, a Commission on Restitution of Land Rights will be created to which all land claims should be addressed. If the land is in the hands of a private owner, the court has the power to adjudicate the dispute. The section clearly stipulates that there has to be compensation given to the owner if the land is taken away, and the court will set the limit of the compensation. The reality is that the overwhelmingly white judiciary appointed by the apartheid era are given the power to preside over land disputes and guaranteed compensation to white landowners at market value. Moreover, the section does not say where the compensation is to come from. The indigent African who has been forced off his land is unlikely to be able to come up with money to buy back what he claims originally belonged to him. It is possible that the judges could read the Interim Constitution in a way that freezes the economic status quo, particularly the present property relationship. In terms of the Interim Constitution, the composition and work of the Constitutional Court are crucial in ensuring the proper orientation and development of the new order. Human rights and democracy in a new South African order cannot be realized through constitutional guarantees that protect minority property rights acquired under the apartheid order. This leads to the next salient issue contained in schedule 4, namely, the reference to provincial rights.

The basic postulate of this study is that a future constitution should provide for a strong government equipped and mandated to tackle the serious economic and social problems created under apartheid. The National Party and its traditional allies such as the former homeland leaders have always insisted that the final constitution should be a federal constitution. The institutions associated with the federal arrangement have certain features that will act to immobilize the central government, which again would favor the economic status quo. For example, under their scheme of federalism major decisions in the realm of housing, education, social welfare, and land distribution have to be taken at the regional level as opposed to the state level.

In adopting the Interim Constitution the idea of federalism was not totally given up. There are provisions in schedule 4 and in other parts of the Interim Constitution such as section 174 that could allow the Constitutional Court to demand that federalism be accommodated in the final constitution. Articles XVIII and XIX of schedule 4 speak about the powers, boundaries, and functions of the national government that have to be protected. Article XIV speaks about the functions of national and provincial governments that shall include exclusive and concurrent powers. Section 174 stipulates that the parliament of the provincial legislature shall not encroach upon the powers, functions, and structures of a local government so "as to compromise the fundamental status, purpose and character of local government." Moreover, section 176 of the Interim Constitution states that at the local government level all budget decisions must be taken by a two-thirds majority. The real danger is that the Constitutional Court may read all these provisions to require a constitutional system where maximum autonomy must devolve to the regions and local units on a number of subjects. Under this rationale of local autonomy, it is possible for white enclaves to erect restrictive covenants and other barriers to protect their exclusive neighborhoods, schools, and other facilities. In the United States, right up to the New Deal era, the Supreme Court operated on the notion of "dual federalism" and interpreted the Constitution as limiting the federal government from regulating matters of concern to the states. If the courts in South Africa interpret the Interim Constitution in the same manner, a majority central government would conceivably be unable to effect national policies in the areas of housing, education, development, and more important, redistribution without the consent of the local regions. This brings us to the role of the Constitutional Court.

The Constitutional Court occupies a very important position under the Interim Constitution, which necessitates that this body be properly constituted with justices who depart from the apartheid tradition. Unfortunately, the Interim Constitution creates rules for appointment of the Constitutional Court that threaten to stack the court with judges from the old order. There will be eleven members on the Constitutional Court. The president will appoint four judges to the court. However, in exercising this power he has to make his choices from sitting judges, which means that he has to choose judges to serve on the Constitutional Court who owe their position as judges to the National Party. The remaining seven members of the court, including the president of the court, will be appointed by the president from a list nominated by a Judicial Service Commission (JSC). The composition of the JSC is also stacked in favor of the old order, because, apart from four persons designated by the president (the minister of justice and four senators), the JSC is made up of two representatives of the attorney's profession, two representatives from the advocate's profession, the chief justice, a judge president, designated by all the judge presidents, and a representative of the deans of law schools.

The success of the Interim Constitution and the nature and success of the final constitution will greatly depend on the caliber of people who are appointed to serve on the Constitutional Court. This is particularly the case since the Interim Constitution does not offer an adequate safeguard against federalism creeping into the final constitution, nor does it empower the government to effect socioeconomic redistribution, particularly land distribution without providing compensation. To the extent that the Constitutional Court acts to prevent socioeconomic change, or insists on federalism as a device to allow a minority to prevent the majority at the center from effecting change, the constitutional system will experience a legitimacy crisis that could cause a rupture in the entire system.

APPENDIX

■ ■ ■

Definition of the Term Black

The Population Registration Act 30 of 1950 provided for a classification of every person by the director of the census as a "white," "colored," or a "native" person. In addition, every "colored" and "native" person is further categorized in terms of an ethnic or other subgroup. For example, within the "colored" group a person could be categorized as "Cape colored," "Malay," "Indian," etc. Within the "native" group a person could be classified into one of nine additional subcategories, such as Zulu, Xhosa, Shangaan, Sotho, etc.

There are no scientific criteria that exist for classification of people into any of the above groups, and the drafters of the statute had to resort to artificial and sometimes arbitrary criteria such as "general acceptance" and "obvious acceptance" in order to classify people into the various categories.

In terms of the statute the first criterion to determine a person's classification would be paternity. If both parents are white an individual would be classified as white. If a person has one white parent and the other is from a different category, the person would be classified as "colored." A "colored" person is defined as a person "who is not a white person or a native." A "native" person is defined as one who is "generally accepted as a member of any aboriginal race or tribe in Africa." A white person is defined as one "who in appearance obviously is, or is generally accepted as a white person but does not include a person who, although in appearance is obviously a white person, is generally accepted as a colored person."

The preceding statement is a brief overview of the Population Registration Act that determined an individual's political, social, and economic rights in South Africa. This act was, in many quarters, regarded as the cornerstone of apartheid. It is noteworthy that the act did not mention the term *African* or *black*. The absence of the term African can perhaps be explained by the dominant white group in South Africa calling itself Afrikaaners, which translated from Afrikaans means Africans. Right up to the 1970s the official government term for the indigenous African people was *Bantu*, which translated from one of the dialects means people. The term *Bantu* was rejected by the African population as a derogatory label imposed on them by the white rulers. The government referred to all those persons who were not white as nonwhites (that is, Indians, coloreds, and Africans).

The early 1970s was a period of intense political activity in South Africa that was spurred on by the Black Consciousness Movement (BC) led by the late Steve Biko. It was a period that witnessed the rise of a new black intelligentsia that began to examine critically the condition of the oppressed and exploited masses. The emerging movement saw the psychological oppression of black people as the single greatest obstacle to physical liberation. This called for a radical change in the oppressed's perception of themselves and a critical questioning of the concepts and terminologies adopted by the oppressor. The new movement called on the oppressed to rid themselves of the value systems and definitions of the oppressor. Therefore there was a rejection of the term *nonwhite* as a categorization of the oppressed (and those people who were not white). The term *nonwhite* was seen as a negative description, with a connotation that black people were not as good as white people and had to be defined in terms of what they were not. This negative self-image had the result of leading black people toward white ideals and of emulating white people. So long as black people carried this psychological baggage (of not being proud of themselves for what they were) they would continue to aspire toward whiteness as opposed to fighting for liberation. Thus, the rejection of the negative term *nonwhite* was replaced by a positive assertion of being black.

The BC Movement saw in the term *black* a revolutionary and unifying potential. For the first time the oppressed and exploited were called upon to shed all the real or imaginary differences that divided them and unite on the basis of their common experiences of oppression and exploitation. The term *black* was to transcend so-called ethnic or tribal differences (such as Zulu, Indian, Sotho, colored, etc.) and to mobilize the oppressed into one solid unit.

The introduction of the term *black* into the South African vocabulary must be attributed to the Black Consciousness Movements (the South African Students Organization [SASO] and the Black Peoples Convention [BCP]). In the late 1970s the South African government dropped its use of the term *Bantu* when referring to the African population and resorted to the term *black*. The term *Bantu* fell into disuse after the 1976 Soweto uprisings and the rejection of Bantu Education by the African students. The government's narrow use of the term *black* to refer to only a part of the oppressed population obviously had as its intention the furthering of the government's policy of making different sections of the oppressed view themselves as separate entities. For a while the white-controlled media also adopted the term *black* in the narrow sense of referring to African people. The term *black* has since been adopted by the major political organizations (namely, the ANC and AZAPO) to refer in the main to all the oppressed peoples. The use of the term *black* by the white liberal media has been inconsistent, and they sometimes use black to address all the oppressed while on other occasions only to address Africans. This study has used the term *black* to refer to all the people who were politically oppressed in South Africa—Africans, coloreds, and Indians. To many people in the opressed community, the terms *colored* and *Indian* are derogatory. This study has not used such labels unless necessary.

SELECTED BIBLIOGRAPHY

■　■　■

Books

Aaby, Peter. *The State of Guinea-Bissau: African Socialism or Socialism in Africa?* Uppsala: Scandinavian Institute of African Studies, 1978.

Adam, Heribert. *South Africa: Sociological Perspectives.* London: Oxford University Press, 1971.

African Affairs Research Group. *Save the Congo, Save Africa!* Sierra Leone: African Affairs Research Group, 1965.

Agresto, John. *The Supreme Court and Constitutional Democracy.* New York: Cornell University Press, 1985.

Amissah, Austin. *The Contribution of the Courts to Government: A West African View.* Oxford: Clarendon Press, 1981.

Andrews, William G. *Constitutions and Constitutionalism.* 3d ed. Princeton, N.J.: Van Nostrand, 1968.

Andrews, William G. and Franz D. Scholz. *Soviet Institutions and Policies: Inside Views.* Princeton, N. J. : Van Nostrand, 1966.

Apter, David E. *Choice and the Politics of Allocation: A Developmental Theory.* New Haven: Yale University Press, 1971.

Awogu, F. Olisa. *Political Institutions and Thought in Africa: An Introduction.* New York: Vantage Press, 1975.

Awolowo, Obafemi. *Thoughts on the Nigerian Constitution.* London: Oxford University Press, 1966.

Azikiwe, Nnamdi. *Zik: Selections from the Speeches of Nnamdi Azikiwe.* Cambridge: Cambridge University Press, 1961.

255

Babu, Abdul Rahman Mohamed. *African Socialism or Socialist Africa?* London: Zed Press, 1981.

Banton, Michael. *Political Systems and the Distribution of Power.* London: Association of Social Anthropologists, 1968.

Barghoorn, Frederick C., and Thomas F. Remington. *Politics in the USSR.* 3d ed. Boston: Little Brown, 1986.

Barkan, Joel D., and John J. Okumu. *Politics and Public Policy in Kenya and Tanzania.* New York: Praeger, 1979.

Barker, Ernest. *Social Contract: Essays by Locke, Hume and Rousseau.* London: Oxford University Press, 1952.

———. *Principles of Social and Political Theory.* Oxford: Clarendon Press, 1952.

Basson, Dion A., and Henning P. Viljoen. *South African Constitutional Law.* Cape Town: Juta & Co., 1988.

Bayly, Joseph T. *Congo Crisis.* Grand Rapids, Mich.: Zondervan Publishing House, 1966.

Beard, Charles A. *An Economic Interpretation of the Constitution of the United States.* New York: Free Press, 1986.

Beirne, Piers, and Richard Quinney. *Marxism and Law.* New York: Wiley, 1982.

Bell, Derrick, A. *Race, Racism and American Law.* Boston: Little, Brown, 1980.

Benjamin, Roger W., and Stephen L. Elkin. *The Democratic State.* Lawrence, Kans.: University Press of Kansas, 1985.

Benyon, John, ed. *Constitutional Change in South Africa: Proceedings of a Conference on Constitutional Models and Constitutional Change in South Africa.* Pietermaritzburg: University of Natal Press, 1978.

Berg-Schlosser, Dirk. *The Distribution of Income and Education in Kenya: Causes and Potential Political Consequences.* Munchen: IFO-Institut fur Wirtschaftsforschung, 1970.

———. *Tradition and Change in Kenya: A Comparative Analysis of Seven Major Ethnic Groups.* Paderborn: F. Schoningh, 1984.

———. *Political Stability and Development: A Comparative Analysis of Kenya, Tanzania and Uganda.* Boulder, Colo.: Lynne Rienner, 1990.

Beshir, Mohamed Omer. *Diversity, Regionalism and National Unity.* Uppsala: Scandinavian Institute of African Studies, 1979.

Bienen, Henry. *Kenya: The Politics of Participation and Control.* Princeton, N.J.: Princeton University Press, 1974.

Bihari, Otto. *The Constitutional Models of Socialist State Organization.* Budapest: Akademiai Kiado, 1979.

Bombwall, K. R. *The Foundations of Indian Federalism.* London: Asia Publishing House, 1967.

Boukema, H. J. M. *Good Law: Towards a Rational Lawmaking Process.* Frankfurt am Main: P. Lang, 1982.

Boulle, Laurence J. *Constitutional Reform and the Apartheid State: Legitimacy, Constitutionalism, and Control in South Africa.* New York: St. Martin's Press, 1984.

Bowles, Samuel, and Herbert Gintis. *Democracy and Capitalism: Property, Community and the Contradictions of Modern Social Thought.* New York: Basic Books, 1986.

Brewer-Carias, Allan R., and Donald F. Bur. *Judicial Review in Comparative Law.* Cambridge: Cambridge University Press, 1989.

Brock, William R. Welfare, *Democracy and the New Deal*. Cambridge: Cambridge University Press, 1988.

Bromlei, Ivlian V., et al. *Sovremennye etnicheskie protsessy v SSSR*. Akademiia nauk SSSR: Institut etnografii, 1977.

Brookes, Edgar Harry, and J. B. Macauley. *Civil Liberty in South Africa*. Westport, Conn.: Greenwood Press, 1973.

Brown, Brendon, F. *The Natural Law Reader*. New York: Oceana Publications, 1969.

Bryde, Brun-Otto. *The Politics and Sociology of African Legal Development*. Frankfurt am Main: Metzner, 1976.

Burg, Steven L. *Conflict and Cohesion in Socialist Yugoslavia: Political Decision Making Since 1966*. Princeton, N.J.: Princeton University Press, 1983.

Burnheim, John. *Is Democracy Possible?: The Alternative to Electoral Politics*. Berkeley: University of California Press, 1985.

Burns, Alan C. *Parliament as an Export*. London: Allen & Unwin, 1966.

Busia, Kofi A. *Africa in Search of Democracy*. New York: Praeger, 1967.

―――. *The Position of the Chief in the Modern Political System of Ashanti: A Study of the Influence of Contemporary Social Changes on Ashanti Political Institutions*. London: Cass, 1968.

Buthelezi Commission. *The Requirements for Stability and Development in KwaZulu and Natal*. Durban: H & H Publications, 1982.

Cain, Maureen, and Alan Hunt, eds. *Marx and Engels on Law*. London: Academic Press, 1979.

Cairns, Huntington. *Legal Philosophy from Plato to Hegel*. Baltimore: Johns Hopkins University Press, 1949.

Cameron, George D. *The Soviet Lawyer and His System: A Historical and Bibliographic Study*. Ann Arbor: Division of Research, Graduate School of Business Administration, University of Michigan, 1978.

Cappelletti, Mauro, and William Cohen. *Comparative Constitutional Law: Cases and Materials*. Indianapolis, Ind.: Bobbs-Merrill, 1979.

Carter, Gwendolen M. *African One-Party States*. Ithaca, N.Y.: Cornell University Press, 1962.

Cecil, Henry. *The English Judge*. London: Stevens, 1970.

Centre for Development Research. *Beyond Apartheid: Discussion Papers on a Democratic Development in South Africa*. Copenhagen: Centre for Development Research, 1992.

Cliffe, Lionel. *One Party Democracy: The 1965 Tanzania General Elections*. Nairobi: East African Publishing House, 1967.

Codding, George A. *The Federal Government of Switzerland*. Boston: Houghton Mifflin, 1961.

Cohen, Ronald, and John Middleton, eds. *Comparative Political Systems; Studies in the Politics of Pre-Industrial Societies*. Garden City, N.Y.: Natural History Press, 1967.

Conant, Michael. *The Constitution and Capitalism*. St. Paul: West Publishing Co., 1974.

Conference on New Approaches in Social Anthropology. *Political Systems and the Distribution of Power*. New York: F. A. Praeger, 1965.

Connolly, William E. *Legitimacy and the State*. New York: New York University Press, 1984.

Conradt, David P. *The German Polity*. New York: Longman, 1986.

Cooray, L. J. Mark. *Conventions: The Australian Constitution and the Future*. Sydney: Legal Books, 1979.

Corder, Hugh, ed. *Essays on Law and Social Practice in South Africa*. Cape Town: Juta, 1988.

——. *Judges at Work: The Role and Attitudes of the South African Appellate Judiciary, 1910–1950*. Cape Town: Juta, 1984.

Cowan, L. Gray. *The Dilemmas of African Independence*. New York: Walker, 1968.

Cowen, Denis V. *Constitution-Making for a Democracy*. Johannesburg: Anglo-American Corp. of South Africa, 1960.

Cowen, Denis V. *The Foundations of Freedom, with Special Reference to Southern Africa*. Cape Town: Oxford University Press, 1961.

Cunningham, Robert L. *Liberty and the Rule of Law*. 1st ed. College Station, Tex.: Texas A&M University Press, 1961.

Currie, David P. *The Constitution of the United States: A Primer for the People*. Chicago: University of Chicago Press, 1988.

Dahl, Robert A. *Who Governs? Democracy and Power in an American City*. New Haven: Yale University Press, 1961.

Dalberg-Larsen, Jorgen. *The Welfare State and Its Law*. Berlin: Tesdorpf, 1987.

Davidson, Basil. *Crossroads in Africa: Basil Davidson Talks to Antonio Bronda*. Nottingham: Spokesman Books, 1980.

——. *Growing from Grass Roots: The State of Guinea-Bissau*. London: Committee for Freedom in Mozambique, Angola and Guinea, 1974.

Dean, W. H. B., and Dirk Van Zyl Smit, eds. *Constitutional Change in South Africa*. Cape Town: Juta, 1983.

De Smith, S.A., and Rodney Brazier. *Constitutional and Administrative Law*. 6th ed. New York: Penguin Books, 1989.

De Smith, S.A. *The New Commonwealth and Its Constitutions*. London: Stevens, 1964.

Dhavan, Rajeev, et al., eds. *Judges and the Judicial Power: Essays in Honour of Justice V. R. Krishna Iyer*. London: Sweet and Maxwell, 1985.

Dhavan, Rajeev. *President's Rule in the States*. Bombay: N. M. Tripathi, 1979

Dicey, Albert V. *Introduction to the Study of the Law of the Constitution*. 5th ed. London: Macmillan, 1897.

Duchacek, Ivo D. *Comparative Federalism : The Territorial Dimension of Politics*. New York: Holt, Rinehart and Winston, 1970.

——. *Power Maps: Comparative Politics of Constitutions*. Santa Barbara, Calif.: ABC-Clio, 1973.

Duggan, William R., and John R. Civille. *Tanzania and Nyerere: A Study of Ujamaa and Nationhood*. Maryknoll, N. Y. : Orbis Books, 1976.

Earle, Valerie A., and George W. Carey. *Federalism: Infinite Variety in Theory and Practice*. Itasca, Ill.: F. E. Peacock, 1968.

Eckstein, Harry, and David E. Apter. *Comparative Politics: A Reader*. New York: Free Press of Glencoe, 1963.

Edinger, Lewis J. *Politics in West Germany*. 2d ed. Boston: Little, Brown, 1977.

Eidlin, Fred H., and Henry W. Ehrmann. *Constitutional Democracy: Essays in Comparative Politics—A Festschrift in Honor of Henry W. Ehrmann*. Boulder, Colo.: Westview Press, 1983.

Elias, T. O. *Nigeria: The Development of Its Laws and Constitution*. London: Stevens, 1967.

Elster, Jon, and Rune Slagstad. *Constitutionalism and Democracy*. Cambridge: Cambridge University Press, 1988.

Fanon, Frantz. *Toward the African Revolution: Political Essays*. New York: Grove Press, 1967.

Fatton, Robert. *Black Consciousness in South Africa: The Dialectics of Ideological Resistance to White Supremacy*. Albany: State University of New York Press, 1986.

Fine, Bob. *Capitalism and the Rule of Law: From Deviancy Theory to Marxism*. London: Hutchinson, 1979.

———. *Democracy and the Rule of Law: Liberal Ideals and Marxist Critiques*. London: Pluto Press, 1984.

Finer, Samuel E., ed. *Five Constitutions*. Brighton, Sussex: Harvester Press, 1979.

Forsyth, C. F. *In Danger for Their Talents: A Study of the Appellate Division of the Supreme Court of South Africa from 1950–1980*. Cape Town: Juta, 1985.

Friedman, Milton. *Free to Choose: A Personal Statement*. New York: Harcourt Brace Jovanovich, 1980.

Friedrich, Carl J. *Constitutional Government and Politics*. 4th ed. Waltham, Mass.: Blaisdell Pub. Co., 1968.

———. *Limited Government: A Comparison*. Englewood Cliffs, N.J.: Prentice-Hall, 1974.

———. *The Impact of American Constitutionalism Abroad*. Boston: Boston University Press, 1967.

———. *The Philosophy of Law in Historical Perspective*. 2d ed. Chicago: University of Chicago Press, 1963.

Friedrich, Carl J., and Robert R. Bowie. *Studies in Federalism*. Boston: Little Brown, 1954.

Galli, Rosemary, and Jocelyn Jones. *Guinea-Bissau: Politics, Economics and Society*. Boulder, Colo.: Lynne Rienner Press, 1987.

Georges, Telford. *Law and its Administration in a One Party State: Selected Speeches*. Ed. R. W. James and F. M. Kassam. Nairobi: East African Literature Bureau, 1973.

Gertzel, Cherry J. *The Politics of Independent Kenya, 1963–1968*. Evanston, Ill.: Northwestern University Press, 1970.

Ghai, Yash P. *Constitutions and the Political Order in East Africa*. Dar es Salaam: University College, 1970.

Gierke, Otto Friedrich von, and Ernst Troeltsch. *Natural Law and the Theory of Society 1500–1800*. Boston: Beacon Press, 1957.

Glendon, Mary A., et al., eds . *Comparative Legal Traditions: Text, Materials and Cases on the Civil Law, Common Law, and Socialist Law Traditions, with Special Reference to French, West German, English and Soviet Law*. St. Paul, Minn.: West Publishing Co., 1985.

Gonidec, P. F. *African Politics*. Boston: M. Nijhoff, 1981.

Graham, Keith. *The Battle of Democracy: Conflict, Consensus and the Individual*. Brighton: Wheatsheaf, 1986.

Greenstein, Fred I., and Nelson W. Polsby. *Handbook of Political Science*. Reading, Mass.: Addison-Wesley Pub. Co., 1975.

Griffith, J. A. G. *The Politics of the Judiciary*. Atlantic Highlands, N.J.: Humanities Press, 1977.

Grimal, Henri. *Decolonization: The British, French, Dutch, and Belgian Empires, 1919–1963.* Trans. Stephen De Vos. Boulder, Colo.: Westview Press, 1978.

Gwyn, William B. *The Meaning of the Separation of Powers: An Analysis of the Doctrine from its Origin to the Adoption of the United States Constitution.* New Orleans: Tulane University, 1965.

Haasbroek, David J. P. *Apartheid: Myth or Reality.* Kwadlangezwa: University of Zululand, 1981.

Hahlo, H. R., et al. *The Union of South Africa: The Development of Its Laws and Constitution.* London: Stevens, 1960.

Hamilton, William B. *The Transfer of Institutions.* Durham, N. C.: Duke University Press, 1964.

Hanf, Theodor, et al. *South Africa, the Prospects for Peaceful Change: An Empirical Enquiry Into the Possibility of Democratic Conflict Regulation.* Trans. John Richardson. London: R. Collins, 1981.

Harden, Ian, and Norman Lewis. *The Noble Lie: The British Constitution and the Rule of Law.* London: Hutchinson, 1986.

Harding, Arthur L., ed. *The Rule of Law.* Dallas: Southern Methodist University Press, 1961.

Hartley, Trevor C., and J. A. G. Griffith. *Government and Law: An Introduction to the Working of the Constitution in Britain.* London: Weidenfeld and Nicholson, 1975.

Hayek, Friedrich August von. *The Political Ideal of the Rule of Law.* Cairo: 1955.

———. *The Road to Serfdom.* Chicago: University of Chicago Press, 1980.

Hayward, Jack. *The One and Indivisible French Republic.* London: Weidenfeld & Nicholson, 1973.

Hazard, John N. *Communists and Their Law: A Search for the Common Core of the Legal Systems of the Marxian Socialist States.* Chicago: University of Chicago Press, 1969.

Hazlewood, Arthur. *African Integration and Disintegration.* London: Oxford University Press, 1967.

Henkin, Louis, and Albert J. Rosenthal, eds. *Constitutionalism and Rights: The Influence of the United States Constitution Abroad.* New York: Columbia University Press, 1990.

Hicks, Ursula K. W. *Federalism—Failure and Success: A Comparative Study.* London: MacMillan, 1978.

Hinden, Rita. *Africa and Democracy.* London: Encounter, 1962.

Hirst, Paul Q. *Law, Socialism, and Democracy.* London: Allen & Unwin, 1986.

Holden, Barry. *The Nature of Democracy.* New York: Barnes & Noble Books, 1974.

Holliday, N. *Federate or Fail: Key to a Peaceful, Politically Scientific Change for South Africa.* Alice, Ciskei: Lovedale Press, 1985.

Holmes, Marjorie Jean, and Campbell Sharman. *The Australian Federal System.* Sydney: G. Allen & Unwin, 1977.

Holt, Robert T., and John E. Turner, eds. *The Methodology of Comparative Research.* New York: Free Press, 1970.

Horwitz, Ralph. *The Political Economy of South Africa.* New York: Praeger, 1967.

Hough, Jerry F., and Merle Fainsod. *How the Soviet Union Is Governed.* Cambridge, Mass.: Harvard University Press, 1979.

Howe, Irving, ed., *Beyond the Welfare State.* New York: Schocken Books, 1982.

Hughes, Christopher, ed. *The Federal Constitution of Switzerland.* Oxford: Clarendon Press, 1954.

————. *The Parliament of Switzerland.* London: Cassell, 1962.

Hund, John, and Henrik W. Van der Merwe. *Legal Ideology and Politics in South Africa: A Social Science Approach.* Lanham, Md.: University Press of America, 1986.

Huntington, Samuel P. *Political Order in Changing Societies.* New Haven: Yale University Press, 1968.

International Legal Center, Research Advisory Committee on Law and Development. *Law and Development: The Future of Law and Development Research.* Stockholm: Almquist & Wiksell International, 1974.

International Commission of Jurists. *African Conference on the Rule of Law, 1st Lagos.* Geneva: ICJ, 1961.

Jackson, John D. *Justice in South Africa.* London: Secker & Warburg, 1980.

Jaffe, Louis L. *English and American Judges as Lawmakers.* Oxford: Clarendon Press, 1969.

Jambrek, Peter. *Development and Social Change in Yugoslavia: Crisis and Perspectives of Building a Nation.* Lexington, Mass.: Lexington Books, 1975.

Johnson, Frederick A. *Class, Race, and Gold: A Study of Class Relations and Racial Discrimination in South Africa.* London: Routledge & Kegan Paul, 1976.

Journal of African Marxists. *Independent Kenya.* London: Zed Press, 1982.

Kahn, Ellison, ed. *Fiat Iustitia: Essays in Memory of Oliver Deneys Schreiner.* Cape Town: University of Witwatersrand, 1938.

Kainz, Howard P. *Democracy, East and West: A Philosophical Overview.* New York: St. Martin's Press, 1984.

Kantor, Brian, et al. *South African Economic Issues.* Cape Town: Juta, 1982.

Kanza, Thomas R. *Conflict in the Congo: The Rise and Fall of Lumumba.* Harmondsworth: Penguin Books, 1972.

Keller, Edmond J., and Donald Rothchild, eds. *Afro-Marxist Regimes: Ideology and Public Policy.* Boulder, Colo.: Lynne Rienner Publishers, 1987.

Kenyan Ministry of Cooperatives and Social Services. *Cooperative Development Policy for Kenya.* Nairobi, 1970.

King, Preston T. *Federalism and Federation.* London: Croom Helm, 1982.

Kommers, Donald P. *The Constitutional Jurisprudence of the Federal Republic of Germany.* Durham, N.C.: Duke University Press, 1989.

Kovacs, Istvan. *New Elements in the Evolution of Socialist Constitution.* Trans. J. Decsenyi. Budapest: Akademiai Kiado, 1968.

Kuper, Leo, and M. G. Smith, eds. *Pluralism in Africa.* Berkeley: University of California Press, 1969.

Laclav, Ernesto, and Chantal Mouffe. *Hegemony and Socialist Strategy: Towards a Radical Democratic Politics.* Trans. Winston Moore and Paul Cammack. London: Verso, 1985.

Lenin, V. I. *What is to be Done?* Trans. Joe Fineberg and George Hanna. London: Penguin Books, 1988.

Lindsay, Alexander D. *The Essentials of Democracy.* Westport, Conn.: Greenwood Press, 1980.

Lipset, Seymour M., ed. *Politics and the Social Sciences.* New York: Oxford University Press, 1969.

———. *The First New Nation: The United States in Historical and Comparative Perspective*. New York: Basic Books, 1963.

Locke, John. *Two Treatises of Government*. Ed. Peter Laslett. London: Cambridge University Press, 1960.

Lofchie, Michael F., ed. *The State of the Nations: Constraints on Development in Independent Africa*. Berkeley: University of California Press, 1971.

Lombard, Johannes A. *Freedom, Welfare and Order: Thoughts on the Principles of Political Cooperation in the Economy of Southern Africa*. Pretoria: Benbo, 1978.

Louw, Leon, and Frances Kendall. *After Apartheid: The Solution for South Africa*. San Francisco, Calif.: ICS Press, 1987.

Machel, Samora. *Establishing People's Power to Serve the Masses*. Toronto: Toronto Committee for the Liberation of Southern Africa, 1976.

Macridis, Roy C. *Modern Political Systems: Europe*. 5th ed. Englewood, N.J.: Prentice-Hall, 1983.

———. *The Study of Comparative Government*. Garden City, N.Y.: Doubleday, 1955.

Magubane, Bernard. *The Political Economy of Race and Class in South Africa*. New York: Monthly Review Press, 1979.

Malherbe, Paul N. *Multistan: A Way Out of the South African Dilemma*. Cape Town: David Philip, 1974.

Marais, D., and D. Riekert. *Constitutional Development of South Africa*. Johannesburg: Macmillan, 1981.

Marcus, Gilbert. *The Freedom Charter: A Blueprint for a Democratic South Africa*. Johannesburg: University of the Witwatersrand, 1985.

Markovitz, Irving L. *Power and Class in Africa: An Introduction to Change and Conflict in African Politics*. Englewood Cliffs, N.J.: Prentice-Hall, 1977.

Marquard, Leopold. *A Federation of Southern Africa*. London: Oxford University Press, 1971.

———. *The Peoples and Policies of South Africa*. 4th ed. London: Oxford University Press, 1969.

Marsh, David C. *The Welfare State*. London: Longman, 1970.

Marsh, Jan. *Stop the War Against Angola and Mozambique: Chronological Account of Acts of Aggression Against the Front Line States by Apartheid South Africa, 1975–1981*. London: Campaign to Stop the War Against Angola and Mozambique, 1981.

Marshall, Geoffrey. *Constitutional Theory*. Oxford: Clarendon Press, 1971.

Marx, Karl. *A Contribution to the Critique of Political Economy*. London: Lawrence and Wishart, 1971.

———. *Political Writings*. Ed. David Fernbach. Harmondsworth: Penguin Books, 1973.

Marx, Karl, et al. *On the Dictatorship of the Proletariat: A Collection*. Moscow: Progress Publishers, 1984.

Marx, Karl, and Frederich Engels. *The Communist Manifesto*. Trans. Samuel Moore II. New York: New York Labor News, 1948.

Mathews, Anthony S. *Law, Order and Liberty in South Africa*. Berkeley: University of California Press, 1977.

May, Henry John. *The South African Constitution*, 3d ed. Westport, Conn.: Greenwood Press, 1970.

Mazrui, Ali Al'Amin. *Cultural Engineering and Nation-Building in East Africa.* Evanston, Ill.: Northwestern University Press, 1972.

McAuslan, Patrick and John F. McEldowney. *Law, Legitimacy and the Constitution: Essays Marking the Centenary of Dicey's Law of Constitution.* London: Sweet & Maxwell, 1985.

McHenry, Dean E. *Tanzania's UJAMAA Villages: The Implementation of a Rural Development Strategy.* Berkeley: University of California Press, 1979.

McIlwain, Charles H. *Constitutionalism, Ancient and Modern.* Rev. ed. Ithaca, N.Y.: Cornell University Press, 1947.

McRae, Kenneth D. *Conflict and Compromise in Multilingual Societies.* Waterloo, Ont.: Wilfrid Laurier University Press, 1983.

McWhinney, Edward. *Supreme Courts and Judicial Law-making: Constitutional Tribunals and Constitutional Review.* Dordrecht: M. Nijhoff, 1986.

Melson, Robert, and Howard Wolpe, eds. *Nigeria: Modernization and the Politics of Communalism.* East Lansing: Michigan State University Press, 1971.

Merryman, John Henry. *Comparative Law, Western European and Latin American Legal Systems: Cases and Materials.* Indianapolis, Ind.: Bobbs-Merrill, 1978.

Miliband, Ralph. *Class Power and State Power.* London: Verso, 1983.

———. *Marxism and Politics.* Oxford: Oxford University Press, 1977.

———. *The State in Capitalist Society.* London: Weidenfeld & Nicholson, 1969.

Mill, John Stuart. *Considerations on Representative Government.* Ed. Currin V. Shields. New York: Liberal Arts Press, 1958.

Mosca, Gaetano. *The Ruling Class.* New York: McGraw-Hill Book Co., 1939.

Mueller, Susanne D. *Government Opposition in Kenya, 1966–1969.* Boston: African Studies Center, Boston University, 1983.

Muller, Ingo. *Furchtbare Juristen: die Unbewaltigte Vergangenheit Unserer Justiz.* Munchen: Kindler, 1987.

Neumann, Franz. *The Rule of Law: Political Theory and the Legal System in Modern Society.* Dover, N.H.: Berg, 1986.

Nkrumah, Kwame. *Africa Must Unite.* New York: F. A. Praeger, 1963.

Nwabueze, Benjamin O. *Constitutionalism in the Emergent States.* London: C. Hurst, 1973.

———. *A Constitutional History of Nigeria.* Essex: Longman, 1982.

———. *Judicialism in Commonwealth Africa: The Role of the Courts in Government.* London: C. Hurst, 1977.

Nwatu, Dennis N. *Development of Parliamentary Democracy in Nigeria.* Enugu, Nigeria: Chuka Printing Co., 1986.

Nyerere, Julius K. *Man and Development.* Dar es Salaam: Oxford University Press, 1974.

———. *Freedom and Unity.* London: Oxford University Press, 1967.

Odinga, J. Oginga. *Not Yet Uhuru: The Autobiography of Oginga Odinga.* London: Heinemann, 1967.

Ogwurike, Chijioke. *Concept of Law in English-Speaking Africa.* New York: NOK Publishers International, 1979.

Ojuka, Aloo, and William Ochieng, eds. *Politics and Leadership in Africa.* Kampala: East African Literature Bureau, 1975.

Okpaku, Joseph, ed. *Nigeria: Dilemma of Nationhood.* New York: Third Press, 1972.

Omand, Roger. *The Apartheid Handbook.* New York: Penguin Books, 1985.

Osbun, Lee Ann. *The Problem of Participation: A Radical Critique of Contemporary Democratic Theory.* Lanham, Md.: University Press of America, 1985.

Pan African Congress. *Resolutions and Selected Speeches from the 6th Pan African Congress.* Dar es Salaam: Tanzania Publishing House, 1976.

———. *Time for Azania.* Toronto: Norman Bethune Institute, 1976.

Pateman, Carole. *Participation and Democratic Theory.* Cambridge: Cambridge University Press, 1970.

Pennock, J. Roland, and John W. Chapman, eds. *Constitutionalism.* New York: New York University Press, 1979.

———. *Liberal Democracy.* New York: New York University Press, 1983.

Pheko, Motsoko. *Apartheid: The Story of a Dispossessed People.* London: Marram Books, 1984.

Phillips, Owen Hood, and Paul Jackson. *Constitutional and Administrative Law.* 6th ed. London: Sweet & Maxwell, 1978.

Pizzorusso, Alessandro, et al., eds. *Law in the Making: A Comparative Study.* Berlin: Springer-Verlag, 1988.

Polley, James A., ed. *The Freedom Charter and the Future: Proceedings of the National Conference on the Freedom Charter and the Future.* Johannesburg: Ad. Donker, 1988.

Potekhin, I. I. *African Problems: Analysis of an Eminent Soviet Scientist.* Moscow: Nauka Publishing House, 1968.

Potholm, Christian P. *The Theory and Practice of African Politics.* Englewood Cliffs, N.J.: Prentice-Hall, 1979.

Pylee, Moolamattom V. *India's Constitution.* 3d ed. Bombay: Asia, 1979.

Ramet, Pedro, ed. *Nationalism and Federalism in Yugoslavia, 1963–1983.* Bloomington, Ind.: Indiana University Press, 1984.

———. *Yugoslavia in the 1980's.* Boulder, Colo.: Westview Press, 1985.

Ramundo, Bernard A. *The Soviet Legal System: A Primer.* Chicago: ABA, 1971.

Randall, Peter, ed. *South Africa's Political Alternatives.* Johannesburg: SPRO-CAS, 1973.

Record, Wilson. *Race and Radicalism: The NAACP and the Communist Party in Conflict.* Ithaca, N.Y.: Cornell University Press, 1964.

Riker, William H. *Federalism: Origin, Operation, Significance.* Boston: Little Brown, 1964.

Rivkin, Arnold. *Nation-Building in Africa: Problems and Prospects.* Ed. John H. Morrow. New Brunswick, N.J.: Rutgers University Press, 1969.

———. *Nations by Design: Institution-Building in Africa.* Garden City, N.Y.: Anchor Books, 1968.

Rockefeller, Nelson A. *The Future of Freedom: A Bicentennial Series of Speeches.* Washington: U.S. Government Printing Office, 1976.

Ronen, Dov, ed. *Democracy and Pluralism in Africa.* Sevenoaks, Kent: Hodder and Stoughton, 1986.

Rotberg, Robert I., and John Barratt, eds. *Conflict and Compromise in South Africa.* Lexington, Mass.: Lexington Books, 1980.

Rubin, Leslie, and Brian Weinstein. *Introduction to African Politics: A Continental Approach.* New York: Praeger, 1977.

Sachs, Albie. *Justice in South Africa.* London: Sussex University Press, 1973.

Sartori, Giovanni. *Democratic Theory.* Westport, Conn.: Greenwood Press, 1973.

Saul, John S. *The State and Revolution in Eastern Africa: Essays*. New York: Monthly Review Press, 1979.

Sawyerr, G. F. A., ed. *East African Law and Social Change*. Nairobi: East African Publishing House, 1967.

Schmidhauser, John R., ed. *Comparative Judicial Systems: Challenging Frontiers in Conceptual and Empirical Analysis*. London: Butterworths, 1987.

Schrenk, Martin, et al. *Yugoslavia: Self-Management Socialism and the Challenges of Development*. Baltimore: Johns Hopkins University Press, 1979.

Schwartz, Bernard. *Constitutional Law: A Textbook*. 2d ed. New York: Macmillan, 1979.

Selucky, Radoslav. *Marxism, Socialism, Freedom: Towards a General Democratic Theory of Labour-Managed Systems*. New York: St. Martin's Press, 1979.

Serapiao, Luis B., and Mohamed A. El-Khawas. *Mozambique in the Twentieth Century: From Colonialism to Independence*. Washington, D.C.: University Press of America, 1979.

Sharlet, Robert. *Soviet Constitutional Crisis: From De-Stalinization to Disintegration*. Armonk, N.Y.: Sharpe, 1992.

Shevtsov, Viktor S. *The State and Nations in the USSR*. Trans. Lenina Ilitskaya. Moscow: Progress Publishers, 1982.

Silveira, Onesimo. *Africa South of the Sahara: Party Systems and Ideologies of Socialism*. Stockholm: Raben & Sjogren, 1976.

Skurnik, W. A. E., ed. *African Political Thought: Lumumba, Nkrumah, Touré*. Denver: University of Denver, 1968.

Smith, Adam. *An Inquiry into the Nature and Causes of the Wealth of Nations*. Ed. Edwin Cannan. New York: The Modern Library, 1937.

Smith, Joel, and Lloyd D. Musolf, eds. *Legislatures in Development: Dynamics of Change in New and Old States*. Durham, N.C.: Duke University Press, 1979.

Smith, Edwin William. *The Golden Stool: Some Aspects of the Conflict of Cultures in Africa*. London: Holborn Publishing House, 1927.

Somerville, Keith. *Angola: Politics, Economics and Society*. London: F. Pinter Publishers, 1986.

Sontheimer, Kurt. *Deutschland Zwischen Demokratie und Antidemokratie*. Trans. Fleur Donecker. London: Hutchinson, 1972.

Spiro, Herbert J. *Government by Constitution: The Political Systems of Democracy*. New York: Random House, 1959.

Stankiewicz, W. J. *Approaches to Democracy: Philosophy of Government at the Close of the Twentieth Century*. New York: St. Martin's Press, 1981.

Steinberg, Jonathan. *Why Switzerland?* Cambridge: Cambridge University Press, 1976.

Stewart, William H. *Concepts of Federalism*. Lanham, Md.: University Press of America, 1984.

Strong, Charles F. *Modern Political Constitutions: An Introduction to the Comparative Study of their History and Existing Form*. 6th rev. ed. London: Sidgwick & Jackson, 1963.

Suckling, John, and Landeg White, eds. *After Apartheid: Renewal of the South African Economy*. Trenton, N.J.: Africa World Press, 1988.

Suttner, Raymond, et al. *30 Years of the Freedom Charter*. Johannesburg: Ravan Press, 1985.

Tambo, Oliver. *Preparing for Power.* New York: G. Braziller, 1988.

Teubner, Gunther, ed. *Dilemmas of Law in the Welfare State.* Berlin: Walter de Gruyter, 1986.

Thomas, Wolfgang H. *Plural Democracy: Political Change and Strategies for Evolution in South Africa.* Johannesburg: South African Institute of Race Relations, 1977.

Thompson, Edward P. *Whigs and Hunters: The Origin of the Block Act.* Harmondsworth: Penguin, 1977.

Tirucheluam, Neelan, and Radhika Coomaraswamy, eds. *The Role of the Judiciary in Plural Societies.* London: F. Pinter, 1987.

Tsamerian, Ivan P. *Equality Between the Races and Nationalities in the USSR.* Paris: UNESCO, 1962.

U. S. Congress. *House Committee on International Relations. Subcommittee on Africa. Perspectives on Mozambique: Hearing Before the Subcommittee on Africa of the Committee on International Relations, House of Representatives, Ninety-Fifth Congress, Second Session, 16 May 1978.* Washington: U.S. Government Printing Office, 1978.

Vail, Irina M. *Pravo i Bor'ba idei v sovremennom mire: Kritika Sovremennykh Burzhuaznykh Kontseptsii prava.* Moskva: Int gosudarstva i prava, 1980.

―――. *Praktika Burzhuaznogo Konstitutsionalizma: Kriticheskie Ocherki.* Moskva: Akademiia nauk SSSR, Int gosudarstva prava, 1982.

Van Rooyen, J. C. W. *Censorship in South Africa: Being a Commentary on the Application of the Publications Act.* Cape Town: Juta, 1987.

Van Vuuren, D. J., et al. , eds. *Change in South Africa.* Durban: Butterworths, 1983.

Van Vuuren, D. J., and D. J. Kriek, eds. *Political Alternatives for Southern Africa.* Durban: Butterworths, 1983.

Van Zyl Slabbert, F., and David J. Welsh. *South Africa's Options: Strategies for Sharing Power.* New York: St. Martin's Press, 1979.

Vile, Maurice J. C. *Constitutionalism and the Separation of Powers.* Oxford: Clarendon Press, 1967.

Wade, E. C. S., and G. Godfrey Phillips. *Constitutional and Administrative Law.* 10th ed. London: Longman, 1985.

Wallerstein, Immanuel M. *Africa, The Politics of Independence: An Interpretation of Modern African History.* New York: Vintage Books, 1961.

Waltman, Jerold L., and Kenneth M. Holland. *The Political Role of Law Courts in Modern Democracies.* New York: St. Martin's Press, 1988.

Watts, Ronald L. *New Federations: Experiments in the Commonwealth.* Oxford: Clarendon Press, 1966.

Wheare, Kenneth C. *Modern Constitutions.* 2d ed. London: Oxford University Press, 1966.

―――. *Federal Government.* 4th ed. New York: Oxford University Press, 1964.

Wiseman, Herbert V. *Parliament and the Executive: Analysis with Readings.* London: Routledge & Kegan Paul, 1966.

Wraith, Ronald E. *Corruption in Developing Countries.* New York: Norton, 1964.

Ybema, Seerp B. *Constitutionalism and Civil Liberties.* Leiden: Leiden University Press, 1973.

Articles

Asante, I. "Nation Building and Human Rights in Emergent African Nations," *Cornell International Law Review* 2 (1969): 100.

Aspaturian, V. "The Theory and Practice of Soviet Federalism," *Journal of Politics* 12(1950): 41.

Ayoade, J. A. A. "Federalism in Africa, Some Chequered Fortunes," *Plural Societies* 9(1)(Spring 1978): 3.

Barongo, Y. "Alternative Approaches to African Politics," *Political Science in Africa* (1983): 141.

Blenck, J. "Republic of South Africa: Partition a Solution?" *Aussen Politiek* 27(1976): 29.

Budlender, J. "A Common Citizenship," *South African Journal of Human Rights* (1985): 210.

Cameron, G. "Legal Chauvinism, Executive-Mindedness and Justice L. C. Steyn's Impact on South African Law," *South African Law Journal* 99(1982): 42.

———. "Nude Monarchy: The Case of South African Judges," *South African Journal of Human Rights* 3(1987): 339.

Claassen, C. J. "Retain the Bar and Side-Bar," *South African Law Journal* 99(1982): 652.

Cowling, A. "Judges and the Protection of Human Rights in South Africa: Articulating the Inarticulate Premise," *South African Journal of Human Rights* 3(1987): 181.

Dugard, J. "Some Realism About the Judicial Process and Positivism—A Reply," *South African Law Journal* 98(1981): 385.

———. "The Judicial Process, Positivism, and Civil Liberty," *South African Law Journal* 88(1971): 183.

———. "The Judiciary and National Security," *South African Law Journal* 99(1982): 657.

Geldenhuys, D. "South Africa's Constitutional Alternatives," *South African International* (1981): 213.

Giliomee, H. "The Last Trek? Afrikaaners in the Transition to Democracy," *South African International* (January 1992): 117.

Gordon, M. "Class and Economics of Crime," *Review of Radical Economics* 3(3) (1971): 52.

Gupta, A. "Political Systems and the One-Party State of Tropical Africa," *India Quarterly* 31(2) (1975): 160.

Hough, M. "Forms of State, Government, and Authority," *South African Journal of African Affairs* 9(3/4) (1979): 160.

Hudson, P. "The Freedom Charter and Socialist Strategy in South Africa," *Politikon* 13(1) (1986): 75.

Kaba, W. "Guinean Politics: A Critical Overview," *The Journal of Modern African Studies* 15(1) (1977): 31.

Kentridge, S. "Telling the Truth About Law," *South African Law Journal* 99(1982): 652.

Klug, H. "The South African Judicial Order and the Future," *Hastings International and Comparative Law Review* 12(1988): 223.

Levanthal, H. "Courts and Political Thickets," *Columbia Law Review* 77(1977): 345.

Lijphart, A. "Consociational Democracy," *World Politics* 21(1969): 216.

Livingston, W. S. "A Note on the Nature of Federalism," *Political Science Quarterly* 67(1952): 91.

Lofchie, M. F. "Representative Government, Bureaucracy, and Political Development: The African Case," *African Administrative Studies* 16(1976): 131.

Mayer, W. "Federalism and Party Behavior in Australia and Canada," *Western Political Quarterly* 23(1970): 795.

Meillasoux, C. "A Class Analysis of the Bureaucratic Process in Mali," *Journal of Development Studies* 6(2) (1970): 96.

Miller, A. "On Politics, Democracy, and the First Amendment: A Commentary on First National Bank v. Bellotti," *Washington and Lee Law Review* 38(1981): 23.

Mokgatle, D. "The Exclusion of Blacks from the South African Judicial System," *South African Law Journal* 3(1987): 48.

Motala, Z. "Human Rights in Africa: A Cultural, Ideological and Legal Examination," *Hastings International and Comparative Law Review* 12(1989): 382.

Osakwe, C. "Equal Protection of Law in Soviet Constitutional Law and Theory—A Comparative Analysis," *Tulane Law Review* 59(1985): 974.

Parsons, T. "Evolutionary Universals in Society," *American Sociological Review* 29(1965): 353.

Raz, J. "The Politics of the Rule of Law," *Ratio Juris* 3(1990): 3.

Rex, J. "The Plural Society: The South African Case," *Race* 40(1971): 404.

Robson, W. A. "The Transplanting of Political Institutions and Ideas," *Political Quarterly* 35(1964): 407.

Rose, R. and H. Mossawir, "Voting and Elections: A Functional Analysis," *Political Studies* 85(June 1967): 177.

Sachs, A. "Changing the Terms of the Debate: A Visit to a Popular Tribunal in Mozambique," *Journal of African Law* 28(1984): 99.

——. "Towards a Bill of Rights for a Democratic South Africa," *Hastings International and Comparative Law Review* 12(1989): 322.

Sartori, G. "Constitutionalism: A Preliminary Discussion," *American Political Science Review* 56(1962): 853.

Slovo, J. "General Secretary of SACP," *Umsebenzi* 6(1) (1990): 4.

South African Communist Party, "The Road to South African Freedom," *African Communist* (1963): 41.

Tarlton, C. "Symmetry and Asymmetry as Elements of Federalism: A Theoretical Speculation," *Journal of Politics* 27(1965): 861.

Thomas, W. H. "South Africa Between Partition and Integration," *Aussen Politiek* (1979): 313.

Trapido, S. "South Africa in a Comparative Study of Industrialization," *Journal of Development Studies* 7(1971): 313.

Tsion, F. "Highlights of the Constitution of the People's Republic of Ethiopia (PDRE): A Critical Review of the Main Issues," *Review of Socialist Law* 14(1988): 129.

Venter, S. "Some of South Africa's Political Alternatives in Consociational Perspective," *South African International* (1981): 131.

Vosloo, W. B. "Consociational Democracy as a Means to Accomplish Peaceful Change in South Africa," *Politikon* 6(1) (1979): 14.

Index

∎ ∎ ∎

269

271